THE Presidents,
First Ladies, AND
Vice Presidents

THE Presidents, First Ladies, AND Vice Presidents

White House Biographies, 1789–2005

Daniel C. Diller and Stephen L. Robertson

CQ PRESS

A Division of Congressional Quarterly Inc.
Washington, D.C.

CQ Press
1255 22nd Street, N.W., Suite 400
Washington, D.C. 20037

(202) 729-1900; toll-free, 1-866-4CQ-PRESS (1-866-427-7737)

www.cqpress.com

♾ The paper used in this publication exceeds the requirements of the American National Standard for Information Sciences—Permanence of Paper for Printed Library Materials, ANSI Z39.48-1992.

Printed and bound in the United States of America

09 08 07 06 05   5 4 3 2 1

Cover and book design: Naylor Design, Inc.

Illustration credits and acknowledgments appear on page 265, which constitutes a continuation of the copyright page.

Cover illustration credits: Dolly Madison, Library of Congress; Thomas Jefferson, Library of Congress; Ronald Reagan, White House; Abraham Lincoln, Library of Congress; Frances Cleveland, Library of Congress; Lyndon Johnson, Lyndon B. Johnson Library; George W. Bush, AP/Worldwide

Library of Congress Catalog Number: 2004029355

ISBN 1-56802-984-5 (cloth)
ISBN 1-56802-985-3 (paper)

Contents

Boxes

On January 6, 2005, Congress formally counted the electoral votes as follows: 286 for George W. Bush, 251 for John Kerry, and 1 for John Edwards.

Preface

In the months leading up to the 2004 presidential election, political pundits debated the parallels between the presidencies of George H. W. Bush and his son George W. Bush, theorizing whether the younger Bush would repeat his father's experience and lose his bid for a second term. John Quincy Adams—the son of President John Adams and the first son of a president to be elected to the presidency (in 1824)—became the first son to lose a reelection bid (in 1828). George W. Bush—the second son of a president to be elected president (in 2000)—became the first son to win reelection.

The election of 2004 generated fervor, anxiety, and anger like few before it. A number of issues—terrorism, the war in Iraq, the economy, and, as it turns out, "moral values"—energized an avalanche of new voters, led to unprecedented amounts of campaign contributions and spending, and produced a race for the presidency whose winner could not be predicted. Bush ultimately defeated Democrat John Kerry in the electoral college, winning 286 votes to Kerry's 252.

Thus far in U.S. history, forty-two individuals have served as president. History views some of them, such as George Washington, Abraham Lincoln, and Franklin D. Roosevelt, as great because of the leadership they exhibited in, respectively, guiding the formation of the U.S. government, fighting to preserve the Union, and steering the nation from depression to economic recovery. The majority of past presidents have been capable chief executives, governing in times of peace and prosperity. A few have been categorized as failures, yet the lives of every U.S. president, whether great or barely noteworthy, remain fascinating because they are so closely tied to the history of the nation.

Along with the president, the first lady has always been one of the most prominent individuals in the United States. Americans have generally watched and admired how these women handled their responsibilities as wives and mothers while fulfilling that of White House hostess. In the modern era, in addition to performing traditional roles assumed by the first lady, women in this position have taken on more public ones, such as traveling abroad as a representative of the United States, promoting social causes, or participating in the work of the administration.

The Constitution originally awarded the vice presidency to the second-place finisher in the electoral college vote. Highly respected American leaders John Adams and Thomas Jefferson were first elected vice president before later becoming president. After passage in 1804 of the Twelfth Amendment, which requires a separate vote for president and vice president, what little luster accompanied the vice presidency disappeared, and the position sank in esteem. In the twentieth and twenty-first centuries, however, with the advent of the nuclear era and homeland security issues, the importance of the vice president's role as successor to the president reemerged. Since 1945 three vice presidents—Harry S. Truman, Lyndon B. Johnson, and Gerald R. Ford—have assumed the presidency after the death or resignation of an elected president. In the wake of the September 11, 2001, attacks against the United States, Vice President Richard Cheney often spent time in an "undisclosed location" as a security measure, should anything happen to the president. Given the importance of presidential succession post–September 11, and with the vice presidency now widely seen as a stepping-stone to a presidential nomination, the office has gained in stature and influence.

The first chapter of *The Presidents, First Ladies, and Vice Presidents: White House Biographies, 1789–2005* opens with a short look at the president's day-to-day living and work arrangements in the White House, including discussions of recreational activities and the new structure and procedures of the Secret Service following the September 11 attacks.

In the second chapter, biographies of the presidents examine their early lives, political careers and campaigns, and years in the White House, focusing especially on events during their terms in office. In addition to presenting biographies of the first ladies, the third chapter profiles presidents' wives who were not first ladies (page 148), White House hostesses for presidents who did not have wives during their terms in the White House (page 154), and surrogate White House hostesses for first ladies who were unable, usually

for health reasons, to fulfill their social duties (page 162). Biographies of the vice presidents comprise the final chapter. Photographs accompany all the biographies.

New to this edition are updated biographies for President George W. Bush, First Lady Laura Bush, and Vice President Richard Cheney; the Secret Service's transfer from the Department of the Treasury to the Department of Homeland Security and other post–September 11 security-related issues; and updated information on former office-holders, including Ronald Reagan's death, Jimmy Carter's Nobel Prize, and the post-presidential career of Bill Clinton and that of former first lady Hillary Rodham Clinton. A detailed index rounds out the volume.

This edition of *Presidents, First Ladies, and Vice Presidents* owes much to writer Deborah Kalb, who researched and updated the chapters and biographies, and to Jessica Forman, Joan Gossett, Grace Hill, Belinda Josey, Kerry Kern, Lorna Notsch, Steve Pazdan, Paul Pressau, Robin Surratt, Shana Wagger, and Margot Ziperman at CQ Press.

THE Presidents,
First Ladies, AND
Vice Presidents

Daily Life of the President

By Stephen L. Robertson

Although in theory just another citizen, the president does not live like one. The first family occupies the White House, a fully staffed, 132-room structure that combines personal living quarters and an office complex. Located at 1600 Pennsylvania Avenue in Washington, D.C., the Executive Mansion sits on an immaculate eighteen-acre estate, which is maintained by the National Park Service. The American Association of Museums has recognized the White House as a museum of American history and culture. Within its walls are thousands of beautiful items of furniture, art, china, and antiques, many of which are invaluable. Should the president or first lady not like the paintings on the walls, the National Gallery of Art will provide new ones.

WHITE HOUSE LIFE

Newly elected presidents receive $50,000 to spend over the course of their presidency on redecorating the White House. Because the redecorating allowance does not go very far, some presidents and first ladies have conducted campaigns to raise private funds and material donations, such as furniture, for the mansion. In addition to offices and the first family's living quarters, the Executive Mansion houses exercise rooms and recreational facilities for the president, who may invite guests or staff to use them as well. On the ground floor are an office for the president's physician and the White House Medical Unit, which has a staff of more than twenty and is adequate for routine medical care. (Major or specialized treatment is available at one of Washington's hospitals.) There are also a dental clinic, a barbershop, a tailor's shop, a cafeteria, laundry rooms, a carpenter's shop, a machine shop, a painter's shop, and a bomb shelter.

If the president needs a few moments with nature to meditate or clear his mind, just outside the mansion are grounds that hold the Rose Garden and the Jacqueline Kennedy Garden, where the chefs sometimes gather herbs to season the first family's meals.

Presidential Perquisites and Expenses

The president draws an annual salary of $400,000 (increased from $200,000 in 2001), an expense account of $50,000, and a travel allowance of $100,000. In reality, because the president travels almost exclusively on government transportation, the cost of which is covered by government agencies such as the Department of Defense, most of the president's travel allowance is available for other uses. The president has access to more than a dozen limousines and cars—including an armor-plated limousine with a detachable roof—which are leased by the manufacturer to the government at a small fee. Family members and designated staff on official business may also use the cars, and up to six presidential assistants may be named to "portal to portal" privileges: being chauffeured from their home to the White House door. The president also may use a Marine Corps helicopter for short trips such as to Camp David, the presidential retreat in Maryland.

For longer journeys, a small fleet of airplanes is available, including *Air Force One,* the primary jet, which was replaced during the administration of George Bush at a cost of $500 million. (There are actually two planes; the one that the president is aboard at any given time is designated *Air Force One.*) The new *Air Force One* is a modified Boeing 747 that can travel at six hundred thirty miles an hour, carries up to seventy passengers, and has a special crew of twenty-three. It has comfortable compartments with desks, sofas, and beds, a presidential suite, a conference room, a computer center, food service facilities, medical facilities (including an operating room for an emergency), an entertainment room, seven bathrooms, and communications equipment, including eighty-five telephones, some of which are secure, and one fax machine, for constant access to the rest of the world. The president's family and invited guests may fly on these official aircraft; however, unless they are on official business, they must pay their own way. By custom of the White House Military Office, which operates the aircraft, the fare is calculated at the commercial airlines' first-class rate plus one dollar. The cost of maintaining the plane is about $40,000 per hour.[1]

A flight with the president is an enormous status symbol, and one that is eagerly sought by almost everyone in the administration and in Congress. The new *Air Force One* was originally designed to hold up to 140 passengers, but it was scaled back because the Reagan administration (which ordered the jet) feared that a larger plane would enormously multiply the demands to hitch a ride with the president. Naturally, for a ride on *Air Force One* to be a status symbol, there needs to be proof of it:

> Those who get a ride have a tangible way of letting folks know. They can swipe special M&Ms with the presidential seal and "Air Force One" on the box, then leave the candy in plain view at home or office. . . . In 1988 the White House contacted M&M-Mars Company and asked it to design a presidential candy box in time for Reagan's trip to the Moscow summit.[2]

Security and communications considerations dictate that the president use government transportation almost exclusively. The president's guardians, the Secret Service, have discouraged the use of private transportation by the president since the Truman administration. When President Harry S. Truman's mother-in-law died, Truman, seeking privacy, wanted to return to his Missouri home on a commercial train, but the Secret Service refused to allow it.

The expenses incurred in operating the White House itself are paid by the government. For example, the electric bills, which can total more than $180,000 per year, are paid by the federal Treasury. Similarly, the White House telephone service, which operates through an in-house switchboard and is among the best in the world, is provided at no charge to the president. In fiscal year 2004, $12.4 million was appropriated for the executive residence at the White House.

Despite the lavish accommodations and generous perks that presidents receive, the many items that the government does not pay for can be a serious drain on the president's personal resources. As a general rule, personal items—toiletries, clothing, gifts, and so on—must be purchased by the president. The presi-

AN EVENING AT THE BUSH WHITE HOUSE

An invitation to a White House state dinner—a black tie affair hosted by president and first lady for visiting heads of state—is one of the most prized in the capital. The invitees, who generally bring a spouse or other dinner companion, usually are a mix of top administration officials, members of Congress (from both parties), prominent individuals with dealings with the invited nation, friends of the president, business leaders, and other celebrated Americans.

For the state dinner on September 5, 2001, that the Bushes hosted for Mexican president Vicente Fox and his wife, along with a handful of Mexican ministers and dignitaries, top U.S. officials included Vice President Dick Cheney, Secretary of State Colin Powell, National Security Adviser Condoleezza Rice, and U.S. Ambassador to Mexico Jeffrey Davidow. Other high-ranking Americans included Chief Justice William Rehnquist, Senate Majority Leader Tom Daschle, Speaker of the House J. Dennis Hastert, and Federal Reserve Chairman Alan Greenspan. There were also distinguished members of the Mexican American business, education, and artistic communities. Celebrities included singer Placido Domingo, actor Clint Eastwood, and football player Darrell Green.

White House chef Walter Scheb III, who had been serving up "healthier" American cuisine for the president for seven years, planned the dinner for the evening. "If there is a way to get the fat out without making the taste or texture suffer, we do it," Scheb said.[1] Also working was pastry chef Roland Mesnier, who had been dazzling guests with his dessert works of art since the Carters. At the 2001 state dinner for the Mexican president, the White House served the following menu:

Maryland crab and chorizo pozole
Summer vegetables
Pepita-crusted bison
Poblano-whipped potatoes
Fava bean and chanterelle ragout
Apple chipotle sauce
Salad of gold and red tomatoes
Mache and micro greens with sherry
   dressing
Mango and coconut ice cream dome and
   peaches
Red chile pepper sauce
Tequila sabayon

Three Californian wines, including one from a Mexican American winery in Napa Valley, were served with dinner. The tables in the State Dining Room were set with the white and gold Clinton china and the Morgantown crystal. For flatware, the Bushes used the White House's collection of vermeil, gilded pieces of solid silver. Working with the White House florist Nancy Clarke, the first lady had selected the floral arrangements of cream hydrangea, white Casablanca lilies, white roses, and limes.

In the East Room following the dinner, opera singer Dawn Upshaw, accompanied by pianist Stephen Prustman, entertained the guests with songs by twentieth-century American, Latin American, and Spanish composers. Later in the evening the Bushes entertained the Foxes on the Truman Balcony where they viewed fireworks over the Washington Monument.[2]

1. Marian Burros, "At Dinner: Hot Lights, Light Food," *New York Times,* September 28, 1994, A6.
2. The White House, 2001.

dent also must absorb the cost of the food served to the first family and their personal guests, as well as the maintenance of personal items such as appliances and furniture that the first family brought to the White House.

A similar distinction exists in White House entertainment. The government will pay for official entertaining. The tab for a state dinner, for example, will be picked up by the State Department. Any nongovernmental function must be paid for by someone else. For any strictly political functions the president's political party may help defray expenses (these must be paid in advance). In some cases, the president may host an event that is actually sponsored by an outside group, which then reimburses the government. Since 1998 Congress has required that interest and penalties be imposed on anyone not making prompt payment. The cost of any other entertaining, however, such as receptions, dinners, recitals, or parties, is covered by the president. Thus, a White House reception honoring a Nobel laureate or a party for thirty members of Congress would be a private expense. Although a military band is always available, and many entertainers and performers gladly donate their time to the White House, the expense of entertaining easily can be thousands of dollars a month. *(See box, An Evening at the Bush White House, p. 3.)*

Despite the size of the president's salary and benefits, living in the White House is far from inexpensive, as first families learn to their dismay. Rosalynn Carter wrote of her shock when the food bill for her first ten days in the White House in 1977 came to $600.[3] Thus, they look for ways to economize: Bess Truman scrutinized every line of the budget, and Mamie Eisenhower searched newspaper advertisements for bargains. Lady Bird Johnson's cook sometimes made the round of supermarkets looking for specials. When Mrs. Johnson's daughter Luci once asked for a second dress to wear to a festival, the first lady, citing the budget, refused to buy it. Although most were fairly wealthy, each first lady has echoed

Jacqueline Kennedy's orders to her staff: "I want you to run this place just like you'd run it for the chinchiest president who ever lived."[4]

Some presidents take their desire to save money even further. To symbolize his concern for economy in government, Lyndon B. Johnson constantly harassed staff and family alike to turn off the lights in the White House when they were not needed. The harassment continued until finally Johnson came home one night to a blacked-out White House; the only light in the entire mansion was a single candle on the table where his brother, Sam Houston Johnson, was writing. Other presidents have taken steps to save resources, if not actually money. President Jimmy Carter tried to save energy by ordering all the White House thermostats turned down in the winter, and President Bill Clinton started recycling the family trash.

Purchases for the White House, including many of the president's personal wants, are made by the staff. For example, the first family's food is bought wholesale from selected stores (limited in number partly because of security). After the White House menu is fixed, government trucks visit the stores, where White House staff members and carefully screened store employees collect the food. Such purchases are paid with the president's personal check. Other types of purchases are made in a similar way.

It is rarely possible for the president or the first lady to go on public shopping trips. As late as the 1920s Grace Coolidge shopped virtually unnoticed. On one such trip she even encountered another customer who told her that she resembled the first lady. Such informality rapidly disappeared, however. In 1945 Bess Truman drove herself around Washington, but she soon began to cause traffic jams and had to stop. In 1977 Rosalynn Carter tried to fly quietly on a commercial airliner to New York City to buy some clothes, only to find a mob of journalists waiting for her when she left the store. More recently, in December 1993 President Clinton created pandemonium at a nearby Washington, D.C., mall when

CHIEF USHER OF THE WHITE HOUSE

The chief usher of the White House has one of the most varied jobs anywhere in the government, as seen in the following job description taken from the U.S. Civil Service Commission's position description form:

Subject only to the general direction of the President of the United States, serves as "Chief Usher" of the White House. As such is the general manager of the Executive Mansion, and is delegated full responsibility for directing the administrative, fiscal, and personnel functions involved in the management and operation of the Executive Mansion and grounds, including construction, maintenance, and remodeling of the Executive Mansion.

Is responsible for the preparation and justification of budget estimates covering administrative and operating expenses, and for the construction and maintenance projects of the Executive Mansion . . . , as well as for the allotment, control, and proper expenditure of funds appropriated for these purposes.

Is responsible for the direction and supervision of the activities of approximately one hundred employees of the President's household including their selection, appointment, placement, promotion, separation, disciplinary action, etc. In addition, exercises responsibility over the mechanical and maintenance forces in connection with the maintenance and repair of buildings and grounds.

Serves as the receptionist at the White House, and as such is responsible for receiving and caring for all personal and official guests calling on the President or the First Lady. These guests include, among others, members of the Congress and their families, members of the Judicial Branch, governors, foreign dignitaries, and heads of state. Is responsible for arranging for accommodations for house guests, their comfort, their acquaintance with customs of the household, etc. Is responsible and arranges for all personal and official entertainments, receptions, dinners, etc., in the Executive Mansion, which frequently include the heads of sovereign states, and several hundred persons. Is responsible for the procurement of all food consumed by the President's family and their guests. Makes personal appointments for the President and other members of his official family.

Is responsible for answering a large volume of correspondence regarding the Executive Mansion, its history and furnishings, historical subjects, sightseeing, Congressional requests with regard to the Mansion and Grounds, State function, etc.

Is completely responsible for the efficient operation, cleanliness, and maintenance of the 132 rooms of the Executive Mansion containing 1,600,000 cubic feet. . . .[1]

1. J. B. West, *Upstairs at the White House: My Life with the First Ladies* (New York: Coward, McCann, and Geoghegan, 1973), 10–11.

he shopped for Christmas presents for his wife and daughter.

The Executive Mansion is fully staffed. The White House domestic staff has nearly one hundred permanent, full-time employees who remain from president to president and whose primary loyalty is to the presidency itself. Although this staff is not protected by civil service status, staffers are fired infrequently. Moreover, because jobs within the White House have a certain prestige, turnover is low. Accounts indicate that the staff takes great pride in serving the president.

The most important member of the White House domestic staff is the chief usher. Responsible for the general operation of the White House, the chief usher manages the mansion's budget; hires, directs, and dismisses personnel; and oversees the various White House activities under way. Should the president or the first family want something done around the White House, they seek out the chief usher. Chief ushers have been charged with coordinating the mansion's redecoration, organizing a president's last-minute reception for hundreds of people, supervising a president's funeral, and even acquiring animals for the president's children. Despite the pressure of the job, chief ushers have taken great pride in their work and turnover is very low; there were only five chief ushers during the twentieth century. *(See box, Chief Usher of the White House, p. 5.)*

Below the chief usher is the large permanent White House workforce, including butlers, maids, cooks, operating engineers, electricians, carpenters, plumbers, painters, floral designers, and a seamstress. In recent years, the total for staff salaries averaged nearly $4 million annually. The staff is sufficiently diversified to handle most problems internally. On occasion, however, other government employees may be drafted to supplement the domestic staff. An unusually large dinner party, for instance, may necessitate extra butlers. When President Johnson, at the end of the period of mourning for John F. Kennedy, decided suddenly to invite the entire Congress to the White House for a Christmas party, additional government personnel had to be brought in to assist with the preparations.

The first family is permitted to place a small number of personal servants on the government payroll. These employees, although paid temporarily

by the government, are in fact distinct from the rest of the domestic staff. They are employed by the president and first lady and leave with them. Their pay is generally on a par with that of the permanent staff; some, however, may live in the White House itself and therefore draw a smaller salary. Included among such employees would be the president's valet(s), personal cook, and barber, and the first lady's personal secretary and maids.

The President's Workday

The workload of the president has changed a great deal during the twentieth century. Although it is probably true, as George Reedy, Lyndon Johnson's press secretary, has said, that no president has ever died from overwork, the load certainly seems to have been much heavier after 1930 than before.

Before 1930 most presidents had a fairly light workload. Congress dominated American government, and the president was expected to do little. Indeed, the federal government as a whole was not expected to do much, for most government activities took place at the state and local levels. In general, people expected the federal government to take a hands-off attitude to most problems. Consequently, presidents did not have to work very long or hard.

In the 1800s a schedule such as Benjamin Harrison's was typical: arrive at the office around nine in the morning, work for two or three hours, and take the rest of the day off. Later, in 1905, Theodore Roosevelt disposed of government business in the morning and devoted his afternoons to exercise and his evenings to reading. Calvin Coolidge spent fairly little time in his office from 1923 to 1929 because he felt the government should do little. There were exceptions—James K. Polk (1845–1849) worked so long and hard that he ruined his health and died three months after leaving the presidency at age fifty-three, thereby perhaps disproving Reedy's dictum. However, most presidents in the nineteenth and early twentieth century did not find the job terribly taxing. Fighting off the would-be officeholders was more demanding.

The presidential workload began to increase in the 1930s when problems arose that were beyond the capacities of the states. The Great Depression, followed by World War II, led to new expectations of the federal government, which increased its role in society and the economy with each passing year. Concurrently, people began to look to the president more than to Congress for direction and solutions. Just as the federal government was expected to solve the nation's problems, so the president was expected to lead the government. Longer presidential workdays were therefore inevitable. Herbert Hoover (1929–1933) spent many more hours in the Oval Office than most of his predecessors, and his successor, Franklin D. Roosevelt (1933–1945), spent all day at work, with brainstorming sessions often held over meals. Harry Truman (1945–1953) arose at five-thirty in the morning, exercised, had breakfast by eight o'clock, and went straight to work. Although he did not labor under the same pressures as Roosevelt, he worked a full day.

By 1952 the public viewed the presidency as a full-time job. Many Americans therefore found Dwight D. Eisenhower's approach to the job somewhat disconcerting. Relying on his extensive staff, Eisenhower (1953–1961) tried to return to the old work patterns. He concentrated his work into the mornings and tried to take afternoons off as much as possible. Unlike Roosevelt and Truman, Eisenhower avoided working on weekends. He argued that a rested president made better decisions than an overworked one, but not everyone agreed. He was criticized for the amount of time he spent playing golf, and a bumper sticker appeared, which read: "Ben Hogan for President. If We're Going to Have a Golfer, Let's Have a Good One."

For the most part, John F. Kennedy (1961–1963) did not work long hours either. As a senator he had

Eisenhower plays golf at a club in Newport, Rhode Island, while onlookers watch and take pictures.

had a reputation as a four-day legislator; as president he consistently took weekends off. Kennedy worked through the morning, paused in the afternoon for a swim, lunch, and a nap, and then returned to the office for a time in the late afternoon.

Life under Lyndon Johnson (1963–1969) was not so relaxed. A driven man who possessed almost superhuman energy, Johnson wanted to accomplish more than any other president and drove himself, and everyone else, accordingly. He arose early and held bedroom meetings with selected staff members; he then spent the morning in his office. After lunch he took a nap, on doctor's orders, from two to four. Thus refreshed, he started the day all over again, frequently working late into the night. It was not at all unusual for LBJ to hold staff meetings at nine or ten in the evening and to work until after midnight. He drove his staff as hard as himself, demanding that they be available at all times of the night and day.

Although Richard Nixon (1969–1974) was not as frantic as Johnson, he too worked long hours. He generally arose at seven-thirty in the morning and was at his office by eight-thirty. Meetings began at nine and lasted throughout the morning. After a brief lunch, Nixon would resume work until early evening. A workday of ten to eleven hours, with perhaps an hour for lunch, was common. At times, Nixon would return to his office around nine in the evening to read and work another hour or two. He generally went to bed between midnight and one in the morning.

The habit of presidents working long days continued with Gerald R. Ford (1974–1977) and Jimmy Carter (1977–1981), both of whom put in full days and not a few nights. By then it was believed that the president had to work twelve-hour days because the burdens of government were so great. One of Carter's commercials during his 1980 reelection campaign illustrated and played on that belief; it pictured a dark White House late at night, with a solitary light where Carter worked alone.

The workday of Ronald Reagan (1981–1989), in contrast, was usually over by four in the afternoon. He also generally took Wednesday and Friday afternoons off and took frequent vacations. Like Eisenhower, he did not care to immerse himself in details and thought he made better decisions with less work. However, by the 1980s the public had become accustomed to more workaholic presidents, and there was criticism from many quarters about Reagan's "banker's hours" approach to the presidency. It is worth noting, however, that even though

Reagan had a shorter workday than his immediate predecessors, he labored longer than most presidents before 1930.

Reagan's two immediate successors, both more hands-on presidents, worked longer hours. For George Bush, the workday began at about seven in the morning and lasted until six or six-thirty in the evening. He tried to take weekends off, generally preferring to leave Washington altogether. Clinton worked even more. A man who needed only about five hours sleep a night and who, in one associate's words, "works whenever he's awake," Clinton started his workday after his morning jog and continued until late at night. It was common for Clinton to be on the telephone conducting business well after midnight. He rarely took weekends off, and Saturday and Sunday became regular workdays at his White House. (At the start of yet another frenetic weekend, a Clinton aide joked that there were "only two more days until Monday.")

When he became president in 2001, George W. Bush tried to use the same schedule that had been successful for him when he was governor of Texas. He started his day with his morning run at six, after which he would take his wife coffee in bed. A stickler for promptness (he referred to his presidency as "the on-time administration"), he began his daily meetings promptly at 8:00 a.m. Clay Johnson, Bush's personnel director and an old personal friend, described the president's schedule as "two hard half-days": work from 8:00 a.m. until 11:30 a.m., break for lunch, exercise, and relaxation, and then work again from 3:30 p.m. to 6:00 or 6:30 p.m.[5] By 10:00 p.m., Bush would generally retire for the night; late-night calls to his aides were rare. Fridays were often short days; weekend work was minimized, especially before the terrorist attacks in September 2001.

While this schedule might not seem consistent with the image of the president struggling mightily with great issues, it fit Bush's view of his job. Equating the presidency with a chief executive officer of a major corporation, Bush, like Reagan before him, saw his role as providing broad direction for the ship of state, and thus there was no reason to spend hours mastering innumerable details of policy. In his mind, a workload like Clinton's was counterproductive; a president, like anyone else, needs adequate downtime to "recharge the batteries." The difference in work habits between Clinton and the younger Bush was seen in the time each spent on his first budget:

> By [chief of staff Andrew] Card's estimation, Mr. Bush devoted in the 'neighborhood of five hours' in meetings to discuss his budget proposal. By contrast, Gene Sperling, who for years was a top economic adviser to Mr. Clinton, said the former president spent at least 25 hours in official meetings and 50 hours more in casual settings. Mr. Bush left it to [Vice President Richard] Cheney to preside over a small group of aides who actually drafted the proposal.[6]

The long workdays most presidents keep put enormous stress on the president's staff, who must work at least as long and hard as the president does. George Bush's staff averaged between a fifty- and an eighty-hour workweek, frequently working from six in the morning until eight at night. Bush domestic policy adviser Roger B. Porter at one point was sleeping in his office during the week. For the Clinton staff, it was worse. Because the boss worked weekends, so did the staff, and so twelve to fifteen hours per day, seven days a week, was not an uncommon schedule. In addition, Clinton's erratic personal schedule meant that he would call aides at all sorts of odd hours to discuss policy. On the other hand, George W. Bush encouraged his staff to reduce working hours whenever possible. So far as the president is concerned, of course, the Oval Office is only a one-minute walk from the Executive Residence, and the president can always retreat there to snatch a few minutes' respite during the busy day. White

House staffers, most of whom have an average commute to the office of forty-five minutes to an hour, have no such luxury.[7]

During the past century, the demands on the presidency have increased enormously, so that a few hours' work in the morning is no longer sufficient. All modern presidents have worked longer hours than most nineteenth-century presidents. Even those, such as Reagan and George W. Bush, who tried to minimize their workload, ended up working more than they originally planned. The expanded responsibilities of the United States government demands it, and the public tends to expect it. Today, in a "24/7" world, most presidents find themselves working long hours indeed. In fact, George W. Bush, in a debate with his 2004 Democratic challenger, Sen. John F. Kerry, repeatedly said that being president was "hard work."

The President's Recreation

With its long hours and psychological burden, the modern presidency is a stressful job. Consequently, rest and relaxation are important to the well-being of the president.

Among the recreational facilities available at the White House is a heated outdoor swimming pool, built with private funds by President Ford. The original White House swimming pool was built in 1933 with publicly donated funds for Franklin Roosevelt, who used it frequently, at least during his early years in office. Truman, Kennedy, and Johnson also used the pool often, but Eisenhower did not. Nixon later eliminated the pool to make space for a press room. During the Clinton administration, a hot tub was built next to the pool.

The White House also contains a small gymnasium, a tennis court that was built originally for Theodore Roosevelt, and a one-lane bowling alley that was particularly popular with Nixon. There is a movie theater where the first family and their guests can watch their favorite movies. Presidential requests for movies that are in current release are filled quickly by the film studios.

The White House library regularly receives new books from publishing houses, which send titles that match each president's interests. For example, when the Eisenhowers moved into the White House the library was flooded with western and romance titles, which were the favorites of the president and first lady, respectively.

Presidents have managed to relax in a variety of ways. Benjamin Harrison took walks or used the billiard table in the basement of the White House. In fact, the entire Harrison family played the game, despite the terrible condition of the basement in the 1890s. Harrison's successor (and predecessor), Grover Cleveland (1885–1889; 1893–1897), also relaxed at the billiard table, and he enjoyed taking carriage rides through the city as well. Although Cleveland spent more time at his desk than many previous presidents, he still got away for hunting and fishing.

Because of the time he spent caring for his frail, epileptic wife, William McKinley (1897–1901) was unable to indulge in many recreational activities. He took walks and, like Cleveland, enjoyed an occasional carriage ride. He also enjoyed visits from his friends and an infrequent game of cards. His greatest pleasure, however, was the cigar that was his constant companion. It was perhaps the one indulgence he permitted himself.

A "man's man," Theodore Roosevelt walked and hiked regularly, jogged often, excelled at horsemanship, hunted, swam in the Potomac, and played tennis on the White House courts with invited guests. Roosevelt's tennis guests were members of Congress, diplomats, cabinet members, and other political figures. An invitation to play tennis with Roosevelt was a privilege, and only those who played well were invited back. Roosevelt also enjoyed fencing, boxing, and wrestling, and he often devoted

entire afternoons to any one of them. He even practiced the martial arts and once set up a contest between American wrestling and Japanese jujitsu to see which was superior. Yet he also loved to read and frequently devoted his evenings to a book or the latest magazines. The entire Roosevelt household read with him.

William Howard Taft (1909–1913), not being a fan of the strenuous life, preferred less demanding recreation. Taft took walks and occasional automobile rides, and he enjoyed reading the newspapers and having massages. A baseball fan, Taft was the first president to open a season by tossing out the first pitch. He also played golf often.

For Woodrow Wilson (1913–1921) golf was never more than an amusement; he never tried to be good at it. Rides in his car, billiards, solitaire, particularly Canfield, and the theater were among his other favorite pastimes. Warren G. Harding (1921–1923) played golf and walked a little for exercise, but he preferred spending his spare time playing cards—poker and bridge—with old cronies from Ohio.

Calvin Coolidge relaxed by taking walks and working jigsaw puzzles. One of his Secret Service agents taught him to fish and he became an avid angler, although all he did was hold the rod. His agents baited the hook and removed the fish for him. One day, when he noticed someone catching fish from the stream in front of his South Dakota vacation house, he sent the Secret Service to confiscate them and tell the trespassers, "They are my fish." His favorite relaxation, however, was sleeping. Coolidge slept at least eleven hours a day, getting nine hours a night and taking two- to four-hour naps each afternoon.

Herbert Hoover, who spent his 1929–1933 term grappling unsuccessfully with the Great Depression, seems to have relaxed very little in the White House. Irwin Hood "Ike" Hoover (no relation to the president), then chief usher at the White House, noted that the president "labored practically all his waking hours and never spent any time with his family."[8] Hoover worked out with a medicine ball in the mornings, however, and read often. It was his complaint about being unable to find adequate reading material in the White House that led to publishers' donations. And the Hoovers apparently enjoyed dinner companions; in fact they rarely ate alone.

Franklin Roosevelt's inability to walk because of polio limited the forms of recreation he could enjoy. At first, Roosevelt swam frequently in the White House swimming pool, but as the cares of his office mounted, he used the pool less and less; he had largely abandoned it by 1945. In the way of hobbies Roosevelt was a skilled bird-watcher, and he liked to collect stamps, books, and models of sailing ships. His White House study in fact was filled with these things, much to the dismay of the housekeeping staff.[9] Roosevelt also relaxed by taking weekend trips to his mountain hideaway, Shangri-La (now Camp David), in the Maryland countryside. He also frequently enjoyed the quiet and privacy of long automobile rides in the country, and he liked to fish from the presidential yacht. Roosevelt's yacht was one of several vessels that had been maintained by the navy and made available to presidents since the Theodore Roosevelt administration. President Carter sold the last of these boats during his administration, and now there is no presidential yacht.

President Truman maintained an exercise regime while in the White House. He began the day with an hour's brisk walk at six, followed by a swim in the pool, a workout on the rowing and exercise machines, some calisthenics, and another dip in the pool. From 1949 to 1950 part of the well-publicized daily walks were devoted to viewing the renovation of the White House, which had to be almost totally rebuilt because of accumulated structural problems. (During the renovation, the Trumans lived at Blair House, which is situated across Pennsylvania Avenue from the White House.) The walks stopped after an

aborted assassination attempt on Truman in 1950. Truman also relaxed by playing the piano during quiet evenings with his family.

Believing that proper rest was vital to effective work, Eisenhower carefully guarded his leisure time while president. An avid golfer, he made a putting green out of the lawn outside the Oval Office—he threatened to shoot the squirrels that kept burying nuts there—and practiced his swing on the South Lawn. He played golf often at the Burning Tree Country Club in Bethesda, Maryland. The president also enjoyed painting and set up a studio in the White House. He liked to watch movies, particularly westerns; preferred to read westerns, mysteries, and cookbooks; and was the first president to spend much time watching television.

President Kennedy relaxed by leaving Washington. Almost every weekend he was off to his family's property in Massachusetts or Florida, a friend's home in rural Virginia, or Camp David. Many of these holidays were taken without his wife, who often vacationed separately. While at the White House itself, Kennedy used the White House pool. He would take a nude swim in the afternoon, return to his room for a nap, go back to work, and then return to the pool afterward. J. B. West, chief usher at the White House from 1957 to 1969, wrote that Kennedy followed this routine every day that he was at the mansion.[10] Because the president had a chronically bad back that hampered his physical activity, he exercised regularly to strengthen it, and he kept a rocking chair in the Oval Office for relief from his back pain. But despite his ailment, Kennedy enjoyed sailing and was a good golfer.

Lyndon Johnson was a human dynamo who never seemed to need rest. For Johnson, a man always on the move, work itself seemed to be a form of relaxation. When he sought some other form of activity, he swam in the pool, played an occasional game of dominoes, and sometimes watched a movie. The president also enjoyed dancing; at parties he took turns dancing with different partners and often danced with his daughters, Luci and Lynda. Because Johnson liked a good massage, when he left the White House he arranged to have his masseur, a navy officer, transferred to Bergstrom Air Force Base near his Texas ranch.

The more sedate Richard Nixon rarely swam and had the pool filled in. Nixon, however, watched an occasional movie, sometimes played golf, and used the White House bowling alley. Moreover, he went out frequently on the White House yacht. Nixon also often read for relaxation and seemed to find comfort in the White House fireplaces, which were used even in the summer; the air-conditioning was turned up to compensate. In the way of spectator sports, Nixon liked baseball and greatly enjoyed football. In fact, he was an avid fan of the Washington Redskins and followed the team closely when he could. He even suggested plays to the Redskins' coaching staff. According to Dennis McCarthy, a member of Nixon's Secret Service detail, one evening after a game Nixon came outside and sat on the porch with him "just like two guys getting together over a couple of beers to discuss the game, except there was no beer." [11]

Gerald Ford was a former football player who enjoyed watching the game, but he also liked more active recreation. An outdoor swimming pool was built during Ford's term, and the president lifted weights, rode an exercise bicycle, and skied in the winter. Ford's greatest pleasure, however, was golf. He played whenever he could and unfortunately developed a reputation as a rather erratic player after hitting a spectator or two with his golf shots.

Like many of his predecessors, Jimmy Carter relaxed with a swim. He jogged on the White House grounds, bowled in the bowling alley, and played tennis on the mansion's courts. The Carter family particularly enjoyed the movie theater, which by Rosalynn Carter's account became one of their favorite places to escape. The family frequently retreated there with popcorn or an entire meal to watch movies, including to-be-released titles with the director or an actor as a guest. Carter enjoyed classical and some pop music, and, as a speed reader who could read two thousand words per minute with 95 percent retention, he could read three or four books a week.

After the attempt on his life, Ronald Reagan regularly followed an exercise routine that actually increased his muscular strength while he was president. Evenings with friends were a favorite pastime; he was an excellent storyteller who loved a good joke. Reagan also enjoyed the outdoors, particularly riding horses and working at his California ranch in the Santa Ynez Mountains.

George Bush seemed to attack his recreation time. Perhaps because he had been the captain of the baseball team at Yale, he developed a preference for active relaxation and pursued it with zest. He spent time playing golf, often speeding around the course, and had an artificial putting green installed on the mansion's grounds. He jogged regularly, swam, played some softball, and made frequent use of the White House tennis court. He enjoyed hunting and fishing and sometimes raced his powerboat off the Maine coast. Having developed a passion for horseshoes, he had a horseshoe pit built at the White House and played often.

On the other hand, workaholic Bill Clinton sometimes seemed never to relax at all. However, he did have a morning jog each day, sometimes on a special track built on the South Lawn. (Before the track was built, Clinton would take his morning runs through the streets of Washington, even stopping a few times at McDonald's for breakfast—to the displeasure of the Secret Service.) He was an avid reader, particularly of mysteries and novels, a sports fan, especially of the University of Arkansas basketball team, and played the saxophone. He also played golf and occasionally fished, hunted, and went biking or boating.

George W. Bush, an avid baseball fan, shakes hands with St. Louis Cardinals catcher Mike Matheny after throwing out the first pitch before the Milwaukee Brewers and St. Louis Cardinals baseball game at the Busch Stadium in St. Louis in April 2004.

George W. Bush, a dedicated jogger, made regular use of the White House track, running three miles a day. He had to cut back somewhat on his running after suffering knee problems. Bush also enjoyed reading, lifting weights, and working outdoors and bike riding at his Texas ranch. His greatest passion was baseball: he was an avid and lifelong baseball fan, and for several years was part-owner of the Texas Rangers baseball team.

Alternatives to the White House

When the pressures of the presidency become too great, it may not be enough to retreat to the movie theater or the swimming pool. Presidents often feel the need to leave the White House altogether to put their problems behind them. For that purpose the government maintains a presidential retreat in the mountains of Maryland, known as Camp David.

Originally named Shangri-La, Camp David was built for Franklin Roosevelt, who traveled there frequently. Eisenhower renamed it Camp David in honor of his grandson, Dwight David Eisenhower II, and made it his weekend home for the early part of his administration.

Subsequent presidents, particularly since Johnson, have found Camp David an invaluable source of solitude for self-renewal. It also has been a place where presidents can retreat to meditate on problems, design programs, and write speeches. For example, it was at Camp David that FDR plotted much of the strategy for the Normandy invasion of World War II. The retreat also has been used to conduct business and even for international diplomacy. In 1978 Carter hosted an important summit meeting there between Egyptian president Anwar Sadat and Israeli prime minister Menachem Begin, which led to the signing of the Camp David peace accords.

A PRESIDENT'S VACATION

All presidents face the problem of how to get away from it all and escape the pressures of the office. To some extent, it is impossible to escape, for some presidential matters cannot be delayed "until next week." Even when on vacation, presidents still receive daily intelligence briefings. In addition, presidents cannot simply "take off" like an average American; because they are recognized everywhere they go and everyone wants to see them, they cannot easily find solitude.

George W. Bush, Ronald Reagan, and Lyndon Johnson were able to get away to their ranches where they could relax outside of the public eye. John Kennedy went to the family compound in Massachusetts, Richard Nixon had a vacation home in California, and George Bush retreated to Maine. Bill Clinton, who did not own a family residence until his last year in office, was faced with finding summer vacation spots for his family every year.

In 1993 and 1994, and 1997–2000, the Clintons vacationed for about one week each August at Martha's Vineyard, off the coast of Massachusetts. The island was chosen because of its relative seclusion and because the inhabitants are so used to the rich and famous that a president would hardly seem worthy of notice. During his time on the island, Clinton was able to unwind by walking the beach, playing golf, being with his family, and sleeping late. However, predictions that the glitterati would ignore the president's presence were wrong; Clinton was wined and dined by local residents and spent a lot of his time at parties and dinners.

In 1995 and 1996 the Clintons vacationed in a more remote location, Jackson Hole, just south of the Grand Teton National Park, in Wyoming.

When first used in 1942, the buildings at Camp David looked unfinished and were filled with furniture from the White House attic. The modern Camp David complex, which is far from rustic, is designed to let the president relax in comfort. It has a four-bedroom, air-conditioned lodge and additional guest cabins. Conference rooms are also provided. There is a 130-seat chapel (built with private funds). Like the White House, Camp David has a swimming pool, bowling alley, and tennis court. For presidents who like to fish, there is a stream stocked with trout; for shooting, there is an archery and skeet-shooting range; and for playing golf, there is a par-three hole. Jacqueline Kennedy, a skilled rider, particularly appreciated the camp's riding stables.

Most important, Camp David is private. It is thirty minutes by helicopter from the White House, but it contains adequate communications equipment to keep in touch with the rest of the world. The grounds are surrounded by a chain link fence topped with barbed wire and are patrolled by Marine guards. No one enters without an invitation from the first family; even the omnipresent White House press corps is left outside the compound. As President Reagan noted, Camp David is one of the few places where a president can just step outside and go for a walk. Camp David is run by the Navy at an estimated cost of $3 million annually.[12]

Even with the availability of Camp David, most presidents like the alternative of a private home for

The Clintons hiked and rode horseback, went whitewater rafting down the Snake River, and toured Grand Teton and Yellowstone. Jackson Hole is remote, but not remote enough to escape the trappings and burdens of the presidency. There were still neighbors who wanted the president to dine with them; there were still the aides, the media, and the Secret Service surrounding him; there were still the daily briefings. There were still national problems to deal with, as when Clinton took time out in 1995 to direct the federal response to wildfires on Long Island.

The Clinton experience indicates that presidents cannot truly escape from the pressures of their office; they can, at most, briefly put them in the background. Although G. W. Bush spent nearly the entire month of August 2001 at his 1,600-acre ranch in Crawford, Texas, he also did not leave his presidential responsibilities behind in Washington. In addition to "enjoying a little downtime" with family and friends, Bush took a few one- or two-day trips to parts of the Southwest to talk with Americans, gave a nationwide televised address on his decision to allow limited federal funding of stem cell research, and met with Russian president Vladimir Putin.

After the terrorist attacks of September 11, 2001, Bush continued to spend much of each August on "working vacations" in Crawford. In 2002 he used his ranch as a base while pursuing other work-related activities, such as speaking at fund-raisers around the country for GOP candidates running for office in the midterm elections and convening an economic summit in Texas. In 2003 Bush spent the bulk of August in Crawford, while also traveling to appear at fundraisers. With his reelection effort in high gear, Bush spent much of August 2004 on the campaign trail; the month concluded with the start of the Republican National Convention in New York.

rest and relaxation. Such homes, popularly known, for example, as the western (Nixon) or Georgia (Carter) White House, are equipped with communications and security facilities at public expense. Whereas Camp David is used frequently for weekend escapes, a president generally will use the alternate White House for extended vacations.

Almost every recent president has had at least one such retreat. FDR withdrew to his family estate in Hyde Park, New York, or to Warm Springs, Georgia, where he could undergo physical therapy. Truman went home to Independence, Missouri, or traveled to the Key West, Florida, naval base when he took a vacation. Eisenhower sometimes vacationed in Denver, Colorado, near his wife's family. He was there when he suffered a heart attack in 1955. Eisenhower had a Gettysburg farmhouse that he had purchased and remodeled, and before he left office it had become his weekend and vacation retreat.

Kennedy used several retreats. Originally avoiding Camp David because he was sure he would not like it if the Eisenhowers had, he vacationed instead at his family's compound at Cape Cod, Massachusetts, his father's house in Palm Beach, Florida, or at a friend's house, leased for his use, at Glen Ora, Virginia. After leaving the Glen Ora house the Kennedys decided to build their own retreat near Glen Ora, and it was virtually finished when they decided they liked Camp David after all. Kennedy and his wife made news with their separate vacations. Mrs. Kennedy traveled without the president to India, Italy, and the Mediterranean.

Johnson retreated to the LBJ Ranch on the Pedernales River in the Texas hill country. He loved to oversee the operation of his spread, speeding around it in his car and showing it off to visitors. The president also enjoyed hosting barbecues, sometimes on the spur of the moment. He challenged his Secret Service detail to speedboat races on the ranch's lake. The service always let him win the races so that they could secretly keep the fastest boat.

President Nixon had two retreats: a home in Key Biscayne, Florida, and one in San Clemente, California. The Nixon homes became involved in the Watergate controversy, when it was charged that funds were used improperly in their purchase. Other critics claimed that the remodeling of the Nixon homes, done in the name of security, in fact increased their resale value at the taxpayers' expense.

President Ford maintained only one retreat, a home in California, and President Carter went back to his longtime home in Plains, Georgia, for a break from Washington. Ronald Reagan enjoyed his California ranch while president and vacationed there frequently. In fact, Reagan enjoyed his ranch so much that he was criticized for taking too many vacations; he spent some 200 days there in his first term.

President George Bush escaped White House pressures by retreating to Houston, Texas, where he stayed in a house he rented from friends. The Bushes' retirement home in Houston was not ready for occupancy until after he left the presidency. Much of his vacation time was spent in Kennebunkport, Maine, where he had a summer home on land his family had owned since 1902. Bush's Kennebunkport retreat had a large house, two smaller ones, a swimming pool, and a tennis court.

Thinking that he would not like the atmosphere of the retreat with its military guards, President Clinton rarely used Camp David early in his presidency, although he went there more as time passed. As his second term developed, Camp David became a welcome refuge from the controversy surrounding his behavior with Paula Jones and Monica Lewinsky.

Unlike many of his predecessors, Clinton had no private estate to use for vacations. He was part owner of a house in Little Rock, Arkansas, and toward the end of his presidency the Clintons bought homes in Chappaqua, New York, and Washington, D.C. The first family took summer vacations at Martha's Vineyard, Massachusetts, and Jackson Hole, Wyoming, and shorter vacations in the Virgin Islands, Hawaii, and ski resorts in Utah.

Like his father, President George W. Bush had access to the family's compound at Kennebunkport, Maine. He also made good use of Camp David, especially on weekends after the terrorist attacks of September 2001 to decide on the American military response. After winning reelection in November 2004, Bush opted to spend a long weekend relaxing at Camp David. However, his preferred retreat was to the ranch that he and his wife owned near the small town of Crawford, Texas. *(See box, A President's Vacation, p. 14)*

In August 2001 Bush spent a month at his ranch on what was termed a "working vacation," the longest such break from Washington taken by a president since Nixon (which led to criticism in the press and a decline in his approval ratings). Besides being a refuge where the first couple could host barbecues for old friends, the informal setting of the Crawford ranch was also used for diplomacy; Bush met with Russian president Vladimir Putin to discuss Russo-American relations and with Saudi Crown Prince Abdullah in 2002 to discuss the problems in the Middle East. Among other world leaders who visited Crawford during Bush's first term were British prime minister Tony Blair, Spanish prime minister Jose Maria Aznar, and Mexican president Vicente Fox.

PROTECTING THE PRESIDENT: THE SECRET SERVICE

One of the major benefits provided presidents is the full-time personal protection for them and their families. While the bulk of the president's security is provided by the U.S. Secret Service, other government agencies also contribute to the effort to protect the president.[13] The Federal Bureau of Investigation (FBI) points out to the Secret Service those people within the United States who might pose a threat to the president, and the Central Intelligence Agency (CIA) provides information on potential assassins in other countries, a source of increasing concern to the service.

Because the number of Secret Service personnel is insufficient to fill all the human resource demands of protecting the president, local and foreign police may be used, depending on where the president travels. The air force provides a fighter escort for *Air Force One;* the navy furnishes backup in case an emergency develops while the president flies over the ocean; the army provides communication equipment; and the Marine Corps posts a detachment to guard Camp David. Finally, the General Services Administration (GSA) arranges for any renovations needed to improve security at a presidential residence.

Although all these agencies contribute to the president's safety, the central body is the Secret Service, which coordinates their activities. Any measures taken by GSA, for example, are at the request of the service, and it is the service that provides the human shield needed to protect the president.

Origins of the Secret Service

What is now known as the Secret Service was created in July 1865 to reduce the wholesale counterfeiting of U.S. currency. By the end of the Civil War, counterfeiting had reached such proportions that as many as one-third of all bills in circulation may have been bogus. In one of the last official acts of his life, President Abraham Lincoln agreed to the creation of a unit within the Treasury Department that would have the permanent task of catching forgers and counterfeiters. The Secret Service Division proved quite successful at this task. During its first few years it captured more than two hundred counterfeiters a year.

Because at that time the service was the only federal government agency that acted as a general law enforcement body, it found that its role expanded rapidly. By 1874 it was investigating fraud, peonage, and slavery cases, as well as the Ku Klux Klan. The service also began to acquire the form and structure of a bureaucratic institution and, unfortunately, a reputation for unsavory tactics; agents freely made searches and arrests without warrants and even spied on Andrew Johnson while he was still in the White House. In 1874 a distrustful Congress stripped it of all but its original functions.

The Secret Service languished until 1898 and the Spanish-American War, when President McKinley, needing an intelligence agency to gather information about the Spanish, asked for its help. During the war the service operated as both a military espionage body and a domestic counterintelligence body, and by the end of the war it had established itself as one of the best such units in the world. After the war the intelligence role was de-emphasized, but it was restored during World War I. Although the Secret Service worked well with the State Department during the conflict, it found itself out of the spy game by World War II. The growth of the FBI and military intelligence rendered the service's activities in that area superfluous.

The service's quite active anticounterfeiting operations remained intact throughout this period, however. In 1917 alone it obtained more than one thousand arrests and convictions and seized nearly $300,000 in fraudulent money. It also conducted

Secret Service agents accompany George W. Bush on a raised walkway leading to the stage at a campaign rally for Bush's reelection in Parkersburg, West Virginia, in September 2004.

investigations into official misconduct and played a major part in uncovering the Teapot Dome scandal during the Harding administration.

Protection of the president was not part of the service's original function. For many years presidents who wanted bodyguards had to hire them themselves, and most did without. Confronted with a would-be assassin in 1835, President Andrew Jackson himself attacked his assailant and drove him off. On the night he was killed, President Lincoln was guarded by a single District of Columbia policeman; the guard had wandered off when assailant John Wilkes Booth arrived. Secret Service agents were nearby when Presidents James A. Garfield and McKinley were shot, but none of them were responsible for protecting the president. In McKinley's case there were three agents next to him, but their only job was crowd control. Indeed, early efforts by the service to protect the president were rebuffed by Congress, and it was not

until 1906 that the first presidential detail was authorized.

The coverage given by the service gradually expanded through the years, and with the decline in its intelligence role, protection became its second major function. In 1940 the service survived a threat to that function from the FBI, which had taken on the job of protecting the vice president from 1929 to 1932, when a proposed relocation of the service into the Justice Department failed. In fact, the Secret Service was only permanently granted the job of presidential protection in 1951; until that time its authorization had to be renewed annually.

Organization and Personnel

Because of its original anticounterfeiting role, the Secret Service was for a long time an arm of the Treasury Department, which administered the service with a very light touch. In the wake of the 2001 terrorist attacks, President George W. Bush in June 2002 proposed creating a new cabinet-level domestic security office that would include the Secret Service; the Secret Service became part of the new Department of Homeland Security on March 1, 2003.

As of 2004, the Secret Service employed about 2,100 elite special agents. Other employees included the Uniformed Division, about 1,200 officers, and approximately 1,700 other staff members. The service has had a small but growing number of female special agents assigned to every aspect of the service's work, including the presidential detail. In 2004 the service named a woman to be deputy director.

The fiscal year 2004 budget for the service totaled $1.14 billion. Its budget has been steadily increasing as the service tries to respond to more demands. Budgeting can be difficult because it is hard to know in advance exactly how much protection may be needed. The total varies with the changing number of protectees and the activities in which they engage.

The service's investigative mission includes the divisions of counterfeit, financial crimes, and forensic services. Among the crimes the service's experts investigate are credit-card fraud, computer fraud, and money laundering. In addition, forensic examiners analyze documents and identify fingerprints.

The service's protective responsibilities include the compilation of data on individuals who, for whatever reason, have come to the service's attention as potential threats to its protectees. Its files contain more than forty thousand people, about 1 percent of whom are on a "watch list" as serious threats. Others are singled out depending on the president's travel plans. In addition to identifying dangerous persons to be monitored, the service also conducts searches to ensure that any environment the president will occupy is safe and secure, without dangerous objects such as explosives or surveillance devices.

Individual divisions are responsible for a particular protectee. The division for the president contains the White House detail. Other divisions are responsible for the vice president, each of the living former presidents, and any widowed first ladies. Should a protectee die or decline coverage, his or her division is disbanded. The service is also responsible for protecting announced presidential candidates and foreign heads of state.

The Uniformed Division originally was part of the District of Columbia Police Department. President Harding, who wanted better control over it, removed it from the department in 1922. In 1930, after a stranger walked unchallenged into President Hoover's dining room one evening, the Secret Service was given authority over the division. The Uniformed Division is responsible for the White House security guards, and since 1970 it has also provided protection for foreign embassies in Washington. When the service provides protection for an embassy, it protects only that; guards do not leave the grounds, and they take action only if someone trespasses onto the property.

Most Secret Service employees have demanding jobs, and the training for special agents is particularly arduous. To be a special agent an applicant must be younger than thirty-seven years old when appointed and be able to pass a physical exam, the Treasury Enforcement Agent Exam or U.S. Marshal's Enforcement Exam, an extensive interview, and a security check, among other procedures. Candidates who pass the initial screening undergo an intensive training program to prepare them for both parts of the service's mission. They are first sent to the Federal Law Enforcement Training Center in Glynco, Georgia, to learn about criminal law and investigative techniques. Then they move on to the service's 420-acre school in Beltsville, Maryland, to learn the details of investigation and protection. A superb training ground, the Beltsville facility has classrooms and laboratories in which

Secretary of Homeland Security Tom Ridge receives a ceremonial flag from Secretary of the Treasury John Snow in Washington, D.C., February 25, 2003. The event marked the ceremonial handing over of control of the U.S. Secret Service, U.S. Customs Service, and the Federal Law Enforcement Training Center from the Treasury Department to the new Department of Homeland Security.

sophisticated methods for detecting forgeries are taught.

To prepare for their protective role, prospective agents are taught such subjects as emergency medical principles, abnormal psychology, hand-to-hand combat, investigative techniques, and evasive driving tactics. They also become firearms experts. They study movies of previous assassination attempts and engage in simulations in which their own responses are videotaped and studied. Using full-size mock-ups of the White House and of a city street, new agents can refine their skills.

Secret Service agents are civil service employees and are paid according to the federal government's General Schedule (GS). Depending on experience and education, agents usually begin at the GS5, 6, or 7 levels, which starts at between $24,000 to $29,000 per year. Advancement to GS10 or higher is usually fairly rapid; within six to eight years, an agent may earn more than $50,000 annually.

Agents start in a field office, move to a protective detail after a few years if they are good enough, and after a few more years go back to a field office and eventually an administrative job. For people on protective details, particularly the president's, the stress can be extreme; thus agents tend to be rotated regularly. Moreover, the hours can be long and irregular; agents may find themselves on duty for sixteen hours and more. Because an agent can be called on duty on short notice and sent anywhere around the world, a normal family and personal life is often difficult at best. Indications of this are found in the fact that the average age of an agent is only thirty-five, and that the service teaches its agents the warning signs of psychological disorders and alcoholism.[14]

The Roles of the Secret Service

With its roles of defender of the nation's currency and protector of the president, the Secret Service is in a sense two agencies in one: a criminal investigation unit and a bodyguard service. Unfortunately, the two roles do not always fit together very well, and some agents are not equally comfortable in both. The skills required to crack a counterfeiting ring are not the same as those needed to foil an assassination attempt. The service thinks the juxtaposition is useful, but not everyone agrees.

Because relatively few agents regularly participate in the protective role, the major task for many agents is the prevention of counterfeiting and forgery. The service attempts to break counterfeiting rings before the bogus bills go into service, targeting the big distributors. It also investigates cases of forged checks and documents and has recently investigated food stamp fraud. Of particular interest are cases involving stolen government checks and bonds. The service tries to combine public awareness with the latest technology to control these crimes. It obtains convictions in 98 percent of the cases it prosecutes.

The better-known part of the service's mission is protection of the president. That role has expanded considerably since its inception. The first White House detail, assigned to Theodore Roosevelt in 1901, had only two agents. The detail expanded to ten by 1918 and to thirty-seven by 1940. In 1989 it numbered seventy. The protection has broadened as well. Originally, it included just the president, but in 1908 it was extended to the president-elect, in 1917 to the president's immediate family, and since 1962 has included the vice president and the vice president–elect. Protection for these four individuals is mandatory; by law, they may not refuse it. Further additions to the service's workload were made in 1965, when retired presidents, widows of presidents, and their children under age sixteen were protected. Coverage was extended to presidential candidates in 1968, to foreign heads of state in 1971, and to candidates' wives (on a limited basis) in 1976. In addition, the president in 1971 was granted the right to request protection for anyone thought to need it, as Jimmy Carter did for Edward Kennedy in 1980 before the senator became an official presidential candidate. Any

of these people can refuse Secret Service protection, but few do; one of those few was Richard Nixon, who terminated his protection in 1985. Bill Clinton will be the last president with lifetime Secret Service protection; under a 1997 law, former presidents serving after that time will receive protection for ten years after they leave the White House.

Because of extensions of coverage and increased travel and activity by public figures, the demand for protection results in a considerable load for the service, particularly in election years, when it may be forced to borrow from elsewhere to meet its obligations. This is true even though the service normally protects only those candidates who can raise enough campaign funds to warrant matching funds from the federal Treasury.

Occasionally, the service finds itself with other tasks. During World War II, for example, it was responsible for protecting the original Constitution and the Declaration of Independence on display at the National Archives in Washington, D.C. Similarly, when Leonardo da Vinci's painting *Mona Lisa* toured the United States in 1962, it was guarded by the service.

Protecting the President: Tactics and Problems

All the training undertaken by agents in the Secret Service's operations divisions is aimed at keeping the president alive and unharmed. The service has adopted numerous tactics to ensure the president's continued safety in a world filled with dangers.

The service prefers, of course, that the president remain in the White House, where there are numerous safeguards and a controlled environment. Although the service does not reveal any details, it is clear that White House security arrangements are elaborate. Anyone entering the mansion on business is checked; anyone working there, including presidential aides, must wear a photo badge. All incoming packages and visitors are also carefully monitored; bomb-sniffing dogs are available to check suspicious packages or vehicles. Armed guards and plainclothes agents keep watch around the premises, and sharpshooters are posted on the roof. The grounds are protected by reinforced fences, guardhouses, television cameras, and electronic sensors. In recent years, a bicycle patrol has been added. There is a Doppler radar system that looks directly up to detect any parachute assault, antiaircraft weapons (reportedly heat-seeking, shoulder-fired Stinger missiles), and a bomb shelter. Finally, should the president need help, there is a "panic button" under the desk in the Oval Office that can unobtrusively summon agents at any time.

Despite the trained agents and all of the equipment, the system sometimes fails. In 1977 an intruder was able to walk up to the windows outside the Oval Office and speak directly to President Carter. In 1981 a man with a history of mental illness gained access to the White House grounds and was there unchallenged for ten minutes; he made it to the mansion itself before he was stopped.[15] In the early morning on September 12, 1994, a man flying a small airplane eluded radar detection and crashlanded on the White House grounds. The pilot was killed as the plane crumpled up against the mansion itself, directly under the president's bedroom. The first family was not in the White House at the time, and it was not certain whether the incident was an attack on President Clinton or a failed stunt. Nonetheless, security measures were carefully reevaluated. In 1995, in an effort to protect against vehicular attack, part of Pennsylvania Avenue in front of the White House was closed to traffic and converted into a pedestrian mall. Incidents still occur: in February 2001 agents were forced to shoot (not fatally) a man carrying a gun outside on the South Lawn. In the wake of the September 2001 terrorist attacks, greater security measures were put in place at the White House. Tours were suspended

(they later were resumed) and access became more limited around the complex. In addition, a plan was implemented whereby President Bush and Vice President Richard Cheney were rarely in the same place at the same time. For security reasons, Cheney spent much of his time in what was described as an "undisclosed location." But by the time of the Bush-Cheney 2004 reelection effort, Cheney was a key presence on the campaign trail and his whereabouts generally were public knowledge.

When the president travels, the challenges for the service are greater because the variables that can be easily controlled are fewer. The White House detail and the field offices in the areas where the president plans to travel must make extensive security arrangements. Working with the local police, they secure the airport where the president will arrive and depart. They carefully plan and survey the routes to be traveled, secure the buildings in which the president will appear, and arrange that rooftops and other overlooks be patrolled. Sharpshooters may be posted on roofs. Procedures for screening onlookers are introduced. The service's files are checked for any people known to be a possible threat to the president; some of them may be watched during the visit. Preparations extend to identifying a hospital to use in case of emergency and ensuring that it has adequate supplies of the president's blood type.

In recent years security arrangements have not permitted publicity about the president's travel plans. Formerly, in an effort by political supporters to ensure the largest crowds possible, it was customary to publicize the president's travel route. For example, President Kennedy's exact route through Dallas on November 22, 1963, was available to anyone who picked up a Dallas newspaper. This is no longer true. When the president travels today, the arrival and departure times and the itinerary are not public knowledge.

The most visible part of the presidential protection effort is the cordon of agents that surrounds the president. These agents are with the president at almost all times, even in the White House, except the family quarters. They stand guard both inside and outside of every room occupied by the president. When the president leaves the White House, the agents form (as best they can) a human shield around the chief executive. The service tries to maintain what it calls a "safe zone" or clear space around the president, so that the agents have a better chance to spot a potential assailant. Their efforts to keep a safe zone have sometimes led to criticism of their tactics.

Because these agents represent the last line of defense for the president, they are under enormous pressure. Beyond watching for any known dangerous people who may be around, agents scan the crowds in search of unusual or threatening behavior: a man wearing an overcoat on a warm day, a person carrying a newspaper in a strange way, a woman too eager to get close to the president, or even a face that keeps reappearing in different places. Because the goal of the service is prevention, not retribution, agents must develop a sixth sense to anticipate trouble. An instinct for danger and quick reactions are critical to keeping the president safe.

Should an attack occur, agents shield the president first, then subdue the assailant, and finally, once the president is safely removed, secure the area and assist any injured bystanders. Agents are trained to become a human shield for the president. As he watched agents stand to practice with firearms, President Reagan commented that they made a very large target that way; he was told that that was the point. In Dallas in 1963 agent Rufus W. Youngblood covered Vice President Lyndon Johnson with his own body when the presidential motorcade came under attack. Videotapes of the 1981 assassination attempt on President Reagan show agent Timothy J. McCarthy, with arms and legs spread wide, walking directly toward the assailant, John W. Hinckley Jr., thus blocking his view of the president. (McCarthy was shot, but he recovered.)

The service has encountered several serious difficulties in its efforts to protect the president, and several of these have had to do with presidents themselves. Some presidents have been quite cooperative with the service, but others have balked at its requests, generally for two reasons.

One reason is strictly political. Most presidents like crowds, and even if they do not, it is simply good politics for them to be seen mingling with their adoring supporters. Thus, while the service probably would prefer that presidents spent their days in one room in the White House, political realities dictate that presidents get out and "press the flesh." The more they do that, the harder it is for the service. President Johnson, for example, loved to dive into crowds, much to his bodyguards' dismay. On that fateful day in Dallas in 1963, Kennedy had the protective cover removed from his limousine so that the crowds could see him better.

Even a president like Nixon, who was something of a loner and thus easier to protect, was a problem for political reasons. Nixon's staff constantly wanted to show how much Nixon was loved by the people and looked for close public contacts to prove it. Thus, the staff consistently fought the service over security arrangements, which it regarded as too restrictive for its aims. One argument over where the crowd restraining line was to be placed was so bitter that the chief of Nixon's protective detail threatened to arrest Chief of Staff H. R. Haldeman for his interference.

The second reason for the lack of cooperation with the service is the presidents' desire for privacy. Agents are a constant intrusive presence in the president's life, which may lead to presidential resentment and resistance. President Johnson complained that the service would not hesitate to occupy his bedroom, and when he was at his ranch, he would often try to lose his detail by jumping in the car and ordering his driver to drive as fast as possible. When at Kennebunkport, President Bush would sometimes zoom off in his powerboat, leaving his guardians behind. The issue of a president's privacy emerged during the Kenneth Starr investigation of President Clinton in 1998, when Secret Service agents assigned to his detail were required to testify before a grand jury.

The Secret Service has ways to get around presidents and first ladies who may find their protection particularly burdensome. Eleanor Roosevelt, for example, flatly refused to accept her protective detail. Finally, the service worked out a deal: if she would carry and learn to fire a handgun, the service would stop tailing her. In fact the gun stayed in her dresser drawer, and the service put undercover agents at her every stop. Early in his term Harry Truman liked to walk to the bank, but the service did not like the fact that he waited on street corners for the lights to change, so agents fixed all the traffic lights on his route to turn red in all directions at once—thus Truman would never have to wait on a corner again. He soon caught on, however, and ordered the service to stop.[16] Pat Nixon tried to keep the number of agents with her on trips around Washington smaller than the service wanted, but her wishes were ignored. When one day she noticed the second car of agents that was accompanying her, she was reassured that it was only there in case her car had engine trouble.[17]

Presidents also tend to be fatalistic, further complicating the service's job. Many presidents, in fact, begin to feel that personal risk is part of the job. The feeling expressed by Lyndon Johnson that "all a man needs is a willingness to trade his life for mine" seems common to most presidents. This sense that "no amount of protection is enough" in the face of a determined assassin makes the service's job more difficult, for it leads presidents to be less cautious than their guardians would like. Not all presidents are fatalistic to the same degree, but those who are prove quite difficult for the service. Indeed, one of the most fatalistic of presidents, John Kennedy, was also one of the hardest to protect.

Another problem the service faces is trying to identify a potential assassin, a critical step in preventing an attack on the president. The master files maintained by the service of anyone who may pose a risk to the president—for example, people who have made threats, mentally disturbed and violent people, or members of political extremist groups—are updated constantly and sorted by degree of threat. Before the president moves from the White House, a watch list is put together of anyone in the files who resides where the president is going, and the agents in charge account for everyone they can and keep special watch for the rest.

In practice, however, this system has several flaws. First, the service has to rely on the FBI for much of the information that goes into its files, and communication between the two agencies sometimes fails. The service also must rely on local police for information about individuals, and the quality of the data obtained may vary.

Second, the service, which is a rather small agency, lacks the human resources to evaluate reports as carefully as it would like. Thus, the watch list has been limited to about four hundred people, primarily because the agents cannot handle many more. After the attempt on President Reagan in 1981, some critics argued that John Hinckley's arrest for trying to carry a gun onto an airplane in 1980 should have put him on the watch list. Unfortunately, the agency lacked the people necessary to investigate that case and evaluate the risk.

The major problem, however, is that there is no consistent way to identify an assassin, either in the files or among the public at large. Despite its best efforts, the service has never managed to develop any statistical or psychological techniques that would allow it to distinguish unerringly a real assassin from all the false alarms in its own files, nor does it have any sure way to spot one in a crowd. In fact,

despite the impressive progress in the fields of computer technology and psychiatry, the service has few clues as to how to look for potential assassins. Without a reliable set of profiles or indices that can be used to identify those who are actually dangerous, as opposed to potentially dangerous, neither the agents nor their computers can derive much benefit from increased quantities of intelligence data.[18]

Such profiles simply do not exist. Thus, compilation of a watch list becomes a matter of subjective judgment by the agents in charge, as does the determination of which reports warrant inclusion in the master files. With no foolproof guide to help evaluate information, truly dangerous people can be and are overlooked. In fact, none of the people who have shot at service protectees since 1960—Lee Harvey Oswald (President Kennedy, 1963), Sirhan Sirhan (Robert Kennedy, 1968), Arthur Bremer (Gov. George Wallace, 1972), Lynette Alice Fromme (President Ford, 1975), Sara Jane Moore (President Ford, 1975), and John Hinckley (President Reagan, 1981)—were in the agency's files before the attack.

Complicating the service's mission further is the increased threat of foreign terrorist activity against the president, particularly after the attacks on the New York World Trade Center and the Pentagon in September 2001 and the color-coded system of alerts that developed in the aftermath. Although such threats may be mostly hypothetical, the service cannot take chances and must treat them seriously. Even two decades before the 2001 attacks, in late 1981, the service spent two months in a state of constant alert because of reports that Libya's Muammar Qaddafi had sent a "hit team" to kill President Reagan. Rumors flew about the nature and location of the team. In the end, however, nothing happened, and the hit squad may never have existed. This case indicates the additional burden thrown on the service in an era of international terrorism. Given the agency's limited resources, such a threat spreads the service thin and makes its job even more difficult.

Today, presidents frequently travel abroad, which also increases the problems for the Secret Service. The service must then coordinate its activities with those of a foreign country's security agencies; the difficulty of anticipating and spotting potential assassins is multiplied by the unfamiliar environment. That there are risks is shown in the attempt on former president Bush's life in April 1993. While on a visit to Kuwait, Bush was the target of a car bomb that was planted by the Iraqi intelligence service, in retribution for his role in leading Desert Storm. The plot failed and the bomb was never detonated, but the attempt indicates the potential danger and the difficulties of the service's job in protecting presidents and their families.

Notes

1. See Bradley H. Patterson Jr., *The White House Staff: Inside the West Wing and Beyond* (Washington, D.C.: Brookings, 2000), 379, and Christopher Georges, "Executive Suite," *Washington Monthly,* January/February 1993, 36.
2. Fred Barnes, "All the President's Perks," *New Republic,* September 2, 1991, 25.
3. Rosalynn Carter, *First Lady from Plains* (Boston: Houghton Mifflin, 1984), 144.
4. Quoted in J. B. West, *Upstairs at the White House: My Life with the First Ladies* (New York: Coward, McCann, and Geohegan, 1973), 209.
5. Carl M. Cannon and Alexis Simendinger, "Flextime at the White House," *National Journal,* February 17, 2001, 496.
6. Richard L. Berke, "Bush Is Providing Corporate Model for White House," *New York Times,* March 11, 2001, A1.
7. Some description of the life of the staff can be found in two pieces by Burt Solomon: "The Work's Hard, the Hours Long, But the Rewards Are Worthwhile" (*National Journal,* February 17, 1990, 406–407) deals with the George Bush staff, and "When the Next H-Hour Strikes, Will Clinton's Aides Be Awake?" (*National Journal,* June 11, 1994, 1362–1363) deals with Clinton's.
8. Irwin Hood Hoover, *Forty-Two Years in the White House* (Boston: Houghton Mifflin, 1934), 267.
9. West, *Upstairs at the White House,* 20.

10. Ibid., 204–205.
11. Dennis V. McCarthy, *Protecting the President: The Inside Story of a Secret Service Agent* (New York: Morrow, 1985), 195.
12. Patterson, *The White House Staff,* 370.
13. The discussion of the Secret Service that follows relies heavily on Philip H. Melanson's *The Politics of Protection: The U.S. Secret Service in the Terrorist Age* (New York: Praeger, 1984), an excellent study of the origins and operations of the service.
14. For a firsthand account of the stress of a service job, see McCarthy, *Protecting the President,* especially chap. 5.
15. Melanson, *The Politics of Protection,* 92.
16. Ibid., 128.
17. McCarthy, *Protecting the President,* 172.
18. Melanson, *The Politics of Protection,* 115.

Biographies of the Presidents

By Daniel C. Diller

The Constitution requires only that a president be at least thirty-five years of age, a natural-born citizen or a citizen at the time of the adoption of the Constitution, and a resident within the United States for fourteen years. Although these constitutional requirements disqualify few Americans, the forty-two persons who have become president have come from a relatively narrow slice of American society.

All presidents have shared several important characteristics. First, all have been men. Through the 2004 election, no woman had been nominated for president by a major political party. Second, each of the forty-two presidents descended from northern European ancestors. Moreover, of the forty-two, only five trace their roots to continental Europe. The ancestors of Martin Van Buren, Theodore Roosevelt, and Franklin D. Roosevelt were Dutch; Herbert C. Hoover's were Swiss; and Dwight D. Eisenhower's were German. The forebears of the thirty-seven other presidents came to America primarily from the British Isles. Third, no president has reached the presidency without significant experience as a public servant. Most presidents have served in at least one elective office at the national or state level. Twenty-four presidents have been members of Congress; seventeen have been governors of a state; and fourteen have been vice presidents. Presidents

have also served as cabinet members, diplomats, state legislators, mayors, judges, sheriffs, and prosecutors on their way to higher office. Because George Washington was the first president, he did not have the opportunity to run for Congress, but he served the nation as a general and a delegate to the Continental Congress.

Three presidents—Zachary Taylor, Ulysses S. Grant, and Eisenhower—were career generals without civilian political experience. Two others, William Howard Taft and Hoover, never had been elected to a national political office or a governorship but had served the nation as cabinet officers. Taft was Theodore Roosevelt's secretary of war; Hoover was secretary of commerce under Warren G. Harding and Calvin Coolidge.

Beyond these three characteristics common to each of the first forty-two presidents, two characteristics have been shared by all but one of them: marriage and Protestantism. James Buchanan was the only president who never married. Five others entered the presidency without a wife: Grover Cleveland did not marry until after he became president, and Thomas Jefferson, Van Buren, Andrew Jackson, and Chester A. Arthur took office as widowers. Not until the election of Ronald Reagan in 1980, however, did the American people elect a president who had been divorced. There have been two father-son combinations—John Adams and John Quincy Adams, and George Bush and George W. Bush—and one grandfather-grandson pair, William Henry Harrison and Benjamin Harrison.

Until John F. Kennedy became the first Catholic president in 1961, all chief executives had come from Protestant backgrounds with the Episcopalian, Presbyterian, and Unitarian denominations predominating. Although all presidents have professed their belief in God, they have varied widely in their religious convictions and practices. Jefferson's political opponents accused him of being an atheist—a charge he denied. Although Abraham Lincoln frequently quoted the Bible in his speeches, he belonged to no specific denomination and felt compelled early in his political career to make a statement declaring his belief in God. A few presidents have been outwardly religious men. James Garfield was a lay preacher for the Disciples of Christ before beginning his congressional career. Jimmy Carter described himself as a born-again Christian during the 1976 presidential campaign.

If one considers all these characteristics together, a distinct profile of the American president emerges. Presidents typically have been American-born, married men who were at least forty-two years old (Theodore Roosevelt being the youngest to hold office), descended from northern European, Protestant ancestors, and have had some type of public service career at the state or national level. From this well-defined societal group, however, presidents have come into office from a variety of personal backgrounds. Some presidents descended from the American aristocracy, including Jefferson, James Madison, John Quincy Adams, John Tyler, William Henry Harrison and his grandson Benjamin Harrison, the Roosevelts, Taft, Kennedy, George Bush, and George W. Bush. These presidents had the advantages of wealth and family connections when building their political careers. Other presidents, including Jackson, Lincoln, Andrew Johnson, and Garfield, were self-made men from poor, sometimes destitute circumstances. Several presidents, such as Hoover, Richard Nixon, Reagan, and Bill Clinton, did not grow up in poverty but received little financial support from their parents as they started their careers.

The educational background of presidents ranges from that of Woodrow Wilson, who earned a Ph.D. from Johns Hopkins University, to Andrew Johnson, who never attended a school of any type. Other presidents, such as Washington and Lincoln, received only rudimentary formal education. Thirty-three presidents attended college, including every twentieth-century president except Harry S. Truman.

Presidents also have worked in all types of professions before starting their careers in public service. The most common profession for presidents has been law; twenty-five were admitted to the bar. More than half the presidents had some experience in agriculture, either as a plantation owner, dirt farmer, rancher, field worker, or son of a farming family. Seven presidents were teachers. Several others were professional soldiers, merchants, surveyors, or journalists. Like his father before him, George W. Bush made his first fortune as owner of an oil company in Texas.

Presidents have made progress toward the presidency at different times in their lives. Jackson and Nixon, for example, began their political careers with election to the U.S. House of Representatives at the ages of twenty-nine and thirty-three, respectively, and Clinton was elected attorney general of Arkansas at age thirty. In contrast, Wilson and Reagan were not elected to their first political offices—governor of New Jersey and governor of California, respectively—until they were in their mid-fifties. No one could have foreseen in 1922 that Truman, then the owner of a failing haberdashery who had never gone to college or run for public office, would be president in twenty-three years. In contrast, twenty-three years before John Quincy Adams became president, he had graduated Phi Beta Kappa from Harvard, served as minister to Holland and Prussia, been elected to the Massachusetts State Senate, and narrowly lost election to the U.S. House of Representatives. Thus, despite the presidents' similarities, each has come to office at a different pace, under different circumstances, and with different experiences.

Just as the prepresidential experiences of the chief executives have varied, so have their postpresidential experiences. While many chief executives have retired from public life after leaving the presidency, a few have continued their political careers, and several have run again for president. Cleveland was the only president to be reelected president after leaving office. Van Buren, Millard Fillmore, and Theodore Roosevelt ran unsuccessfully for reelection after leaving office. Former president Ulysses S. Grant came close to receiving the Republican nomination in 1880, but the Republican National Convention chose dark-horse candidate Garfield instead.

Two former presidents were elected to Congress after retiring from the presidency. John Quincy Adams was elected to the U.S. House of Representatives in 1830 and served there until 1848; he died in the Capitol after suffering a stroke. Andrew Johnson was elected to the Senate in 1875 and served briefly before his death that year. Tyler was elected to the Confederate Congress in 1861 but died before taking his seat.

Taft fulfilled his highest personal ambition when Harding appointed him chief justice of the United States in 1921. Taft served on the Court until he retired in 1930. Most former presidents have served as unofficial advisers to their party or to the incumbent president. Several, including Taft and Hoover, have served on advisory commissions or administrative boards appointed by the incumbent president. One former president, Carter, has taken on numerous diplomatic missions as a personal envoy of the incumbent president. And since Coolidge,

every president who has survived his term has written an autobiography or memoirs about his time in office.

George Washington

Born: February 22, 1732; Westmoreland County, Virginia
Party: Federalist
Term: April 30, 1789–March 4, 1797
Vice President: John Adams
Died: December 14, 1799; Mount Vernon, Virginia
Buried: Mount Vernon

George Washington was born into a moderately wealthy family, who owned several plantations in northern Virginia. His father, Augustine, had ten children, six with Mary Ball, of which George was the eldest, and four by a previous marriage. When the eleven-year-old George's father died, he was left in the custody of his eldest half brother, Lawrence, whom he loved and admired.

George's early education was adequate, though far from exceptional. He was tutored and attended school on an irregular basis from ages seven to fifteen but had no formal education beyond grammar school. George's exposure to the well-mannered intellectual atmosphere created by Lawrence compensated for the youngster's limited book learning. He also received an education in the outdoor occupations of Virginia. In his early teens he was already a skilled woodsman, tobacco planter, and surveyor. When George was sixteen, he joined the first of several survey expeditions that he would make to the Virginia frontier.

In 1751 George took the only overseas trip of his life, to Barbados with Lawrence, who was suffering from tuberculosis and thus hoping that the Caribbean climate would relieve his condition. There George contracted a mild case of smallpox,

which left him scarred. Lawrence died in July 1752, after he and George returned to the colonies.

The following November, Washington began his frontier military career as a major in the Virginia militia. His first assignment was to inform the French commander at Fort Le Boeuf in Pennsylvania that unless the French evacuated the Ohio Valley they risked war. The French refused to budge, ensuring hostilities with the British.

After returning from the mission Washington was promoted to lieutenant colonel with the help of influential friends. In early 1754 he marched west with 160 recruits to reinforce British troops at the fork of the Ohio and Monongahela rivers. During this journey his men fired what many historians regard as the first shots of the French and Indian War. The nervous recruits ambushed a detachment of thirty French soldiers, killing ten, including their commander, Coulon de Jumonville. The attack gained Washington a measure of infamy because

Jumonville was on a diplomatic mission to the British. Six weeks later Washington's force was besieged and defeated at Fort Necessity. Before allowing his men to return to Virginia, the French forced Washington to sign a statement written in French, which he did not understand. In it he admitted to being an assassin. Washington's reputation was damaged by the episode, especially among British military officers. Upon returning to Virginia, Washington resigned his commission.

In December 1754 Lawrence's last living child died, and Washington inherited the right to rent Lawrence's estate at Mount Vernon from his late half brother's remarried widow, Ann Lee. In 1761, when Mrs. Lee died, he inherited Mount Vernon outright.

Washington returned to military service in the spring of 1755 when he was appointed aide-de-camp to Maj. Gen. Edward Braddock. After several years of service in the French and Indian War, in which he achieved the rank of colonel, Washington resigned in 1758 to run for the Virginia House of Burgesses. He served there for nine years. He was not known as a dynamic or creative legislator, but he gained the admiration of his colleagues and firsthand knowledge of representative government.

Revolutionary War

As tensions mounted between the British and the colonies, Washington became increasingly involved in the patriot cause. In 1769 Washington helped lead a movement to establish restrictions on the importation of British goods throughout the colonies. And in 1774 he attended the First Continental Congress in Philadelphia as a delegate from Virginia. Afterward, he returned to Virginia and began training militia forces using his own money. On June 16, 1775, Washington accepted a commission from the Second Continental Congress as the commanding general of the Continental army. Patriot leaders hoped the choice of a military leader from a southern state would unite the colonies behind the rebellion that already had begun in New England.

As a general, Washington's inspirational and administrative abilities were more exceptional than his military knowledge. He made several tactical blunders during the war, including the ill-considered deployment of part of his army in an exposed position on Long Island in 1776, which resulted in the loss of five thousand troops and the British occupation of New York City. Yet despite his lack of experience in commanding large forces, Washington did show flashes of strategic brilliance. The celebrated triumphs of his army at Boston, Trenton, Princeton, and Yorktown demonstrated his superior generalship. Nevertheless, Washington's skill at maintaining morale, inspiring loyalty, and holding his army together, as exemplified during the harsh winter of 1777–1778 at Valley Forge, Pennsylvania, was more crucial to the success of the Revolution than his tactical abilities.

After the decisive defeat of the British at Yorktown in 1781, discontent within the Continental army became the primary threat to the young nation. Many soldiers believed that Congress had not compensated them adequately or recognized their service to the nation. In May 1782 Washington angrily rejected an idea proposed by one of his officers that he allow himself to be crowned king. In March 1783 a more serious threat to Republican government emerged. Many officers were considering using the army to depose Congress and set up their own government. Washington addressed an assembly of his officers on March 15 in Newburgh, New York, where he persuaded them to give up their plan and support Congress.

With the war officially ended by the Treaty of Paris, signed on September 3, 1783, Washington retired to Mount Vernon. He managed his plantation until 1787, when he agreed to accept an appointment as one of Virginia's delegates to the Constitutional Convention in Philadelphia. His presence lent

legitimacy to the convention, and its delegates unanimously elected him presiding officer. After a long summer of debate during which Washington said little, the convention agreed on a new constitution. Washington and his fellow delegates signed the document on September 17, 1787.

Presidency

Washington was the inevitable choice of his nation to be the first president under the new constitution. He alone had the nonpartisan reputation needed to transcend sectional and ideological conflicts, so that the United States would have time to establish effective government institutions and gain the trust of the people. In early 1789 presidential electors unanimously elected Washington president. After a triumphant overland journey from Mount Vernon to New York City, during which he was met by cheering crowds at every stop, Washington took the oath of office in New York on April 30, 1789.

During Washington's first term Congress passed the Bill of Rights, and the states that had not yet ratified the Constitution did so. In an attempt to inspire confidence in the federal government and to establish a spirit of national unity Washington toured the northern states in late 1789 and the southern states in the spring of 1791. Mindful of the problems caused by the weakness of the federal government under the Articles of Confederation, Washington was careful throughout his presidency to assert the primacy of the federal government over the states.

Washington was usually deferential toward Congress; he believed that the president should veto a bill only if it were unconstitutional. He often made decisions after listening to his two most important and eloquent advisers, Secretary of State Thomas Jefferson and Secretary of the Treasury Alexander Hamilton, debate an issue. Secretary of War Henry Knox, Attorney General Edmund Randolph, and Postmaster General Samuel Osgood completed the cabinet. Although Washington endeavored to avoid any partisanship, he usually agreed with Hamilton on important issues. In particular, he backed Hamilton's plans to have the federal government assume the wartime debts of the states and to establish a national bank. After much debate Congress passed both measures, and Washington signed the debt assumption bill in 1790 and the bank bill in 1791.

Washington's primary goal in foreign policy was maintaining the neutrality of the United States in the war between France and Great Britain. Washington believed that the young nation had to avoid alliance entanglements if it were to survive and remain united during its early years. Secretary of State Thomas Jefferson urged that the United States aid France, which had helped the colonies defeat the British in the Revolutionary War, but Washington rejected Jefferson's counsel. The president issued a neutrality proclamation on April 22, 1793, which declared that the United States would be "friendly and impartial" toward the belligerents. Jefferson's disputes with Washington's policies led him to resign at the end of 1793. The following year Congress passed the Neutrality Act of 1794, which endorsed Washington's policy of neutrality. In 1795 Washington signed the Jay Treaty with Great Britain. The agreement, which had been negotiated in London by Chief Justice John Jay, increased commerce between the two nations and settled several disputes. The treaty was highly unpopular, however, with pro-French Democratic-Republicans who attacked Washington for concluding what they perceived as a pro-British agreement.

In 1794 Washington faced a domestic crisis when a rebellion broke out in western Pennsylvania over the federal tax on whiskey. Washington believed that he had to put down the rebellion quickly to avoid the impression that the federal government was weak. Thus, he ordered the governors of Pennsylvania, Maryland, New Jersey, and Virginia to supply the federal government with fifteen thousand militia

and rode to Pennsylvania to oversee their preparations personally. The show of force was sufficient to quell the Whiskey Rebellion, and Washington never had to lead the militia into battle.

During his presidency Washington strove to avoid partisan politics; he believed that political factions could destroy the unity of the young nation. Thus, in his famous Farewell Address published on September 17, 1796, he cautioned against excessive partisanship as well as foreign influence and permanent alliances. But despite his efforts to prevent the development of parties, before his presidency had ended two factions had already emerged in American politics: the Federalists, with whom Washington most closely identified, led by Alexander Hamilton and Vice President John Adams, and the Democratic-Republicans, led by Thomas Jefferson and House member James Madison.

Retirement

In 1796 Washington refused to consider running for a third term. He had been wounded during his second term by criticism from the Democratic-Republican press over the Jay Treaty and other issues and was anxious to return to the quiet life of a gentleman farmer at Mount Vernon. He spent the last years of his life managing his estate and entertaining friends. In 1799, when war seemed imminent with France, President John Adams asked Washington to accept an appointment as lieutenant general and commander in chief of the army. Washington accepted on the condition that he would not have to take active command of the forces except in an emergency. War with France was averted, and Washington's retirement was not disturbed.

On December 12, 1799, after riding about his estate on a cold day, he suddenly fell ill, probably with pneumonia. His condition deteriorated rapidly, and he died on December 14 at Mount Vernon.

Washington married Martha Dandridge Custis on January 6, 1759. Martha was a wealthy widow, who added fifteen thousand acres to Washington's estate. The couple had no children, but they raised Martha's two surviving children from her previous marriage. Martha's daughter, Patsy, died in 1773 as a teenager, and when her son John died in 1781, George and Martha assumed custody of his two children. Thomas Jefferson, looking back on Washington's life in 1814, wrote:

> His mind was great and powerful without being of the very first order; his penetration strong, though not so acute as that of a Newton, Bacon, or Locke; and as far as he saw, no judgement was ever sounder. It was slow in operation, being little aided by invention or imagination, but sure in conclusion. . . .
>
> Perhaps the strongest feature in his character was prudence, never acting until every circumstance, every consideration, was maturely weighed. . . . His integrity was most pure, his justice the most inflexible I have ever known.

John Adams

John Adams

Born: October 30, 1735; Braintree (now Quincy),
    Massachusetts
Party: Federalist
Term: March 4, 1797–March 3, 1801
Vice President: Thomas Jefferson
Died: July 4, 1826; Quincy, Massachusetts
Buried: Quincy

John Adams was born into a well-established family of farmers whose descendants had immigrated to Massachusetts from England a century before his birth. He was the oldest of three sons born to John and Susanna Adams. Young John received a grammar school education designed to prepare him for college. He enrolled in Harvard University in 1751 intending to become a Congregational minister. However, before he graduated in 1755 he had decided against a career in the ministry in favor of either law or medicine. After briefly teaching school in Worcester, Adams began studying law. By 1758 he had been admitted to the Massachusetts bar and was practicing law in Braintree.

Adams soon became recognized throughout Massachusetts as an outspoken advocate of colonial causes. He authored Braintree's protest against the British Stamp Act of 1765, which was used as a model for similar protests by many other Massachusetts towns. Adams also published a series of anonymous letters in the *Boston Gazette* in which he theorized that the rights of English citizens were derived solely from God, not from the British monarchy or parliament.

In 1770 Adams demonstrated his commitment to due process of the law when he defended the British soldiers on trial for the murder of colonial citizens at the Boston Massacre. His reputation withstood the unpopularity of his action, and the following year he was elected by an overwhelming margin to the Massachusetts state legislature. In 1774 Adams became a delegate to the First Continental Congress. He was an early and influential advocate of separation from Britain and was appointed to the committee assigned to draft a declaration of independence. Adams retired from Congress in November 1777, intending to return to Massachusetts and his law practice. Within a month, however, Congress appointed him to the American commission in France. He set sail to join Benjamin Franklin and Arthur Lee in Paris on February 13, 1778, but a treaty of alliance had already been concluded by the time he arrived. Adams spent a year in Europe before returning to America in the summer of 1779. Upon his arrival he was elected as a delegate to the Massachusetts constitutional convention. He almost single-handedly wrote the first draft of the new state constitution, which the convention adopted with only minor changes. He returned to Europe in 1780 where he would spend the next eight years in various diplomatic posts, including minister to Holland and minister to Great Britain. He signed the armistice ending war with the British in 1783 and negotiated several loans and commercial treaties with the European powers.

Adams was serving as envoy to Great Britain when the Constitutional Convention was held, but his *Defense of the Constitutions of Government of the United States,* written while he was in Europe and published in 1787, contained insights into constitutional theory that were cited by delegates to the convention. When Adams received a copy of the Constitution in Great Britain, he immediately gave it his support. By this time he had grown tired of the unwillingness of the British government to improve relations with the United States. He resigned his post and returned to the United States.

When he arrived in Boston on June 17, 1789, he had already been elected to Congress under the new Constitution. He never served in this capacity, because he would also be elected vice president by virtue of his second-place finish to George Washington in the balloting for president. Adams was dismayed at winning the vice presidency with only thirty-four votes. The disparity between his total and the unanimous sixty-nine received by Washington was caused by the machinations of Alexander Hamilton, who persuaded many delegates to scatter their second vote to dilute Adams's influence.

Adams dutifully fulfilled his constitutional function of presiding over the Senate. Since the original Senate had only twenty-two members, the vice president was often in a position to break tie votes as prescribed by the Constitution. During Adams's two terms he had twenty-nine opportunities to decide issues with his tie-breaking vote, more than any subsequent vice president. However, he was seldom consulted by Washington on important issues and complained that the vice presidency was an insignificant and mechanical job—a lament of many of the men who would follow Adams in office. Nevertheless, Adams's relationship with Washington remained cordial.

After eight years as vice president, Adams was Washington's heir apparent. Fellow Federalist Alexander Hamilton, however, attempted to arrange the election of a candidate more agreeable to him than Adams. He persuaded a number of Federalist delegates to vote for intended vice-presidential candidate Thomas Pinckney, but not for presidential candidate John Adams. Hamilton hoped that Adams would lose the presidency to Pinckney, who Hamilton believed would be more receptive to his influence. But the maneuver backfired when many of Adams's supporters withheld their second votes from Pinckney to ensure Adams's victory, thereby allowing Democratic-Republican candidate Thomas Jefferson to finish second and win the vice presidency.

The most important and contentious issue of Adams's presidency was an impending war with France. French vessels had been preying on American shipping since 1795, and, just before Adams's inauguration, Paris issued a decree legitimizing the seizure of virtually any American ship. Adams faced intense political pressure from pro-British Hamiltonians who believed that the United States should join Britain in fighting to prevent French domination of Europe and to preserve American dignity. Jefferson's Democratic-Republicans opposed a war with France, but they did not have the votes in Congress to stop a declaration of war if Adams had wanted one. Adams chose to strengthen the nation's military, particularly the navy, while continuing negotiations with the French. He dispatched John Marshall, Charles C. Pinckney, and Elbridge Gerry to Paris in the summer of 1797 to seek an agreement that would avoid war and end French attacks on American shipping. But the diplomatic mission failed when the American representatives were greeted with demands for a bribe for French foreign minister Talleyrand, a loan to France, and an official apology for Adams's criticisms.

In April 1798 Adams's release of documents relating to the incident (which came to be known as the XYZ affair) aroused American opinion against France and rallied public support behind Adams. By this time an undeclared naval war between the two nations had already begun, and Congress granted Adams's request for further defense measures, including the establishment of the Navy Department. But he resisted calls for a full-scale declared war against France, even though he could have bolstered his own political fortunes by yielding to the militant sentiment of the American public.

While Adams was enthusiastic about building a strong navy, he grudgingly agreed to the enlargement of the army. He asked George Washington to come out of retirement to command it. Washington accepted on the conditions that he would not have

to take the field until there was fighting and that Alexander Hamilton would be his second in command in charge of building and training the army. Adams feared giving the powerful and ambitious Hamilton control of the army, but he believed if war did occur Washington's presence was indispensable to the unity of the country, so he assented to Washington's conditions.

In early 1799 France began sending conciliatory signals, which prompted Adams to send another peace commission before the year was over. Hamilton had tried to rally Federalist support for war with France and had proposed a joint British-American venture against Spanish holdings in North America. But increased taxes to support war preparations had diminished public enthusiasm for military adventurism. Adams stood by his policy of avoiding a declared war unless it was forced upon him by the French. The following May, when the immediate danger of a land war with France had passed, Adams ordered a drastic reduction in the army. In November word reached the United States that the American delegation had successfully concluded a treaty of peace and commerce with France.

By this time the Democratic-Republicans had taken control of the state legislatures of several key states, thus setting the stage for Adams's defeat in the 1800 presidential election. One of the reasons for the growing disaffection with the Federalist Party was its support of the Alien and Sedition Acts. In 1798 the Federalist majority in Congress attempted to put an end to the vituperative attacks on Federalist members of Congress and cabinet members in the Democratic-Republican press. The Sedition Act provided for imprisonment and fines for individuals who wrote, published, or uttered anything false or malicious about federal government officials. The Sedition Act together with the Alien Act of the same year, which gave the president broad authority to deport aliens suspected of subversive activity, constituted the greatest legislated suppression of freedom of expression in the history of the United States. Adams signed these bills into law but was not active in enforcing them.

Despite the disunity of the Federalist Party and the unpopularity of the Alien and Sedition Acts, the 1800 election was close. Adams received sixty-five electoral votes, eight fewer than Jefferson and Aaron Burr.

Before leaving office Adams pushed for judicial reforms and appointed more than two hundred new judges, attorneys, clerks, and marshals. Some of these "midnight appointments" were removed by Jefferson, but many retained their offices. Adams also appointed John Marshall chief justice of the United States, a selection Adams was especially proud of in his later years.

When Adams's term ended, he returned to his farm in Massachusetts without attending Jefferson's inauguration. Adams spent much of his retirement writing his autobiography and corresponding with former colleagues about politics, philosophy, and religion.

He wrote a letter of reconciliation to Thomas Jefferson at the insistence of their mutual friend Dr. Benjamin Rush in December 1811. Jefferson replied immediately, and they established a lasting correspondence. Adams died on July 4, 1826, the fiftieth anniversary of the Declaration of Independence. His last words reportedly were "Thomas Jefferson still lives." Adams had no way of knowing that Jefferson had died only a few hours before.

Adams married Abigail Smith in 1764. Her correspondence with her husband, family, and friends provides a valuable historical record of her husband's activities and the period in which they lived. They had five children: Abigail, John Quincy, Susanna, Charles, and Thomas. Susanna died while she was an infant. John Quincy became a prominent diplomat, congressman, and the sixth president of the United States. Adams's parents were Susanna Boyleston Adams and John Adams, a respected farmer and

shoemaker who was active in local politics. The famous New England radical patriot Sam Adams was John's distant cousin.

Thomas Jefferson

Born: April 13, 1743; Goochland (now Albemarle) County, Virginia
Party: Democratic-Republican
Term: March 4, 1801–March 4, 1809
Vice Presidents: Aaron Burr; George Clinton
Died: July 4, 1826; Charlottesville, Virginia
Buried: Charlottesville

Thomas Jefferson was the eldest son and third of the ten children of Peter and Jane Jefferson. Peter Jefferson was a wealthy plantation owner, and Jane was a member of the prominent Randolph family, which was descended from British royalty.

As a boy, Thomas received instruction in Latin, Greek, French, mathematics, and philosophy from local scholars. When Peter Jefferson died in 1757, Thomas inherited Shadwell, the thousand-acre Virginia estate on which he was born. In 1760, at the age of seventeen, Thomas entered the College of William and Mary in Williamsburg, Virginia. There he studied vigorously for two years under the tutelage of Dr. William Small, a professor of mathematics, history, and philosophy. He left the college in the spring of 1762, however, without taking a degree.

Jefferson then studied law in Williamsburg for five years under the well-respected lawyer George Wythe. During Jefferson's stay in Williamsburg, Wythe and Small introduced him to many members of Virginia's government, including Francis Fauquier, the royal governor of the colony. In 1767 Jefferson was admitted to the Virginia bar and began a successful legal practice. Two years later he took a seat in Virginia's House of Burgesses. During his six years in that body, Jefferson distinguished himself as a powerful literary stylist. His colleagues often called upon him to draft proclamations and legislative documents.

Jefferson brought his reputation as a gifted writer to the Continental Congress in 1775. The following year, at the age of thirty-three, he was appointed by Congress to the committee charged with writing the Declaration of Independence. His fellow committee members—John Adams, Benjamin Franklin, Robert Livingston, and Roger Sherman—chose him to draft the document. Although the committee made minor changes in Jefferson's original draft and the entire Congress asked that several passages be deleted or modified, the Declaration of Independence was largely Jefferson's work.

Jefferson returned to Virginia in 1776 to a seat in the state legislature. In 1779 he became governor of his home state. His first experience as a chief executive was not impressive. In 1781 he was forced to abandon the Virginia capital of Richmond when British troops advanced upon the city. Some Virginians accused him of cowardice, but after a long debate the Virginia legislature passed a resolution stating that Jefferson's retreat was justified. He declined renomination for governor in 1781.

Diplomat and Secretary of State

In 1784 Congress sent Jefferson to Paris as its minister to France. During his five years at this post, Jefferson witnessed the many events of the French Revolution. He applauded the revolution's stated democratic goals and had many friends among its leaders. Jefferson, like John Adams, missed the drafting of the Constitution because of his diplomatic service in Europe.

In 1789 Jefferson returned to the United States to become the country's first secretary of state. In this capacity Jefferson was more than just the nation's leading diplomat. Like the other members of George Washington's cabinet, Jefferson served as

an adviser to Washington on matters outside the area of policy traditionally associated with his position. Washington often preferred to have his cabinet debate issues while he listened dispassionately to their reasoning. In these debates Jefferson was usually pitted against Treasury Secretary Alexander Hamilton. Hamilton, who was closer ideologically to Washington than Jefferson, was undoubtedly the most influential member of the cabinet. On July 31, 1794, Jefferson announced that he would resign at the end of the year because of his disagreements with administration policies. In particular, he objected to Hamilton's creation of a national bank and Washington's strict neutrality between Britain and France despite the 1778 treaty of alliance with France, which Jefferson believed should have been honored.

By 1796 the Democratic-Republican Party, which opposed the Federalists, had begun to emerge with Jefferson as its leader. That year he lost the presidential election to John Adams by three electoral votes, and, according to the original election rules of the Constitution, his second-place finish earned him the vice presidency. In this office he actively opposed the policies of Adams and the Federalists.

Presidency

After the election of 1800 the Twelfth Amendment introduced new election rules, which called for the president and vice president to run as a team, thereby eliminating the possibility of a candidate intended for the vice presidency receiving more votes than the presidential candidate. In the 1800 election, however, Jefferson was paired on the Democratic-Republican ticket with Aaron Burr. When the ambitious Burr received as many electoral votes as Jefferson, he refused to concede to his running mate. The tie gave the House of Representatives, where the Federalists and Alexander Hamilton were still in the majority, the responsibility of electing the president. To Hamilton's credit, he worked for the election of Jefferson, his political archenemy, whom he thought less dangerous and more reasonable than Burr. The tie-breaking process took thirty-six ballots, but Jefferson was elected eventually.

Despite the acrimony between the Democratic-Republicans and the Federalists (outgoing president John Adams did not even attend Jefferson's inauguration), Jefferson entered office preaching reconciliation. He transformed the atmosphere surrounding the presidency from the stiff, regal style of Washington and Adams to his own democratic informality. Jefferson immediately freed all persons who had been jailed under the Alien and Sedition Acts enacted during the Adams administration. The Alien Act gave the president the authority to jail or deport aliens in peacetime, and the Sedition Act gave federal authorities broad power to prosecute persons who criticized the government. He also worked with

Congress, which had come under the control of his party after the 1800 election, to cut the government budget and federal taxes.

In foreign policy Jefferson acted decisively to meet the threat to American shipping in the Mediterranean from pirates operating from the Barbary Coast of North Africa. American and European nations had been paying tribute to the governments of Morocco, Algiers, Tunis, and Tripoli to protect their ships from harassment. Jefferson, however, refused demands for increased tribute payments and sent a squadron of warships to the Mediterranean to protect U.S. shipping. After U.S. forces defeated Tripoli in a naval war, a treaty was concluded in 1805 that ended tribute payments to that state. The United States continued tribute payments to other North African states, however, until 1816.

Jefferson's most important act during his first term as president was the Louisiana Purchase. In 1803 the French owned the port of New Orleans as well as a vast area that stretched from New Orleans to present-day Montana, known as the Louisiana Territory. Jefferson, fearing that the French could block U.S. navigation of the Mississippi and threaten American settlements in the West, sent ambassadors to France in the hope of purchasing the port of New Orleans. The French instead offered to sell the entire Louisiana Territory. The American representatives, James Monroe and Robert Livingston, saw the opportunity to create an American empire and improve the security of the western frontier. Thus, they struck a deal with French emperor Napoleon to buy all of the Louisiana Territory for $15 million.

Jefferson recognized that to support the agreement he would have to ignore his own principles of strict constructionism, since the Constitution did not specifically authorize the president to acquire territory, and Congress had not appropriated money for the purchase. He believed that the purchase would greatly benefit the nation and that the offer from Napoleon might be withdrawn if he hesitated. Therefore, Jefferson approved the deal and urged Congress to ratify it and appropriate funds for the purchase. In the fall of 1803 Congress bowed to his wishes and appropriated the $15 million. With the addition of the 828,000 square miles of the Louisiana Territory, the area of the United States nearly doubled.

In 1804, Jefferson, who was at the height of his popularity, easily won reelection. He lost only two states and defeated Charles C. Pinckney in the electoral college by a vote of 162–14.

Jefferson's second term was troubled by war between Britain and France. In 1806 both powers were blockading each other's ports and seizing American sailors and cargo. Jefferson was determined, however, not to become involved in the war. Thus, he persuaded Congress to pass the Embargo Act of 1807, which prohibited the shipping of U.S. products to other nations. Jefferson hoped that by cutting off all foreign trade he would prevent provocations on the seas that could lead to war.

The Embargo Act was a total failure. It severely hurt American businesses and farmers by denying them export markets. As the U.S. economy stagnated, Federalists and some Democratic-Republicans argued that the federal government's authority to regulate foreign commerce did not give it the power to stop foreign commerce altogether. Many merchants defied the embargo, causing Jefferson to order harsh enforcement measures that led to abuses of civil rights. On March 1, 1809, three days before the end of his term, Jefferson signed the Non-Intercourse Act, which ended the embargo against nations other than Britain and France and made provisions to lift the embargo against those two nations if they stopped violating U.S. neutrality. Despite the unpopularity of the Embargo Act, Jefferson's chosen heir and secretary of state, James Madison, won the 1808 presidential election.

Retirement

When his second term expired Jefferson retired to Monticello, his home outside of Charlottesville, Virginia, which he had designed himself. He devoted his time to managing his estate, entertaining visitors, corresponding with former colleagues, and reveling in his many intellectual pursuits. Jefferson, who suffered from financial troubles caused by his generous entertaining and the defaults by several friends on loans he had cosigned, sold his 6,500-volume library to Congress in 1815. Congress's original collection of books had been burned by the British during the War of 1812. Jefferson's books formed the nucleus of the collection that would become the modern Library of Congress.

In 1819 the University of Virginia was chartered under Jefferson's supervision. He planned the curriculum, chose the faculty, drew up the plans for its buildings, and served as its rector until his death. Jefferson died at Monticello on July 4, 1826, the same day as John Adams and the fiftieth anniversary of the Declaration of Independence. Jefferson is buried at Monticello beneath a gravestone that he willed should read: "Here was buried Thomas Jefferson, Author of the Declaration of American Independence, of the Statute of Virginia for Religious Freedom, and the father of the University of Virginia."

Jefferson married Martha Wayles Skelton, a wealthy twenty-three-year-old widow, on January 1, 1772. The couple had six children, but only two, Martha and Maria, reached maturity. Martha Jefferson's father, John Wayles, died in 1773, leaving a forty-thousand-acre estate to the Jeffersons that doubled their landholdings. Wayles was heavily in debt, however, and Jefferson struggled for many years to pay off the balance. On September 6, 1782, Martha Jefferson died at the age of thirty-three. Little is known about Martha, and there is no authentic portrait of her in existence. Jefferson never remarried.

In November 1998 the British scientific journal *Nature* reported that a DNA analysis of blood samples taken from descendants of both Jefferson and his slave, Sally Hemings, indicated it was likely Jefferson had fathered a son by Hemings. The article said an unusual Y chromosome found in the blood of both lines of descendants seemed to link the president to Hemings's son, Eston.

James Madison

Born: March 16, 1751; Port Conway, Virginia
Party: Democratic-Republican
Term: March 4, 1809–March 4, 1817
Vice Presidents: George Clinton; Elbridge Gerry
Died: June 28, 1836; Orange County, Virginia
Buried: Orange County

James Madison, oldest of the ten children of James and Eleanor Madison, was raised at Montpelier, the family plantation in Virginia. Young James Madison was an excellent scholar. He graduated from the College of New Jersey (now Princeton University) in 1771 and spent an extra six months studying theology under John Witherspoon, president of the college. In 1772 James returned to Virginia to continue his study of law and religion. Like John Adams, he considered entering the ministry after college, but the lure of a political career and the urgency of the patriot cause led him away from the ministry and into public service.

In 1775 he assumed his first government office, a slot on the committee of public safety of his native Orange County. By the spring of 1776 he had earned sufficient notice and respect to be elected as a delegate to Virginia's constitutional convention. There he served on the committee that drafted a declaration of rights and was primarily responsible for the constitutional article on religious freedom. As a member of the state constitutional convention,

Madison automatically became a state legislator in the new Virginia government. There he met Thomas Jefferson, who became his close friend and political mentor. In 1777 Madison was defeated in his attempt to be elected to the state legislature, but the same year he was elected to the governor's council, an advisory body in which he served governors Patrick Henry and Thomas Jefferson.

Father of the Constitution

In 1780 Madison's political focus was broadened when he was chosen to serve in the Continental Congress, where he worked to bring greater organization to the federal government under the new Articles of Confederation. During this period, however, Madison began to believe that the articles had to be strengthened if the government was going to survive. Congress had no means of implementing its decisions and was completely dependent on the goodwill of the states. For example, in June 1783 Madison had witnessed a band of Revolutionary War veterans surround the Philadelphia statehouse where Congress was meeting and demand that the legislators vote them back pay. When Congress asked Pennsylvania for militia to disperse the band, the state government refused. Such humiliations convinced Madison that the federal government had to be restructured.

At the end of 1783 Madison returned to Virginia where he was reelected to the state legislature. He served there until 1786. During this period Madison studied the history of government and began to form ideas about how to strengthen the national government. In September 1786 he attended the Annapolis Convention, a national meeting called to consider trade. Only five states were represented at the convention, but the delegates in Annapolis issued a call for a second national convention to be held in Philadelphia the following year.

Madison led a group of nationalists who wanted to establish a broad mandate for the Philadelphia convention. They urged all thirteen states to send delegates, obtained a congressional endorsement of the convention, and enhanced the prestige of the convention by convincing George Washington to attend. At the Constitutional Convention in Philadelphia in 1787, Madison's extensive study and contemplation of political theory paid off for his nation. More than any other individual, he was responsible for the content of the Constitution produced by the convention. The "Virginia Plan," which served as the basis of the Constitution, was submitted to the convention by Edmund Randolph, but it was largely Madison's work.

Following the convention Madison wrote a series of essays, known as the *Federalist Papers,* with Alexander Hamilton and John Jay. These essays explained and defended the new Constitution, which had to be ratified by the states before it could become law. He also led the successful fight for rat-

ification at Virginia's ratifying convention in 1788. That year Madison was prevented from being elected to the new U.S. Senate by powerful state legislator and former Virginia governor Patrick Henry, who had opposed the Constitution.

Madison won election to the U.S. House of Representatives, however. There he proposed nine amendments to the Constitution, which became the basis for the Bill of Rights. Madison legislated according to a strict interpretation of the Constitution; he opposed the government's exercise of powers not specifically granted in the document. He fought unsuccessfully against Treasury Secretary Alexander Hamilton's plans to establish a national bank and have the federal government assume the war debts of the states. He also wrote a series of articles, under the name "Helvidius," that argued against the expansion of presidential power and attacked Washington's proclamation of neutrality toward warring Britain and France in 1793 as unconstitutional.

From his position in Congress, Madison assumed a leading role, second only to Thomas Jefferson, in the formation of the Democratic-Republican Party. In 1797, after four terms, he retired from Congress.

In 1801, newly elected president Thomas Jefferson appointed Madison secretary of state. He served in this post for all eight years of Jefferson's presidency, and he supported all the president's major diplomatic initiatives, including the Louisiana Purchase.

With Jefferson's support, Madison was nominated for president by the Democratic-Republicans in 1808. Although he lost five northern states, Madison received 122 electoral votes to Federalist Charles C. Pinckney's 47.

Presidency

Madison's presidency focused on issues related to the war under way in Europe between Britain and France. British warships were boarding American commercial ships, seizing cargo, and impressing any sailor they suspected of being British.

Members of Congress known as the War Hawks, a group that included Henry Clay and John Calhoun, urged Madison to declare war on the British. The War Hawks, most of whom were from the South and the West, also wanted to launch military adventures into Canada and to halt Indian attacks in the West, which they believed were encouraged by the British.

By 1812 Madison saw no alternative to war, and on June 1 he asked Congress for a declaration of war. The declaration passed on June 18, 19–13 in the Senate and 79–49 in the House.

That fall, Madison ran for reelection against DeWitt Clinton of New York, the nominee of an anti-Madison faction of the Democratic-Republican Party. The Federalists, who did not nominate a candidate, threw their support to Clinton. Madison defeated Clinton 128–89 in the electoral college.

The United States was not prepared for war. Its navy was small compared to the British fleet, and throughout the war the army had great difficulty fulfilling its recruitment goals. Moreover, the nation was not united behind the war effort. The war was opposed by many citizens in the Northeast, who favored the British in their fight with France. In addition, the merchants of that region preferred the occasional seizure of their neutral vessels by the British to a war that could end trade completely. Indeed, some New England Federalists openly discussed secession during the war.

The United States prevailed in several sea battles, and frontier generals William Henry Harrison and Andrew Jackson won decisive victories over Britain's Indian allies, but overall the war went badly for the United States. The worst humiliation occurred in August 1814 when the British occupied Washington, D.C., and burned government buildings, including the Executive Mansion and Capitol. On December 24, 1814, Britain and the United States signed the Treaty of Ghent, which ended the war without resolving the issues for which it had been fought. The British gave no guarantees that they would allow U.S. ships safe passage in the future.

In spite of the many defeats suffered by the United States, the end of the war brought a resurgence of nationalism. The Treaty of Ghent and Andrew Jackson's overwhelming victory over the British at the Battle of New Orleans on January 8, 1815, two weeks after the peace treaty had been signed, convinced many Americans that the war had been won. Federalist opposition to the war crippled that party, leaving Madison's Democratic-Republicans in a commanding position.

Madison's last two years in office were successful ones. Congress backed the president's proposal to appropriate funds to strengthen the armed forces. Madison also supported the establishment of the Second Bank of the United States and increased tariffs to protect U.S. industries.

Retirement

After leaving office Madison returned to Montpelier, his estate in Virginia. He remained a close friend of Thomas Jefferson, who lived thirty miles away. When Jefferson died in 1826 Madison assumed his job as rector of the University of Virginia. In 1829 he cochaired a Virginia convention aimed at revising the state constitution. During his retirement Madison also edited the secret daily record he had kept at the Constitutional Convention, which has been invaluable to historians when reconstructing its events. His wife sold Madison's *Notes on the Federal Convention* to Congress in 1837. The year before Madison had died peacefully at Montpelier at the age of eighty-five.

On September 15, 1794, at the age of forty-three, Madison married widow Dorothea Payne Todd, who was called "Dolley." The couple had no children, but they raised Dolley's one surviving child from her previous marriage. Dolley was an outgoing woman who loved entertaining. As first lady her social charms compensated for her husband's reserved nature. After her husband's death Dolley participated in many Washington social functions until her death in 1849.

James Monroe

Born: April 28, 1758; Westmoreland County, Virginia
Party: Democratic-Republican
Term: March 4, 1817–March 4, 1825
Vice President: Daniel D. Tompkins
Died: July 4, 1831; New York City
Buried: Richmond, Virginia

James Monroe was the eldest of the five children of Elizabeth and Spence Monroe, a well-established Virginia planter of modest means. James entered the College of William and Mary in Williamsburg, Virginia, when he was sixteen but left two years later to join the Continental army. As a lieutenant he fought in numerous battles, including Trenton, Brandywine, Germantown, and Monmouth. At Trenton he was wounded in the shoulder and promoted to captain for his bravery by Gen. George Washington. In 1778 he was promoted again, to lieutenant colonel, but he was not able to recruit enough Virginia volunteers to form a new regiment that he could command.

Monroe left the army in 1780 to study law under Thomas Jefferson, then governor of Virginia. Monroe quickly developed a close personal and professional relationship with his mentor that led to a career in politics and public service. In 1782 he was elected to the Virginia legislature and, a year later, he was chosen along with Jefferson to represent Virginia at the Continental Congress in New York City. While in Congress Monroe became an expert on frontier issues after making two fact-finding journeys into the Ohio Valley. When Monroe's third term expired in 1786, he moved to Fredericksburg, Virginia, where he established a law practice. That year Monroe was again elected to the Virginia legislature.

Although Monroe attended the national convention in Annapolis, Maryland, which created momentum for the writing of the Constitution, he was not a delegate to the Constitutional Convention of 1787. His belief that the Constitution gave the president and Senate too much power led him to oppose the document vigorously at Virginia's ratifying convention in 1788. Nevertheless, after ratification by Virginia, he ran for the U.S. House of Representatives but lost to James Madison.

Monroe soon adopted a national political perspective, and when Virginian William Grayson, an anti-Federalist, died in 1790, Monroe was appointed to his Senate seat. In the Senate Monroe worked against Treasury Secretary Alexander Hamilton's fiscal policies. Monroe helped Jefferson and Madison establish the foundations of the Democratic-Republican Party that would challenge the Federalists after George Washington's retirement.

In 1794 Washington appointed Monroe ambassador to France. In Paris, however, his outspoken support of the French conflicted with Washington's careful policy of neutrality in the Franco-British war. After the president recalled him in 1796, Monroe published *A View of the Conduct of the Executive,* in which he attacked the administration's policies toward France. In 1799 Monroe was elected governor of Virginia and served effectively for three years.

Thomas Jefferson was elected president in 1800, ushering in a period of Democratic-Republican dominance over national affairs. In January 1803, after Monroe's third term as governor of Virginia had expired, Jefferson asked him to travel to France to negotiate the purchase of New Orleans. When Napoleon offered to sell not just New Orleans but the entire Louisiana Territory, Monroe and Ambassador Robert Livingston seized the opportunity to double the size of the United States. Acting without authority, they closed the deal for $15 million. The purchase added 828,000 square miles to the United States. Monroe continued to function as a special ambassador in Europe for four more years. He tried unsuccessfully to purchase the Floridas from the Spanish and to conclude a treaty with the British ending that country's capture of American vessels.

Monroe returned to Virginia in 1807 and practiced law until he was again elected governor in 1811. When newly elected president James Madison offered Monroe the post of secretary of state, however, he resigned the governorship to return to national service. Monroe helped write Madison's request for a declaration of war against the British in 1811. The United States was ill-prepared, however, for the War of 1812. The first two years of fighting brought several humiliating defeats, including the capture and burning of Washington, D.C., by the British in August 1814. In September of that year

Madison appointed Monroe secretary of war in addition to his duties as secretary of state. Monroe then worked tirelessly to reorganize the nation's defenses and to end the confusion that had prevailed in the War Department. In March 1815, three months after the war ended, an exhausted Monroe resigned as secretary of war and went to his home in Virginia for a rest. He returned to Washington six months later and resumed his duties as secretary of state.

With Madison's backing, Monroe was nominated as the Democratic-Republican presidential candidate in 1816. He easily defeated the Federalist candidate, Sen. Rufus King of New York, 183–34 in the electoral college. Less than three months after taking office, Monroe followed George Washington's example and toured the Middle Atlantic and New England states. Reacting to the enthusiastic reception of the president in the North, a Boston newspaper declared the time to be a political "era of good feelings." These good feelings extended to the 1820 presidential election. Monroe ran unopposed and received all but one electoral vote that was cast for John Quincy Adams by an elector who wished to preserve George Washington's distinction as the only president ever to be elected unanimously.

Monroe's presidency, however, was not without its problems. When Missouri sought admission to the United States as a slave state, sectional tensions over the slavery issue erupted. Monroe was a slaveholder who believed that the institution should eventually be abolished. He also believed, however, that new states entering the Union had the constitutional right to determine for themselves if they would permit slavery. In 1820, after a lengthy debate, Congress passed the Missouri Compromise. The plan allowed Missouri to enter the Union as a slave state simultaneously with the admission of Maine as a free state. The compromise also prohibited slavery north of latitude 36° 30' in the territory acquired in the Louisiana Purchase. Monroe doubted the constitutionality of the plan, but he approved it because he considered it the best way to avoid sectional conflict and possibly the secession of southern states.

In foreign policy Monroe's administration had several notable successes. The Rush-Bagot Agreement signed with Great Britain in 1817 limited the number of warships each country could deploy on the Great Lakes and led to the demilitarization of the Canadian frontier. In 1819 Secretary of State John Quincy Adams concluded a treaty in which Spain transferred control of the Floridas to the United States and agreed to a border dividing the United States and Spanish territory in western North America.

Monroe's administration is best known, however, for the foreign policy doctrine that bears his name and continues to influence U.S. policy toward Latin America. In October 1823 Great Britain suggested that the United States join it in resisting European intervention in Latin America, where several revolutions had succeeded in overthrowing Spanish colonial rule. Although former presidents Jefferson and Madison advised Monroe to accept the British proposal, Monroe was swayed by the arguments of Secretary of State Adams, who advocated an independent U.S. declaration against European intrusions into the Western Hemisphere. In his annual message to Congress in 1823 Monroe announced that the United States intended to stay out of European conflicts and would not interfere in the existing Latin American colonies of the European powers. Monroe warned the Europeans, however, that any attempt to establish new colonies in the Western Hemisphere or interfere in the affairs of independent American nations would be regarded by the United States as an "unfriendly" act.

At the time the Monroe Doctrine was issued it had little force because the United States did not possess the military strength to defend Latin America. As the nation developed, however, the Monroe

Doctrine became a cornerstone of U.S. foreign policy.

While serving in the Continental Congress in New York in 1785 Monroe met his wife-to-be, Elizabeth Kortright; they married in 1786. The Monroes raised two daughters and had one son who died at the age of two. Monroe experienced financial difficulties after he retired from the presidency and was forced to sell Ash Lawn, one of his two Virginia homes in 1825. After his wife died in 1830, he sold his other Virginia estate, Oak Hill, and moved to New York City to live with his daughter and her husband. On July 4, 1831, Monroe became the third president, along with John Adams and Thomas Jefferson, to die on Independence Day.

John Quincy Adams

Born: July 11, 1767; Braintree (now Quincy),
    Massachusetts
Party: Democratic-Republican
Term: March 4, 1825–March 4, 1829
Vice President: John C. Calhoun
Died: February 23, 1848; Washington, D.C.
Buried: Quincy

John Quincy Adams was the oldest son and second child of John and Abigail Adams. He was the first son of a president to become president himself. As a boy in Massachusetts, John Quincy lived through the early stages of the Revolutionary War and was an eyewitness to the battle of Bunker Hill. He lived in Europe from 1778 to 1785 while his father served as a diplomat. He was educated in France and the Netherlands and learned to speak several languages. In 1781, when he was fourteen, he left his family for two years to serve as secretary and translator for Francis Dana, the first U.S. ambassador to Russia.

When Adams returned to America in 1785 he enrolled in Harvard University and graduated two

John Quincy Adams

years later. After passing the bar in 1790, he established a law practice in Boston. His distinguished diplomatic career began in 1794 when George Washington appointed him ambassador to the Netherlands. In 1796 he was about to move to Portugal to become ambassador when his father was elected president. President Adams reassigned his son to the post of minister to Prussia, which he held throughout his father's term.

When Thomas Jefferson defeated John Adams in his try for reelection in 1800, John Quincy returned to the United States where he embarked on a legislative career as a Federalist. In 1802 he was elected to the Massachusetts Senate, which sent him to the U.S. Senate the following year. Adams, however, angered his fellow Federalists by insisting on considering each issue independently, rather than voting with the party. When he supported President Jefferson's Embargo Act in 1807, the Massachusetts legislature elected his successor six months before his

term expired. Adams thus resigned in protest and returned to Massachusetts to practice law and teach at Harvard University.

Despite Adams's Federalist background, he was appointed minister to Russia in 1809 by Democratic-Republican President James Madison. While in St. Petersburg, Adams witnessed Napoleon's disastrous invasion of Russia and declined an appointment to the U.S. Supreme Court. In 1814 Adams was sent to Ghent to head the U.S. delegation to the negotiations seeking an end to the War of 1812. The treaty negotiated by Adams and his delegation and signed on December 24, 1814, extricated the United States from the embarrassing war without having to make significant concessions. Adams was then sent to London where he served as minister to Great Britain until 1817.

President James Monroe called Adams home from London in 1817 to become secretary of state. Adams distinguished himself in this post by conducting successful negotiations with Spain on the cession of the Floridas. The Adams-Onis Treaty with Spain, concluded on February 22, 1819, provided for the transfer of East and West Florida to the United States and the establishment of a border between Spanish and U.S. territory running from the Gulf of Mexico to the Rocky Mountains and along the forty-second parallel to the Pacific Ocean. Historians regard the treaty as a brilliant act of diplomacy, and Adams himself called its conclusion "the most important event of my life." Adams also was the mind behind the Monroe Doctrine, which warned that the United States would oppose any European interference in the internal affairs of an American nation or further European colonization of territory in the Western Hemisphere.

The 1824 presidential election was one of the most confused in U.S. history. The remnants of the Federalist Party had faded away during Monroe's presidency, leaving the Democratic-Republican Party the only significant party in existence. The

Democratic-Republican congressional caucus nominated W. H. Crawford of Georgia as the party's candidate, but several state caucuses refused to be guided by the judgment of this group. Consequently, John Quincy Adams, Andrew Jackson, and Henry Clay were nominated as regional candidates. The four-candidate race split the electoral vote, and no one received the majority required to be elected. Jackson led Adams 99 to 84 votes, with Crawford and Clay receiving 41 and 37 votes, respectively. This stalemate threw the election into the House of Representatives. There Henry Clay, a powerful member of the House, gave his support to Adams, who emerged victorious despite having received less than one-third of the popular vote. Jackson's supporters were furious that their candidate had been denied the presidency. When Adams selected Clay to be his secretary of state, the new president's opponents charged that he had made a "corrupt bargain."

Despite the absence of an electoral mandate and the disadvantage of a Congress poised to oppose him, Adams attempted to implement a program of public improvements. To stimulate the economy he advocated construction of a federally funded system of roads and canals and the implementation of high protective tariffs. He also called for federal funding of a national university, a national observatory, and scientific expeditions. The president's proposals failed, however, to attract significant support. Adams gained respect from certain groups for his antislavery and American Indian rights stands, but he was out of step politically with the majority of the American public, especially in the South and West. By his own admission he was not a popular president. When he ran for reelection in 1828 against Andrew Jackson, he did well in his native New England but lost the South and West, and therefore the election, by a landslide.

In 1830 the Twelfth District of Massachusetts elected the former president to the U.S. House of Representatives. Adams welcomed the chance to get back into national politics, free of the burdens and constraints of the presidency. He wrote, "No election or appointment conferred upon me ever gave me so much pleasure." Although not a radical abolitionist, Adams won respect for his conscientious opposition to slavery. He also was a leading congressional critic of the annexation of Texas and the Mexican War. Adams's life of public service ended in February 1848 when he became ill at his desk in the House chamber, fell into a coma, and died two days later in the Capitol.

While serving as a diplomat in Europe in 1797 Adams married Louisa Catherine Johnson, the daughter of Joshua Johnson, a merchant who was also the American consul general in London. They had four children. Their youngest son, Charles Francis Adams, had a distinguished diplomatic career, serving as minister to Great Britain during the American Civil War.

Andrew Jackson

Born: March 15, 1767; Waxhaw, South Carolina
Party: Democratic
Term: March 4, 1829–March 4, 1837
Vice Presidents: John C. Calhoun; Martin Van Buren
Died: June 8, 1845; Nashville, Tennessee
Buried: Nashville

Andrew Jackson was the youngest of the three sons of Andrew and Elizabeth Jackson, who had emigrated from Ireland. The couple were poor farmers in the Waxhaw region of South Carolina. The boy's father died a few days before Andrew was born from internal injuries sustained while lifting a heavy log. Andrew was raised by his mother, with the help of his uncle and older brother.

By the time he was five Andrew had learned to read at a country school, but he received only a rudimentary education. When he was just thirteen

Andrew Jackson

Andrew and his older brother Robert joined the militia. Their oldest brother Hugh had already been killed in the Revolutionary War, and Andrew and Robert were wounded and captured by the British in 1781. While a prisoner, Andrew was scarred on the hand by a British officer who struck him with a saber for refusing to clean the officer's boots. Because the boys contracted smallpox while in a British prison in South Carolina, they were allowed to return to their mother. Andrew's experiences during the war caused him to develop a hatred toward the British that he would feel for the rest of his life.

Andrew's brother Robert died two days after being released by the British, and his mother died later that year. Andrew was then left in the care of his mother's relatives. When he was sixteen he received an inheritance worth several hundred pounds from his paternal grandfather in Ireland. By this time, however, Andrew had adopted a wild lifestyle, and he gambled much of the money away.

In 1784 Jackson moved to Salisbury, North Carolina, where he began studying law in the office of Spruce Macay. He was admitted to the bar and began practicing law in 1787. In 1788 he moved to the new settlement of Nashville, where he became the prosecuting attorney of the Western District of North Carolina, which would become the state of Tennessee.

In 1796 Jackson became a member of the convention that drafted Tennessee's constitution, and that same year he was elected without opposition as Tennessee's first representative to the U.S. House of Representatives. Because Tennessee had become a state shortly before regular congressional elections were to be held, Jackson's term lasted only from December 1796 until March 1797. During his brief tenure in the House he was one of a handful of members to vote against a farewell tribute to George Washington. Jackson was critical of Washington's support for the Jay Treaty, which he believed allowed the British to continue preying on American shipping.

Although Jackson declined to run for reelection and returned to Tennessee when his brief term ended, within months he was elected to fill a vacant Senate seat. He served in the Senate from November 1797 to April 1798, when he again resigned. He then returned to Tennessee because of financial difficulties and his dislike of being separated from his family. In November of that year he was appointed to a seat on the Tennessee Superior Court. He served there until 1804, when he resigned to manage his estate. Although Jackson had become a prominent citizen, he still possessed the temper of his youth. During his years in Tennessee he was involved in several duels and fights. Some of these incidents came to nothing, including a duel in 1803 with Tennessee governor John Sevier in which no shots were fired. In 1806, however, Jackson fought a duel with Charles Dickenson, who had questioned the propriety of Jackson's marriage. Dickenson fired first, wounding Jackson in the chest. The athletic

Jackson shrugged off his wound, straightened himself, and mortally wounded Dickenson with his volley. Because Dickenson's bullet was lodged near Jackson's heart, it could not be removed and caused Jackson periodic pain for the rest of his life. In 1813 Jackson got into a fight with Thomas Hart and Jesse Benton in Nashville. He emerged from the brawl with two bullet wounds, one that almost forced the amputation of his arm.

Military Career

Since 1802 Jackson had held the rank of major general of the Tennessee militia. When the United States declared war on Great Britain in 1812, Jackson offered the services of his militia against the British. The government was slow to accept his offer but eventually sent Jackson to fight the Creek Indians, who were allied with the British. Jackson, whose troops had earlier nicknamed him "Old Hickory" in tribute to his toughness, engineered a five-month campaign that culminated in the decisive defeat of the Creeks at the Battle of Horseshoe Bend, Alabama, on March 27, 1814. Soon after, he was commissioned as a brigadier and then major general in the U.S. Army.

Following a brief campaign in which Jackson's forces captured Pensacola, Florida, from the British, the general was ordered west to defend New Orleans. After a large British force landed near the city, Jackson launched a surprise attack on December 23, 1814, which slowed the British advance. He then ordered his forces to retire to earthen fortifications blocking the route to New Orleans. When the British attacked on January 8, 1815, Jackson's motley army of U.S. regulars, Tennessee backwoodsmen, free blacks, friendly Indians, and pirate Jean Lafitte's crew laid down a deadly fire that left the canefield where the battle was fought littered with British dead. In about a half hour over two thousand British troops were killed or wounded. Only about forty of Jackson's men were killed, wounded, or missing. The decisive victory at New Orleans raised the morale of the nation, which had suffered many embarrassing military defeats during the war, and made Jackson a folk hero.

After the war Jackson remained military commander of the Southern District of the United States. In late 1817, acting on vague orders to defend the frontier near Spanish Florida from Indian attacks, Jackson launched an invasion of Florida that led to the capture of several Spanish posts. When Spain protested, the general was in danger of being reprimanded for exceeding his orders and infringing upon the right of Congress to declare war. Secretary of State John Quincy Adams, however, defended Jackson's actions, which he recognized increased pressure on the Spanish to cede the territory to the United States. President James Monroe stated his qualified support of Jackson's campaign, and in 1819 Adams concluded a treaty in which Spain renounced its claims to the Floridas.

Presidency

Although Jackson denied any interest in seeking the presidency, his supporters in Tennessee maneuvered to make him a candidate. In 1823 Jackson was elected to the U.S. Senate by the Tennessee legislature, sending him back to Washington as an obvious contender for the presidency.

The 1824 election was a confusing affair in which all the candidates were Democratic-Republicans and no one received a majority of electoral votes. With 133 electoral votes needed for election, Jackson, the leading vote-getter, received only 99 votes. John Quincy Adams finished second with 84, and William Crawford and Henry Clay received 41 and 37 votes, respectively. The election was thus thrown into the House of Representatives. Jackson lost the election when the House elected Adams after Clay threw his support to the second-place finisher.

The 1828 presidential election, in which Jackson defeated incumbent Adams, was a watershed in American politics. Jackson was not only the first person from the West to be elected president, but also he was the first to have been elected with the overwhelming support of the masses of common farmers and citizens who recently had been enfranchised in most states. Tens of thousands of voters descended on Washington for Jackson's inauguration. After his swearing-in Jackson opened the White House to his supporters, whose rowdy behavior confirmed the perceptions of many members of the conservative eastern political establishment that the country had succumbed to mob rule. The jubilant throngs at the White House broke furniture and china, muddied carpets, and forced Jackson to evacuate the premises for his own safety.

Jackson, like many presidents of his era, faced sectional tensions. In 1832 Congress had passed a high tariff despite the opposition of many southern states. Southerners objected to high tariffs because they protected the manufacturing interests in the North, while trade reprisals from Europe denied the South markets for its agricultural products. In response to the tariff law, the South Carolina legislature declared that the federal tariff was null in that state. Jackson met the challenge to the Constitution by denouncing nullification and requesting authority from Congress to send troops to South Carolina if needed to enforce the tariff. Congress granted this authority, which helped convince South Carolina to accept a compromise tariff bill backed by Jackson. The episode led to the estrangement of Jackson from his vice president, John C. Calhoun, who had supported South Carolina's nullification of the tariff.

Although Jackson defended the primacy of the federal government, he did not support all its activities. In 1832 he vetoed the bill that would have rechartered the Second Bank of the United States on the grounds that the bank was unconstitutional and a monopoly benefiting the rich. Jackson's opponents

hoped the issue would hurt him in the 1832 election, but the popular president easily defeated Whig Henry Clay. Unfortunately, the lack of a central bank weakened controls over state and local banks and contributed to the inflation and overspeculation that were partially responsible for the severe depression that began in 1837 after Jackson left office.

On January 30, 1835, Jackson became the first president to be the target of an assassination attempt. As Jackson was emerging from the Capitol, Richard Lawrence fired two pistols at him at point-blank range. Miraculously, both misfired. Jackson went at his assailant with his walking stick as onlookers seized Lawrence. The deluded young man, who claimed Jackson was preventing him from assuming the British throne, later was committed to an insane asylum.

When Jackson's second term expired, he retired to the Hermitage, his estate near Nashville. Although he never again sought public office and suffered from several ailments that left him weak, he retained his avid interest in politics. His support was important to the presidential victories of Martin Van Buren in 1836 and James K. Polk in 1844. Jackson died in 1845 at the Hermitage.

When Jackson met Rachel Donelson Robards in Nashville in 1788, she was separated from but still married to Lewis Robards. But when Jackson married her in 1791, they believed she had been granted a divorce. In late 1793, however, they learned that Rachel's divorce had not become legal until a few months before. Thus, to avoid any legal difficulties Andrew and Rachel repeated their wedding ceremony in January 1794.

Although the couple had no children, in 1810 they adopted Rachel's nephew, whom they renamed Andrew Jackson Jr. During the 1828 presidential campaign, Jackson's political opponents dredged up old accusations that Jackson's marriage was improper. Rachel was upset by the scrutiny of her past and longed for a quiet life in Tennessee with her husband. The charges may have affected Rachel's health, for it grew progressively worse, and she eventually died of a heart attack on December 22, 1828, after Jackson had been elected president but before his inauguration.

Martin Van Buren

Born: December 5, 1782; Kinderhook, New York
Party: Democratic
Term: March 4, 1837–March 4, 1841
Vice President: Richard M. Johnson
Died: July 24, 1862; Kinderhook
Buried: Kinderhook

Martin Van Buren was the third child of Abraham and Maria Van Buren. Martin's father was a farmer and tavern keeper who had fought in the Revolution. His mother, who had been widowed before marrying Abraham, had two sons and a daughter by her previous marriage.

Van Buren, the first president not of British descent, was raised in the Dutch community of Kinderhook, New York. Despite having received only a rudimentary education as a child, he began studying law when he was only fourteen under Francis Silvester. He moved to New York in 1801 and continued his law studies. After being admitted to the bar in 1803 he returned to Kinderhook and opened a law practice.

In 1808 Van Buren moved to Hudson, New York, where he was appointed surrogate of Columbia County. He began his rapid rise to power in New York politics in 1812 when he was elected to the state senate. He was appointed state attorney general in 1815 and retained his Senate seat while serving in that post. By 1820 Van Buren had become one of the most powerful politicians in New York. Before pursuing a national political career, Van Buren organized the "Albany Regency," a political

machine that controlled New York politics through patronage, party newspapers, and a tightly controlled Democratic caucus in the state legislature.

In 1821 the New York State legislature elected Van Buren to the U.S. Senate as a member of the Democratic-Republican Party. He was reelected in 1827. While serving in the Senate, Van Buren was one of the most vocal critics of President John Quincy Adams.

Van Buren's rise to the presidency was aided by his association with Andrew Jackson. Although Van Buren and Jackson had little in common but political skill, they became close allies. By 1827 Van Buren had become Jackson's most powerful supporter from the northeastern states. In 1828 Van Buren resigned from the Senate to help Jackson's presidential campaign in New York by running for governor. Jackson was elected president and Van Buren won the governorship, but Van Buren resigned after only three months to become Jackson's secretary of state.

As secretary of state, Van Buren was the most influential member of Jackson's cabinet. He not only became a successful diplomat respected by foreign governments for his discretion and negotiating ability, but he also continued to be Jackson's principal political adviser. In 1831 Van Buren further endeared himself to Jackson when he concurred with Jackson's defense of Peggy Eaton, Secretary of War John Eaton's wife, who had been rejected by Washington society for her alleged past promiscuity. Soon after the Eaton affair Van Buren resigned from his office to allow Jackson to reconstruct his cabinet free of supporters of Van Buren's political rival, Vice President John C. Calhoun. Jackson then appointed Van Buren ambassador to Great Britain, but when the Senate confirmation vote resulted in a tie, Calhoun voted against confirming Van Buren, who had already arrived in London.

In 1832 Van Buren replaced Calhoun as Jackson's vice-presidential running mate. The Jackson–Van Buren team was elected easily, and Van Buren continued to exercise influence over Jackson's policies.

In 1836, with President Jackson's backing, Van Buren received the Democratic presidential nomination. The Whig Party, believing that no single candidate had a good chance to beat Van Buren, nominated several regional candidates, hoping to divide the electoral vote and force the election into the House of Representatives. Van Buren, however, won a majority of the popular and the electoral vote. He needed 148 electoral votes to win the election outright, and he received 170 votes, with William Henry Harrison, his closest Whig opponent, receiving 73 votes.

Van Buren pledged at his inauguration to continue the policies of Jackson, and he reappointed Jackson's cabinet. The former president's economic policies, however, contributed to the depression that dominated Van Buren's presidency and did not subside until he had been defeated for reelection. In 1832 Jackson had vetoed the bill to recharter the

National Bank. Without the central control provided by the National Bank, many state and local banks engaged in wild speculation that led to financial disaster.

In 1837 overspeculation and a natural downturn in the business cycle caused many banks and businesses to fail. While unemployment soared, Van Buren followed the conventional economic wisdom of the period by cutting government expenditures. But these restrictive fiscal policies only deepened the depression.

Like his mentor, Van Buren also opposed a national bank, but he believed the federal government should handle its own funds rather than placing them in state banks as Jackson had done. He therefore proposed an independent federal treasury system. After several years of political maneuvering and debate Congress passed the Independent Treasury Act in July 1840. It established subtreasuries in seven U.S. cities.

On the issue of slavery Van Buren promoted the moderate course of allowing slavery to continue where it existed but blocking its extension. His opposition to the annexation of Texas, which would have added another slave state to the Union, avoided conflict with Mexico but cost him support in the South and West and damaged his relationship with Andrew Jackson.

Van Buren also had to deal with conflict on the U.S. border with Canada. He refused to support a movement by some U.S. citizens to aid a Canadian attempt to overthrow British rule in Canada. He defused the crisis by issuing a neutrality proclamation and sending Gen. Winfield Scott to Buffalo to enforce the peace. In 1839 a dispute developed over the uncertain legal boundary between Maine and Canada. Maine's governor, John Fairfield, called up a force of Maine militia and was preparing to fight with the Canadians over the issue when Van Buren intervened by negotiating an agreement with the British ambassador to the United States and sending

General Scott to Maine to block any military adventure by Fairfield.

In 1840 Van Buren was renominated unanimously by the Democratic Party, but Whig William Henry Harrison was a formidable opponent. Not only was Harrison a national hero for successfully fighting American Indians before and during the War of 1812, but also he was portrayed as the candidate of the common man who was truer to Jacksonian principles than Van Buren. Although Van Buren won 47 percent of the popular vote, Harrison trounced him in the electoral college 234–60. Van Buren even failed to win his home state of New York.

Despite his defeat in 1840 Van Buren did not retire from presidential politics. He attempted to run again for his party's nomination in 1844 but was defeated by dark-horse candidate James K. Polk, who outflanked Van Buren by openly advocating the annexation of Texas.

In 1848 Van Buren ran for president as the candidate of the new antislavery Free Soil Party. His long-shot candidacy split the Democratic vote in New York, helping Whig Zachary Taylor win the state and defeat Democrat Lewis Cass by 163–127 electoral votes. In 1850 Van Buren returned to the Democratic Party, and he supported Franklin Pierce's presidential candidacy in 1852.

Van Buren was the first former president to tour Europe. From 1853 to 1855 he visited Britain, France, Italy, Belgium, Holland, and Switzerland. During his retirement he wrote *Inquiry into the Origin and Course of Political Parties in the United States.* The manuscript was unfinished when he died in 1862 after suffering severe asthma attacks, but it was edited by his sons and published in 1867.

Van Buren married his childhood sweetheart and distant cousin Hannah Hoes on February 21, 1807. They had four sons and a fifth child who died soon after birth. Hannah died in 1819 before her husband attained national prominence. Van Buren never remarried, and the role of White House hostess was performed by Angelica Singleton Van Buren, the wife of his oldest son and White House secretary, Abraham.

William Henry Harrison

Born: February 9, 1773; Berkeley, Virginia
Party: Whig
Term: March 4, 1841–April 4, 1841
Vice President: John Tyler
Died: April 4, 1841; Washington, D.C.
Buried: North Bend, Ohio

William Henry Harrison was the youngest of the seven children of Benjamin and Elizabeth Harrison. William's father, a prosperous Virginia planter who served as a member of the Continental Congress and governor of Virginia, also signed the Declaration of Independence.

When William was fourteen his parents sent him to Hampden-Sydney College in his home state. Before graduating, however, he left for Philadelphia to study medicine under Dr. Benjamin Rush, a prominent physician and signer of the Declaration of Independence. When his father died in 1791, Harrison quit medicine to join the army. He was commissioned as a lieutenant and assigned as an aide to Gen. Anthony Wayne at Fort Washington near Cincinnati. In 1794 Harrison fought in the Battle of Fallen Timbers where General Wayne's forces defeated eight hundred American Indians. Harrison was promoted to captain in March 1795 and was given command of Fort Washington late that year.

In 1798 President John Adams appointed Harrison secretary of the Northwest Territory. The following year Harrison traveled to Washington, D.C., as the delegate of the Northwest Territory to Congress. There he worked successfully for legislation that separated the Indiana Territory from the

Northwest Territory. In 1800 Adams appointed Harrison governor of the Indiana Territory, a post that he held until 1812. In November 1811 Harrison led the Indiana territorial militia in a battle fought near Tippecanoe Creek against a confederation of American Indians under the Shawnee chief Tecumseh. The battle was inconclusive, but it made Harrison a nationally famous Indian fighter. During the War of 1812 Harrison was appointed brigadier general in command of the U.S. Army in the Northwest. Two years after the Battle of Tippecanoe Harrison again met Tecumseh, who had formed an alliance with the British. At the battle of the Thames in Ontario, Harrison's troops decisively defeated the Indians. Tecumseh was killed, and the federation of American Indians was broken. The importance of the Thames battle was overshadowed, however, by Harrison's earlier fight against the Indians, which had earned him the catchy nickname "Tippecanoe."

After the war Harrison was elected first to the U.S. House of Representatives, then to the Ohio Senate, and finally to the U.S. Senate. In 1828 Andrew Jackson appointed him ambassador to Colombia, but Harrison served there only eight months before returning to North Bend, Ohio, to manage his farm. In 1834 he accepted an appointment as clerk of his county's court of common pleas to help pay his heavy debts. While serving in this relatively insignificant post, he began campaigning actively for the 1836 presidential nomination of the Whig Party.

After witnessing the ease with which popular Democrat Andrew Jackson won two presidential elections, leaders of the Whig Party decided that they too needed a candidate who was a war hero from the West. The Whigs thus ran several regional candidates, including Harrison, against Jackson's chosen successor, Martin Van Buren. Van Buren won the election, but Harrison demonstrated his appeal by winning seven states.

Harrison's strong showing in the 1836 presidential election made him the logical Whig candidate in 1840. Even with Andrew Jackson's endorsement, Van Buren's hold on the presidency was vulnerable because of an economic depression that had started in 1837. The Whig's campaign of 1840 was a study in political manipulation of the electorate. Party leaders promoted "Tippecanoe" as a champion of the common man and war hero who was raised in a log cabin and preferred to drink hard cider. Meanwhile, they portrayed Van Buren as the rich person's candidate who lived like a king in the White House. The Whigs buried political issues under a mountain of slogans, songs, picnics, stump speeches, and parades. And the strategy worked, with Harrison receiving 234 electoral votes to Van Buren's 60.

Harrison's inaugural address, delivered on March 4, 1841, while hardly the most memorable in presidential history, was probably the most fateful. A driving rainstorm soaked Harrison as he rode to the

Capitol on a white horse and it continued throughout his address, which was the longest inaugural speech ever delivered. It contained over eight thousand words and lasted an hour and forty-five minutes. Ironically, in his speech, he advocated a constitutional amendment limiting presidents to one term in office and pledged to serve only one himself. Harrison caught a severe cold from his long exposure to the elements. On March 27 his condition deteriorated, and he was confined to his bed with what doctors diagnosed as pneumonia. He died on April 4, exactly one month after his inauguration.

Harrison married Anna Symmes on November 25, 1795, while he was an army lieutenant stationed in Ohio. They had six daughters and four sons. One of their sons, John Scott, was the father of Benjamin Harrison, who became the twenty-third president.

John Tyler

Born: March 29, 1790; Charles City County, Virginia
Party: Whig
Term: April 6, 1841–March 4, 1845
Vice President: None
Died: January 18, 1862; Richmond, Virginia
Buried: Richmond

John Tyler had much in common with his 1840 presidential running mate, William Henry Harrison. Both men were born in Charles City County, Virginia, and both were sons of prominent Virginia planters who had served as governor of that state.

John was the sixth of the eight children born to John and Mary Tyler. His mother died when he was just seven years old. Throughout his early life John set high goals for himself and attempted to follow his father's example of an active life of public service. He attended William and Mary College in Williamsburg, Virginia, graduating in 1807 when he was just seventeen. He then studied law under his father and was admitted to the bar two years later.

In 1811 Tyler was elected to the Virginia House of Delegates as a Jeffersonian Democratic-Republican. He was reelected five times and remained in office until 1815. During the War of 1812 he served briefly as captain of a Virginia militia company, but he saw no action. In November 1816 he was elected to the U.S. House of Representatives, but he retired from Congress in 1821, citing poor health. During his early political career Tyler was noted for his support of slavery and states' rights.

In 1823 Tyler was again elected to the Virginia House of Delegates, where he served until he was elected governor in 1825. After he resigned the governorship in 1827 he won a seat in the U.S. Senate, which he held until 1836.

As a senator, Tyler promoted the compromise tariffs that eased the nullification crises in South Carolina in 1832. Although he doubted that the states could legally nullify federal laws, he vigorously opposed Jackson's threats to use force against South Carolina. In 1836 Tyler resigned his Senate seat after refusing to follow the instructions of the Virginia legislature that he vote for the deletion of an 1833 censure of Andrew Jackson from the Senate *Journal*. The Senate had censured Jackson for his removal of public funds from the Second Bank of the United States without proper congressional approval.

Tyler's unhappiness with Jackson and the Democratic Party led him to join the Whig Party, despite the antislavery and nationalistic positions of many of its leaders. As one of several regional Whig vice-presidential candidates in 1836, Tyler received forty-seven electoral votes. Democrats Martin Van Buren and Richard Johnson won the presidency and vice presidency, respectively.

Considering their similar beginnings, it is ironic that Tyler was chosen as Harrison's running mate to balance the ticket. Harrison was promoted by the Whigs as "Old Tippecanoe," a tough Indian fighter who, like Andrew Jackson, was a champion of the common people. Tyler added southern gentility and a proslavery background that the Whigs hoped would appeal to the South. The Whig campaign of 1840 avoided policy issues and promoted its candidates through parties, parades, songs, and catchy slogans such as "Tippecanoe and Tyler too." The Whig ticket easily defeated President Martin Van Buren, whose popularity had been damaged by an economic depression that had lasted throughout his term.

Tyler appeared destined to have a small role in the Harrison administration. Daniel Webster, Henry Clay, and other Whig leaders had planned to exercise considerable influence over the aging Harrison, and there would be little place for Tyler, whose views were outside the Whig mainstream. Tyler, however, was thrust into the presidency when Harrison died only one month after taking office. The Constitution did not specify whether a vice president was to become president upon the death of an incumbent or merely assume the powers and duties of the office. Since Tyler was neither a Democrat nor a true Whig, leaders of both parties sought to limit his power. Many members of Congress and other national leaders contended that Tyler should be recognized only as acting president. But Tyler ignored his critics and assumed not only the duties of the presidency but also its title and all of its power.

Unlike the aging William Henry Harrison, who would likely have been dominated by Whig Party leaders, Tyler adopted policies that were entirely his own. His strict constructionist principles led him to oppose the major goals of the Whig leadership, including the National Bank, high tariffs, and federally funded internal improvements. As a result, he was excommunicated from the Whig Party while still president.

Although Tyler had little influence in Congress, he wished to make Texas, which had declared its independence from Mexico in 1836, a part of the United States. He thus oversaw the negotiation of a treaty of annexation with Texas in early 1844. On April 22 of that year he submitted the treaty to the Senate for approval. The Senate, however, rejected the treaty on June 8.

Tyler wished to run for reelection in 1844, but neither of the major political parties wanted to nominate him. He therefore organized a new Democratic-Republican Party dedicated to states' rights and the annexation of Texas. He gave up his candidacy, however, when the Democrats nominated James K. Polk, who had the support of Andrew Jackson and also advocated annexing Texas.

On December 4, Tyler, now a lame-duck president, sent his last State of the Union message to Congress. In it he proposed that the Texas annexation treaty be approved by a simple majority of both houses. The proposal was controversial not only because annexation of Texas would have implications for the slavery issue, but also because such a method of granting congressional consent would ignore the constitutional provision requiring a two-thirds vote by the Senate for approval of treaties. The House passed the joint resolution by a vote of 120–98 on January 25, 1845, and the Senate followed suit by a vote of 27–25 on February 27, 1845. Tyler's strategy had worked, and an important legislative precedent was set. Tyler signed the bill into law on March 1, three days before leaving office.

When his term expired, Tyler retired to Sherwood Forest, his Virginia estate. As a private citizen, he remained an outspoken advocate of southern interests. He believed that states had a constitutional right to secede, but he worked to preserve the Union.

In early 1861 he presided over the Washington Peace Conference, an eleventh-hour attempt to resolve sectional differences and avoid civil war. When Virginia seceded, however, he pledged his loyalty to the South.

In November 1861 Tyler was elected to the new Confederate Congress in Richmond, Virginia. He died there in a hotel room on January 18, 1862, before he could take his seat.

Tyler married Letitia Christian in 1813 on his twenty-third birthday. They had eight children. Mrs. Tyler died in the White House in 1842 after an extended illness. Several months after his first wife's death, Tyler became infatuated with Julia Gardiner, a young socialite from New York. After a year of courtship they were married in New York on June 26, 1844. Tyler had seven children by his second wife giving him a total of fifteen, the most of any president.

Tyler's second marriage caused a minor scandal in the capital because his bride was only twenty-four years old. Their wedding came in the wake of a tragic accident on the Potomac River in which Julia's father, David Gardiner, and several members of Tyler's cabinet were killed. In fact, many members of Washington society, including Julia and the president, were also on board at the time of the accident, when a cannon that was being demonstrated on board the navy frigate *Princeton* exploded.

James K. Polk

Born: November 2, 1795; Mecklenburg County, North Carolina
Party: Democratic
Term: March 4, 1845–March 4, 1849
Vice President: George M. Dallas
Died: June 15, 1849; Nashville, Tennessee
Buried: Nashville

James Knox Polk was the eldest of the ten children born to Samuel and Jane Polk. Samuel Polk was a prosperous North Carolina farmer who was interested in politics. When James was ten his family moved to Duck River, Tennessee, a settlement without a school on the edge of the frontier. There his parents taught him mathematics and reading.

As a boy, Polk was frail and often ill. When he was seventeen he survived an operation to remove gallstones without the benefit of anesthesia. His health improved dramatically after the surgery.

In 1818 Polk graduated from the University of North Carolina with honors. He then moved to Nashville, Tennessee, where he studied law for two years in the office of Felix Grundy before being admitted to the bar.

Polk began his political career in the Tennessee legislature in 1823 at the age of twenty-seven. Two years later he was elected to the U.S. House of Representatives from Andrew Jackson's former district. Polk rose quickly to positions of power in the House, becoming chairman of the Ways and Means Committee, majority leader, and finally Speaker in 1835. During his years in the House he earned the nickname "Young Hickory" because of his unswerving support for Andrew Jackson. In 1839 he left the House when the Democratic Party in Tennessee

drafted him as its candidate for governor. He won that election and served a two-year term. He ran for reelection in 1841 and 1843 but was defeated both times by the Whig candidate.

At the 1844 Democratic National Convention in Baltimore Polk's political career was resurrected dramatically from those gubernatorial defeats. Martin Van Buren was favored to receive the Democratic presidential nomination, but neither he nor his chief rival, Lewis Cass, could muster the two-thirds vote required to secure the nomination. With the balloting hopelessly deadlocked, the convention turned unanimously to Polk as a compromise candidate on the ninth ballot. He thus became the first dark-horse presidential candidate of a major party.

Polk campaigned on an expansionist platform that advocated annexation of Texas and a settlement with Britain that would fix the northern boundary of Oregon at 54° 40'. He also received the invaluable endorsement of Andrew Jackson. Polk defeated his better-known Whig opponent, Henry Clay, 170–105 in the electoral college. The election, however, was closer than the electoral vote indicates. Polk received only forty thousand votes more than Clay, and he won New York's thirty-six electoral votes—which would have given Clay a 141–134 victory—by just five thousand votes.

The most important issue confronting the new president was westward expansion. Polk and most of the nation wished to resolve the Oregon boundary question with Great Britain, acquire California and other lands in the Southwest from Mexico, and annex Texas. An agreement signed in 1818 provided for joint U.S.-British ownership of the Oregon Territory, which extended from California to above the fifty-fourth parallel. Although Polk had campaigned on the slogan "54° 40' or fight," the battle cry of those who wanted all of the Oregon Territory, he offered to divide Oregon with the British at the forty-ninth parallel. When the British refused, Congress, at his request, terminated the joint ownership agreement on April 23, 1846. Realizing that lack of a settlement could mean war, the British accepted Polk's original offer.

Three days before Polk's inauguration, President Tyler had signed a joint resolution annexing Texas, as Polk had advocated during his campaign. The southern border of Texas, however, remained in dispute, and tensions with Mexico over Texas and other territories in the Southwest threatened to lead to war. In 1846 Polk sent U.S. troops under Gen. Zachary Taylor into the territory between the Nueces River and the Rio Grande. The action was provocative, since the area was claimed by both Mexico and Texas but occupied by Mexicans. Polk had already decided to ask Congress for a declaration of war when news reached Washington that Mexican forces had attacked the American contingent. The president then claimed that Mexico was the aggressor and asked Congress to declare war, which it did, despite opposition from some northern lawmakers. American forces under Gen. Zachary Taylor and Gen. Winfield Scott won major victories over the Mexican army and eventually occupied Mexico City.

In 1848 Mexico agreed to the Treaty of Guadalupe Hidalgo, which ceded California and New Mexico to the United States in return for $15 million and recognized the Rio Grande as the boundary of Texas.

In domestic policy Polk also achieved his major goals. With his backing, Congress narrowly passed the Walker Tariff Act in 1846, which greatly reduced tariffs. Although the bill was opposed in the North, it stimulated trade and the U.S. economy. Polk also persuaded Congress to pass an independent treasury bill in 1846, which reestablished a system of subtreasuries first set up under Van Buren to handle government funds. Before Polk reestablished the subtreasuries, these funds had been deposited in state banks.

At the beginning of his term, Polk reputedly had told a friend that his four main goals as president were resolution of the territorial dispute over Oregon, acquisition of California and New Mexico, a lowered tariff, and reestablishment of a subtreasury system. He successfully achieved all four goals, and historians generally believe that he provided the strongest presidential leadership between the terms of Presidents Jackson and Abraham Lincoln.

Upon entering office, Polk had declared that he would not run for a second term. He kept his promise in 1848 by not seeking the Democratic presidential nomination. After attending Zachary Taylor's inauguration, the former president left Washington and toured the South on his way to his recently purchased home in Nashville. Polk, who worked long hours and almost never took a day off during his presidency, was not to enjoy a long retirement. The stress of the presidency and his work schedule may have weakened his health. He died in Nashville at the age of fifty-three, only three and a half months after leaving office.

Polk married Sarah Childress on January 1, 1824. She served not only as White House hostess but also as the president's personal secretary. The Polks had no children. After her husband's death Sarah retired in Nashville, Tennessee, where she lived as a widow until her death in 1891.

Zachary Taylor

Born: November 24, 1784; Orange County, Virginia
Party: Whig
Term: March 4, 1849–July 9, 1850
Vice President: Millard Fillmore
Died: July 9, 1850; Washington, D.C.
Buried: Louisville, Kentucky

Zachary Taylor was born into a prominent family of Virginia planters related to both James Madison and Robert E. Lee. His father, Richard Taylor, had served as an officer in the Revolutionary War. When Zachary's mother, Sarah, was pregnant with him, the Taylors left Virginia to establish a farm near Louisville, Kentucky. Zachary, the third of nine children, was born at a friend's home along the way. Because the Kentucky frontier lacked schools, Zachary was given a rudimentary education by occasional tutors and his well-educated parents.

In 1808 at the age of twenty-three Taylor was commissioned as a lieutenant in the army. He participated in William Henry Harrison's campaigns against American Indians in the Indiana Territory and fought in the Ohio Valley during the War of 1812. After the war he resigned from the army over a dispute about his rank but returned a year later when he was recommissioned as a major. He then served in a series of garrison posts on the frontier. In 1832 Taylor was promoted to colonel during the Black Hawk War and was among the officers who accepted Chief Black Hawk's surrender. He was reassigned in 1837 to Florida where the army was

fighting the Seminole Indians. On Christmas Day of that year his troops defeated the Seminoles in a major battle that earned him a promotion to brigadier general, and on May 15, 1838, he assumed command of all forces in Florida. In 1841 Taylor was given command of the southern division of the army and reassigned to Baton Rouge, Louisiana, where he bought a large plantation.

When the United States annexed Texas in 1845, President James K. Polk ordered Taylor to defend it against a Mexican invasion. In January 1846 Polk instructed the general to take the provocative step of deploying his forces on territory claimed by Mexico between the Nueces River and the Rio Grande. When Mexico declared war and launched an attack against Taylor's army, the general invaded Mexico and won a series of quick victories at Palo Alto, Resaca de la Palma, and Monterrey.

Taylor's victories earned him a promotion to major general and popularity among the American

public. President Polk, however, recognized that Taylor's heroics made him an attractive Whig presidential candidate and maneuvered to prevent further boosts to the general's reputation. The president ordered Taylor to command a small force of five thousand troops in northern Mexico, while Gen. Winfield Scott was given most of the troops who had served under Taylor and the more glamorous duty of leading an expedition to capture Mexico City. Taylor, however, turned this assignment to his advantage when his soldiers routed twenty thousand Mexicans at Buena Vista in February 1847. The victory made Taylor a hero in the United States, and, as Polk had feared, the Whig Party sought to capitalize on "Old Rough and Ready's" popularity by offering him its nomination for president.

Taylor declared that he disliked partisan politics and preferred to run without party affiliation. Eventually, however, he accepted the Whig Party's nomination but announced that he thought of himself as a national candidate rather than a Whig candidate. Taylor's reputation as a war hero was enough to earn him a close 163–127 electoral vote victory over Democratic candidate Lewis Cass. Martin Van Buren's third-party candidacy contributed to Taylor's victory by splitting New York's Democratic vote, thereby allowing Taylor to capture the state's thirty-six electoral votes that would have given Cass a majority.

Taylor's primary weakness as a chief executive was his lack of political experience. At Taylor's inauguration James Polk found the general to be "exceedingly ignorant of public affairs." Despite this handicap Taylor refused to be just a Whig figurehead. Among his proposals were greater government aid for agriculture and the development of a transcontinental railroad.

The major issue confronting Taylor was whether slavery would be allowed to exist in the West where territories soon would be applying for statehood. Southerners feared that new states entering the

Union, particularly California, would outlaw slavery and upset the equilibrium between slave and free states in Congress. Congressional leaders, led by Henry Clay of Kentucky, attempted to legislate a compromise that would satisfy both the North and the South. Taylor, however, supported the right of states to decide for themselves whether they would permit slavery. He also hoped that the bestowal of statehood on California would bring order to that territory, where local government had been unable to cope with the thousands of settlers who came after the discovery of gold there. He thus encouraged New Mexico and California to apply for statehood and declared that he would oppose the compromise plan being developed by Congress.

Although Taylor was a slave-owning southerner, he believed the Union must be preserved at all costs. He warned southern leaders that if their states rebelled against federal authority because of California statehood or any other issue, he would use the army to enforce the law and preserve the Union. Taylor never had to veto a congressional compromise plan or confront the secession of southern states, however. After sitting through ceremonies at the Washington Monument on a hot Fourth of July he fell ill and died in the White House five days later at the age of sixty-five. His vice president, Millard Fillmore, succeeded to the presidency and threw executive support behind the Compromise of 1850, which held the Union together temporarily by making concessions to the South in return for California's entrance into the Union as a free state.

In 1810, while a young army officer, Taylor married Margaret Mackall Smith. They had six children, two of whom died as infants. Their only son, Richard, served as a general in the Confederate army. One of their daughters, Sarah Knox, married Jefferson Davis, who would become president of the Confederacy. She died of malaria only three months after the wedding.

Millard Fillmore

Born: January 7, 1800; Cayuga County, New York
Party: Whig
Term: July 10, 1850–March 4, 1853
Vice President: None
Died: March 8, 1874; Buffalo, New York
Buried: Buffalo

Millard Fillmore was the second oldest of the nine children of Nathaniel and Phoebe Fillmore, a poor New York farm couple. When Millard was fourteen he was apprenticed to a clothmaker, but he bought his freedom from apprenticeship for thirty dollars and took a job teaching school. While teaching, he studied law with a local county judge and was admitted to the bar in 1823.

Fillmore began his political career as a member of New York's Anti-Masonic Party, which opposed secret societies in the United States. In 1828 he was elected to the New York State Assembly with the support of Anti-Masonic Party boss Thurlow Weed. While in the legislature, Fillmore drafted a bill that abolished imprisonment for debtors; it eventually became law. After being reelected twice he left the legislature to establish a lucrative law practice in Buffalo with his future postmaster general, Nathan K. Hall. From 1833 to 1835 and 1837 to 1843 Fillmore served in the U.S. House of Representatives. In 1834 he followed Weed into the Whig Party and soon became a prominent member of its northern wing. While in the House, Fillmore was an ally of Sen. Henry Clay (Whig-Ky.). In 1843 Fillmore returned to New York to practice law and enter state politics. He was defeated narrowly for the governorship in 1844 by Democrat Silas Wright but won election as New York's comptroller three years later.

In 1848 the Whigs nominated Mexican War hero Zachary Taylor as their presidential candidate. The party's search for a vice-presidential candidate to balance the ticket with the slave-owning Taylor led to Fillmore, who had impressed many party leaders with his good looks and political skills. The Taylor-Fillmore ticket then narrowly defeated Democrats Lewis Cass and William Butler.

As vice president, Fillmore was excluded from policymaking in the Taylor administration, but he dutifully presided over the Senate as that body struggled with the slavery issue. Fillmore was a staunch opponent of slavery, but he believed a moderate course was necessary to preserve the Union. He therefore supported the Compromise of 1850 devised by Sen. Henry Clay. The plan sought to relieve sectional tensions by making concessions to both the North and the South. President Taylor, however, opposed the compromise and was prepared to veto it and use force to put down any rebellions in the South that might result. Fillmore foresaw a close vote in the Senate and informed the president that if a tie vote should occur his conscience obligated him to vote for the compromise despite Tay-

lor's opposition. Before the Senate could vote on the plan, Taylor died suddenly on July 9, 1850.

Because Fillmore believed Taylor's cabinet was against the compromise, he accepted the resignations of all seven men and appointed a new cabinet that supported it. With Taylor dead, the threat of a presidential veto of Clay's plan was removed and work on the compromise moved forward. In September 1850 Fillmore signed a series of bills that made up the Compromise of 1850. Under the compromise, California was admitted to the Union as a free state, the territories of Utah and New Mexico were established without mention of slavery, and Texas was paid $10 million for surrendering its claim to New Mexico. Other provisions made federal officials responsible for capturing and returning runaway slaves and outlawed the slave trade in the District of Columbia while affirming the right to own slaves there. Many southerners objected to the compromise because it set a precedent: it allowed the federal government to pass legislation on slavery rather than leaving the issue to the states. Abolitionists, however, thought the compromise favored the South. They especially detested the Fugitive Slave Law, which Fillmore felt obligated to enforce despite his recognition that in doing so he was committing political suicide. The president believed the compromise would work only if the federal government upheld all of its provisions with equal force.

No one was entirely satisfied with the Compromise of 1850, which did nothing to resolve the slavery issue. It resulted, however, in a few years of relative calm. During this period Fillmore oversaw the modernization of the White House, worked to secure federal funds for railroad construction, and opposed the efforts of private U.S. citizens to overthrow Spanish rule in Cuba. Before Fillmore left office in 1853 he sent Commodore Matthew Perry on a cruise across the Pacific to open up Japan to American trade.

In 1853 Fillmore lost not only his wife but also his party. After the election of 1852 the Whig Party disintegrated. Their most visible leaders, Daniel Webster and Henry Clay, had died in 1852, and Fillmore's enforcement of the Fugitive Slave Act had disaffected many northern Whigs who helped form the new Republican Party in 1854. Fillmore declined to join the Republicans and instead accepted the 1856 presidential nomination of the ultraconservative American or "Know-Nothing" Party. The Know-Nothings were named for their practice of responding "I know nothing" to questions about their rituals. The party was based on an opposition to immigrants and Catholics. The Know-Nothings believed these groups threatened the United States by plotting against the government and promoting radical ideologies. In the election Fillmore received over 800,000 popular votes but just eight electoral votes. He thus finished a distant third behind Democrat James Buchanan and Republican John Fremont.

After this embarrassment Fillmore retired from politics. In 1858 he married Caroline McIntosh, a wealthy forty-four-year-old widow, and settled in Buffalo. He died of a stroke on March 8, 1874. Fillmore had one son and one daughter by his first wife, Abigail Powers.

Franklin Pierce

Born: November 23, 1804; Hillsboro, New Hampshire
Party: Democratic
Term: March 4, 1853–March 4, 1857
Vice President: William R. King
Died: October 8, 1869; Concord, New Hampshire
Buried: Concord

Franklin Pierce was the sixth of the eight children born to Anna and Benjamin Pierce. His father, who would become governor of New Hampshire, married Anna after the death of his first wife. Pierce's parents sent him to private schools as a child, and at the age of fifteen he enrolled at Bowdoin College in Brunswick, Maine. Pierce did well at Bowdoin, graduating third in his class in 1824. After college he studied law and was admitted to the bar in 1827. In 1829 he was elected to the New Hampshire legislature while his father was governor.

When he was elected to the U.S. House of Representatives in 1833, Pierce left the New Hampshire legislature, where he had become Speaker of the House. Although Pierce's loyal support of the Jackson administration earned him a second term, he served only a few months because the New Hampshire legislature elected him to the U.S. Senate in 1836. In 1842, however, he retired from the Senate at the urging of his wife and returned to New Hampshire to practice law. In 1844 President James K. Polk appointed Pierce U.S. district attorney for New Hampshire.

As district attorney and chairman of the Democratic Party in New Hampshire, Pierce remained a powerful political figure, but he refused a series of important political appointments, partly because his wife did not want to move back to Washington, D.C. When the president appointed Sen. Levi Woodbury (D-N.H.) to the Supreme Court in 1845, Pierce declined to replace Woodbury in the Senate. The same year he turned down the New Hampshire Democratic gubernatorial nomination. In 1846 Polk offered him the U.S. attorney generalship, but Pierce again refused so he could remain in New Hampshire with his family. After the United States declared war on Mexico, however, Pierce accepted a commission as a colonel and began recruiting a New England regiment. Before he sailed for Mexico in May 1847, he was promoted to brigadier general. Pierce saw little action during his five and one-half months in Mexico because of an intestinal ailment and an injury sustained when his horse fell. Nevertheless, in January 1848 he returned to a hero's welcome in Concord where he resumed his law practice. That same year he again refused the Democratic nomination for governor.

Pierce's rise to the presidency was sudden and unexpected. The 1852 Democratic nominating convention produced a stalemate between James Buchanan, Lewis Cass, William Marcy, and Stephen A. Douglas. Because none of these candidates was able to garner a majority of the votes, the convention began searching for a fifth candidate. On the forty-ninth ballot the Democrats nominated Franklin Pierce, who several months before had announced he would not turn down such a nomination. As a northerner with southern sympathies and a spotless record, Pierce was an acceptable compromise candidate, although he had not served in an elective office since 1842. His Whig opponent was Gen. Winfield Scott, a hero of the Mexican War. Scott's campaign, however, was crippled by the defection of many northern Whigs to the Free Soil

Party. Pierce remained in New Hampshire during the months before the election, letting his fellow Democrats, who had united behind his candidacy, campaign for him. The uncontroversial Democratic platform of strict observance of the Compromise of 1850 gained Pierce a 254–42 victory in the electoral college.

Pierce took office advocating tranquility and prosperity at home and the extension of U.S. territories and commercial interests abroad. Most of his domestic policies favored the South. In his inaugural address he had declared his belief that slavery was constitutional and that "states where it exists are entitled to efficient remedies" to enforce it. The Compromise of 1850 enacted under Millard Fillmore had calmed temporarily tensions over the slavery issue, but that calm did not last through Pierce's presidency. In 1854 Pierce signed the Kansas-Nebraska Act into law. It repealed the 1820 Missouri Compromise that had outlawed slavery north of 36° 30', thereby enabling Kansas to declare itself a slave state if its citizens favored that course. Pierce, who believed that each state should decide for itself whether to permit slavery, strongly supported the act, which had been sponsored by Illinois senator Stephen A. Douglas. The act, however, turned Kansas into a war zone. Proslavery southerners and abolitionist northerners raced into Kansas hoping to seize control of the territory's government for their side. Many atrocities were committed by both groups, causing the territory to be dubbed "Bleeding Kansas."

In international affairs Pierce supported Millard Fillmore's initiative of sending Commodore Matthew Perry to Japan to open that country's ports to Western trade. Perry negotiated a treaty that gave U.S. ships access to two ports and guaranteed humane treatment of U.S. sailors shipwrecked off Japan's coasts.

After leaving the presidency in 1857 Pierce never again sought public office. He and his wife, Jane

Means Appleton Pierce, traveled in Europe from 1857 to 1859 and then retired to their Concord, New Hampshire, home. They had three sons, two of whom died in infancy. Their third son, eleven-year-old Benjamin, was killed when a train on which he and his parents were passengers wrecked near Andover, Massachusetts, a few weeks before Pierce's inauguration. The tragedy deeply affected Pierce's wife, who remained in a state of mourning during the first two years of Pierce's presidency. Pierce was a close college friend of American author Nathaniel Hawthorne, who wrote Pierce's campaign biography. Pierce was at Hawthorne's bedside when the writer died in 1864.

James Buchanan

Born: April 23, 1791; Stony Batter, Pennsylvania
Party: Democratic
Term: March 4, 1857–March 4, 1861
Vice President: John C. Breckinridge
Died: June 1, 1868; Lancaster, Pennsylvania
Buried: Lancaster

James Buchanan was the second oldest child and oldest son of the eleven children born to James and Elizabeth Buchanan. Young James grew up working in the family's thriving frontier trading post in Mercersburg, Pennsylvania.

James received an elementary education at common schools and attended a secondary school in Mercersburg before entering Dickinson College in Carlisle, Pennsylvania, in 1807. A year later he was expelled for disorderly conduct, but he was reinstated with the help of the president of the college's board of trustees. James graduated with honors in 1809 and returned to Lancaster to study law. In 1812 he was admitted to the bar, and the following year he was appointed assistant prosecutor for Lebanon County, Pennsylvania.

In August 1814, after the British burned Washington, D.C., Buchanan joined a company of men from Lancaster that marched to Baltimore to fight the British. The British withdrew from Baltimore soon after the company arrived. The unit was disbanded, and Buchanan returned to Pennsylvania where he was elected to the state assembly. He served two terms before leaving politics to establish a successful law practice.

Buchanan began his national political career in 1820 with his election to the U.S. House of Representatives as a Federalist. He served in the House for ten years. He was a staunch opponent of John Quincy Adams and in 1828 gave his allegiance to Andrew Jackson and the Democratic Party. Jackson appointed Buchanan minister to Russia in 1831. While in St. Petersburg, Buchanan negotiated a treaty of commerce favorable to the United States. He returned home in 1833 and was elected to the U.S. Senate by the Pennsylvania legislature the following year. He quickly became a leading conservative Democrat and chairman of the Foreign Relations Committee. Buchanan chose to stay in the Senate despite President Martin Van Buren's offer of the attorney generalship and President John Tyler's offer of a seat on the Supreme Court. When President James K. Polk, for whom Buchanan had campaigned, offered Buchanan the post of secretary of state, however, he accepted. As secretary of state, Buchanan took a leading role in the negotiations with Britain that produced a compromise on fixing the boundary of the Oregon Territory.

After losing the 1848 Democratic presidential nomination to Lewis Cass, Buchanan retired to Lancaster. In 1853, however, he accepted an appointment from President Franklin Pierce as minister to Great Britain. While in Britain, Buchanan collaborated with the U.S. ambassadors to Spain and France in writing the Ostend Manifesto of 1854. This diplomatic report advocated the acquisition of Cuba from Spain by force if Spain refused to sell it. Its intent was to prevent the possibility of a slave uprising on the island that might spread by example to the United States. The document, which was not acted upon, was denounced in the North but increased Buchanan's popularity in the South.

After returning from Britain in 1856, Buchanan was nominated for president by the Democrats. His absence from the country during the bloody fighting in Kansas precipitated by the Kansas-Nebraska Act made him more acceptable than either President Pierce or Sen. Stephen Douglas, both of whom had supported the act. Buchanan faced John Fremont of the newly formed Republican Party and former president Millard Fillmore of the right-wing American (Know-Nothing) Party. Buchanan received only 47 percent of the popular vote but won every southern state in defeating Fremont 174–114 in the electoral college.

Buchanan's presidency was dominated by the tensions between North and South over the slavery issue. Although Buchanan considered slavery to be unjust, he believed people in the southern states had the constitutional right to own slaves. He was a committed Unionist who tried to steer a middle course between the forces for and against slavery, but most of his policies appeared to northerners to favor the South. He enforced the Fugitive Slave Act, tried to quell northern antislavery agitation, and supported the Supreme Court's Dred Scott decision. The latter denied the citizenship of slaves, recognized the right of slaveowners to take their slaves wherever they chose, declared the Missouri Compromise restricting slavery to below 36° 30' to be unconstitutional, and implied that neither Congress nor the territorial governments created by Congress had the authority to exclude slavery from the territories. Buchanan not only supported the 7–2 decision, but also lobbied Associate Justice Robert Grier to support it.

The Dred Scott case did not resolve the slavery question as Buchanan had hoped. In 1858 Buchanan split his party when he sent a proslavery constitution written by the minority southern faction in Kansas to Congress and recommended that Kansas be admitted as a slave state. Many Democratic leaders, including Stephen Douglas, denounced the constitution and distanced themselves from Buchanan. The Senate approved the plan to admit Kansas under the proslavery constitution, but the House rejected it. Kansas remained a territory until 1861 and continued to inspire conflict between North and South.

The 1860 election produced the secession crisis that Buchanan had hoped to prevent. When Abraham Lincoln of the antislavery Republican Party was elected, southerners began to debate secession. Buchanan supported compromise solutions proposed by members of Congress and other leaders. He backed a proposal to reestablish the Missouri Compromise line and a constitutional amendment that would guarantee the right to own slaves in states that wanted it, but none of the plans was acceptable.

After Lincoln's election secessionists seized most federal forts in the South without much resistance. Buchanan considered secession to be unconstitutional, but he believed that the right to rebel against unjust rule was a basic right of all people and was even embodied in the Declaration of Independence. He also believed that the federal government could not wage war against a state or group of states. Therefore, he refrained from responding with force to the acts of rebellion. He did request, however, the power to call out the militia and increase the size of the armed forces, but Congress refused. By the time Buchanan's term ended, seven states had seceded, and the nation was headed toward civil war.

After Lincoln's inauguration Buchanan retired to Wheatland, his home in Lancaster, Pennsylvania. He corresponded with friends and political associates but was not active in public affairs. During his retirement the northern press criticized him for failing to prevent the Civil War and accused him of allowing federal forts to remain vulnerable and participating in plots to arm the South before the war. In an attempt to justify his actions and the policies of his administration, he published his memoirs, *Mr. Buchanan's Administration on the Eve of the Rebellion,* in 1866. Buchanan believed that he vindicated himself through his book, which placed primary blame for the war on northern radicals. Buchanan died at Wheatland in 1868.

Buchanan was the only president never to marry. His close relationship with William R. King, who became vice president under Franklin Pierce, has led some historians to speculate that Buchanan was homosexual. His niece, Harriet Lane, served as White House hostess during his administration. In 1819, while practicing law, he became engaged to Ann Coleman, who was from a wealthy Lancaster family. But after a quarrel with Buchanan she broke the engagement and left for Philadelphia to visit her sister. She died mysteriously a few days later on December 9, 1819, amid rumors that she committed suicide. Her family did not allow Buchanan to attend her funeral.

Abraham Lincoln

Born: February 12, 1809; near Hodgenville, Kentucky
Party: Republican
Term: March 4, 1861–April 15, 1865
Vice Presidents: Hannibal Hamlin; Andrew Johnson
Died: April 15, 1865; Washington, D.C.
Buried: Springfield, Illinois

Abraham Lincoln was born in a one-room log cabin on a backwoods farm in Kentucky. He was the second of the three children of Nancy and Thomas Lincoln, a poor farmer who also did carpentry work. Abe's younger brother died in infancy, and his mother died when he was nine. In 1819 his father married Sarah Bush Johnston, who was a loving stepmother to Abe. She brought her three children by her previous marriage into the family.

During Abe's childhood the Lincolns lived on farms in Kentucky and Indiana. Abe attended country schools sporadically, learning to read, write, and do elementary math. He possessed a quick, inquisitive intellect, however, and spent much free time reading the family Bible and whatever books he could borrow. Abe worked at numerous odd jobs while in his teens, including farmhand, grocery store clerk, and ferry boat rower. In 1828 and 1831 he took trips down the Mississippi River to New Orleans as a flatboat deck hand. While in New Orleans during the second trip he reputedly developed his hatred of slavery after witnessing the maltreatment of slaves.

Abe had moved with his family to a farm near Decatur, Illinois, in 1830, but after returning from New Orleans in 1831, he settled in New Salem, Illinois. There he worked in a store and became known

Abraham Lincoln

for his prowess as a storyteller and wrestler. In 1832, Lincoln volunteered to fight Sauk Indians led by Chief Black Hawk. After serving several months in the army, he was discharged without participating in any combat. He returned to New Salem from his military service and made an unprepared attempt to win a seat as a Whig in the Illinois state legislature, but he was defeated.

Later in 1832 Lincoln bought half interest in a general store. When the store failed the following year, Lincoln was left with debts that he would not be able to pay off completely for seventeen years. After his failed business venture, Lincoln was appointed postmaster of New Salem and also worked as a surveyor.

Early Political Career

In 1834 Lincoln ran again for the state legislature and this time won a seat. He began studying law by

reading borrowed law books. Shortly after being reelected to a second term in 1836, Lincoln was licensed to practice law. In 1837 he moved to Springfield, Illinois, and began practicing law when the legislature was not in session. He was reelected to the legislature in 1838 and 1840, serving for a time as Whig floor leader.

In 1846 Lincoln was elected to the U.S. House of Representatives. Despite the popularity of the Mexican War in his district, he joined fellow Whigs in denouncing the war as unjust. Lincoln also opposed the extension of slavery into the territories but did not advocate abolishing slavery where it already existed. Lincoln had promised Illinois Whig Party leaders that he would serve only one term, so when his term expired he returned to Springfield. He spent the next several years reading and developing his successful law practice.

In 1854 Lincoln ran for the Senate but backed out of the race when his candidacy threatened to split the antislavery vote. Two years later, Lincoln joined the new Republican Party, which had formed in 1854. He campaigned for its 1856 presidential candidate, John C. Fremont, who lost to Democrat James Buchanan.

The Illinois Republican Party nominated Lincoln for senator in 1858. He faced incumbent Democrat Stephen A. Douglas, author of the Kansas-Nebraska Act of 1854, which was favored by many proslavery Democrats. The act gave the people in the territories of Kansas and Nebraska the option to permit slavery.

Lincoln challenged Douglas to a series of seven debates focusing on slavery that were attended by huge crowds. In the debates Lincoln questioned the morality of slavery and firmly argued against its expansion into territories where it did not exist already. The state legislature elected Douglas over Lincoln 54–46, but the debates made Lincoln famous throughout the country and a credible candidate for the Republican presidential nomination in 1860.

During the next two years he made several highly publicized speaking tours, including one to the East in early 1860. His name was placed in nomination at the Republican National Convention in Chicago in 1860, but he trailed New York senator William Seward on the first and second ballots. On the third ballot, however, Lincoln secured the nomination.

The Democratic Party, meanwhile, split into two factions. Stephen Douglas was nominated by northern Democrats, and Vice President John C. Breckinridge of Kentucky was nominated by southern Democrats. The remnants of the Whig and Know-Nothing Parties further complicated the election by joining to nominate John Bell as the candidate of their new Constitutional Union Party. Lincoln won the four-candidate race with less than 40 percent of the popular vote. He captured eighteen northern states with 180 out of the total 303 electoral votes. Breckinridge and Bell followed with 72 and 39, respectively. Douglas, who finished second to Lincoln in the popular vote, won only Missouri's 12 electoral votes.

Presidency

Lincoln's election precipitated the secession crisis that the nation had feared for several decades. In December 1860, South Carolina left the Union, followed by six more states early in 1861. The rebelling states formed a confederacy and elected Jefferson Davis as their president.

Lincoln tried to ease southern fears that he intended to abolish slavery. He declared in his first inaugural address that he had no intention or authority to "interfere with the institution of slavery where it already exists." But he warned the Southern states that he did not recognize their secession and would enforce federal law and defend the Union. He declared, "In your hands, my dissatisfied fellow-countrymen, and not in mine, is the momentous issue of civil war." War came when rebels attacked and captured Fort Sumter in Charleston harbor in April 1861. The attack on the federal fort signaled the South's unwillingness to return to the Union. On April 15, Lincoln called for seventy-five thousand volunteers to put down the rebellion. Soon after, four more Southern states seceded, raising the number of states in the Confederacy to eleven.

During the next three months Lincoln refused to call Congress into session, while he took extraordinary actions to prepare for war, many of which violated the Constitution. He blockaded the South, doubled the size of the armed forces, suspended the writ of *habeas corpus* in some areas, and spent Treasury funds, all without congressional approval. Finally, on July 4, he convened Congress, which ratified most of his war measures.

Lincoln and the North hoped that the rebellion could be put down quickly, but the war turned into a protracted and bloody conflict. The Union won victories in the West under Gen. Ulysses S. Grant; but in the East, Union generals were repeatedly outmaneuvered by Robert E. Lee and other Confederate generals. On January 1, 1863, Lincoln issued the Emancipation Proclamation, which declared that the slaves in the rebellious states were free. So that the proclamation would have greater credibility, he had waited to make this move until after the Union won a victory, which came at the battle of Antietam in September 1862.

In July 1863 the Union victory at Gettysburg, Pennsylvania, put the Confederacy on the defensive. Lincoln traveled to Gettysburg on November 19, where he delivered his famous Gettysburg Address during a ceremony to dedicate the battlefield's cemetery. The short address—one of the nation's greatest creedal statements—stressed the equality of all citizens and the transcendency of the Union.

In 1864 Lincoln took an important step toward winning the war when he ordered Grant east to take command of all Union armies. That year Lincoln ran for reelection against Democratic candidate

George B. McClellan, one of his former generals. Lincoln had relieved McClellan of his command of the Union army in 1862 because the general was overcautious and ineffective. During the spring of 1864 Lincoln's reelection had been in doubt as Grant's army fought a series of indecisive and costly battles in Virginia at the Wilderness, Spotsylvania, and Cold Harbor. But by September, Union general William T. Sherman had captured Atlanta, and Grant had besieged Petersburg, Virginia. Voters sensed that the Union was close to victory and reelected the president. Lincoln won all but three states and defeated McClellan 212–21 in the electoral college.

During the final year of the war, Grant fought a battle of attrition against Lee's forces in Virginia, while Sherman's army drove through Georgia and North and South Carolina destroying Southern crops and industries. Finally, on April 9, 1865, Lee surrendered to Grant at Appomattox Court House in Virginia, ending the war.

In his second inaugural address, delivered on March 4, 1865, Lincoln had proposed a magnanimous peace, saying "with malice toward none, with charity for all, with firmness in the right as God gives us to see the right, let us strive on to finish the work we are in, to bind up the nation's wounds."

Lincoln, however, did not have the opportunity to implement his generous reconstruction plans. On April 14, 1865, while watching a production of the play *Our American Cousin* at Ford's Theater in Washington, D.C., he was shot in the back of the head at close range by actor John Wilkes Booth. After shooting Lincoln, Booth jumped from the presidential box to the stage, fled the theater, and rode south. On April 26 federal troops surrounded and killed him at a farm in Virginia. Booth, who had sympathized with the Confederacy, was part of a conspiracy to kill several government officials, including Vice President Andrew Johnson. With the exception of Secretary of State William Seward, who received a non-

fatal stab wound at his home, the other targets of assassination escaped harm.

Lincoln was treated by a doctor at the theater, then carried across the street to a house where he died the next morning, April 15, without regaining consciousness. Vice President Johnson took the oath of office later that day. Lincoln's body lay in state in the Capitol and White House before being carried back to Illinois on a train viewed by millions of mourners.

Lincoln married Mary Todd on November 4, 1842. Of their four sons, only Robert, their eldest, reached adulthood. He served as secretary of war under Presidents James A. Garfield and Chester A. Arthur and minister to Great Britain under Benjamin Harrison. Their second son, Edward, died at the age of three; their third son, William, died of typhoid fever in the White House in 1862 at the age of eleven. Their youngest son, Thomas (Tad), survived his father but died at the age of eighteen in 1871.

Lincoln originally had been engaged to marry Mary Todd on January 1, 1841, but their wedding did not take place for reasons that are unclear. Afterwards, Lincoln suffered an emotional and physical breakdown and lived in Kentucky for a period while he recovered. In 1842 Lincoln resumed his relationship with Mary, and they married that year. Their marriage was a stormy one that was complicated by the deaths of their children and Mary's lavish spending, superstitions, and bouts with depression.

Andrew Johnson

Born: December 29, 1808; Raleigh, North Carolina
Party: Democratic
Term: April 15, 1865–March 4, 1869
Vice President: None
Died: July 31, 1875; Carter's Station, Tennessee
Buried: Greeneville, Tennessee

Andrew Johnson was the younger of the two sons born to Jacob and Mary Johnson. Andrew's father, who died when he was three, was a laborer, and his mother was a seamstress. Neither parent could read or write, and Johnson received no formal education.

When Andrew was thirteen he was apprenticed to a tailor in Raleigh, North Carolina, his birthplace. Andrew's fellow workers taught him to read, although he did not learn to write until several years later. In 1824, after two years as an apprentice, Andrew ran away from his master, James Selby, and worked as a journeyman tailor in Laurens, South Carolina. Although Selby was still offering a reward for his return, Johnson came back to Raleigh in 1826 and convinced his mother and stepfather to move west with him. They settled in Greeneville, Tennessee, where Johnson opened a tailor shop.

In 1828 the people of Greeneville elected the young tailor alderman. After two years on the city council, Johnson was chosen mayor at the age of twenty-one. In 1835 he made the step up to state politics when he was elected as a Democrat to the Tennessee legislature. He espoused the ideals of Andrew Jackson, became an advocate of the common farmer and small business owner, and earned a reputation as a powerful orator. In 1837 he was defeated for a second term in the Tennessee legislature, but he won reelection in 1839. Two years later he was elected to the state senate, and in 1843 his congressional district sent him to the U.S. House of Representatives.

In Washington, Johnson supported the Mexican War and the Compromise of 1850. He served four terms in the House, but an 1853 Whig redistricting plan made his reelection impossible. Consequently, Johnson ran for governor of Tennessee and won two terms before the Tennessee legislature sent him to the U.S. Senate in 1857.

In 1860 Johnson was proposed as a presidential candidate, but he withdrew his name from nomination and supported John Breckinridge. When Abraham Lincoln was elected, Johnson surprised many of his fellow southerners by declaring his loyalty to the Union. He campaigned against the secession of Tennessee, and when his state did secede in June 1861, he was the only southern senator to remain in the Senate. In 1862, after Union forces had captured most of Tennessee, Lincoln appointed Johnson military governor of his state. With Johnson's urging, Tennessee became the only seceding state to outlaw slavery before the 1863 Emancipation Proclamation.

Johnson's loyalty to the Union was rewarded with a vice-presidential nomination in 1864. Lincoln's first-term vice president, Hannibal Hamlin, wanted to be renominated, but Lincoln refused to back his candidacy. Delegates to the National Union convention in Baltimore (the Republican nominating convention expanded to include Democrats loyal to the Union) hoped that having a southern

Democrat on the ticket would attract support from northern Democrats and voters in border areas.

Lincoln and Johnson defeated Democrats George McClellan and George Pendleton by 212–21 electoral votes. Some Johnson supporters, however, changed their minds about him when he showed up drunk for the inauguration on March 4, 1865. Lincoln shrugged off the incident and expressed confidence in his vice president.

Johnson served as vice president only six weeks before President Lincoln died on April 15 from a gunshot wound inflicted by assassin John Wilkes Booth. The new president thus faced the immense problem of reconstructing a broken South, which had surrendered six days before. Johnson tried to implement the lenient Reconstruction program envisioned by Lincoln, but he was blocked by radical Republicans in Congress who were intent upon punishing the region and limiting the influence of white southerners in national politics. Johnson successfully vetoed several harsh Reconstruction bills early in his presidency, but in the 1866 congressional elections the radical Republicans gained overwhelming control of Congress and were in a position to override the president's vetoes.

On March 2, 1867, Congress passed the first Reconstruction Act over Johnson's veto. It established martial law in the South, granted universal suffrage to blacks, and limited the voting rights of Southern whites. The same day Congress overrode Johnson's veto of the Tenure of Office Act, which prohibited the president from removing without Senate approval any appointee who had been confirmed by the Senate. Johnson's defiance of this act forced a showdown between the president and Congress. On August 12, 1867, while Congress was in recess, Johnson replaced Secretary of War Edwin Stanton with Gen. Ulysses S. Grant without the Senate's approval.

On January 13, 1868, the Senate declared the president's action illegal and reinstated Stanton. Gen.

Grant complied with the Senate's order, but Johnson again dismissed Stanton and ordered Maj. Gen. Lorenzo Thomas to take Stanton's place. Three days later, on February 24, 1868, the House voted 126–47 to impeach the president. Radical Republicans had been searching for an excuse to impeach Johnson since early 1867.

The president's fate was then in the hands of the Senate, which could remove him from office with a two-thirds vote. On March 13 Johnson's trial began in the Senate chambers with Chief Justice Salmon P. Chase presiding. The Senate voted 35–19 for the impeachment articles, one vote short of the necessary two-thirds needed for conviction. Although Johnson's radical Republican opponents controlled the Senate, seven believed that the charges against Johnson did not warrant his removal and voted against conviction despite the consequences for their political careers. The decisive vote belonged to freshman Sen. Edmund G. Ross (R-Kan.), whose "not guilty" acquitted Johnson.

Although Johnson's presidency was dominated by Reconstruction and his battles with Congress, he and his secretary of state, William H. Seward, achieved a notable foreign policy success in 1867 when they negotiated the purchase of Alaska from Russia for only $7.2 million.

When Johnson's term expired in 1869 he returned to Tennessee, where he ran for the U.S. Senate. He lost that year and was defeated for a seat in the House in 1872. Finally, in 1874 the Tennessee legislature elected him to the Senate. He returned to Washington, where he resumed his fight for more lenient Reconstruction policies. Johnson only served five months of his Senate term before he died of a stroke in 1875 while visiting his daughter at Carter's Station, Tennessee.

Johnson married sixteen-year-old Eliza McCardle on May 17, 1827, in Greeneville, Tennessee, where he had opened a tailor shop. She had received some primary education and was able to teach Johnson, who could already read, to write and do elementary mathematics. The couple had three sons and two daughters. Eliza died in Tennessee less than six months after her husband.

Ulysses S. Grant

Born: April 27, 1822; Point Pleasant, Ohio
Party: Republican
Term: March 4, 1869–March 4, 1877
Vice Presidents: Schuyler Colfax; Henry Wilson
Died: July 23, 1885; Mount McGregor, New York
Buried: New York City

Ulysses S. Grant was the eldest of the six children born to Jesse and Hanna Grant. Jesse Grant was a tanner, but his son disliked the business and preferred doing chores on the family farm. Grant attended a series of schools as a child, and received an appointment to the United States Military Academy at West Point, New York, in 1839 through the efforts of his father. Although Grant had no interest in a military career, he accepted the appointment.

Grant's name at birth was Hiram Ulysses, but when he enrolled at West Point he reversed the order of these two names. The school, however, officially recorded his name as Ulysses S. Grant. Rather than correct the mistake, Grant adopted West Point's version of his name without expanding his new middle initial. In 1843 Grant graduated twenty-first in his class of thirty-nine at West Point. He did well in mathematics and hoped one day to be a math teacher. He also was recognized for his outstanding handling of horses, a skill he had developed as a boy on his father's farm. His class rank, however, was not high enough to earn him an appointment to the cavalry.

Grant's first assignment was as a second lieutenant in an infantry regiment stationed near St. Louis. In 1844 his unit was transferred to Louisiana, and from

there to Texas in 1845. He was among the troops under Gen. Zachary Taylor ordered by President James Polk to occupy the disputed area north of the Rio Grande. When Mexican forces attacked Taylor's forces, Polk persuaded Congress to declare war. Although Grant had deep reservations about the Mexican War's morality, he fought in most of its major battles including Palo Alto, Resaca de la Palma, Monterrey, Vera Cruz, Cerro Gordo, and Chapultepec. He was recognized for his bravery and promoted to first lieutenant after the capture of Mexico City in September 1847.

In July 1848, Grant returned to the United States and was stationed at several posts around the country. In 1852 he reluctantly left his wife and children behind in St. Louis when he was transferred to California. Grant hated being separated from his family and drank heavily to ease his loneliness. Finally, in 1854 after a drinking episode, his commanding officer forced him to resign his commission.

The next few years were humbling ones for Grant. He returned to his family in Missouri, where he failed as a farmer and as a real estate broker. In 1860 his younger brother offered him a job as a clerk in their father's hardware and leather store in Galena, Illinois. With no better options, Grant accepted the salary of $800 per year and moved his family to Galena.

Civil War

In April 1861 Grant had worked in the store only eleven months when President Abraham Lincoln called for volunteers to put down the insurrection in the South. Because of his military experience, Grant was appointed colonel of an Illinois regiment in June. He impressed his superiors and in August was promoted to brigadier general. Grant obtained permission from Gen. Henry Halleck in January 1862 to launch a military campaign into the South. On February 6, Grant's troops defeated Confederate forces at Fort Henry, Tennessee. Ten days later he won the first major Union victory of the war, when his forces captured Fort Donelson on the Cumberland River in Tennessee. The battle netted Grant fifteen thousand Confederate prisoners, a promotion to major general, and a national reputation. Grant's demand that the Confederates surrender unconditionally earned him the nickname "Unconditional Surrender" Grant.

Grant moved his troops deeper into Tennessee where on August 6 and 7, 1862, they repelled a furious Confederate surprise attack at Shiloh Church near Pittsburg Landing. Heavy Union casualties at Shiloh prompted some of Lincoln's advisers to urge the president to relieve Grant of his command. Lincoln dismissed their advice, saying, "I can't spare this man. He fights." In July 1862 Grant had gained command of all Union forces in the West when Halleck was promoted to general in chief and transferred to Washington, D.C. During the next twelve months, Grant slowly maneuvered to capture the imposing Confederate fortifications at Vicksburg, Mississippi.

On July 4, 1863, the Confederate commander at Vicksburg and twenty thousand troops surrendered to Grant. The victory gave the Union control of the Mississippi River and split the South in two.

In March 1864 President Lincoln promoted Grant to lieutenant general and appointed him general in chief of the army. Grant used his army's numerical superiority to fight a battle of attrition in Virginia against the main body of the Confederate army under Gen. Robert E. Lee. After a year of heavy fighting in which tens of thousands of troops on both sides were killed or wounded, Lee surrendered to Grant at Appomattox Court House in Virginia on April 9, 1865.

After the war Grant toured the South and issued a report advocating a lenient Reconstruction policy. In 1866 he was promoted to the newly established rank of general of the armies of the United States. The following year Grant, who throughout his military career had tried to remain aloof from politics, became involved in a political controversy. President Andrew Johnson had fired Secretary of War Edwin M. Stanton in violation of the Tenure of Office Act, which required the approval of Congress for dismissal of a cabinet member. In August Johnson appointed Grant to take Stanton's place, but the general resigned when Congress reinstated Stanton. Johnson felt betrayed by Grant, whom he hoped would stay in office to force a court battle over the Tenure of Office Act. The split with the Democratic president moved Grant closer to the Republicans. In 1868 they nominated him as their candidate for president. Grant, whose Civil War record had made him the most idolized person in America, received 52.7 percent of the popular vote and defeated Democrat Horatio Seymour 214–80 in the electoral college.

Presidency

When Grant took office, Reconstruction of the South was the primary issue confronting his administration. Grant supported the Reconstruction laws enacted during Andrew Johnson's administration and the ratification of the Fifteenth Amendment giving African Americans the right to vote. The amendment was ratified on March 30, 1870. Although Grant opposed blanketing the South with troops to guarantee the rights of blacks and to oversee other aspects of Reconstruction, he did respond to violations of the law with force. As Grant's term progressed, however, many northerners came to believe that federal attempts to keep southern whites from controlling state governments could not go on forever and were causing southern whites to use intimidation and terror to achieve their ends. Grant, therefore, was less willing and able to rally support for an activist Reconstruction policy.

Grant also pursued a conservative financial course. In March 1869, he signed the Public Credit Act, which pledged the government to redeem its debts in gold rather than paper money issued during the Civil War. Grant also advocated a gradual reduction of the public debt left over from the war.

In foreign affairs, Grant and Hamilton Fish, his capable secretary of state, successfully negotiated the Treaty of Washington with Great Britain. The treaty, signed in May 1871, provided for the settlement of U.S. claims against Great Britain for destruction caused during the Civil War by the *Alabama* and other ships built in Britain for the Confederacy. Grant was unsuccessful, however, in his attempts to annex Santo Domingo. His personal secretary, Orville Babcock, negotiated a treaty of annexation, but it was rejected by the Senate.

Grant retained his popularity during his first term and in 1872 won an overwhelming victory over Horace Greeley, editor of the *New York Tribune*. Greeley had been nominated by the Democratic Party and the Liberal Republican Party, a faction of former Republicans pledged to fight corruption and implement a conciliatory policy toward the South. Grant defeated Greeley, 286 electoral votes to 66. Greeley died less than a month after the election.

Like his former commander, Zachary Taylor, Grant had no political experience before becoming president. Although Grant himself was honest, many of his appointees and associates were not; and Grant's administration, particularly his second term, is remembered for its scandals. Before Grant's second inauguration, the Crédit Mobilier scandal was revealed. Grant's outgoing vice president, Schuyler Colfax, and incoming vice president, Henry Wilson, both were implicated in the bribery scheme, which involved skimming profits made from the construction of the transcontinental railroad. In 1875 a Treasury Department investigation revealed that several prominent Republicans, including Orville Babcock, were involved in the Whiskey Ring, a group that had used bribery to avoid taxes on liquor. In 1876 Grant's secretary of war, William Belknap, resigned just before being impeached by the House of Representatives for accepting bribes. In his last annual message to Congress in 1876, Grant acknowledged that he had made mistakes during his presidency but assured its members that "failures have been errors of judgement, not of intent."

Retirement

Upon leaving office Grant embarked with his wife on a round-the-world tour. He traveled in Europe, Africa, and Asia for two and a half years. He received a hero's welcome in foreign capitals and was entertained like royalty by many heads of state. The trip repaired Grant's popularity in the United States, and he was the preconvention favorite for the 1880 Republican presidential nomination. On the first ballot at the Republican convention in Chicago, Grant received 304 of the 378 votes necessary for nomination. Despite the support of Sen. Roscoe Conkling and his New York political machine, the anti-Grant factions had enough strength to prevent the former president's nomination on subsequent ballots. The convention remained deadlocked until the thirty-fifth ballot, when compromise candidate James A. Garfield was nominated.

After the convention, Grant retired from politics and moved to New York City. In May 1884 a brokerage firm in which he was a silent partner failed, and he was forced to sell much of his property to pay his debts. In August of that year he was diagnosed as having cancer. He began writing his memoirs in an attempt to give his family financial security before his death. Although suffering extreme pain, Grant lived longer than his doctors had predicted and finished his memoirs on July 19, 1885, four days before his death. The two-volume *Personal Memoirs of U.S. Grant* sold 300,000 copies and earned Grant's widow nearly a half million dollars in royalties.

Grant married Julia Boggs Dent on August 22, 1848, in St. Louis after he returned from the Mexican War. She was the sister of his West Point roommate. They had three sons and one daughter. Their eldest son rose to the rank of major general in the U.S. Army and served as minister to Austria-Hungary during Benjamin Harrison's administration.

Rutherford B. Hayes

Born: October 4, 1822; Delaware, Ohio
Party: Republican
Term: March 4, 1877–March 4, 1881
Vice President: William A. Wheeler
Died: January 17, 1893; Fremont, Ohio
Buried: Fremont

Rutherford Birchard Hayes was the youngest of the five children of Rutherford Hayes, a merchant who died two months before his son's birth. His father's estate was substantial, and his mother, Sophia, was able to send her children to private schools. Hayes enrolled at Kenyon College in Gambier, Ohio, when he was sixteen and graduated four years later,

in 1842, as the valedictorian of his class. He studied law for a year at a law firm in Columbus, Ohio, before enrolling in Harvard Law School. In 1845 he graduated and was admitted to the Ohio bar.

In 1846 Hayes practiced law in Lower Sandusky (now Fremont), Ohio, but moved in 1850 to Cincinnati, where he established a thriving law office whose clients included several fugitive slaves. Hayes joined the Republican Party when it was formed in the mid-1850s. In 1858 the city council of Cincinnati appointed Hayes to an unexpired term as city solicitor, his first public office. He won reelection to the post in 1859 but was defeated in 1861.

When the Civil War began Hayes was commissioned as a major and given command of a regiment of the Twenty-third Ohio Volunteers, which he had helped organize. He was promoted to lieutenant colonel in October 1861 and colonel in September 1862 after he led a charge at the Battle of South Mountain, Maryland, despite being shot in the arm. In August 1864 he was nominated for the U.S. House of Representatives. When Ohio Republican leaders suggested that he take a furlough to campaign, Hayes replied, "An officer fit for duty, who at this crisis would abandon his post to electioneer for a seat in Congress, ought to be scalped." Hayes's devotion to duty and his bravery in battle, where on several occasions he joined with his troops in hand-to-hand combat against the enemy, impressed voters more than any campaign speech he could have made. After being elected, however, he still refused to leave the army until the war was over. In October 1864, after the battle of Cedar Creek, Virginia, where he was wounded for the fourth time, he was promoted to brigadier general. On June 8, 1865, two months after Robert E. Lee had surrendered at Appomattox, Hayes finally resigned from the army to take his seat in Congress.

Hayes served two terms in the House before being elected governor of Ohio in 1867 in a close race. He was reelected two years later but declined to run for a third term. In 1872 he was defeated in his try for a House seat and turned down an offer from President Ulysses S. Grant of the post of assistant Treasury secretary. He retired to Fremont in 1873 and a year later inherited a large estate from his uncle, Sardis Birchard. Although Hayes did not seek the 1875 Republican nomination for a third term as governor of Ohio, he accepted his party's draft and was elected.

In March 1876 Hayes was put forward as a favorite son presidential candidate by the Ohio delegation at the Republican convention. James G. Blaine of Maine, the preconvention favorite, received the most votes on the first ballot but fell short of the number required for nomination. Blaine's opponents recognized they had to coalesce behind a single candidate and chose Hayes primarily because he was uncontroversial and free of scandal. Despite trailing four other candidates on the first ballot, Hayes was nominated on the seventh.

Hayes's chances for election were weakened by the scandals of the Grant administration, poor economic conditions, and the infrequency of his own campaign appearances. When the votes had been counted, Tilden had beaten Hayes by about 260,000 votes in the popular election and 203–166 in the electoral college. Republican leaders, however, were determined to retain the presidency and challenged the results in Florida, Louisiana, and South Carolina on the grounds that blacks had been intimidated from going to the polls. If the electoral votes of these three states were given to Hayes he would triumph 185–184. Southern Republican election officials from the three disputed states disqualified votes from Democratic precincts and declared Hayes the winner. Democratic leaders from these states accused the Republicans of corruption and sent rival sets of electoral votes to Congress, which was left to deal with the mess. With no way to determine who really deserved the electoral votes, members of Congress struck a deal. Democratic members agreed to the formation of an election commission that favored the Republicans in return for secret assurances that federal troops would be withdrawn from the South. The commission voted 8–7 for Hayes, who was officially declared president on March 4, 1877, just two days before his inauguration.

When Hayes became president he honored the agreement made with the Democrats to withdraw federal troops from the South. This move ended the Reconstruction era and enabled white Democrats to reestablish their political control over the southern states.

Hayes was a well-intentioned president, but the stigma of the deal that had made him president, his quarrels with conservatives in his party, and Democratic control of the House from 1877 to 1879 and the Senate from 1879 to 1881 limited his ability to push legislation through Congress. When Congress tried to stimulate the economy by coining overvalued silver coins, Hayes, an advocate of sound money, vetoed the inflationary measure. Congress, however, passed the bill over Hayes's veto. The president's calls for civil service reform also had little effect, as Congress refused to act on his proposals. In 1877, however, Hayes demonstrated his ability to take decisive action when he dispatched federal troops to stop riots that had broken out in several cities as a result of a nationwide railroad strike.

When his term expired, Hayes retired to Fremont, Ohio, where he managed several farms he had bought. He also promoted humanitarian causes, including prison reform and education opportunities for southern black youth. While returning to Fremont from a business trip, Hayes had a heart attack aboard a train on January 14, 1893. He died three days later.

Hayes married Lucy Ware Webb December 30, 1852, in Cincinnati, Ohio. They had seven sons and one daughter; three of their sons died in infancy. Lucy Hayes was deeply religious and lived according to strict moral principles. Her refusal to allow alcoholic beverages to be served at White House functions made her a symbol of the Women's Christian Temperance Union and earned her the nickname "Lemonade Lucy." She was the first college-educated first lady, having graduated from Wesleyan Female College in Cincinnati.

James A. Garfield

Born: November 19, 1831; Orange, Ohio
Party: Republican
Term: March 4, 1881–September 19, 1881
Vice President: Chester A. Arthur
Died: September 19, 1881; Elberon, New Jersey
Buried: Cleveland, Ohio

James Abram Garfield was born in a log cabin on an Ohio farm. When he was one year old, his father, Abram, died, leaving his mother, Eliza, to raise James and his three older siblings. After she sold fifty acres of the farm to pay family debts, the Garfields survived by farming just thirty acres. James worked on the farm during the summer months and attended elementary schools in the winter. When he was seventeen he spent a year driving horse and mule teams that pulled barges on the Ohio and Erie Canal.

In 1849 Garfield entered Geauga Seminary in Chester, Ohio, a local denominational secondary school. He paid for his tuition by working as a carpenter. Two years later he enrolled in the Western Reserve Eclectic Institute (later Hiram College). After a semester the school hired him as an English teacher. He taught and studied there until September 1854, when he had saved enough money to enroll at Williams College in Williamstown, Massachusetts. He graduated with honors in 1856 and returned to Hiram, Ohio, where he became president of Western Reserve Eclectic Institute with its five-member faculty. While presiding over the school, Garfield studied law and became known as an eloquent public speaker and preacher. He was elected to the Ohio Senate as a Republican in 1859 and was admitted to the bar in 1860.

When the Civil War began in 1861 Garfield received a commission as a lieutenant colonel and command of a regiment of Ohio volunteers. After being promoted to colonel, he led a brigade to a dramatic victory over a superior number of Confederate troops at the battle of Middle Creek, Kentucky, on January 10, 1862. Garfield's success brought him a promotion to brigadier general. He participated in the Battle of Shiloh on April 7, 1862, before falling ill and returning to Ohio in July.

In September 1862, Garfield was elected to the U.S. House of Representatives, but he declined to retire from military service. After the Battle of Chickamauga in September 1863, he was promoted to major general for his bravery, although he had endorsed the battle plan of Gen. William S. Rosecrans that led to the Union defeat.

Garfield resigned his commission in December to take his seat in the House. There his oratory and leadership on important committees made him a prominent Republican member of Congress. Garfield dramatically demonstrated his rhetorical skills on April 15, 1865, the day after President Lincoln was assassinated. When a New York mob threatened to avenge Lincoln's death by destroying the headquarters of the *New York World,* a newspaper that had been a severe critic of Lincoln, Garfield quieted the crowd with a short speech given from the balcony of the New York Stock Exchange. It concluded: "Fellow citizens, God reigns and the government of Washington still lives."

Garfield served in the House until 1880. During this time he supported the harsh Reconstruction policies of the radical wing of his party. In 1877 he served on the election commission formed to decide the disputed outcome of the Hayes-Tilden presidential election of 1876. In fact he helped craft the backroom political deal that made Hayes president. While the Democrats controlled the House during the Hayes presidency, Garfield held the post of Republican minority leader.

At the 1880 Republican National Convention the party was sharply divided over whom to nominate for president. President Hayes had declined to run for reelection and could not have won the nomination had he tried. The radical Stalwart faction of the Republican Party, headed by New York senator Roscoe Conkling, a powerful political boss, supported former president Ulysses S. Grant, while the less radical Half-breed faction backed Sen. James G. Blaine (R-Maine). Garfield, who had been elected to the Senate earlier in the year but had not yet taken his seat, had promoted the compromise candidacy of John Sherman of Ohio. The convention, however, nominated Garfield himself on the thirty-sixth ballot. In a gesture to the Stalwarts the convention nominated Chester A. Arthur, a Conkling associate, for vice president.

Garfield faced Democrat Winfield Scott Hancock of Pennsylvania, a hero of the battle of Gettysburg, in the general election. During the campaign the Democrats tried to capitalize on Garfield's role in the Crédit Mobilier bribery scandal that occurred during the Grant administration. Garfield had received a $329 dividend check in 1868 from the Crédit Mobilier holding company but had not actually bought stock in it. The scandal had ruined several other politicians, including Grant's first vice president, Schuyler Colfax, but Garfield's relatively minor role had not crippled his career. Despite the corruption charges and his unpopularity in the South, where he lost every state, Garfield won in the electoral college, 214–155. In the popular vote, however, Garfield received just ten thousand more votes than Hancock.

As president, Garfield's broad-based appointments and support for anticorruption measures angered Stalwarts. On March 23 he appointed Conkling's political rival, William Robertson, to the coveted post of collector of the port of New York. Although Garfield had appointed many Conkling supporters to patronage positions, the powerful senator was determined to block Robertson's confirmation. When Robertson was about to be confirmed, Conkling resigned his seat in protest. The move backfired, however, when the New York State legislature refused to reelect Conkling to the Senate as he had expected.

On July 2, 1881, as Garfield was in the Baltimore and Potomac railroad station in Washington, D.C., on his way to deliver the commencement address at his alma mater, Williams College, he was shot by Charles J. Guiteau. Guiteau shot the president once in the back and fired another bullet that grazed his arm. Garfield was taken to the White House, where he remained for two months while doctors unsuccessfully probed for the bullet that was lodged near his spine. On September 6 the president asked to be moved to Elberon, New Jersey, in the hope that the sea air would help him recover. He died in Elberon on September 19. Ironically, Garfield probably would have survived if his doctors had left the bullet undisturbed rather than searching for it with unsterile instruments, which spread infection.

Guiteau had been captured at the time of the assault and was put on trial in Washington, D.C., two months after the president's death. At the time of the attack the assassin had shouted, "I am a Stalwart; now Arthur is president!" Guiteau, however, was not associated with Roscoe Conkling and the Stalwarts. The assassin believed his distribution of pro-Republican Party literature during the 1880 presidential campaign entitled him to a diplomatic appointment. Repeated rejections by the White House angered him, and he claimed to have received a divine vision instructing him to kill the president. The assassin's

lawyers argued that their client was insane and should be acquitted, but the jury found him guilty and sentenced him to death. Guiteau was hanged in Washington, D.C., on June 30, 1882.

Garfield married Lucretia Rudolph of Hiram, Ohio, on November 11, 1858. They had five sons and two daughters; two of the children died in infancy. One of their sons, James Rudolph Garfield, served as secretary of the interior under President Theodore Roosevelt.

Chester A. Arthur

Born: October 5, 1830; Fairfield, Vermont
Party: Republican
Term: September 20, 1881–March 4, 1885
Vice President: None
Died: November 18, 1886; New York City
Buried: Albany, New York

Chester Alan Arthur was one of the nine children of Malvina and William Arthur, a Baptist minister who had emigrated from Northern Ireland. Arthur claimed to have been born in Fairfield, Vermont, but some political enemies claimed that he actually had been born in Canada, where his father had lived at one time. This charge, if true, would have disqualified him for the presidency, but it was never substantiated.

In 1845 at the age of fifteen Arthur enrolled as a sophomore at Union College in Schenectady, New York, where he studied Greek and Latin. He graduated three years later and was one of six in his class to be elected to Phi Beta Kappa, a national honor society. He settled in North Pownal, Vermont, where he taught school at the North Pownal Academy, becoming principal in 1849. While teaching, Arthur studied law, and in 1853 he joined the New York City law firm of Parker and Culver as a clerk. The following year he passed the bar and became a

member of the firm. As a lawyer, he often defended fugitive slaves and free blacks who suffered discrimination.

Arthur attended the first New York Republican National Convention in 1856 and became an active supporter of Republican candidates. In 1860 New York Republican governor Edward D. Morgan rewarded Arthur's political work by appointing him state engineer in chief with the military rank of brigadier general. During the Civil War Arthur served as assistant quartermaster general, inspector general, and finally quartermaster general of the troops of New York. He excelled in these administrative posts, spending state funds efficiently and keeping scrupulous books. He resigned his commission at the beginning of 1863 and returned to his law practice when Democrat Horatio Seymour became governor. He continued his rise in the New York Republican Party, however, and by the time Ulysses S. Grant was elected president in 1868, he was Sen. Roscoe Conkling's principal lieutenant in the state's Republican machine.

In 1871, with Conkling's support, President Grant appointed Arthur to one of the most lucrative and coveted offices in government—collector of the port of New York. In this post Arthur oversaw the activities of almost one thousand officials, was in charge of collecting about two-thirds of the country's tariff revenue, and earned an average income of $40,000 per year. But despite Arthur's administrative abilities and basic honesty, President Hayes fired him from the customhouse in 1878 as part of his fight against the spoils system.

The Republican National Convention of 1880 pitted New York boss senator Roscoe Conkling and his radical party faction known as the Stalwarts against James G. Blaine and the slightly more moderate Half-breed faction. Conkling supported former president Ulysses S. Grant for the nomination, but after thirty-six ballots the convention turned to a dark-horse candidate, James A. Garfield of Ohio. In an effort to appease the Stalwarts and unify the party, Republican leaders offered the vice presidency to Levi P. Morton, one of Conkling's associates. Conkling, however, was not in a mood to be appeased, and he convinced Morton to reject the offer. When the same offer was made to Arthur, who had never held elective office, he gratefully accepted the nomination despite the objections of Conkling. Garfield and Arthur defeated the Democratic ticket of Winfield Scott Hancock and William H. English by less than ten thousand votes but won in the electoral college, 214–155.

Garfield served only 199 days of his presidential term, however. On July 2, 1881, he was shot by an assassin in Washington, D.C. The gunman, Charles J. Guiteau, declared after the attack, "I am a Stalwart; now Arthur is President!" Garfield initially survived his wounds but died on September 19, after months of failed attempts by his doctors to remove the bullet.

Although Arthur had no connection to Guiteau, he was sensitive to charges that he and the Stalwarts may have been involved in Garfield's death. Therefore, once Arthur had assumed the presidency, he severed his ties to Conkling and the New York political machine. The new president demonstrated his independence by backing the investigations of post office scandals in which several Stalwarts were implicated.

Arthur was not, however, ready to embrace civil service reform, which had been the cause of James Garfield. He advocated instead a continuation of the partisan system of dispensing patronage. Nevertheless, on January 16, 1883, Arthur signed the Pendleton Civil Service Reform Act. The act set up a commission to develop and administer examinations for many federal positions previously filled through patronage.

In economic policy Arthur sought to reduce the government's continuing budget surplus that took money out of the economy. He proposed reducing tariffs, building up the navy, and reducing the federal debt with the surplus. Arthur succeeded in making moderate improvements to the navy and reducing the national debt, but Congress rejected his proposals to cut tariffs.

Upon leaving office Arthur returned to New York City to practice law. He soon accepted the presidency of the New York Arcade Railway Company, which was trying to construct a subway in New York City.

In February 1886 Arthur retired after a medical examination revealed that he had Bright's disease, a life-threatening kidney ailment. He died later that year in New York City.

Arthur married Ellen Lewis Herndon on October 25, 1859. They had two sons and one daughter, but their first son died in infancy. Ellen Arthur died on January 12, 1880, five months before her husband was nominated for the vice presidency. Arthur's sister, Mary Arthur McElroy, acted as White House hostess.

Grover Cleveland

Born: March 18, 1837; Caldwell, New Jersey
Party: Democratic
Terms: March 4, 1885–March 4, 1889; March 4, 1893–March 4, 1897
Vice Presidents: Thomas A. Hendricks; Adlai E. Stevenson
Died: June 24, 1908; Princeton, New Jersey
Buried: Princeton

Grover Cleveland was the fifth of the nine children born to Ann and Richard F. Cleveland, a Presbyterian minister. Grover was originally named Stephen Grover, but he dropped his first name early in his life. In 1853, the year his father died, Grover moved to New York City, where he got a job at a school for the blind. After a year, however, he returned to his family in Holland Patent, New York.

In the spring of 1855 Cleveland traveled west to seek work in Cleveland, Ohio. On the way he stopped to visit relatives in Buffalo, New York, where he decided to stay when his uncle, Lewis F. Allen, offered him a job as a farmhand. A few months later Cleveland went to work as an apprentice clerk in a local law firm. In 1859 he was admitted to the bar and promoted to chief clerk in his firm.

Cleveland had been drafted to fight in the Civil War, but in accordance with the draft laws he had hired a substitute for $300 so he could continue to help support his mother and younger siblings. In 1863 Cleveland accepted an appointment as assistant district attorney of Erie County, New York. Two years later he was defeated in an election for district attorney. With the exception of a two-year term as sheriff of Buffalo from 1871 to 1873, he practiced law for the next sixteen years.

In 1881 he was elected mayor of Buffalo and immediately took action to reform the city administration. His well-deserved reputation as an uncompromising reformer earned him the Democratic nomination for governor of New York in 1882. He easily won the election and assumed office on January 3, 1883. As governor, Cleveland combated corruption and the spoils system with his veto power. He formed an alliance with Theodore Roosevelt, a Republican member of the New York State Assembly, to enact legislation reforming New York City's government.

The governor's successes and reform principles made him an attractive presidential candidate in 1884. The Republicans nominated James G. Blaine, a Republican senator from Maine, who had been linked to several scandals. Cleveland's supporters argued that if the Democratic Party nominated the reform governor, the reform-minded Republicans, known as Mugwumps might desert their party in sufficient numbers to elect a Democrat to the presidency for the first time since the Civil War. The Democratic delegates at the national convention in

Chicago agreed with this strategy, and Cleveland was nominated on the second ballot.

Cleveland's election hopes were damaged, however, when a newspaper report disclosed that he had fathered an illegitimate child, whom he continued to support. Cleveland admitted his paternity and instructed his campaign workers to "tell the truth." Cleveland also was attacked for not serving in the Civil War, although Blaine had avoided service as well. Blaine lost many Catholic votes when he failed to repudiate a supporter's accusation less than a week before the election that the Democrats represented "rum, Romanism, and rebellion." In the end Cleveland received just sixty thousand more votes than Blaine and defeated him 219–182 in the electoral college.

During his first term Cleveland attempted to bring to the presidency the same reformist principles that he had followed as governor of New York. For example, he implemented the Pendleton Civil Service Act, signed into law by Chester A. Arthur, which shifted thousands of government jobs from patronage to a merit system of hiring. He also vetoed numerous private pension bills for individual Civil War veterans. Cleveland was unsuccessful, however, in lowering the tariff, which he considered to be unfair to farmers and workers and unnecessary given the large federal budget surplus.

In 1888 Cleveland ran for reelection against Indiana Republican Benjamin Harrison. Despite defeating Harrison by 100,000 votes, Cleveland lost to Harrison in the electoral college 233–168. Had Cleveland won his home state's thirty-six electoral votes as he did in 1884, he would have won the election.

After leaving office Cleveland moved to New York City, where he practiced law. Four years later he was again nominated for president by his party. The 1892 election featured a rematch between Cleveland and President Benjamin Harrison. Cleveland easily defeated Harrison in the electoral college by 277–145 votes but received only 46.3 percent of the popular vote because the third-party candidacy of James Baird Weaver of the People's Party drew more than one million votes.

Soon after Cleveland took office for the second time the Panic of 1893 sparked a deep economic depression. More than five hundred banks failed, and unemployment rose sharply as businesses went bankrupt. Cleveland believed the depression was caused by inflation and an erosion of business confidence. Thus, with the support of many congressional Republicans, he convinced Congress in 1893 to repeal the mildly inflationary Sherman Silver Purchase Act. He also authorized the purchase of several million ounces of gold from private holders to replenish the government's shrinking gold reserves. Cleveland's policies, however, did not ease the depression.

In 1894 the economic situation worsened when a local strike at the Pullman Palace Car Company near Chicago led to a debilitating railroad strike throughout the Midwest. When violence erupted in Chicago, Cleveland sent federal troops there to break the strike despite the protests of Illinois governor John P. Altgeld. Cleveland's action earned him support from the business community but the enmity of labor organizations. Although the depression had greeted Cleveland as he entered office, he received much of the blame for the nation's economic troubles. After Republicans gained congressional seats in the 1894 midterm elections, Cleveland had difficulty exerting much control over Congress or even his party. The 1896 Democratic convention nominated William Jennings Bryan for president, and many Democratic candidates distanced themselves from Cleveland.

In foreign affairs Cleveland withdrew in March 1893 a treaty negotiated in the closing months of the Harrison administration that would have annexed Hawaii. He considered the treaty unfair

and blocked any further attempt to annex the islands. He also resisted the temptation to yield to public pressure and go to war with Spain over their suppression of a rebellion in Cuba that began in 1895.

Upon leaving office for the second time Cleveland settled in Princeton, New Jersey. He devoted his time to fishing, delivering lectures, and writing books and articles. In 1901 he was appointed to the board of trustees of Princeton University, and in 1904 he became the president of that board while future president Woodrow Wilson served as president of the university. In 1907 Cleveland was elected president of the Association of Presidents of Life Insurance Companies. During his last years Cleveland's heart and kidneys weakened. He died of a heart attack in Princeton, New Jersey, in 1908.

Cleveland married Frances Folsom, the twenty-one-year-old daughter of his former law partner, on June 2, 1886, in a White House ceremony. The couple had three daughters and two sons. Two of the children were born during Cleveland's second term.

Benjamin Harrison

Born: August 20, 1833; North Bend, Ohio
Party: Republican
Term: March 4, 1889–March 4, 1893
Vice President: Levi P. Morton
Died: March 13, 1901; Indianapolis, Indiana
Buried: Indianapolis

Benjamin Harrison was born at his grandfather's home at North Bend, Ohio, the second of the ten children of John and Elizabeth Harrison. Four of the ten children died in infancy. The Harrison family also included John's two surviving daughters from a previous marriage. When Benjamin was seven, his grandfather, William Henry Harrison, became the ninth president of the United States but died after one month in office. Benjamin's great-grandfather, Benjamin Harrison, had been governor of Virginia and a signer of the Declaration of Independence.

After receiving a primary education at a country school and from tutors, Benjamin attended Farmer's College in Cincinnati from 1847 to 1850. He then transferred to Miami University in Oxford, Ohio. He graduated with honors in 1852 and began studying law at a firm in Cincinnati. In 1854 he moved to Indianapolis and established his own practice. A year later he formed a law partnership with William Wallace, a more established Indianapolis lawyer. Within a few years their firm had become one of the most respected in the city.

Soon after moving to Indianapolis Harrison became active in the Republican Party. In 1857 he was elected Indianapolis city attorney. The following year he served as secretary of the Indiana Republican central committee, and in 1860 he was elected reporter of the Indiana Supreme Court.

In 1862, during the Civil War, Harrison was commissioned as a colonel and given command of the Seventieth Indiana Volunteers, which he had helped recruit. His regiment guarded railroads in Kentucky and participated in the Atlanta campaign. He gained a reputation as a cold disciplinarian and was unpopular with many of his troops. His unit fought well, however, and he was promoted to brigadier general in 1865.

When the war ended Harrison returned to Indianapolis, where his legal skill, war record, and speeches on behalf of Republican causes made him one of the most famous men in Indiana. In 1876 Harrison received the Republican nomination for governor but lost by five thousand votes to Democrat James D. Williams. Harrison had not sought the nomination and was happy to return to his law practice. He presided over the Indiana Republican convention in 1878 and was chairman of his state's delegation to the Republican National Convention in 1880.

In 1881 Harrison was elected to the U.S. Senate, where he chaired the committee on territories. In this capacity he defended the interests of homesteaders and Native Americans against the railroads. Harrison also was a strong advocate of Civil War veterans and worked to protect and expand their pensions. Harrison ran for reelection in 1886, but the Democrats had gained control of the Indiana legislature two years before and voted him out of office.

At the 1888 Republican National Convention in Chicago Harrison was nominated on the eighth ballot to run for president against incumbent Grover Cleveland. The primary issue of the campaign was the tariff, which Harrison promised to raise if elected. Harrison lost the popular vote but won in the electoral college 233–168 with the help of a narrow victory in New York that gave him that state's thirty-six electoral votes.

Harrison enjoyed the luxury of having both houses of Congress controlled by his party. As a result, he was able to implement much of his economic program. In July 1890 he signed the Sherman Antitrust Act and the Sherman Silver Purchase Act. The former outlawed trusts and business combines that restrained trade, while the latter required the Treasury to purchase large quantities of silver with notes that could be redeemed in gold. The silver purchase was inflationary and strained the nation's gold reserves, but Harrison and the Republicans resisted the more damaging proposal of free coinage of silver desired by many indebted farmers from the South and West. Later, in 1890, Harrison signed the McKinley Tariff Act, which was sponsored by House member and future president William McKinley. The act sharply raised tariffs as Harrison had promised, providing protection to some U.S. industries but raising prices for many consumer goods. Harrison constructed several compromises that led to passage of the act.

In foreign policy the Harrison administration enjoyed several successes. Harrison's secretary of state, James G. Blaine, presided over the InterAmerican Conference in Washington, D.C., in 1889 and 1890, out of which came the Pan American Union. Blaine also secured an agreement in 1889 with Britain and Germany to preserve the independence of the Samoa Islands under a tripartite protectorate. In 1892 Harrison demanded and received an apology and reparations from Chile for an attack by its citizens on U.S. sailors who were on shore leave in Valparaiso, Chile. He failed, however, in his attempt to annex Hawaii late in his term. An 1893 coup, in which Americans participated, had led to the overthrow of the Hawaiian queen. Thus, the U.S. minister in Hawaii hastily concluded a treaty of ratification with the new provisional government, but Democrats in the Senate blocked the treaty until Harrison's term expired. Incoming president Grover Cleveland withdrew the treaty.

At the end of his term Harrison attended the inauguration of Grover Cleveland, who four years

before had accompanied Harrison to the Capitol as the outgoing president. Harrison then returned to Indianapolis, where he resumed his lucrative law practice. In the spring of 1894 he delivered a series of law lectures at Stanford University in Palo Alto, California. Supporters encouraged him to seek the Republican presidential nomination in 1896, but he refused to allow his name to be placed in nomination. From 1897 to 1899 he represented Venezuela in a boundary dispute with Great Britain that was to be decided by an international arbitration tribunal. After he traveled to Paris in 1899 to present his case, the tribunal upheld most of Venezuela's claims. Harrison then toured Europe with his second wife. He died in Indianapolis in 1901 from pneumonia.

On October 20, 1853, Harrison married Caroline Lavinia Scott, whom he had met while attending Miami University. The couple had two children, Russell and Mary. Mrs. Harrison died in the White House on October 25, 1892. Three years after he left office on April 6, 1896, Harrison married thirty-seven-year-old Mary Scott Lord Dimmick, a niece of his first wife. They had one daughter, Elizabeth, who was born when Harrison was sixty-three.

William McKinley

Born: January 29, 1843; Niles, Ohio
Party: Republican
Term: March 4, 1897–September 14, 1901
Vice Presidents: Garret A. Hobart; Theodore
  Roosevelt
Died: September 14, 1901; Buffalo, New York
Buried: Canton, Ohio

William McKinley was the seventh of the nine children born to Nancy and William McKinley, an iron founder. The McKinleys moved from Niles, Ohio, to Poland, Ohio, when William was nine. There he attended Union Seminary, a local private school. He enrolled in Allegheny College in Meadville, Pennsylvania, in 1859 but dropped out the following year because of illness and financial problems. William returned to Poland, where he taught in a country school and worked in the post office.

When the Civil War began in 1861, McKinley enlisted as a private in the Twenty-third Ohio Volunteers—the same unit in which Rutherford B. Hayes began his service as a major. McKinley steadily worked his way up through the ranks, becoming an officer in September 1862 after the battle of Antietam in Maryland. When the war ended he was a twenty-two-year-old major who had been decorated for bravery.

McKinley chose to leave the army, however, to study law. He worked for two years in the law office of a Youngstown, Ohio, attorney and then polished his legal skills at Albany Law School in New York for a term. He was admitted to the bar in 1867 and opened a law practice in Canton, Ohio. He ran for prosecuting attorney of Stark County as a Republican in 1869 and won despite the county's traditional Democratic voting record. Two years later, however, he was narrowly defeated for reelection.

From 1871 to 1876, McKinley practiced law in Canton and campaigned for Republican candidates. In 1876, when his old commanding officer, Rutherford B. Hayes, was elected president, McKinley won a seat in the U.S. House of Representatives. He served seven consecutive terms in the House until 1891. As a member of Congress, McKinley supported civil service reform, voting rights for African Americans, and government coinage of silver. He was best known, however, for his staunch support of high tariffs as a means of protecting U.S. industries. While serving as the chairman of the House Ways and Means Committee he sponsored the McKinley Tariff Act of 1890, which raised tariff rates to new highs. The tariff brought higher prices for con-

William McKinley

sumers and contributed to voter disaffection for the Republican Party. McKinley was voted out of office along with many other Republican members of Congress in 1890.

McKinley returned to Ohio, where he ran for governor successfully. He served two two-year terms, during which he was increasingly promoted as a presidential candidate. In 1892 he served as the chairman of the Republican National Convention in Chicago. President Benjamin Harrison was nominated on the first ballot, but McKinley came in second in the balloting.

McKinley's presidential nomination in 1896 did not result from a spontaneous movement on the floor of the Republican convention. With McKinley's approval, Ohio party boss Mark Hanna and other leading Republicans actively promoted McKinley's candidacy in the months leading up to the convention. His nomination was almost ensured when the St. Louis convention convened in June

1896, and the delegates nominated him on the first ballot.

Although McKinley had favored the coinage of silver, he renounced his former position and supported the gold standard in order to win conservative Democrats away from the Democratic nominee, William Jennings Bryan, who was an ardent silver advocate. McKinley waged his campaign from his front porch, speaking to crowds that came to Canton by railroad. In contrast, Bryan traveled more than eighteen thousand miles and delivered hundreds of speeches during his campaign. The Republican nominee received the strong support of business and financial leaders who feared that a Bryan presidency would bring inflation. They helped raise a formidable war chest for McKinley, who won in the electoral college 271–176.

McKinley was severely criticized by Democrats and some Republicans for appointing aging Ohio senator John Sherman as his secretary of state. The appointment was seen as a political payoff to Mark Hanna, who promptly was elected to the vacant Senate seat by the Ohio state legislature.

McKinley's top priority upon entering office was the economy, which had been mired in a depression during much of Cleveland's second term. Congress quickly passed the Dingley Tariff Act of 1897 in response to McKinley's requests. Thereafter, the economy began to grow. Although the tariff bill may not have been the cause of the recovery, McKinley took credit for the improvement of economic conditions.

McKinley's first term, however, was dominated by the Spanish-American War and its results. Americans were disturbed by numerous press accounts of atrocities perpetrated by Spanish colonialists upon Cuban natives. McKinley responded to public pressure for war by sending a war message to Congress on April 11, 1898. Congress declared war two weeks later on April 25. Although the United States was not prepared for the war, victory came easily. Spanish control of Cuba was broken, and the U.S. Asiatic squadron under Commodore George Dewey destroyed the Spanish Pacific fleet in the Battle of Manila Bay. The fighting was over by August. On December 10, 1898, Spain signed a treaty freeing Cuba and ceding the Philippines, Puerto Rico, and Guam to the United States. McKinley agonized over how to deal with the Philippines but decided to take possession of them rather than grant them their independence. He resolved to "uplift and civilize and Christianize" the Filipinos. Insurgents in the Philippines, however, were determined to gain their independence. In 1899 they launched a guerrilla war against the U.S. occupying force, which ended in 1902 with the defeat of the insurgents. The bloody conflict cost more American lives and money than the Spanish-American War.

McKinley took several important steps in other parts of Asia and the Pacific. He oversaw the annexation of Hawaii in 1898 and the partition of the Samoan Islands with Germany in 1899. Secretary of State John Hay negotiated an agreement with European nations in 1900 that established an "Open Door" policy toward China, under which all nations doing business with China would enjoy equal trading rights.

McKinley was renominated without opposition in 1900. His close friend and first-term vice president, Garret Hobart, had died in 1899, however, and the Republican National Convention chose Theodore Roosevelt as his running mate. The Democrats again ran William Jennings Bryan, but the nation's economic recovery since McKinley took office gave the Republicans a strong election issue. McKinley improved upon the popular and electoral vote margins of victory he had enjoyed in 1896, defeating Bryan in the electoral college 292–155.

After Roosevelt's nomination, Mark Hanna, who regarded the vice-presidential candidate as an unpredictable reformer, wrote McKinley saying, "Your duty to the country is to live for four years from next March." McKinley would be unable to carry out this duty. Six months after his inauguration, he traveled to Buffalo, New York, to deliver an address at the Pan-American Exposition, a fair celebrating friendship in the Western Hemisphere. The following day the president greeted thousands of people who waited in line to shake his hand at a public reception. Leon Czolgosz, an anarchist disturbed by social injustice, waited in line until it was his turn to shake McKinley's hand. Czolgosz then fired two shots with a concealed .32-caliber revolver that struck McKinley in the chest and stomach.

McKinley was taken first to the emergency medical center at the exposition and then to Milburn House, his Buffalo lodgings. Doctors initially thought the president would recover. Vice President Roosevelt, who had cut his vacation short and rushed to Buffalo upon hearing that the president had been shot, even resumed his holiday when he was informed of the doctors' prognosis. After a week, however, gangrene set in, and McKinley's condition deteriorated. He died early in the morning on September 14.

McKinley married Ida Saxton, the daughter of a banker, on January 25, 1871, in Canton, Ohio. The couple had two daughters, but one died as an infant and the other at the age of four. Ida was afflicted with epilepsy and phlebitis for most of her adult life. Despite occasional seizures and her inability to walk without a cane, she presided over most White House social functions.

Theodore Roosevelt

Born: October 27, 1858; New York City
Party: Republican
Term: September 14, 1901–March 4, 1909
Vice President: Charles W. Fairbanks
Died: January 6, 1919; Oyster Bay, New York
Buried: Oyster Bay

Theodore Roosevelt was the second of the four children and the oldest son of Theodore and Martha Roosevelt. His father was a wealthy New York City banker and merchant. Young Theodore was educated by tutors and enjoyed several trips abroad with the family. Throughout his boyhood, he suffered from asthma and other illnesses. When he was thirteen he began a program of vigorous physical exercise that turned him into a healthy, robust young man. Throughout the rest of his life, he would preach the virtues of a strenuous life.

Roosevelt entered Harvard in 1876. An excellent student, he graduated twenty-first in his class in 1880 and was elected to the Phi Beta Kappa honor society. He then enrolled in Columbia Law School but dropped out after a year of study without taking a degree or seeking admission to the bar.

Roosevelt entered politics in 1881 when he was elected to the New York state legislature at the age of twenty-three. He led a group of reform Republicans who fought corruption in the state government. Roosevelt was reelected in 1882 and 1883 but declined to seek reelection after his wife, Alice, and his mother died within hours of each other on February 14, 1884.

From 1884 to 1886, Roosevelt sought refuge from his grief in the Dakota Territory, where he managed a cattle ranch and served for a period as deputy sheriff. He returned to New York City in 1886 and ran unsuccessfully for mayor. After marrying Edith Kermit Carow, he settled into his home, Sagamore Hill, in Oyster Bay, Long Island. There he wrote books on American history and life in the West. His works include *Hunting Trip of a Ranchman, Life of Thomas Hart Benton, Gouverneur Morris, The Winning of the West,* and *Ranch Life and the Hunting Trail.* During his lifetime, Roosevelt wrote more than forty books.

In 1889 Roosevelt returned to public service when President Benjamin Harrison appointed him U.S. civil service commissioner. He was reappointed in 1893 by Democrat Grover Cleveland and served until 1895. As commissioner, Roosevelt fought against the spoils system, which he considered a source of corruption. He revised civil service exams, doubled the number of government positions subject to examination, and increased government employment opportunities for women.

From 1895 to 1897 Roosevelt served as president of the Police Commission of New York City. He moved to Washington, D.C., in 1897 when President William McKinley appointed him assistant secretary of the navy. In this post he fought to increase the size of the U.S. Navy and advocated war with Spain over that country's suppression of an independence movement in Cuba. On February 25, 1898, with Navy Secretary John Long absent from the capital, Roosevelt ordered the Pacific fleet to go to Hong Kong and prepare to destroy the Spanish fleet in the event of a declaration of war. In issuing the order, Roosevelt overstepped the bounds of his authority,

but when Commodore George Dewey defeated the Spanish fleet in the Battle of Manila Bay on May 1, 1898, Roosevelt's action was vindicated.

Soon after the United States declared war against Spain, Roosevelt resigned from the Navy Department so he could fight in Cuba. He secured the rank of lieutenant colonel and organized a regiment of cavalry that came to be known as the Rough Riders. Although the importance of the Rough Riders to the American victory over the Spanish in Cuba became exaggerated, Roosevelt demonstrated his courage in leading his regiment in the famous charge up one of the San Juan Hills overlooking Santiago. Despite suffering heavy casualties, the Rough Riders captured the hill.

Roosevelt's exploits in Cuba made him a celebrity in the United States. In November 1898 he received the Republican nomination for governor of New York and was narrowly elected. As governor his political independence and refusal to promote the interests of big business disturbed the power brokers of his party, particularly New York Republican boss Thomas Platt.

In 1900 Platt hoped to get rid of Roosevelt by promoting him as a candidate for vice president. Although Roosevelt declared he did not want the job, he was the popular choice at the Philadelphia Republican National Convention, and he accepted the nomination when it was offered to him. Party leaders had mixed feelings about Roosevelt. They recognized that his popularity could win votes for the ticket, but they feared what might happen if McKinley died. Mark Hanna, the Republican national chairman who had overseen McKinley's career, warned his colleagues, "Don't any of you realize that there's only one life between this madman and the White House?"

After the inauguration, Roosevelt presided over a five-day session of the Senate held to confirm presidential appointees. When the session was completed, Congress adjourned until December. Roosevelt, with no other vice-presidential duties to execute, returned to his home on Long Island. On September 6, 1901, Roosevelt was hunting and fishing in Vermont when he learned that President McKinley had been shot. He rushed to Buffalo, where doctors said McKinley would recover from his wounds. Roosevelt wanted to demonstrate to the public that the president was in no danger of death, so he resumed his vacation on September 10. Three days later, however, Roosevelt was informed that McKinley's condition had deteriorated. The vice president arrived in Buffalo on September 14, the day McKinley died. Later in the day he took the oath of office in Buffalo from U.S. District Court Judge John Hazel. At the age of forty-two, Roosevelt became the youngest person ever to serve as president.

Presidency

After McKinley's death, Roosevelt declared, "It shall be my aim to continue absolutely unbroken the policy of President McKinley for the peace, the prosperity, and the honor of our beloved country." Despite retaining McKinley's cabinet, Roosevelt promoted his own policies, which included measures to curb abuses by big business. Soon after taking office he had directed Attorney General Philander Knox to prepare an antitrust suit against Northern Securities Company, a giant railroad trust. The suit was successful in 1904 when the Supreme Court ruled that the company should be dissolved. Although the Roosevelt administration would initiate fewer antitrust suits than the Taft administration, Roosevelt became known as the trustbusting president. In 1902 when a coal strike in Pennsylvania caused shortages and rising coal prices, Roosevelt threatened to take over the mines unless the mine owners submitted to arbitration. The mine owners backed down, and Roosevelt appointed a commission that gave the miners a 10 percent raise.

Roosevelt's most famous act during his first term was his acquisition of land for the Panama Canal. Colombia owned Panama, but in August 1903 the Colombian senate refused to approve a treaty giving the United States the rights to a canal zone six miles wide. Determined to build the canal, Roosevelt later that year supported a revolution in Panama, which, with the help of the U.S. Navy, overthrew Colombian rule. The new Panamanian government agreed to lease the zone to the United States, and construction of the canal began.

In the 1904 presidential election, Roosevelt ran against New York judge Alton B. Parker. Roosevelt lost the South but received over 56 percent of the popular vote, swept the North and West, and easily won in the electoral college, 336–140. He became the first successor president to win the White House in his own right after serving the unfinished term of his predecessor.

During his second term Roosevelt championed many pieces of reform legislation including the Pure Food and Drug Act, the Meat Inspection Act, and the Hepburn Act, which empowered the government to set railroad rates. Roosevelt also continued his conservationist activities begun during his first term. Under Roosevelt the government initiated thirty major federal irrigation projects, added 125 million acres to the national forest reserves, and doubled the number of national parks.

In foreign affairs Roosevelt continued aggressively to promote U.S. interests abroad, often in a manner his critics described as imperialistic. In late 1904 he issued the Roosevelt Corollary to the Monroe Doctrine, which declared that the United States would intervene in Latin American affairs to prevent European nations from intervening there. The following year he put the corollary into practice by taking control of the Santo Domingo customhouses to guarantee that country's European debts. In 1905 he mediated an agreement ending the Russo-Japanese War and was awarded the Nobel Peace

Prize for his efforts. In the face of congressional opposition Roosevelt also sent the U.S. fleet on a world cruise that lasted from late 1907 to early 1909. The show of strength was intended to impress other nations, especially Japan, with U.S. resolve to defend its interests and play an active role in world affairs.

Former President

Roosevelt's friend and secretary of war, William Howard Taft, was elected president in 1908 with Roosevelt's backing. Upon leaving office Roosevelt went to Africa to hunt big game with his son Kermit, then toured Europe with his wife before returning to the United States in June 1910. During the next two years Roosevelt became increasingly alienated from Taft, who he felt had abandoned his policies.

In 1912 Roosevelt declared his interest in the Republican nomination for president. He won most of the primaries, but the Republican National Convention in Chicago was controlled by supporters of President Taft, who received the nomination. Progressive Republicans organized the Progressive Party and persuaded Roosevelt to run. The party was dubbed the "Bull Moose" Party, because candidate Roosevelt declared that he felt "as fit as a bull moose."

On October 14, 1912, while campaigning in Milwaukee, Roosevelt was shot in the chest by an assailant. The candidate insisted on delivering a scheduled speech, which lasted almost an hour. He was then rushed from the amazed crowd to a hospital. Taft and the Democratic nominee, Woodrow Wilson, stopped their campaigns while Roosevelt recovered, but the former president was delivering speeches again within two weeks. Roosevelt's heroic campaigning, however, could not overcome the split he had caused among Republicans. Second-

place Roosevelt and third-place Taft together received over a million more popular votes than Wilson, but with his opposition divided, Wilson won the election.

The Progressives asked Roosevelt to run for president again in 1916, but Roosevelt declined and supported Republican Charles Evans Hughes, who lost to President Wilson. In 1916 Roosevelt had begun to make plans for raising a volunteer division to command if the United States entered World War I. When the United States did enter the war in 1917, he went to the White House to request authority to implement his plans, but Wilson turned him down. During the war, Roosevelt was a leading Republican spokesperson and likely would have been his party's candidate for president in 1920 had he lived. He was hospitalized in November 1918 with a severe attack of rheumatism, an ailment from which he suffered during the last years of his life. He returned to Sagamore Hill for Christmas but remained ill. He died in his sleep on January 6, 1919, from an arterial blood clot.

Roosevelt married Alice Hathaway Lee on October 27, 1880, his twenty-second birthday. Alice died on February 14, 1884, of Bright's disease two days after giving birth to the couple's only child, Alice. Roosevelt's mother, Martha Roosevelt, died the same day of typhoid fever. On February 17, 1906, at the White House, Alice married Rep. Nicholas Longworth, who would serve as Speaker of the House from 1925 to 1931.

Roosevelt married Edith Kermit Carow, whom he had known since childhood, on December 2, 1886. They had four sons and one daughter. Their youngest child, Quentin, was killed during World War I while flying a mission over France. Their oldest child, Theodore Jr., served as assistant secretary of the navy, governor of Puerto Rico, and governor-general of the Philippines during the Harding, Coolidge, and Hoover administrations.

William Howard Taft

Born: September 15, 1857; Cincinnati, Ohio
Party: Republican
Term: March 4, 1909–March 4, 1913
Vice President: James S. Sherman
Died: March 8, 1931; Washington, D.C.
Buried: Arlington National Cemetery, Virginia

William Howard Taft was the second of the five children of Alphonso and Louisa Taft. William's older brother died in infancy. Alphonso Taft was a prominent Cincinnati lawyer, who served as secretary of war and attorney general under Ulysses S. Grant and later was ambassador to Austria-Hungary and Russia.

After excelling as a scholar and an athlete in high school, William enrolled in Yale in 1874. He graduated four years later, second in his class. He returned to Cincinnati, where he studied law in his father's office and at the Cincinnati Law School. He gained admission to the bar in 1880 and was appointed assistant prosecutor of Hamilton County, Ohio, the following year. In 1882 he served briefly as collector of internal revenue for his Ohio district but resigned rather than fire several employees for political reasons. In 1883 he established a law partnership in Cincinnati with a former partner of his father.

Political Career

In 1887 Taft was appointed to a vacancy on the state superior court, winning election to his own two-year term on the court the following year. In 1890 President Benjamin Harrison appointed him U.S. solicitor general. Two years later, Harrison appointed him judge of the U.S. Circuit Court, where Taft remained for eight years. During this period the judge also taught at the Cincinnati Law School.

In 1900 President William McKinley appointed Taft president of the U.S. Philippine Commission, which was charged with establishing a civil government on the islands. Taft was reluctant to leave his judgeship, but McKinley persuaded him to go to the Philippines by offering him an eventual appointment to the Supreme Court.

Taft expected to be in the Philippines only a short time, but in 1901 McKinley appointed him governor-general of the islands. In this capacity, Taft reorganized the Filipino court system, acquired land for the Filipinos from the Catholic Church, improved roads, harbors, and schools, and encouraged limited self-government. While in the Philippines, Taft twice refused appointment to the Supreme Court, the position he coveted most, because he believed he could not abandon the people of the islands. In 1904, however, he accepted Theodore Roosevelt's appointment as secretary of war under the condition that he would be able to continue supervising U.S. policy toward the Philippines.

As secretary of war, Taft's activities ranged beyond oversight of the army. He visited the Panama Canal site in 1904, negotiated a secret agreement with the Japanese in 1905 pledging noninterference with Japan's affairs in Korea in return for Japan's promise to recognize U.S. influence in the Philippines, served as temporary provisional governor of Cuba in 1906, and oversaw relief efforts after the 1906 San Francisco earthquake. By 1908, Taft's wide government experience, his close friendship with Theodore Roosevelt, and his well-known administrative abilities made him the front-runner for the Republican presidential nomination.

Taft was not anxious to run, but Theodore Roosevelt, Republican Party leaders, and his wife persuaded him to seek the presidency. As Roosevelt's chosen successor Taft won the nomination at the 1908 Republican National Convention in Chicago on the first ballot. He then defeated Democrat William Jennings Bryan 321–162 in the electoral college.

Presidency

Upon entering office Taft urged Congress to reduce tariffs. The president, however, angered progressive Republicans, who favored lower tariffs, when he signed the Payne-Aldrich Tariff Act of 1909. The act reduced tariff rates by amounts that most progressives considered insignificant.

Taft showed stronger leadership in his pursuit of antitrust cases. Although Theodore Roosevelt is often remembered as the president who first made wide use of the Sherman Antitrust Act to break up monopolies, Taft's administration brought ninety antitrust suits in four years compared with forty-four during Roosevelt's seven-year presidency. The Standard Oil and American Tobacco companies were among those broken up by the Taft administration. Taft also successfully backed the passage of

the Sixteenth Amendment, which authorized a federal income tax.

In foreign affairs Taft instituted a policy that came to be known as "dollar diplomacy." This policy sought to use investments and trade to expand U.S. influence abroad, especially in Latin America. Taft also was willing to use force to maintain order and to protect U.S. business interests in Latin America. He dispatched ships and troops to Honduras in 1911 and Nicaragua in 1910 and again in 1912 to protect American lives and property threatened by revolution. These interventions contributed to Latin American resentment toward the United States.

In 1911 Taft negotiated a trade reciprocity agreement with Canada, which significantly lowered tariffs between the two countries, but the Canadian parliament rejected the agreement later in the year. Taft suffered another foreign policy defeat in 1911 when the Senate attached crippling amendments to his treaty with Britain and France that would have established a process of arbitration to settle international disputes between the signatories. Taft withdrew the treaty rather than sign it.

Theodore Roosevelt had been one of the harshest critics of the arbitration treaty during the ratification fight. Roosevelt also criticized Taft for what the former president considered conservative departures from his progressive policies toward big business and the environment.

In 1912 Taft was nominated by the Republican Party for reelection. Roosevelt, who had won most of the Republican primaries that year, protested that he had not received a fair chance to win the nomination at the Republican National Convention, which was controlled by Taft supporters. Roosevelt launched a third-party candidacy that doomed Taft's reelection bid. Roosevelt and Taft split the Republican vote, allowing Democrat Woodrow Wilson to capture the presidency. Taft finished in third place with just eight electoral votes.

Former President and Chief Justice

When Taft's term expired, he accepted a professorship of law at Yale University. While teaching, Taft wrote for law journals and other publications and delivered many lectures around the country. In 1913 he was elected president of the American Bar Association. During World War I President Wilson named him joint chairman of the War Labor Board, which resolved wartime labor disputes.

Although Taft enjoyed his time at Yale, he continued to covet an appointment to the Supreme Court. The election of Taft's friend and fellow Republican Warren G. Harding to the presidency in 1920 opened the door to a Supreme Court appointment. When Chief Justice Edward White died on May 19, 1921, Harding chose Taft to take his place. Taft was a highly capable chief justice who usually rendered moderately conservative opinions. He improved the efficiency of the judicial system and fought successfully for passage of the Judiciary Act of 1925, which increased the Supreme Court's discretion in choosing which cases to accept. As chief justice, Taft administered the presidential oath of office to Calvin Coolidge in 1925 and Herbert Hoover in 1929. Taft resigned as chief justice on February 3, 1930, because of his weak heart. He died a few weeks later from heart failure on March 8.

Taft married Helen Herron June 19, 1886. They had one daughter and two sons. Their oldest son, Robert A. Taft, became one of the most powerful Republicans in the Senate during the late 1940s and early 1950s and was considered as a possible presidential candidate in 1940, 1948, and 1952. Their youngest son, Charles Phelps Taft, served as mayor of Cincinnati from 1955 to 1957. In the 1970s Taft's grandson, Robert Taft Jr., served in the Senate, and in 1999 a great-grandson, Bob Taft, became governor of Ohio.

Woodrow Wilson

Born: December 28, 1856; Staunton, Virginia
Party: Democratic
Term: March 4, 1913–March 4, 1921
Vice President: Thomas R. Marshall
Died: February 3, 1924; Washington, D.C.
Buried: Washington, D.C.

Woodrow Wilson was the third of the four children born to Janet and Joseph Wilson, a Presbyterian minister. When Wilson was two, his family moved from Staunton, Virginia, to Augusta, Georgia, where his father became pastor of the First Presbyterian Church. As a boy Wilson witnessed the destruction of the Civil War. He claimed later in life that his earliest recollection was hearing a passerby tell his father that "Mr. Lincoln was elected and there was to be war." Although Joseph Wilson was originally from Ohio, he had strong Southern sympathies and served as a chaplain to Confederate troops in the area. The war prevented Woodrow from attending school until he was nine. In 1870 the Wilsons moved to Columbia, South Carolina, where his father taught at a seminary.

Wilson, who was originally named Thomas Woodrow, dropped his first name as a young adult. He enrolled in Davidson College near Charlotte, North Carolina, in 1873. Before the end of the school year, illness forced him to withdraw. After his family moved to Wilmington, North Carolina, he entered Princeton University in 1875. There he earned recognition as a debater, developed a keen interest in government, and decided not to become a minister like his father. After graduation in 1879, he entered law school at the University of Virginia, but in 1880 poor health again forced him to abandon school. He finished his law degree through independent study while living in Wilmington and was admitted to the bar in 1882. He established a law partnership in Atlanta with a law school friend but quit the profession in 1883 to enroll in Johns Hopkins University as a graduate student of history and government.

Educator and Governor

At Johns Hopkins, Wilson distinguished himself as a brilliant student. In 1885 he published his first book, *Congressional Government,* which argued that Congress had become the dominant branch of government and that it should adopt a system of governing patterned after the British Parliament. The book received critical acclaim and served as Wilson's dissertation. In 1885 Bryn Mawr College near Philadelphia hired Wilson as an associate professor of history. He was awarded his doctorate degree in 1886.

Wilson moved to Wesleyan University in Middletown, Connecticut, in 1888. There he taught his-

tory and political science and coached the football team. In 1890 he accepted a professorship at Princeton University. In 1902 Princeton's trustees unanimously elected him president of the university.

Wilson regarded his new job as an opportunity to implement his ideas about education. He introduced a system providing for small scholarly discussion groups and close faculty supervision of students. His most cherished reform, however, was his plan to reorganize the residential structure of the college around quadrangle units that he believed would refocus the life of the college away from social and sporting activities toward academics.

His "quad plan" was opposed by Princeton's private clubs, which Wilson regarded as bastions of the privileged. Although Wilson's quad plan was eventually rejected, he became known as a crusader for democratic principles in education.

New Jersey's Democratic Party leaders proposed to Wilson that he run for governor in 1910. They hoped the notoriety he had gained while president of Princeton and his eloquence could carry him to the New Jersey statehouse. Once elected, party leaders expected to be able to dominate the scholarly Wilson, who had no political experience. Wilson accepted on condition that he would not have to fulfill any promises of patronage. He resigned from Princeton and was elected governor.

Once in office Wilson quickly demonstrated that he was swayed by no one and was in complete control. He pushed a series of reforms through the legislature that attracted national attention including laws establishing direct primaries, workers' compensation, and antitrust measures. His efforts also led to improved regulation of utilities and the reorganization of the public school system. By 1912 Democrats were considering him as a potential presidential candidate.

Wilson entered the 1912 Democratic National Convention in Baltimore as an underdog to Speaker of the House Champ Clark. Although Clark led

Wilson in the early ballots, he could not muster a majority. On the fourteenth ballot Democratic patriarch William Jennings Bryan abandoned Clark to support Wilson. On the forty-sixth ballot Wilson was finally nominated.

Wilson's election to the presidency was virtually sealed when Teddy Roosevelt split the Republican Party by running for president as the candidate of the Progressive Party. Of the 15 million votes cast, Wilson received only 6.3 million, but Republicans divided their votes between Roosevelt and President William Howard Taft. Wilson received 435 electoral votes, while Roosevelt and Taft received 88 and 8 votes, respectively.

Presidency

Once in office, Wilson demonstrated the same independence and innovation he had shown as governor and university president. He delivered his first annual message to Congress in person on April 8, 1913, which no president had done since John Adams. He also established weekly press conferences.

Wilson fulfilled a campaign promise to lower tariffs by signing the Underwood Tariff Act of 1913. The act cut tariff rates to their lowest levels since before the Civil War and provided for the levying of the first income tax since the Sixteenth Amendment had made such taxes legal. At Wilson's urging Congress passed the Federal Reserve Act of 1913, which created a system of regional federal banks to regulate currency and the banking industry. He supported the establishment of the Federal Trade Commission in 1914 to ensure fair business practices. That year he also signed the Clayton Anti-Trust Act, which strengthened the government's powers to break up monopolies. In 1916 Congress passed the Adamson Act at Wilson's request, which established the eight-hour day for railroad workers.

When World War I began in 1914, Wilson announced that the United States would stay out of

the conflict. German submarines in the Atlantic Ocean, however, were not observing U.S. neutrality. In May 1915, a German submarine sank the British passenger ship *Lusitania* with more than one hundred Americans aboard. The incident led Wilson to issue several diplomatic protests, until the Germans agreed not to prey on passenger ships and to place other restrictions on their submarine warfare.

In 1916 Wilson did not have the luxury of facing a divided Republican Party as he had in 1912. The Republicans nominated Supreme Court justice Charles Evans Hughes, and Theodore Roosevelt declined a second third-party candidacy to campaign for the Republican nominee. Wilson campaigned on his domestic accomplishments and his success in keeping the United States out of war. In one of the closest presidential elections in history, Wilson defeated Hughes 277–254 in the electoral college. Had Wilson lost any of the ten states he won with twelve or more electoral votes he would have lost the election.

Wilson, who tried to mediate an end to the war in Europe, called on January 22, 1917, for a "peace without victory" that would end the fighting and the establishment of a league of nations, an international body that would prevent and settle disputes between members. A week after Wilson's speech, however, the Germans, who expected the United States to enter the war soon, announced they would attack without warning any ship passing through a wide zone in the Atlantic. Wilson responded to the submarine offensive by severing diplomatic relations with Germany on February 3. When the Germans continued their submarine warfare in defiance of Wilson's protests, he asked Congress on April 2, 1917, for a declaration of war. Within four days both houses had overwhelmingly passed the declaration.

Congress delegated broad emergency powers to Wilson to marshal the nation's resources, build an army, and prosecute the war. He pushed the Selective Service Act through Congress, took control of the railroads, established the War Industries Board to oversee the economy, and instituted many other emergency measures.

With the addition of U.S. troops on the Allied side, the war went badly for Germany. An armistice was signed on November 11, 1918. After U.S. entry into the war, Wilson had outlined a plan for territorial adjustment and maintenance of world peace once the war was over. The basis of this plan was his "Fourteen Points," which included freedom of the seas, removal of trade barriers, an end to secret treaties, and a reduction of armaments.

In December 1918, Wilson sailed to France to attend the Versailles peace conference. Europeans hailed the American president as a hero, and he dominated the deliberations of the Allies. Nevertheless, he was forced to make many concessions to European leaders to gain their endorsement of his Fourteen Points and the League of Nations. The treaty produced by the conference imposed a harsh peace on Germany that included heavy war reparations and the loss of its colonies.

Wilson submitted the Treaty of Versailles to the Senate for approval on July 10, 1919, but he could not persuade two-thirds of the Senate to support it. A group of senators led by Republican Henry Cabot Lodge of Massachusetts objected to the provision within the treaty establishing the League of Nations and would not vote for the treaty without attaching reservations that Wilson believed nullified the agreement. On September 4, 1919, Wilson launched a speaking tour of the western states designed to mobilize public support for the treaty. On September 26, after delivering speeches in twenty-nine cities, Wilson became ill in Pueblo, Colorado, and was forced to cancel the rest of his speaking tour. He returned to Washington, D.C., where he suffered a severe stroke on October 2.

The stroke left the president almost entirely incapacitated for several months, and he never completely recovered his strength. While Wilson recuperated, the Senate debated the Treaty of Versailles. Senators split into three major groups: those who supported the treaty, those who sided with Lodge in supporting it only if major reservations were attached, and those who were opposed to the treaty in any form. Wilson refused to compromise with Lodge to gain passage of the treaty and advised his supporters against accepting it with Lodge's reservations. The Senate rejected the treaty on November 19, 1919. Exactly four months later Senate Republican leaders again brought the treaty to a vote in the hope that Democrats would support the Lodge reservations. Democrats in the Senate, however, remained loyal to Wilson and rejected the amended treaty again, while the Republicans blocked the passage of the treaty in its original form. Wilson declared that the American people should decide the issue in the 1920 presidential contest. The public, however, overwhelmingly elected Republican Warren G. Harding over Democrat James M. Cox. Harding refused to back the treaty, and Wilson's fight for U.S. entry into the League of Nations was finished.

When Wilson left office he retired to a home on S Street in Washington, D.C. He formed a law partnership but did not practice. He lived in near seclusion until he died on February 3, 1924, from another stroke.

Wilson married Ellen Louise Axson, the daughter of a Presbyterian minister, on June 24, 1885. They had three daughters. Ellen died on August 6, 1914, in the White House. On December 18, 1915, Wilson married Edith Bolling Galt, a forty-three-year-old widow. After Wilson suffered his stroke in 1919, Edith restricted access to her husband. During Wilson's convalescence he conducted much of his presidential business through Edith. Historians have speculated that she may have made many presidential decisions for her husband.

Warren G. Harding

Born: November 2, 1865; Corsica, Ohio (now
  Blooming Grove)
Party: Republican
Term: March 4, 1921–August 2, 1923
Vice President: Calvin Coolidge
Died: August 2, 1923; San Francisco, California
Buried: Marion, Ohio

Warren Gamaliel Harding was the oldest of the
eight children of Phoebe and George Harding, who
owned a farm in north-central Ohio. Warren did
farm chores and attended local schools as a boy. He
attended tiny Ohio Central College in Iberia, where
he edited the school newspaper.

After Harding's graduation in 1882, he taught in
a country school for one term, before giving up the
profession and moving to Marion, Ohio. There he
tried selling insurance and worked briefly for the
Marion Mirror as a reporter. In 1884 he and two
friends bought the *Marion Star,* a bankrupt, four-
page newspaper. Harding bought out his friends in
1886 when they lost interest in the enterprise. Gradually, he made the paper a financial success and a
political force in Ohio.

In 1892 Harding ran for county auditor but was
defeated badly by his Democratic opponent. He
remained active in state politics, however, frequently
making campaign speeches for Republican candidates. In 1899 he ran for the state senate and was
victorious. He won a second term in 1901 and was
elected lieutenant governor in 1903. Two years later,
however, he refused to be renominated for lieutenant governor in favor of returning to manage his
paper in Marion.

In 1909 Harding ran for governor of Ohio but
was defeated. He gained national prominence in
June 1912 when he delivered the speech nominating William Howard Taft for president at the
Republican National Convention in Chicago. Two
years later, he ran for the U.S. Senate. After winning
the Republican Party's first direct primary for senator in Ohio, Harding was elected.

As a senator, Harding followed the party line,
made many friends, and avoided controversy. He frequently missed roll calls and did not introduce any
important legislation. He voted for Prohibition and
women's suffrage but against the Versailles treaty.
Much of his time in the capital was spent drinking,
playing poker, and developing political allies.

Harding took his undistinguished record to the
1920 Republican National Convention in Chicago.
His was one of many names entered into nomination for president, but he was not among the
favorites in the early balloting. After four ballots,
none of the front-runners could muster a majority
of support. Fearing a deadlock that would threaten
party unity, Republican leaders retired to a "smoke-
filled room" at the Blackstone Hotel. At the urging
of Harding's close friend and political mentor, Harry

Daugherty, they decided to give the nomination to Harding, who possessed good looks, an amiable personality, and a willingness to be led by the party.

During a "front porch" campaign reminiscent of William McKinley's 1896 campaign, Harding promised a "return to normalcy" after the Wilson years. This promise appealed to American voters, who had lived through a difficult period during World War I and were skeptical of outgoing president Woodrow Wilson's internationalist idealism. In the first presidential election in which women could vote, Harding defeated James M. Cox in a landslide, receiving over sixteen million votes to his opponent's nine million. Harding received 404 electoral votes, while Cox managed to win just eleven states, all in the South, for a total of 127 electoral votes.

In 1919 and 1920 the Senate had rejected Woodrow Wilson's Versailles treaty ending World War I because that body objected to U.S. membership in the League of Nations. Consequently, a separate agreement was needed to make formal the end of the war. In 1921 the Harding administration concluded treaties with Germany, Austria, and Hungary, officially making peace with those nations. In 1921 Harding also called the Washington Disarmament Conference. This meeting, masterminded by Secretary of State Charles Evans Hughes, succeeded in producing a treaty that reduced the navies of the United States, Great Britain, France, Germany, Japan, and Italy.

In domestic policy, Harding cut taxes on high incomes and signed the Fordney-McCumber Act, which raised tariff rates that had been lowered during the Wilson administration. A lasting contribution to U.S. government left by Harding was the Bureau of the Budget (now the Office of Management and Budget), which was created by the Budget Act of 1921.

Harding's administration is best known, however, for the scandals that were revealed after his death.

Harding appointed to high government posts many friends and cronies who used their position for personal enrichment. Harding is not known to have participated in the crimes committed by his associates and advisers, but he did little to prevent the corruption within his administration. One of the most famous scandals involved Secretary of the Interior Albert Fall's leasing of government oil reserves at Teapot Dome, Wyoming, and Elk Hills, California, to private interests for a bribe. Fall was later fined and imprisoned for his actions. Secretary of the Navy Edwin Denby, Attorney General Harry Daugherty, and Charles Forbes, head of the Veterans Bureau, also were found to have participated in the scandals.

When the Republicans lost seats in both houses of Congress in the 1922 midterm election, Harding decided to go on a speaking tour in early 1923 to boost his party's and his own popularity. It is also probable that Harding wished to leave Washington to escape the developing rumors about the scandals within his administration.

In Seattle after visiting Alaska, Harding was stricken with pains that were diagnosed as indigestion but which may have been a heart attack. Harding improved but then died suddenly in San Francisco. His doctors suspected a blood clot in the brain may have killed him, but his wife refused to permit an autopsy. The absence of conclusive evidence about his death and the subsequent revelations of scandals led to public speculation that he may have committed suicide or been poisoned, but no evidence of an unnatural death exists. The news of Harding's death brought an outpouring of public grief, and he lay in state at the White House. As details of the scandals of his administration became known in 1923 and 1924, however, Harding's public reputation declined.

Harding married Florence Kling De Wolfe, a divorcée five years his senior, on July 8, 1891, in

Marion, Ohio. The couple had no children but raised Florence's child by her first marriage. Harding carried on an affair with Nan Britton, a woman thirty years younger than he, whom he had known since he edited the *Marion Star.* When Harding was a senator, he helped Britton get a job in New York and often visited her. They had one daughter, who was born on October 22, 1919. Britton disclosed the affair three years after Harding's death in her book *The President's Daughter.*

Calvin Coolidge

Born: July 4, 1872; Plymouth Notch, Vermont
Party: Republican
Term: August 3, 1923–March 4, 1929
Vice President: Charles G. Dawes
Died: January 5, 1933; Northampton, Massachusetts
Buried: Plymouth, Vermont

Calvin Coolidge was the oldest of the two children of Victoria and John Coolidge, who farmed and owned a general store. Calvin was originally named John Calvin after his father, but he dropped his first name when he became an adult. As a boy, Calvin worked on the family farm and attended local public schools. His mother died in 1885 when he was twelve. His younger sister, Abigail, died five years later at the age of fifteen.

As a teenager, Coolidge attended Black River Academy, a local private preparatory school, graduating in 1890. He wanted to attend Amherst College but failed the school's entrance exam that year. He gained admission to Amherst after taking additional courses at St. Johnsbury Academy, another prep school. Coolidge graduated cum laude from Amherst in 1895.

After graduation Coolidge moved to nearby Northampton, Massachusetts, where he got a job as a law clerk. He was admitted to the bar in 1897,

started his own law practice, and became involved in Northampton politics as a Republican. He served as a member of the city council, city solicitor, and chairman of the county Republican committee. He suffered his only political defeat in 1905 when he was beaten for a seat on the Northampton school board. In 1906, however, he was elected to the Massachusetts House of Representatives. After two terms, he returned to Northampton in 1909 and was elected mayor the following year.

In 1911 Coolidge won a seat in the state senate. After four one-year terms he was elected lieutenant governor in 1915. He served three one-year terms in this office before being elected governor by a slim margin in 1918.

In September 1919 the Boston police staged a strike that opened the way for a criminal rampage. After two days, Governor Coolidge called out the state militia to keep order in Boston. When Samuel Gompers, head of the American Federation of

Labor, accused Coolidge of acting unfairly, Coolidge sent him a wire declaring, "There is no right to strike against the public safety by anybody, anywhere, any time." The statement made Coolidge famous across the country.

Although Coolidge was one of many Republicans whose name was placed in nomination for the presidency at the 1920 Republican National Convention in Chicago, he was not a leading candidate for the nomination. The convention was deadlocked between several candidates during the early balloting but eventually turned to Sen. Warren G. Harding of Ohio as a compromise candidate. Harding had been chosen by party leaders who expected their choice for vice president, Wisconsin senator Irvine Lenroot, to be similarly ratified by the convention. When Coolidge's name was put into nomination for vice president after Lenroot's, however, the convention unexpectedly threw its support behind the popular governor. Coolidge received 674 votes to Lenroot's 146 and was chosen on the first ballot.

During the 1920 campaign, Harding and Coolidge promised to raise tariffs to protect U.S. industry and to keep the country out of war and entangling alliances. They won more than 60 percent of the popular vote on their way to a 404–127 victory in the electoral college over Democrats James M. Cox and Franklin D. Roosevelt.

In 1923 Vice President Coolidge was spending the summer in Vermont when a telegraph messenger arrived at his home after midnight on August 3 with the news that President Harding had unexpectedly died in San Francisco. Coolidge's father, who was a notary public, administered the oath of office. The next day Coolidge left for Washington.

Coolidge retained Harding's cabinet, but when the scandals that pervaded the Harding administration were revealed, he asked for the resignations of those involved, including Secretary of the Navy Edwin Denby and Attorney General Harry Daugh-

erty. Coolidge dutifully prosecuted the former Harding administration officials who had committed crimes.

As president, Coolidge quickly became a symbol of simple, practical leadership. Coolidge was fondly called "Silent Cal" by the public because of his quiet, almost sphinx-like demeanor. He was an honest and successful administrator who made the national government more efficient and economical.

Coolidge ran for reelection in 1924 against John W. Davis. Despite the scandals of the Harding administration, Coolidge's personal honesty, his small-town image, and national prosperity carried him to victory. He defeated Davis in the electoral college, 382–136.

During his second term, Coolidge was successful in decreasing the national debt and cutting income taxes. These policies put more money into the hands of consumers and helped stimulate investment. Coolidge's hands-off policies toward business activities, however, deferred needed reforms of the financial industry and encouraged overspeculation that contributed to the stock market crash of 1929 and the subsequent Depression.

In foreign relations, Coolidge reestablished diplomatic relations with Mexico severed under Woodrow Wilson and improved relations with other Latin American nations that had been strained since the turn of the century. Although Coolidge opposed U.S. entry into the League of Nations, he backed the multilateral Kellogg-Briand Pact of 1928, which naively outlawed war between nations.

After leaving office, Coolidge retired to Northampton, Massachusetts, where he bought Beeches, a nine-acre estate. During his short retirement Coolidge wrote newspaper columns and served on the board of directors of the New York Life Insurance Company. In January 1933, less than four years after leaving the White House, Coolidge died of a heart attack.

Coolidge married Grace Goodhue on October

4, 1905. Grace had been a teacher at Clarke Institute for the Deaf in Northampton. She died in Northampton in 1957 at the age of 78. The couple had two sons. Their younger son, Calvin Jr., died in 1924 after developing blood poisoning from a blister formed while playing tennis on the White House court. John, their oldest child, had the distinction of being the oldest living offspring of an American president. He died in June 2000, at ninety-three.

Herbert Hoover

Born: August 10, 1874; West Branch, Iowa
Party: Republican
Term: March 4, 1929–March 4, 1933
Vice President: Charles Curtis
Died: October 20, 1964; New York City
Buried: West Branch

Herbert Clark Hoover was the second of the three children of Jesse and Huldah Hoover. His father, a blacksmith and farm implement merchant, died of typhoid when Herbert was six. When his mother died of pneumonia two years later, he was sent to Oregon to live with an aunt and uncle, who were Quakers like his parents. Herbert attended public schools and worked in his uncle's land settlement office in Salem. He also attended a local business school, where he sharpened his math skills and learned to type.

Hoover took entrance examinations to gain admission to Stanford University, an engineering school being established in California. Despite uneven education, his impressive math skills earned him a spot in Stanford's first freshman class in 1891. Hoover worked his way through college, earning his degree in 1895. After laboring for a few months at a menial mining job in Nevada, Hoover went to San Francisco. There he worked as a typist before an international mining company hired him in 1897 as an engineering assistant. During the next seventeen years, Hoover managed mines in Africa, Asia, Europe, Australia, and the United States. Before the age of forty, he was one of the world's most successful mining engineers and worth several million dollars.

In 1914 when World War I began Hoover was living in London. He served as chairman of a committee of Americans who helped U.S. tourists stranded in Europe to secure passage home. He then became chairman of the Commission for Relief in Belgium, a private charity group. In this capacity he raised funds to aid the people of that war-torn country and made arrangements with the warring nations to distribute the aid.

When the U.S. Congress declared war on Germany in 1917, Hoover returned to the United States, where President Woodrow Wilson appointed him U.S. food administrator. In this post Hoover was responsible for stimulating food production and distributing and conserving food supplies. In 1918 Hoover was appointed chairman of the Allied Food Council, which distributed food to millions of Europeans left impoverished by the war. After the war Hoover attended the Versailles Peace Conference as an economic adviser to President Wilson.

Hoover's relief activities made him one of the most famous and admired Americans of his day and a prospective candidate for public office. But his political affiliation was unclear because he had supported Republican Theodore Roosevelt's third-party candidacy in 1912 and had worked closely with President Wilson, a Democrat. In 1920, however, Hoover declared that he was a Republican and received some support for the party's presidential nomination, which eventually went to Warren G. Harding.

When Harding was elected president, he appointed Hoover secretary of commerce over the objections of Republican conservatives who regarded Hoover as a liberal. Hoover remained in this post for eight years. He reorganized the department and helped solidify the progress toward an eight-hour workday and a prohibition against child labor. He also became a close economic adviser to both President Harding and Vice President Calvin Coolidge, but he remained free of the scandals that plagued their administration.

Hoover was the popular choice of Republicans for the party's presidential nomination in 1928. Despite the opposition of some conservative party leaders, Hoover was nominated at the Kansas City Republican National Convention on the first ballot. He then won the general election over Democrat Al Smith of New York. Hoover received more than twenty-one million popular votes to Smith's fifteen million. Hoover even captured several traditionally Democratic southern states on his way to a 444–87 electoral vote victory.

Hoover had run on a Republican platform that took credit for the prosperity achieved during the 1920s. Ironically, seven months after Hoover's inauguration the October 1929 stock market crash began the economic depression that left about a quarter of the workforce unemployed. After the crash Hoover tried to assure the nation that the economy was sound and that business activity would soon recover, but the Depression grew worse during his term. Although he had not created the conditions that caused the Depression, many Americans blamed him for it.

Hoover tried to fight the growing Depression through limited public works projects, increased government loans to banks and businesses, reductions in the already low income tax, and personal appeals to industry to maintain wages and production levels. But these measures did little to ease the country's economic problems. Hoover's preoccupation with balancing the budget and his belief that federal relief violated the American principle of self-reliance prevented him from taking more sweeping actions. Thus, he opposed federal benefit programs to help the poor and unemployed and deficit spending that would have created jobs. He reluctantly signed the Smoot-Hawley Act of 1930, which dramatically raised tariff rates to protect U.S. industries, thereby initiating a trade war that hurt the American and world economies.

Hoover was nominated by the Republicans for a second term but the nation, desperate for relief from the Depression, turned against him. His Democratic opponent, Franklin D. Roosevelt, won in a landslide.

Hoover returned to his home in Palo Alto, California, in March 1933. During Franklin Roosevelt's presidency Hoover actively criticized Roosevelt's New Deal programs and the U.S. alliance with the Soviet Union during World War II.

In 1946 President Harry S. Truman tapped Hoover's famine relief experience by appointing him chairman of the Famine Emergency Commission, which was charged with preventing starvation in post–World War II Europe.

In 1947 Truman appointed Hoover chairman of the Commission on Organization of the Executive Branch of the Government. The "Hoover Commission" recommended hundreds of organizational changes, many of which were adopted, to make the executive branch more efficient. The commission submitted its final report in 1949, but in 1953 President Dwight D. Eisenhower appointed Hoover to chair a second commission on government organization. The second Hoover Commission functioned until 1955.

Hoover retired from government service after 1955 but continued to write on politics and speak at Republican conventions. In 1964 he died in New York City at the age of ninety. He had the second-longest life of any president, with John Adams living 136 days longer.

Hoover married Lou Henry, a fellow student at Stanford and the daughter of a Monterey, California, banker, on February 10, 1899. Their two sons, Herbert Jr. and Allan, were born while the Hoovers lived in London. Herbert served as under secretary of state from 1954 to 1957.

Franklin D. Roosevelt

Born: January 30, 1882; Hyde Park, New York
Party: Democratic
Term: March 4, 1933–April 12, 1945
Vice Presidents: John N. Garner; Henry A. Wallace; Harry S. Truman
Died: April 12, 1945; Warm Springs, Georgia
Buried: Hyde Park

Franklin Delano Roosevelt was the son of James and Sara Roosevelt. He was his mother's only child, but his father, a widower, had a son by his first wife. James Roosevelt was a wealthy lawyer and railroad executive who had inherited a fortune. Sara was also from a wealthy family and had married the fifty-two-year-old James when she was just twenty-six. She and James's first son were both born in 1854.

Franklin lived a sheltered early life. He received his elementary education from private tutors and traveled frequently with his family to Europe. At age fourteen Franklin enrolled in Groton, a private preparatory school in Groton, Massachusetts. After four years there he entered Harvard University in 1900. Although Franklin did not have a distinguished academic record, he graduated in three years and became editor of the campus newspaper.

Roosevelt stayed a fourth year at Harvard as a graduate student of history and economics. He then studied law at Columbia from 1904 until 1907 but left without graduating when he passed the bar. A New York City firm hired him as a law clerk.

Political Career

In 1910 Roosevelt ran for the New York State Senate as a Democrat from a traditionally Republican district and surprised Democratic Party leaders when he won. He was reelected in 1912 but gave up his seat in 1913, when President Woodrow Wilson appointed him assistant secretary of the navy, a post once held by his distant relative Theodore Roosevelt.

After war broke out in Europe in 1914, Roosevelt argued for greater military preparedness. When the United States entered the war, he twice asked Wilson to transfer him to active service, but the president turned him down saying he was needed where he was. Roosevelt made several trips to Europe to inspect U.S. naval forces. Near the end of the war he developed a plan to hinder German submarine attacks. His "North Sea Mine Barrage," a 240–mile cordon of antisubmarine mines in the Atlantic, reduced allied shipping losses and helped hasten the armistice.

In 1920 Roosevelt resigned from the Navy Department when the Democratic Party nominated him for the vice presidency on the ticket with presidential nominee James M. Cox. Democrats hoped that the promising young politician with the famous name could give the ticket a boost, but Cox and Roosevelt were beaten badly by Republicans Warren Harding and Calvin Coolidge.

After the defeat, Roosevelt became a partner in a New York City law firm and accepted a vice presidency in the Fidelity and Deposit Company of Maryland, a surety bond firm.

In 1921 Roosevelt suffered a personal tragedy. While vacationing in New Brunswick he was stricken with poliomyelitis. The attack left him severely crippled, and his mother urged him to give up politics and retire to the family estate at Hyde Park. Roosevelt, however, struggled to rehabilitate himself. Over a period of years he built up his arms

and chest and eventually was able to walk short distances with the aid of crutches and braces.

On June 26, 1924, Roosevelt returned to national politics when he delivered the presidential nomination speech for New York governor Alfred E. Smith at the Democratic National Convention in New York City. Smith did not receive the nomination, but Roosevelt's courageous appearance on crutches at Madison Square Garden increased his popularity and made him a leading figure in the Democratic Party. Later that year Roosevelt vacationed in Warm Springs, Georgia, where he hoped to regain the use of his legs by swimming in a natural pool of warm spring water. He made numerous trips to Warm Springs during the rest of his life. In 1927 he founded the Georgia Warm Springs Foundation, an inexpensive treatment center for polio victims.

Al Smith, nominated for president in 1928, urged Roosevelt to run for governor in New York to give the Democratic ticket a boost. Roosevelt at first declined, saying he wanted to concentrate on rehabilitating his legs, but he finally agreed to run when he was nominated by acclamation. Questions of Roosevelt's physical ability to function as governor were dispelled by his vigorous campaigning, often conducted from an automobile. Roosevelt won the election despite Republican presidential candidate Herbert Hoover's victory in New York.

As governor, Roosevelt gave tax relief to New York's farmers and lowered the cost of public utilities to consumers. He was reelected in a landslide in 1930. During his second term he concentrated on easing the suffering caused by the Depression.

Roosevelt's success as governor made him a leading candidate for the Democratic presidential nomination in 1932. He entered the convention with a majority of delegates, but he had fewer than the two-thirds necessary to win the nomination. After three ballots he offered to endorse rival John Nance Garner, the Texan Speaker of the House, for vice president, if Garner released his presidential delegates. Garner, recognizing his chances of being nominated for president were slim, accepted the deal and released his ninety delegates to Roosevelt, who was nominated on the fourth ballot. The convention then nominated Garner for vice president.

During the campaign of 1932, Roosevelt exuded confidence and outlined his recovery program, which he called the "New Deal." Although he faced incumbent Republican president Herbert Hoover in the election, Roosevelt was favored to win because many voters blamed Hoover for the severity of the Great Depression. Roosevelt outpolled Hoover by more than seven million votes and won 472–59 in the electoral college.

Before Roosevelt was inaugurated, he became the only president-elect to be the target of an assassination attempt. After Roosevelt had delivered a speech in Florida on February 14, 1933, Giuseppe Zangara, an unemployed bricklayer, fired six shots from a handgun at Roosevelt from twelve yards away. The president-elect, who was sitting in an open car, was uninjured, but five other people were shot, including Chicago mayor Anton Cernak, who was killed. Zangara, who had a pathological hatred for rich and powerful figures, was found guilty of murder and electrocuted.

Presidency

Roosevelt took office at the low point of the Depression. Most of the nation's banks were closed, industrial production was about half of what it had been in 1928, and as many as 15 million people were unemployed. Roosevelt worked with the new Democratic Congress to enact many New Deal bills during the productive opening period of his presidency, known as the "First Hundred Days." He declared a four-day bank holiday to stop panic withdrawals, abandoned the gold standard, increased government loans to farmers and homeowners, and

created federal bank deposit insurance. At Roosevelt's urging, Congress created the Civilian Conservation Corps, which employed tens of thousands of people on conservation projects and passed the Federal Emergency Relief Act, which provided grants to state and local governments for aid to the unemployed. Numerous other measures were passed during the First Hundred Days, which increased public confidence and stimulated the economy.

Business interests feared that the deficit spending required to finance the New Deal would lead to inflation, but injection of federal money into the economy eased the Depression. Roosevelt promoted his policies through "fireside chats," radio addresses to the nation from the White House. A second wave of New Deal programs, including Social Security, unemployment insurance, and federal aid to dependent children, was passed in 1934 and 1935.

Roosevelt's New Deal successes made him a popular president. He defeated Kansas governor Alfred M. Landon in the 1936 presidential election in one of the largest landslides in presidential election history. Landon won only Maine and Vermont.

In 1937 Roosevelt suffered one of the biggest defeats of his presidency and squandered political capital won in the 1936 election when he proposed to expand the Supreme Court from nine to as many as fifteen justices. Roosevelt had been frustrated by the conservative court, which had struck down several of his New Deal measures. If the Court were expanded he could appoint justices who would accept his policies. Neither the public nor Congress, however, would go along with Roosevelt's court-packing scheme. Moreover, the episode hardened resistance to the New Deal from Republicans and conservative Democrats.

In 1940 Roosevelt ran for an unprecedented third term against the progressive Republican nominee, Wendell Willkie of Indiana. Roosevelt defeated Willkie 449 to 82 in the electoral college. His popular margin of victory narrowed from four years before, however, in part because some voters objected to Roosevelt's disregard of the unwritten rule that presidents should serve no more than two terms.

In September 1939 Adolph Hitler's Germany had invaded Poland, starting World War II in Europe. Despite strong neutralist sentiments among members of Congress and the general public, Roosevelt recognized that U.S. national security depended on Great Britain's survival. He promised to keep the United States out of the fighting but pressed for the authority to aid Britain and other allied nations in every way short of going to war. In September 1940 Roosevelt violated two neutrality statutes in trading Great Britain fifty outdated destroyers for the right to lease certain British territory in the western Atlantic for U.S. naval and air bases. In March 1941 Roosevelt persuaded Congress to pass the Lend-Lease Act, which gave the president the power to supply weapons and equipment to "any country whose defense the president deems vital to the defense of the United States." In September of that year, Roosevelt ordered U.S. warships providing protection for supply convoys bound for Britain to attack German vessels on sight. Thus, Roosevelt had engaged the United States in an undeclared naval war months before the nation would enter the war.

On December 7, 1941, the Japanese launched a surprise attack against the U.S. fleet at Pearl Harbor, Hawaii. The next day Roosevelt asked for and received a declaration of war from Congress. Roosevelt shifted his focus and national resources from New Deal reforms to winning the war.

Roosevelt oversaw the development of military strategy and conferred often with British prime minister Winston Churchill. Roosevelt and Churchill met with Soviet leader Joseph Stalin at Tehran in 1943 and Yalta in 1945. At these meetings, the leaders of the three principal Allied nations not only discussed wartime strategy, they planned for the postwar order. At Yalta Roosevelt secured a Soviet promise to enter the war against Japan when Germany was defeated in return for territorial concessions in Asia. The allies also set new Polish borders, scheduled a conference in 1945 to establish the United Nations, and agreed to allow occupied countries to construct new governments based on free elections after the war. Many historians have criticized Roosevelt for being too trusting of Stalin, who established communist puppet states in Eastern Europe after the war.

Although the strain of the wartime presidency had weakened Roosevelt, he ran for a fourth term in 1944. In a fateful move he agreed to the suggestion of his political advisers to drop his third-term vice president Henry A. Wallace, who was considered too liberal. The Democrats nominated Sen. Harry S. Truman from Missouri for vice president in Wallace's place. Roosevelt defeated his fourth Republican opponent, New York governor Thomas E. Dewey, 432–99 in the electoral college.

In April 1945, after returning from Yalta, Roosevelt went to Warm Springs, Georgia, for a rest before the conference on the establishment of the United Nations scheduled for later in the month in San Francisco. On April 12, while sitting for a portrait at his cottage, Roosevelt suddenly collapsed from a cerebral hemorrhage and died a few hours later. The same day in Washington, Truman was sworn in as president. The world mourned the dead president as a train carried his body back to the capital, where it lay in state at the White House. The train then resumed its journey north to Roosevelt's Hyde Park home, where he was buried.

Roosevelt married Anna Eleanor Roosevelt, a fifth cousin, on March 17, 1905. Eleanor's mother and father died when she was a child, so she was given away at her wedding by her father's brother, President Theodore Roosevelt. The Roosevelts had one daughter and five sons, one of whom died in infancy. Eleanor is regarded as the most active first lady in history up to her time. Besides promoting numerous social causes, she served as her crippled husband's representative at many political and ceremonial functions. After the president's death Eleanor continued to fight for social causes. She died on November 7, 1962.

Harry S. Truman

Born: May 8, 1884; Lamar, Missouri
Party: Democratic
Term: April 12, 1945–January 20, 1953
Vice President: Alben W. Barkley
Died: December 26, 1972; Kansas City, Missouri
Buried: Independence, Missouri

Harry S. Truman was the oldest of three children born to Martha and John Truman, a mule trader. Harry's parents wanted to give him a middle name in honor of a grandfather but could not decide between his two grandfathers, Anderson Shippe Truman and Solomon Young. Consequently they gave him the middle initial "S," which stood for nothing.

After living in several towns in Missouri, the Trumans settled in Independence, near Kansas City. Harry's poor eyesight prevented him from joining in some outdoor activities as a boy. Instead he learned to play the piano and became a voracious reader. At the age of sixteen he had his first political experience when he worked as a page at the 1900 Democratic National Convention in Kansas City, which nominated William Jennings Bryan for president.

After graduating from high school Truman held a succession of jobs, including mail room clerk, bank teller, and bookkeeper. He wanted to go to college, but he and his family could not afford it. In 1906, when Truman was twenty-two, he took over the management of his grandmother's 600-acre farm in Grandview, Missouri. He succeeded at farming and became active in local politics and community organizations.

When the United States entered World War I, Truman received a commission as a first lieutenant. He served with distinction in the Vosges and Meuse-Argonne campaigns as commander of an artillery battery and attained the rank of major before leaving the service in 1919.

Political Career

Upon returning to Missouri, Truman opened a haberdashery in Kansas City with a war buddy. When the store failed in 1922 he ran for judge of the eastern district of Jackson County. He won the election with the support of the powerful Kansas City political boss Tom Pendergast. He failed in his bid for reelection two years later but was elected presiding judge of the court in 1926 and was reelected in 1930. These judgeships were administrative rather than judicial positions. Truman controlled hundreds of patronage jobs and millions of dollars' worth of public works projects.

Truman became well known in the Kansas City area. He retained his close connections to Pendergast and the Kansas City machine but also developed a reputation for honesty. Using his Kansas City political base, Truman launched a campaign for the U.S. Senate and was elected in 1934.

In the Senate Truman supported Franklin D. Roosevelt's New Deal legislation. Despite the conviction of Tom Pendergast for income tax evasion, Truman was reelected by a narrow margin in 1940. During his second term, Truman chaired the Special Committee to Investigate the National Defense Program, which sought to eliminate waste and inefficiency among defense contractors. He also supported Roosevelt's efforts to aid the allies before the entry of the United States into World War II.

In 1944 the Democratic Party was set to nominate President Franklin Roosevelt for his fourth term, but the vice-presidential nomination remained in doubt. Vice President Henry Wallace had alienated many Democratic Party leaders, who considered his political views too liberal. Robert Hannegan, national chairman of the Democratic Party, recommended to Roosevelt that Truman be nominated in place of Wallace, and the president agreed. Truman was nominated for vice president on the second ballot at the Democratic National Convention in Chicago. Roosevelt and Truman then defeated Republicans Thomas E. Dewey and John W. Bricker in the general election.

Presidency

Truman served just eighty-two days as vice president. On April 12, 1945, he was summoned to the White House and informed by First Lady Eleanor Roosevelt that the president was dead. Later in the day he took the oath of office at the White House from Chief Justice Harlan F. Stone.

World events forced Truman to become an expert in foreign affairs, an area of policy in which he had little experience before becoming president. Truman's first priority was winning World War II. On May 7 Germany surrendered unconditionally to the allies. In July 1945 Truman traveled to Potsdam, Germany, to discuss the composition of the postwar world with British prime minister Winston Churchill and Soviet premier Joseph Stalin. There the three leaders agreed to divide Germany and its capital, Berlin, into occupation zones.

While at Potsdam, Truman was informed that the United States had successfully tested an atomic bomb. He authorized atomic attacks on Japanese cities to hasten the end of the war. On August 6, 1945, an atomic bomb dropped from a U.S. warplane on Hiroshima killed eighty thousand people. Three days later, another bomb destroyed the city of Nagasaki. Truman's decision to use atomic weapons has been debated by many scholars and military analysts since World War II. Before the bombs were dropped, Japan had sent signals that it might surrender, but Truman believed a quick end of the war was necessary to avoid any need for an invasion of Japan that would cost many U.S. lives. On September 2 the Japanese officially surrendered, ending the war.

Despite U.S.-Soviet cooperation during the war, differences between the two nations developed into a cold war by 1946. The United States objected in particular to the Soviet Union's creation of communist governments in the eastern European states they had occupied while pushing the Nazi armies back into Germany. Truman vigorously protested Moscow's actions and resolved to contain further Soviet expansionism.

In March 1947 when Britain withdrew its assistance to Greek anticommunists for economic reasons, Truman proclaimed the Truman Doctrine and asked Congress for $400 million in economic and military aid to prevent Greece and Turkey from falling to communist insurgents. The Truman Doctrine declared that the United States would aid governments threatened by communist subversion. Later that year Truman and Secretary of State George Marshall asked Congress to expand foreign aid dramatically by approving the Marshall Plan, a multibillion-dollar program to rebuild the economies of western Europe. Congress gave its approval in 1948, and the Marshall Plan became one of the foremost successes of the Truman administration. Later in 1948 when the Soviets closed passage between western Germany and Berlin, which was located within the Soviet occupation zone, Truman used a massive airlift to supply the parts of the city administered by Britain, France, and the United States. The Soviets had hoped to force the United States and its western allies to give up control of their part of Berlin, but Truman's airlift broke the blockade and the Soviets backed down without a military confrontation.

In domestic policy, Truman developed a plan to extend Franklin Roosevelt's New Deal, which the new president called the "Fair Deal." Republicans and conservative Democrats in Congress, however, blocked many of his proposals. He also unsuccessfully backed progressive civil rights legislation. In 1947 Congress overrode Truman's veto of the Taft-Hartley Act, which he claimed unfairly weakened the bargaining power of unions. Five years later he seized and operated steel mills shut down by a strike during the Korean War, a move that the Supreme Court declared unconstitutional. Truman battled postwar inflation with the modest tools at his disposal, but Congress rejected his proposals for more sweeping price-control legislation, and inflation continued to be the most troublesome domestic problem during Truman's years in office.

In 1948 Truman ran for reelection against Thomas E. Dewey. Truman's reelection chances appeared slim when ultraliberal Democrats nominated Henry Wallace for president, and southern Democrats who disliked Truman's strong civil rights

platform formed the "Dixiecrat" Party and nominated Sen. Strom Thurmond of South Carolina. During the campaign public opinion polls indicated that Dewey would win. Truman, however, used a cross-country, whistle-stop campaign to take his message to the people and won a surprise victory, defeating Dewey 303–189 in the electoral college.

Truman's second term was dominated by the Korean War. On June 24, 1950, troops from communist North Korea invaded South Korea. Truman sent U.S. troops to Korea under the auspices of the United Nations. UN forces pushed the North Koreans out of South Korea and drove into North Korea in an attempt to unify the country. Communist China entered the war on the side of the North Koreans in late 1950, however, and pushed UN forces back into South Korea. Eventually the war became deadlocked near the thirty-eighth parallel that had divided the two Koreas before the start of the war. Truman was unable to attain a negotiated peace during his presidency.

In 1951 Truman fired Gen. Douglas MacArthur, commander of UN forces in Korea, for insubordination. MacArthur had criticized the Truman administration's conduct of the war, publicly advocated a provocative invasion of China, interfered with Truman's diplomatic gestures, and disobeyed orders. Nevertheless, MacArthur enjoyed a large following in Congress and among the American public, and Truman's popularity sank after he fired the general.

During Truman's years in office the country became consumed with paranoia over communist subversion. Sen. Joseph R. McCarthy, R-Wis., led a group in Congress who claimed that communist agents had infiltrated the U.S. government, especially the State Department. McCarthy pointed to the failure of the United States to stop the communist revolution in China in 1949 as evidence of the communist sympathies of key U.S. officials. Truman denounced McCarthy but was unable to rally public support against the senator, despite the lack of evidence backing up McCarthy's accusations. After Truman left office, McCarthy became chairman of a Senate investigative subcommittee and accused many citizens of procommunist activities before being censured by the Senate in 1954.

From November 1948 until March 1952 the Trumans lived in Blair House, across Pennsylvania Avenue from the White House, while the executive mansion was being renovated. On November 1, 1950, Harry Truman became the first incumbent president to be the target of an assassination attempt since William McKinley was killed in 1901. Two Puerto Rican nationalists, Griselio Torresola and Oscar Collazo, attacked Blair House with automatic weapons, hoping to fight their way inside to kill the president. Although Truman was not harmed, one Secret Service agent and one of the assassins were killed.

On March 29, 1952, Truman announced that he would not run for reelection in the fall. After leaving office he returned to his home in Independence, Missouri. Truman remained active during his retirement, delivering lectures, commenting on political developments, and overseeing construction of the Truman Library near his home. He published his two-volume memoirs in 1955 and 1956. He died at age eighty-eight in 1972.

Truman married Elizabeth (Bess) Wallace, whom he had known since his boyhood, on June 28, 1919. The couple had one child, Margaret, who was born in 1924. Margaret attended George Washington University and launched a singing career during her father's presidency.

Dwight D. Eisenhower

Born: October 14, 1890; Denison, Texas
Party: Republican
Term: January 20, 1953–January 20, 1961
Vice President: Richard Nixon

Died: March 28, 1969; Washington, D.C.
Buried: Abilene, Kansas

Dwight David Eisenhower was the third of the seven sons of David and Ida Eisenhower. One of Dwight's younger brothers died in infancy. Dwight was born in Texas, but his family lived there for only a short period. When Dwight was a baby, they returned to Kansas, where they had lived before he was born. Settling in Abilene, David Eisenhower got a job as a mechanic in a creamery. Dwight attended public schools and worked in the creamery after classes. At the age of fourteen, he developed blood poisoning from a severely skinned knee. Dwight's doctor wanted-ed to amputate the leg, warning the Eisenhowers that failure to do so could cost Dwight his life. Despite the risk, the boy refused to let the doctor amputate his leg, and he recovered from the blood poisoning.

Eisenhower lacked the money to attend college, so he worked in the creamery full time upon graduation from high school. After a year, he applied for admission to both the Naval Academy and the Military Academy. He was rejected by Annapolis because he was too old, but he was nominated to West Point. He played football and was an above-average student, graduating sixty-fifth in his class of 164 in 1915.

Military Career

When the United States entered World War I in 1917, Eisenhower served as a troop instructor at several bases in the United States. After the war his assignments included a two-year posting in Panama. In 1925 Eisenhower received an appointment to the Army General Staff School in Leavenworth, Kansas. He graduated in 1926 first in his class of 275, an accomplishment that greatly contributed to his advancement through the ranks. He attended the Army War College in Washington, D.C., in 1928 and then served on the staff of the assistant secretary of war until 1932, when he was appointed as an aide to army chief of staff Gen. Douglas MacArthur. When MacArthur went to the Philippines in 1934 to organize a Filipino army, Eisenhower, by this time a major, accompanied him as a staff officer. While in the Philippines he received his pilot's license.

Eisenhower returned to the United States in early 1940 as a lieutenant colonel. During the next three years he would be promoted above hundreds of senior officers on his way to becoming a full general. When the United States entered World War II in 1941, he was a brigadier general serving as chief of staff of the Third Army in San Antonio, Texas. In February 1942 he was called to Washington, D.C., where he took command of the War Plans Division of the War Department's general staff. In this post he helped draft global strategy and a preliminary plan for the invasion of France from Britain. Eisenhower's skill as a tactician and his reputation as a soldier who could unify military leaders holding diverse

points of view led to his appointment in June 1942 as the commanding general of the European Theater of Operations.

In November 1942 Eisenhower directed the successful Allied invasion of North Africa. In 1943 he attained the rank of full general and commanded the Allied invasions of Sicily and Italy. In December 1943 President Roosevelt named Eisenhower supreme commander of all Allied forces in Europe and instructed him to develop a plan for an invasion of France. On June 6, 1944, the forces under Eisenhower's command landed in Normandy in the largest amphibious invasion ever undertaken. The troops gained a beachhead and began driving toward Germany. Eisenhower accepted the surrender of the German army on May 7, 1945.

When the war was over, Eisenhower was one of America's most prominent war heroes. Although he lacked the dramatic presence of Douglas MacArthur, who had commanded U.S. forces in the Pacific during the war, Eisenhower was praised for his ability to rally his troops and his diplomacy with the Allied leaders. After serving as commander of the U.S. occupation zone in Germany, Eisenhower was appointed army chief of staff in November 1945. In 1948 he retired from the military to become president of Columbia University. That year he was approached by both the Democrats and the Republicans as a possible presidential candidate. In 1945 President Harry S. Truman had told Eisenhower that he would support Eisenhower if the general wanted to run for president as a Democrat in 1948. Eisenhower, however, declined all offers to run for office and maintained his political neutrality.

In 1950 President Truman asked Eisenhower to return to active service to become supreme commander of the North Atlantic Treaty Organization (NATO) forces in Europe. During his time in Europe, Eisenhower was again courted by both major political parties. Finally in January 1952 he announced that he would accept the Republican nomination for president if it were offered. He resigned his NATO command in May and was nominated by the Republicans on the first ballot at their national convention in Chicago in July.

Eisenhower's opponent was Gov. Adlai E. Stevenson II of Illinois. Eisenhower avoided detailed discussions of his political positions and relied primarily on his outgoing personality and his popularity as a war hero to win votes. He won a landslide popular vote victory and defeated Stevenson 442–89 in the electoral college.

Presidency

When Eisenhower became president in 1953 a Korean War settlement was within reach. In December 1952, after the election, he had fulfilled a campaign promise to go to Korea to survey the situation. On July 27, 1953, an armistice was signed ending the war.

Although superpower tensions eased somewhat with the death of Soviet leader Joseph Stalin in March 1953 and the Korean War settlement, the cold war continued. Eisenhower endorsed Harry Truman's policy of containing communist expansion but sought to avoid conflict when possible. In 1954 he refused to aid the French garrison surrounded at Dien Bien Phu, Vietnam, by Vietnamese nationalists, who eventually drove the French out of Indochina, and he protested the attack on Egypt by Great Britain, France, and Israel in 1956 over Egypt's nationalization of the Suez Canal. Following the Suez crisis, Eisenhower announced the Eisenhower Doctrine, a commitment by the United States to use force to stop international communist aggression in the Middle East. In accordance with this doctrine, he sent U.S. troops to Lebanon in 1958 when the Lebanese government requested assistance fighting insurgents.

On September 24, 1955, Eisenhower suffered a heart attack that limited his activity for several months. The following June he underwent an operation for an attack of ileitis, an inflammation of the small intestine. Eisenhower's illnesses raised questions about his fitness for a second term. In November 1956, however, the voters reelected him over Democrat Adlai Stevenson by an even larger margin than he had enjoyed in 1952. President Eisenhower was confined to bed a third time in 1957 after suffering a stroke. His periods of disability fueled efforts to develop a procedure for transferring power to the vice president when the president was incapacitated by illness. Such a procedure was established by the Twenty-fifth Amendment, ratified in 1967.

In domestic policy Eisenhower favored antiinflation policies over measures to stimulate economic growth. He produced budget surpluses in three of the eight years of his presidency, an accomplishment that became all the more noteworthy in the three decades after his retirement, when the federal budget was balanced only once. He also warned of the dangers of the development of a "militaryindustrial complex" and sought to limit defense spending. He signed bills that compensated farmers for taking land out of production and that initiated the national interstate highway system. Although he was not a leading opponent of racial segregation, he enforced existing civil rights laws. In 1957 he sent federal troops to Little Rock, Arkansas, when local citizens and state officials tried to block integration of public schools.

Eisenhower held several summits with Soviet leaders in attempting to improve U.S.-Soviet relations. He met with Soviet premier Nikolai Bulganin and Allied leaders in 1955 at Geneva and with Soviet first secretary Nikita Khrushchev in 1959 at Camp David, Maryland. Eisenhower's plans for a 1960 summit, however, were soured when the Soviets shot down an American U2 reconnaissance plane over the Soviet Union on May 1 of that year. Khrushchev protested the U2 overflights and refused to attend a summit in Paris with Allied leaders later that month. Eisenhower took full responsibility for the missions and defended them as vital to the security of the United States.

Eisenhower left office at the age of seventy, the oldest person to serve as president up to that time. He retired to his 230-acre farm near Gettysburg, Pennsylvania, where he enjoyed a quiet retirement. He indulged his love for golf, scoring a hole in one in February 1968, and wrote his memoirs, which were published in two volumes in 1965 and 1966. In November 1965 he suffered two heart attacks but recovered. During the spring and summer of 1968 he had a series of heart attacks that confined him to a hospital. He died in March 1969 from a heart attack, two months after his former vice president, Richard Nixon, was elected president.

Eisenhower married Marie "Mamie" Doud on July 1, 1916. Eisenhower met Mamie, the daughter of a wealthy Denver businessman, shortly after his graduation from West Point. They had two sons, but their first, Doud, died when he was three. Their second son, John Sheldon Eisenhower, was the father of David Eisenhower, who married President Richard Nixon's daughter Julie in 1968. Dwight Eisenhower's youngest brother, Milton, was president of three universities, chaired several government committees, and advised every president from Calvin Coolidge to Richard Nixon.

John F. Kennedy

Born: May 29, 1917; Brookline, Massachusetts
Party: Democratic
Term: January 20, 1961–November 22, 1963
Vice President: Lyndon B. Johnson
Died: November 22, 1963; Dallas, Texas
Buried: Arlington, Virginia

John Fitzgerald Kennedy was the second of the nine children of Joseph and Rose Kennedy. John's moth-

er was the daughter of a former mayor of Boston. His father was a millionaire who had made his fortune in banking, real estate, and other financial ventures. In 1937 Franklin D. Roosevelt appointed Joseph Kennedy ambassador to Great Britain, a position he resigned in December 1940 when he became pessimistic about Britain's chances for survival during World War II. He returned to the United States, where his advocacy of isolationism caused a falling out with Roosevelt, who did not appoint him to another post.

John graduated in the middle of his class from Choate, a preparatory school in Wallingford, Connecticut. After attending the London School of Economics during the summer of 1935, he enrolled at Princeton University, but an illness forced him to withdraw after two months. In 1936 he entered Harvard University, where he studied economics and political science. Kennedy was an average student, but his grades improved dramatically at the end of his college career, and he graduated with honors in 1940. *Why England Slept,* his senior thesis published in book form, was an examination of British appeasement of fascism before World War II.

In 1941 Kennedy tried to enter the army, but he was rejected because of a bad back caused by a football injury. He strengthened his back through exercise and passed the navy's physical later that year. He received a commission as an ensign in October 1941. After attending PT (patrol torpedo) boat training, he was given command of a PT boat in the South Pacific in April 1943. On August 2, 1943, his boat, PT109, was rammed and sunk by a Japanese destroyer. Eleven of his thirteen crew members survived, and he led them on a four-hour swim to a nearby island. During the swim he towed an injured crew member by a life preserver strap. Kennedy and his crew were rescued after friendly natives took a message carved on a coconut to nearby Allied personnel. After the ordeal Kennedy was sent back to the United States, where he was hospitalized for malaria. In 1944 he underwent a disc operation and was discharged the following year.

Kennedy worked briefly as a reporter for the International News Service, then decided to run for Congress from his Massachusetts district. He was elected in 1946 and served three terms before being elected to the Senate in 1952. In 1954 and 1955 he underwent two more operations for his chronic back condition. While convalescing, Kennedy wrote *Profiles in Courage,* a book about senators who had demonstrated courage during their careers. The book became a bestseller and earned Kennedy the 1957 Pulitzer Prize for biography.

In 1956 Kennedy tried to secure the Democratic vice-presidential nomination on the ticket with Adlai Stevenson. After leading on the second ballot at the Democratic National Convention in Chicago, Kennedy lost the nomination to Sen. Estes Kefauver of Tennessee. Despite this defeat Kennedy's political reputation continued to grow. In 1957 he

was assigned to the Senate Foreign Relations Committee, where he gained foreign policy experience. In 1958 he won reelection to the Senate by a record margin in Massachusetts.

By 1960 Kennedy was the leading candidate for the Democratic presidential nomination. His rivals for the nomination were Senate Majority Leader Lyndon Johnson of Texas, Sen. Stuart Symington of Missouri, Sen. Hubert H. Humphrey of Minnesota, and former Democratic presidential candidate Adlai Stevenson. Kennedy prevailed on the first ballot at the Democratic National Convention in Los Angeles in July 1960 and convinced Lyndon Johnson, who had finished second, to be his running mate.

Kennedy's opponent was Vice President Richard Nixon. Kennedy and Nixon engaged in a series of four televised debates, the first in presidential election history. Out of almost 69 million votes cast, Kennedy received only 120,000 more than Nixon. Kennedy won in the electoral college 303–219.

Kennedy was the youngest person ever to be elected president, although Theodore Roosevelt was younger than Kennedy when he succeeded to the presidency after the death of William McKinley. Kennedy's youth, idealism, and attractive family would make him one of the most popular presidents of the twentieth century. His administration came to be known as "Camelot" because of its romantic image.

Soon after entering office Kennedy endorsed a CIA plan developed during the Eisenhower presidency to arm, train, and land 1,400 Cuban exiles in Cuba in an attempt to overthrow the communist regime of Fidel Castro. The April 17, 1961, operation, which came to be known as the Bay of Pigs invasion, was a complete failure as twelve hundred of the Cuban exiles were captured. The president accepted full responsibility for the blunder.

Cuba had been the site of Kennedy's greatest foreign policy failure, but it was also the place of his most memorable foreign policy success. In October

1962 Kennedy was informed that aerial reconnaissance photography proved conclusively that the Soviets were building offensive missile bases in Cuba. Kennedy believed Soviet missiles in Cuba would seriously diminish U.S. national security and increase the chances that the Soviets would try to blackmail the United States into concessions in other parts of the world. The president demanded that the bases be dismantled, but he rejected the option of an air strike against the sites in favor of a naval blockade of the island. The confrontation brought the United States and Soviet Union to the brink of nuclear war, but the Soviets ultimately backed down and agreed to remove the missiles.

Tensions decreased following the Cuban Missile Crisis, but the incident spurred the Soviets to undertake a military buildup that enabled them to achieve nuclear parity with the United States by the late 1960s. In 1963 Kennedy concluded an important arms control treaty with Britain, France, and the Soviet Union that banned nuclear tests in the atmosphere, in outer space, and under water.

Outside of superpower relations, Kennedy increased U.S. involvement in the developing world. In 1961 he established the Peace Corps, an agency that sent skilled volunteers overseas to assist people of underdeveloped countries. He also initiated the Alliance for Progress, an aid program aimed at developing the resources of Latin America.

In domestic policy, Kennedy made substantial progress in furthering the cause of civil rights. He advocated school desegregation, established a program to encourage registration of African American voters, issued rules against discrimination in public housing built with federal funds, and appointed an unprecedented number of blacks to public office. Kennedy used federal troops several times to maintain order and enforce the law in the South during the civil rights movement. He sent federal troops and officials to oversee the integration of the University of Mississippi in 1962 and the University of

Alabama in 1963. That year he proposed sweeping civil rights legislation, but it did not come to a vote during his lifetime.

Kennedy also tried unsuccessfully to convince Congress to cut taxes. The president's advisers convinced him that a tax cut would stimulate the economy and bring growth without large budget deficits or inflation. After Kennedy's death, President Lyndon Johnson was able to secure passage of the Kennedy tax cut and civil rights legislation.

During the fall of 1963 Kennedy made several trips around the country to build political support for his reelection bid the following year. In late November he scheduled a trip to Texas. While riding through Dallas in an open car on November 22, Kennedy was shot once in the head and once in the neck. He died at a nearby hospital without regaining consciousness. Vice President Lyndon Johnson was sworn in as president that afternoon.

Police quickly apprehended the alleged assassin, Lee Harvey Oswald, a former marine who had once renounced his U.S. citizenship and lived in the Soviet Union. Initial investigations concluded that Oswald had shot Kennedy with a rifle from a sixth-story window of the Texas School Book Depository building. Three days after the shooting, Oswald was murdered in front of millions of television viewers by Jack Ruby, owner of a Dallas nightclub. The Warren Commission, a seven-member panel appointed by President Johnson to investigate the assassination, determined that Oswald acted alone. But Oswald's violent death, his unknown motivation, the difficulty of a single marksman firing several accurate shots so quickly, and other peculiarities surrounding the assassination have fostered speculation that Oswald may have been part of a conspiracy.

Kennedy married Jacqueline Lee Bouvier on September 12, 1953. They had three children, but their youngest son, who had been born several weeks prematurely, died of a respiratory ailment two days after birth on August 9, 1963. Kennedy's children, Caroline and John Jr., the first young children of a president living in the White House since the Theodore Roosevelt administration, were favorite subjects of the news media. Kennedy's widow, Jacqueline, married Greek shipping millionaire Aristotle Onassis on October 29, 1968. She died May 19, 1994, at age sixty-four and was buried beside President Kennedy at Arlington National Cemetery. John F. Kennedy Jr. (or "John-John") died on July 16, 1999, when the plane he was piloting crashed into the sea off the Massachusetts coast. His wife and her sister perished with him.

Lyndon B. Johnson

Born: August 27, 1908; Stonewall, Texas
Party: Democratic
Term: November 22, 1963–January 20, 1969
Vice President: Hubert H. Humphrey
Died: January 22, 1973; San Antonio, Texas
Buried: Johnson City, Texas

Lyndon Baines Johnson was the oldest of the five children of Sam and Rebekah Johnson. Lyndon's father and mother were school teachers. His father and both his grandfathers had served in the Texas state legislature. At age five Lyndon moved with his family from Stonewall, Texas, to nearby Johnson City, a small town named for his grandfather. After graduating from high school in 1924, Lyndon traveled to California with a group of friends. He supported himself by working odd jobs, but after a year he hitchhiked his way back to Texas.

Johnson worked on a road gang for a year, then enrolled in Southwest Texas State Teachers College in San Marcos in 1927. He graduated in 1930 and taught high school in Houston for a year before Richard Kleberg, a newly elected member of the U.S. House of Representatives, asked Johnson to

come to Washington, D.C., as an aide. Johnson worked for Kleberg from 1931 until 1935. During this period he learned firsthand about the legislative process and became an ardent supporter of President Franklin D. Roosevelt's New Deal policies. Johnson also studied law at Georgetown University during the 1934–1935 school year. He gave up his law studies and his job with Kleberg, however, when Roosevelt appointed him Texas director of the National Youth Administration in 1935. This program sought to help the nation's unemployed youth find employment and go to school.

In 1937 Johnson suddenly was given the opportunity to run for Congress when James P. Buchanan, the House member from Johnson's Texas district, died. Johnson entered the special election held to fill his seat and beat several candidates by campaigning on a pro-Roosevelt platform.

Johnson won reelection to the House in 1938 and 1940 but was narrowly defeated when he ran for a Senate seat in 1941. After the Japanese attacked Pearl Harbor, Johnson was the first House member to volunteer for active duty in the armed forces. He was commissioned as a lieutenant commander in the navy and sent to the South Pacific, where he undertook a fact-finding mission of the Australian combat zone. Johnson's service was short, however, because in July 1942 President Roosevelt ordered all members of Congress to leave the military and return to Washington.

Johnson served in the House until January 1949, when he took the Senate seat he had won the previous November. After just four years his Democratic colleagues elected him minority leader. In January 1955 he was elected majority leader when the Democrats took control of the Senate. Johnson suffered a severe heart attack in July 1955 but recovered fully. During his six years as majority leader, Johnson became known as one of the most skilled legislative leaders in congressional history. His ability to use flattery, coercion, and compromise to get legislation passed was a valuable asset when he became president.

Johnson ran for president in 1960, but he was defeated for the Democratic nomination by Sen. John F. Kennedy of Massachusetts. Kennedy offered the vice presidency to Johnson, however, and the majority leader accepted. Kennedy and Johnson defeated Republicans Richard Nixon and Henry Cabot Lodge in a close election. Many political observers believed Kennedy might not have won without Johnson on the ticket. Johnson's presence was valuable in helping Kennedy win five southern states, including Texas.

Although Johnson was not an insider in the Kennedy administration, he undertook many diplomatic missions, and the president frequently sought his advice, especially on legislative matters. When Kennedy was shot while he rode in a motorcade through Dallas, Johnson was riding in a car behind the president. He followed the president's car to a hospital, where Kennedy was pronounced dead. Johnson then proceeded to the Dallas airport and boarded *Air Force One*. He decided to take the oath of office immediately, rather than wait until he returned to Washington. While the plane sat on the runway, federal Judge Sarah T. Hughes administered the oath of office to Johnson, who became the thirty-sixth president.

In the days following the assassination, Johnson declared his intention to carry out Kennedy's programs and asked Kennedy's cabinet to remain. Johnson, recognizing that public sentiment for the slain president improved his chances of enacting Kennedy's legislative program, vigorously lobbied Congress to pass a civil rights bill and a tax cut. Congress passed both bills in 1964. The tax cut succeeded in stimulating the economy, and the Civil Rights Act of 1964 protected black voting rights, established the Equal Employment Opportunity Commission, and forbade discrimination on account of race or sex by employers, places of public accommodation, and labor unions.

In 1964 Johnson ran for a presidential term of his own against Republican Sen. Barry Goldwater of Arizona. Many Americans were apprehensive that Goldwater's conservative positions were too extreme. Johnson outpolled Goldwater by more than 15 million votes and defeated him 486–52 in the electoral college.

Johnson regarded his landslide victory as a mandate to enact the "Great Society" social programs that he had outlined in his campaign. Johnson's Great Society was a comprehensive plan designed to fight poverty, ignorance, disease, and other social problems. During his second term he guided numerous bills through Congress establishing federal programs that provided expanded aid for medical care, housing, welfare, education, and urban renewal. Although Johnson had hoped that his administration would be able to concentrate on his Great Society programs, the involvement of the United States in Southeast

Asia soon came to dominate his presidency. The government in North Vietnam and guerrillas in South Vietnam were attempting to unify the country under communist rule by defeating the South Vietnamese regime militarily. Since Vietnam had been split into North and South Vietnam in 1954, the United States had supported the South with weapons, U.S. military advisers, and economic aid. In 1965 Johnson increased the U.S. commitment by sending American combat troops to South Vietnam.

Johnson continued to escalate U.S. involvement in the war in response to communist provocations and the inability of the South Vietnamese government to defend its country. The growing war diverted attention and dollars away from Johnson's domestic programs. Although many citizens supported the war, by 1966 college campuses had erupted in protest against it. Johnson hoped that each increase in U.S. troop strength and expansion of bombing targets would produce a breakthrough on the battlefield that would lead to a negotiated settlement preserving the independence and security of South Vietnam, but the communists refused to give up their goal of reunification.

By early 1968 public opinion had swung decisively against the war and Johnson. He recognized that there was a good chance that he might not be renominated for president by his party. Sen. Eugene J. McCarthy of Minnesota and Sen. Robert F. Kennedy of New York, the late president's brother, were running for the Democratic presidential nomination on antiwar platforms and were receiving substantial support. On March 31, 1968, Johnson delivered a television address in which he announced a partial halt to U.S. air attacks on North Vietnam to emphasize the U.S. desire for peace. He then stunned the nation by saying that he would not seek or accept the Democratic nomination for president.

After leaving Washington in 1969, Johnson retired to his ranch near Johnson City, Texas. He wrote a book about his presidential years, *The Van-*

tage Point, which was published in 1971. On January 22, 1973, Johnson was stricken by a heart attack at his ranch and was pronounced dead on arrival at Brooke Army Medical Center in San Antonio.

Johnson married Claudia Alta Taylor, the daughter of a storekeeper and rancher, on November 17, 1934. During her tenure as first lady, Mrs. Johnson championed efforts to beautify America. Johnson and his wife, who was known as "Lady Bird," had two daughters, Lynda and Luci. Lynda married Charles Robb, who would later serve as governor of and then senator from Virginia.

Richard Nixon

Born: January 9, 1913; Yorba Linda, California
Party: Republican
Term: January 20, 1969–August 9, 1974
Vice Presidents: Spiro T. Agnew; Gerald R. Ford
Died: April 22, 1994; New York City
Buried: Yorba Linda, California

Richard Milhous Nixon was the second of the five sons of Hannah and Francis Nixon, a lemon farmer. When Richard was nine he moved with his family from Yorba Linda to Whittier, California. There his father managed a combination gas station and general store, and Richard and his brothers attended public schools. Nixon entered Whittier College in 1930.

While at Whittier he played football, participated on the debate team, and was elected president of the student body. He graduated second in his class in 1934 with a degree in history. His academic excellence earned him a tuition scholarship to Duke University law school in Durham, North Carolina. In 1937 he graduated third in his class. He returned to California and joined the law firm of Wingert and Bewley in Whittier, eventually becoming a partner.

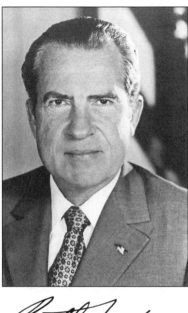

When the United States entered World War II in 1941 Nixon quit the law firm and went to Washington, D.C., to help the war effort. He worked briefly as a lawyer in the Office of Price Administration before applying for a navy commission. He was given the rank of lieutenant (junior grade) and assigned to a navy air transport unit. He served for over a year in the Pacific before being reassigned to the states in 1944. Before leaving active duty in 1946, he had attained the rank of lieutenant commander.

Political Career

In 1945 Nixon was persuaded by a California Republican committee to run for Congress. He faced Democratic House member Jerry Voorhis, who had represented his California district for ten years. In a series of debates Nixon put Voorhis on the defensive by accusing him of being a socialist. Nixon won the election and was reelected in 1948.

In the House Nixon gained a national reputation as an anticommunist crusader. In 1948 he was appointed chairman of a subcommittee of the House Committee on Un-American Activities. His subcommittee investigated charges that several government employees were communists, including Alger Hiss, a former State Department official. In testimony, Hiss denied that he was a communist. President Harry Truman and other top officials, including some Republicans, denounced the hearings. But Nixon pressed the investigation and found discrepancies that led to Hiss's conviction for perjury.

Nixon won a Senate seat in 1950. Democrats accused him of employing dirty campaign tactics, but his aggressive campaigning and his huge margin of victory impressed many Republican leaders. He became an early supporter of Gen. Dwight D. Eisenhower for the 1952 Republican presidential nomination and was chosen as the party's vice-presidential candidate when Eisenhower was nominated.

In September 1952, however, Nixon's vice-presidential candidacy was jeopardized by a *New York Post* story that accused him of using secret funds provided by California business interests for personal expenses. Eisenhower refused to dismiss his running mate but said that Nixon would have to prove that he was "as clean as a hound's tooth." In an emotional televised speech on September 23 viewed by sixty million people, Nixon denied any wrongdoing and said he and his family lived simple lives without the benefit of many luxuries. The address became known as the "Checkers Speech" because, after admitting that he had accepted the gift of a dog his daughter had named "Checkers," he asserted that he would not give it back. The address brought an outpouring of support from the American people and saved Nixon's candidacy.

Dwight Eisenhower's status as a war hero and his pledge to find a settlement to the Korean War brought victory to the Republican ticket. Four years later Nixon was renominated for vice president, despite a "dump Nixon" movement started by several Republican leaders, and was reelected with President Eisenhower. As vice president, Nixon was more visible than many of his predecessors. He chaired several domestic policy committees and made numerous trips overseas, including a 1958 goodwill tour of Latin America and a 1959 diplomatic visit to Moscow, where he engaged in a famous spontaneous debate with Soviet premier Nikita Khrushchev on the merits of capitalism and communism.

Nixon ran for president in 1960 and received the Republican nomination. He and his Democratic opponent, Sen. John F. Kennedy of Massachusetts, engaged in the first televised presidential debates in history. Nixon is considered to have lost the important first debate to Kennedy because he appeared pale and tired on camera. Kennedy defeated Nixon by a slim 120,000-vote margin but won 303–219 in the electoral college.

After the defeat, Nixon returned to California to practice law. In 1962 he ran for governor but lost to Edmund G. Brown. Following the election he told reporters that they would not "have Richard Nixon to kick around anymore."

In 1963 he moved to New York City, where he joined a law firm. Nixon's political ambitions remained alive, however, and he continued to give speeches on foreign policy. He campaigned for Republican candidates in 1966 and maneuvered for the 1968 Republican presidential nomination. At the Republican National Convention in Miami in 1968 he was nominated for president on the first ballot. Nixon promised to end the war in Vietnam and combat rising inflation. In an election that was almost as close as his 1960 loss, Nixon defeated his Democratic opponent, Vice President Hubert H. Humphrey, 301–191 in the electoral college.

Presidency

Nixon's first priority as president was achieving "peace with honor" in Vietnam. He proposed a plan to "Vietnamize" the war by providing the South Vietnamese military with upgraded training and weaponry, while slowly withdrawing U.S. troops from Indochina. Nixon believed that the South Vietnamese armed forces could be built into a force capable of defending their country from North Vietnamese aggression. While this slow withdrawal was taking place, Nixon ordered several controversial military operations, including an invasion of Cambodia in 1970, that increased domestic protests against the war. Nevertheless, the majority of Americans supported Nixon's slow withdrawal. During this period, Nixon's national security adviser, Henry Kissinger, conducted negotiations with the North Vietnamese on ending the war. In January 1973 the Nixon administration finally concluded an agreement that ended direct U.S. participation in the Vietnam War and provided for an exchange of prisoners. Nixon secretly promised South Vietnamese president Nguyen Van Thieu that the United States would not allow his regime to be overthrown by the communists. These commitments would not be met. The communists conquered the South in 1975 after Nixon had left office and Congress had placed strict limitations on U.S. military activities in Southeast Asia.

The most notable successes of the Nixon administration came in relations with China and the Soviet Union. In 1972 he became the first American president to travel to communist China. His summit meeting with Chinese leaders signaled a new beginning for U.S.–Chinese relations, which had been hostile since the communists came to power in 1949. In 1972 Nixon also became the first incumbent president to travel to Moscow. His summit with Soviet leader Leonid Brezhnev was the result of a relaxation of tensions between the superpowers known as détente. Brezhnev and Nixon signed agreements limiting nuclear weapons and antiballistic-missile systems at the Moscow summit. The Soviet leader returned Nixon's visit in June 1973, when he came to Washington, D.C., for a summit meeting.

Nixon's most significant domestic policy action was his imposition of wage and price controls on August 15, 1971. Nixon took this drastic measure to combat rising inflation that he thought might threaten his reelection chances in 1972. The controls initially slowed inflation, but their removal late in Nixon's presidency, combined with a jump in the price of oil caused by an Arab oil embargo, led to sharp increases in inflation. Prices rose 6.2 percent in 1973 and 11.0 percent in 1974.

The 1971 wage and price controls allowed Nixon to stimulate the economy in 1972 without fear that inflation would skyrocket. With unemployment falling, peace at hand in Vietnam, and the memory of Nixon's dramatic 1972 trips to China and the Soviet Union fresh in the minds of voters, the president was reelected in a landslide. Democratic challenger Sen. George McGovern of South Dakota won only Massachusetts and the District of Columbia.

Despite Nixon's overwhelming election victory, his second term soon became consumed by the Watergate scandal. On June 17, 1972, during the presidential campaign, five men with ties to the Committee for the Reelection of the President were arrested while breaking into the Democratic National Committee headquarters in the Watergate Hotel complex in Washington, D.C. Investigations of the burglary and the White House's attempt to cover up its connections to the burglars led to disclosure of numerous crimes and improprieties committed by members of the Nixon administration. Several top Nixon officials, including former attorney general John N. Mitchell, chief of staff H. R. Haldeman, and chief domestic adviser John D. Ehrlichman, were indicted. Nixon claimed he was innocent of any wrongdoing, but evidence showed that he had participated in the coverup of illegal administration activities. In July 1974 the House Judiciary Committee recommended to the full House that Nixon be impeached for obstruction of justice, abuse of presidential powers, and contempt of Congress.

On August 9, 1974, Richard Nixon became the first president ever to resign from office. Vice President Gerald R. Ford became president. Nixon had chosen Ford to replace his first vice president, Spiro T. Agnew, who had resigned in 1973 because of a scandal unrelated to Watergate. Nixon did not have to face criminal proceedings, however, because on September 8 President Ford granted him a "full, free, and absolute pardon."

After leaving the presidency Nixon wrote extensively about his time in office and world affairs. Although he remained tainted by the Watergate scandal, he came to be regarded as an elder statesman by many Americans because of his successes in foreign policy. Presidents of both parties and other officials often asked his advice on dealing with the Soviets and other matters. Nixon died April 22, 1994, at age eighty-one.

Nixon married Thelma Catherine "Pat" Ryan, a high school typing teacher, on June 21, 1940. Nixon met her while acting in an amateur theater group in Whittier. The couple had two daughters, Patricia and Julie. Patricia married Edward Cox in a White House Rose Garden wedding in 1971. Julie married David Eisenhower, the grandson of President Dwight D. Eisenhower. Pat Nixon died June 22, 1993, at age eighty-one.

Gerald R. Ford

Born: July 14, 1913; Omaha, Nebraska
Party: Republican
Term: August 9, 1974–January 20, 1977
Vice President: Nelson A. Rockefeller

Gerald Rudolph Ford was the only child of Dorothy and Leslie King, a wool trader. Ford was originally named Leslie Lynch King Jr., but his parents divorced when he was two, and his mother moved him to her family home in Grand Rapids, Michigan, where she married Gerald R. Ford in 1916. Ford, a paint sales-

Gerald R. Ford

man, adopted young Leslie, who was renamed Gerald Rudolph Ford Jr. Dorothy and Gerald Sr. had three sons in addition to Gerald Jr.

Young Gerald attended public schools in Grand Rapids and became a star football player in high school. He worked in his stepfather's small paint factory and in a restaurant while growing up.

In 1931 Ford enrolled in the University of Michigan. There he studied economics and political science and played center on the football team. Ford played on two national championship teams while at Michigan and was named his team's most valuable player in 1934. He graduated in 1935 with a B average. Several professional football teams wanted Ford to play for them, but he turned down the offers to become Yale University's boxing coach and an assistant on the football coaching staff. In 1938 he was admitted to Yale's law school. He continued to coach to support himself and finished his law degree in 1941.

Ford practiced law in Grand Rapids for less than a year before joining the navy early in 1942. He was commissioned as an ensign and assigned as a physical education instructor in North Carolina. Ford requested sea duty in 1943 and was transferred to the Pacific, where he became a gunnery officer on the light aircraft carrier *Monterey*. He fought in several major naval battles and achieved the rank of lieutenant commander by the end of the war.

Political Career

Ford returned to his Grand Rapids law practice in late 1945. He became involved in local politics and decided to run for the U.S. House of Representatives in 1948. With the support of Michigan's powerful Republican senator, Arthur H. Vandenberg, Ford defeated an isolationist Republican incumbent, Bartel Jonkman, in the primary. Ford's district was solidly Republican, so he had little trouble defeating the Democratic candidate in the general election.

Ford won thirteen consecutive terms in the House, always with at least 60 percent of the vote. He turned down an opportunity to run for the Senate in 1952 because he wished to continue in the House where he was building seniority. Ford rose gradually to leadership positions among House Republicans. In 1963 he became chairman of the House Republican Conference, and in 1964 President Lyndon B. Johnson appointed him to the Warren Commission, which investigated the assassination of John F. Kennedy. The following year, Ford challenged Charles A. Halleck of Indiana for the post of House minority leader. Ford was the choice of most younger Republicans, and he was elected by a vote of 73–67 on January 4, 1965. He remained minority leader for nine years.

In 1973 Vice President Spiro T. Agnew resigned after being accused of income tax evasion and accepting bribes. When the vice presidency is vacant, under terms of the Twenty-fifth Amendment, ratified in 1967, the president nominates a new vice president who then must be confirmed by both houses of Congress. Because the credibility of the administration had been seriously damaged by Agnew and the unfolding Watergate scandal, President Richard Nixon wanted a vice president of unquestioned integrity. He chose Ford, who had developed a reputation for honesty during his years in the House. Nixon announced the appointment of Ford on October 12, 1973, in the East Room of the White House. After two months of scrutiny by Congress, Ford's nomination was approved 92–3 by the Senate and 387–35 by the House. He was sworn in as vice president on December 6.

Presidency

The Watergate scandal forced President Nixon to resign on August 9, 1974. Later that day Ford became the first president to gain that office without being elected either president or vice president. He nominated former New York governor Nelson A. Rockefeller to be vice president. After a congressional inquiry into Rockefeller's finances, he was confirmed and sworn into office on December 19, 1974.

After taking the oath of office, Ford declared that "our long national nightmare is over." Ford's honest reputation, his friendly relations with Congress, and the public's desire for a return to normalcy led to an initial honeymoon with the American public. Seventy-one percent of respondents to a Gallup poll expressed their approval of the new president, while just 3 percent disapproved.

Ford's honeymoon, however, did not last long. On Sunday morning September 8 he announced to a small group of reporters that he was granting Richard Nixon an unconditional pardon. Ford was sensitive to speculation that he had promised to pardon Nixon in return for his nomination as vice

president, so he took the unprecedented action of voluntarily going before a House Judiciary subcommittee to explain the pardon. Ford justified the highly unpopular pardon by saying it was needed to heal the political and social divisions caused by the Watergate scandal. Although no evidence of a secret bargain with Nixon surfaced, the pardon severely damaged Ford's popularity and his chances for election to a term of his own in 1976.

The most pressing domestic problem facing Ford during his term was persistent inflation and a sluggish economy. The president initially attempted to fight inflation by vetoing spending bills and encouraging the Federal Reserve to limit the growth of the money supply. In 1975, however, unemployment had become the more serious problem, and Ford compromised with Congress on a tax cut and a spending plan designed to stimulate the economy. Although inflation and unemployment remained at historically high levels, the economy recovered during late 1975 and 1976.

In foreign affairs Ford attempted to build on President Nixon's expansion of relations with the Soviet Union and China. Congressional restrictions on U.S. military involvement in Southeast Asia prevented Ford from providing military assistance to South Vietnam, which North Vietnam conquered in 1975. When the U.S. merchant ship *Mayaguez* was seized by Cambodia that year, however, he ordered marines to rescue the crew. The operation freed the crew, but forty-one of the rescuers were killed.

In September 1975 Ford was the target of two assassination attempts. On September 5 Lynette Fromme pointed a loaded pistol at the president as he moved through a crowd in Sacramento. A Secret Service agent disarmed her before she could fire. Fromme, a follower of mass murderer Charles Manson, was convicted of attempted assassination and sentenced to life imprisonment. Two weeks later, on September 22, political activist Sara Jane Moore fired a handgun at Ford as he was leaving a hotel in San Francisco. The bullet struck a taxi driver, who received a minor wound. Moore was apprehended by a bystander and two police officers before she could fire a second shot. She, too, was convicted of attempted assassination and sentenced to life in prison.

In early 1976 Ford appeared unlikely to retain the presidency. Even his party's nomination was in doubt, as conservative former California governor Ronald Reagan made a strong bid for the nomination. Ford collected enough delegates in the primaries, however, to narrowly defeat Reagan at the party's convention. In late 1975 Ford had asked Vice President Rockefeller to remove himself from consideration for the vice-presidential nomination in 1976. The president chose Sen. Robert J. Dole of Kansas as his running mate.

Jimmy Carter, the Democratic presidential candidate, was heavily favored to defeat Ford in the general election, but Ford made up ground during the fall campaign. Carter defeated the president, however, 297–240 in the electoral college.

After leaving the presidency, Ford retired to Palm Springs, California. In 1979 he published his autobiography, *A Time to Heal*. Ronald Reagan approached Ford about becoming his vice-presidential running mate in 1980, but Ford turned him down.

Ford did not actively engage in public affairs during his retirement, but he did occasionally campaign for Republican candidates. He also joined with other former presidents to endorse selected policies, including enactment of the revisions to the General Agreement on Tariffs and Trade, the North American Free Trade Agreement, and the deployment of U.S. troops to the former Yugoslavia. He did, however, break with Republican hard-liners in Congress on several issues, including that of the Clinton impeachment; Ford favored a public rebuke of the president in the well of the House of Representatives.

Ford married Elizabeth "Betty" Bloomer Warren, a thirty-year-old divorcee and former professional dancer, on October 15, 1948. The Fords had three sons and one daughter. After undergoing medical treatment for alcoholism in 1978, Mrs. Ford established the Betty Ford Center for Drug and Alcohol Rehabilitation.

Jimmy Carter

Born: October 1, 1924; Plains, Georgia
Party: Democratic
Term: January 20, 1977–January 20, 1981
Vice President: Walter F. Mondale

James Earl Carter Jr. was the oldest of the four children of James and Lillian Carter. From childhood on, James preferred to be called "Jimmy." His father was a storekeeper, farmer, and insurance broker who believed in segregation. His mother, a registered nurse who provided health care to her poor neighbors, held more progressive views on social and racial issues. Jimmy attended public schools and became a member of the First Baptist Church of Plains, Georgia. This evangelical church profoundly influenced Carter's development, although he did not adopt its conservative political philosophy in his political career.

After high school, Carter briefly attended Georgia Southwestern College in Americus before being appointed to the U.S. Naval Academy. Carter graduated fifty-ninth in his class of 820 in 1946. His first assignment was as an instructor aboard battleships anchored at Norfolk, Virginia. In 1948 he applied and was accepted for submarine duty. After two and a half years as a crew member on a submarine in the Pacific, he was selected to work in the navy's nuclear submarine program. He became an engineering officer on the *Sea Wolf*, a new atomic submarine under construction. He also took classes in nuclear

physics at Union College in Schenectady, New York. After his father died in 1953, however, he decided to retire from the navy.

Carter returned to his home in Plains, where he took over the family peanut farm. He gradually increased his land holdings and started several agriculture-related businesses, including a peanut-shelling plant and a farm-supply business. As Carter's wealth grew he became involved in local politics. He was appointed to the Sumter County School Board in 1955 and served there for seven years. He also served as chairman of the county hospital authority.

Political Career

In 1962 Carter ran for the Georgia State Senate. He lost a primary election but challenged the results because he had personally witnessed a ballot box being stuffed by a supporter of his opponent. His protest was upheld, and he became the Democratic

nominee. He was elected and served two terms before declaring his candidacy for governor in 1966. Carter campaigned vigorously but lost in the primary election. In 1970 he surprised political observers by defeating former governor Carl E. Sanders in the Democratic primary, then went on to win the general election.

As governor, Carter openly denounced racial segregation and became a symbol of the "New South." He also reorganized the state government, supported measures to protect the environment, and opened government meetings to the public.

Georgia law prohibited a governor from running for two consecutive terms, so Carter set his sights on the presidency. New federal election laws that provided presidential candidates with campaign funds made it possible for Carter to run for president without the support of wealthy campaign contributors or Democratic Party leaders. One month after leaving the Georgia governorship he announced that he was running for the 1976 Democratic presidential nomination.

Carter's candidacy was a long shot. He was an inexperienced, one-term governor from a southern state who had to defeat several better-known Democrats for the nomination. Carter campaigned tirelessly during 1975 and 1976 and gained national attention by winning the Democratic caucuses in Iowa on January 19, 1976. When he won again in the New Hampshire primary on February 24, he suddenly became the front-runner. Before the June 1976 Democratic National Convention in New York he had earned enough delegates in primaries and caucuses to lock up the nomination.

Carter emerged from the convention with a solid lead in public opinion polls over Republican incumbent Gerald R. Ford, whose candidacy suffered from several years of economic troubles and his pardon of former president Richard Nixon. This gap narrowed as the election approached, but Carter won 297–240 in the electoral college.

Presidency

One of Carter's early presidential goals was to "depomp" the presidency and make it more responsive to the people. He underscored his intention by walking back to the White House from the Capitol after his inauguration. Carter conducted frequent press conferences, held meetings in selected towns across the country, carried his own suit bag, and stopped the tradition of having a band play "Hail to the Chief" when he arrived at an occasion. The public liked Carter's open, informal style, but the president could not sustain his popularity.

In the late summer of 1977 journalists and government investigators disclosed that Carter's budget director, Bert Lance, had engaged in questionable financial practices during his career as a banker before he joined the Carter administration. For several months Carter defended Lance, a close personal friend, but on September 21, 1977, Lance resigned under the weight of the allegations. Lance was ultimately exonerated when a jury acquitted him of bank fraud charges in 1981, but the Lance affair appeared to contradict Carter's claim that he was holding the officials of his administration to a higher ethical standard than previous presidents had.

The state of the economy did even more damage to Carter's presidency. During the 1976 campaign Carter had criticized President Ford for the high inflation and unemployment the country was suffering. Under Carter, however, the economic situation worsened. Prices had risen 6.5 percent the year Carter took office, but they rose 11.3 percent in 1979 and 13.5 percent in 1980. Unemployment, which stood at about 7.7 percent in 1980 during Carter's reelection campaign, was also higher than most Americans would accept.

In foreign policy, Carter achieved notable successes. He mediated negotiations between Prime Minister Menachem Begin of Israel and President Anwar Sadat of Egypt. The talks produced the 1979 Camp David Accords, which established peace between those two countries. He also formalized relations with the People's Republic of China on January 1, 1979, and secured Senate approval in 1978 of treaties transferring control of the Panama Canal to Panama on December 31, 1999.

The last two years of Carter's term, however, brought several foreign policy failures. On June 18, 1979, Carter and Soviet leader Leonid Brezhnev signed a treaty in Vienna to limit strategic nuclear weapons, but the Senate was hesitant to approve this agreement, known as SALT II. In 1980 Carter withdrew the SALT II treaty after the Soviets invaded Afghanistan in December 1979 to prop up a pro-communist government there. In response to the Soviet invasion, Carter also imposed a grain embargo and refused to allow the U.S. team to participate in the 1980 Olympic games in Moscow.

On November 4, 1979, Iranian militants stormed the U.S. embassy in Tehran, taking American diplomats and embassy personnel hostage. Carter's efforts to free the hostages, including an abortive helicopter raid in April 1980 in which eight soldiers died, proved ineffective. The hostage crisis dominated the last year of Carter's presidency, and the Iranians did not release the hostages until January 20, 1981, minutes after Carter had left office.

Despite these problems, Carter fought off a challenge for the 1980 Democratic presidential nomination from Sen. Edward M. Kennedy of Massachusetts. Carter's opponent in the general election was conservative former governor Ronald Reagan of California. Reagan defeated Carter 489–49 in the electoral college, with Carter winning only six states and the District of Columbia.

After leaving the presidency Carter returned to his home in Plains. He lectured and wrote about world affairs, launched the Carter Presidential Center in Atlanta to examine public policy issues, and became involved in several voluntary service projects.

In 1994 Carter carried out a series of high-profile diplomatic missions to North Korea, Bosnia, and Haiti. The Haiti trip produced a last-minute agreement that allowed U.S. military forces, which were set to invade Haiti, to enter the country peacefully. In May 2002 Carter became the first U.S. president—sitting or former—to visit Cuba since Calvin Coolidge in January 1928. Carter gave a speech from Havana calling on the United States to end its forty-year economic embargo against the country. In October 2002 the Nobel Peace Prize was awarded to Carter for his decades of untiring effort to promote world peace, human rights, and economic and social development. As he headed into his eighties, Carter kept up his work at the Carter Center and also continued to write books, including memoirs and fiction.

Carter married eighteen-year-old Rosalynn Smith, a close friend of his sister Ruth, on July 7, 1946. The Carters had three sons and one daughter. President and Mrs. Carter were awarded the Presidential Medal of Freedom in 1999. Several of Carter's relatives became national celebrities. His brother, Billy, capitalized on his brother's fame by making numerous public appearances and marketing "Billy Beer." Carter's mother, who had served in the Peace Corps in the late 1960s and early 1970s, made several overseas journeys to represent her son at state funerals and other occasions.

Ronald Reagan

Born: February 6, 1911; Tampico, Illinois
Party: Republican
Term: January 20, 1981–January 20, 1989
Vice President: George H. W. Bush
Died: June 5, 2004, Los Angeles, California
Buried: Simi Valley, California

Ronald Wilson Reagan was the youngest of the two sons of Nelle and John Reagan, a shoe salesman. When Ronald was nine the family moved from Tampico, Illinois, to nearby Dixon. He attended public schools and worked as a lifeguard at a swimming area in the Rock River. He enrolled in Eureka College near Peoria, Illinois, in 1928. There he played football and was elected president of the student body. He graduated in 1932 with a degree in economics and sociology.

After college Reagan worked as a sportscaster for radio stations in Davenport and Des Moines, Iowa. During a trip to California in 1937 to cover the spring training sessions of the Chicago Cubs baseball team, an agent for Warner Brothers movie studio persuaded Reagan to take a screen test. Reagan won the role of a small-town radio announcer in the movie *Love Is on the Air*. The movie began his twenty-eight-year acting career, during which he would make fifty-five movies, including *King's Row, The Hasty Heart,* and *Knute Rockne, All American.*

In 1942 Reagan entered the U.S. Army Air Corps as a second lieutenant and was assigned to make training films. He was discharged in 1945 with the rank of captain. After the war he continued to act in movies but devoted an increasing share of his time to movie industry politics. In 1947 he was elected president of the Screen Actors Guild, a labor union representing Hollywood actors. He held that office until 1952 and was reelected to a one-year term in 1959. In October 1947 he appeared as a friendly witness before the House Un-American Activities Committee. He supported the blacklist created by Hollywood producers to deny work to actors and writers suspected of having communist ties.

Until the late 1940s Reagan had been a staunch Democrat, supporting presidents Franklin Roosevelt and Harry Truman. In the late 1940s his political sympathies began to shift to the right as he became more concerned about communist subversion. He voted for Dwight Eisenhower in 1952 and 1956 and Richard Nixon in 1960. From 1954 to 1962 he served as a spokesperson for General Electric. In addition to hosting the television show *GE Theater,* he made speeches to factory workers about the virtues of free enterprise and the dangers of too much government regulation. In 1962 Reagan finally abandoned the Democratic Party and registered as a Republican.

Political Career

In 1964 Reagan made a televised campaign speech on behalf of Republican presidential candidate Barry Goldwater. The speech established Reagan as an articulate spokesman for the conservative wing of the Republican Party and led California Republican leaders to ask him to run for governor. Reagan received the 1966 Republican nomination for governor after winning almost 65 percent of

the vote in a five-candidate primary election. He then defeated incumbent Democrat Edmund G. Brown, who had beaten Richard Nixon four years before. Reagan was easily elected to a second term in 1970.

As governor, Reagan succeeded in passing a welfare reform bill that cut the number of Californians on welfare and increased the payments to the remaining welfare recipients. He campaigned for budget cuts and lower taxes, but early in his governorship he signed bills increasing taxes, because he claimed Brown had left the state in financial trouble. Reagan also harshly criticized student protesters on college campuses and cut state funds for higher education during his first term. During his second term, however, the funds were restored, and by the time he left office state support for higher education was double what it had been when he was first elected.

Reagan received some support for the presidential nomination in 1968, but the party nominated Richard Nixon. Reagan backed President Nixon in 1972, but after declining to run for a third term as governor in 1974 he began campaigning for the presidency. Despite running against incumbent president Gerald R. Ford, Reagan came close to winning the 1976 Republican presidential nomination. Ford received 1,187 delegate votes to Reagan's 1,070 delegate votes at the Republican National Convention in Kansas City. When Ford lost the election to Democrat Jimmy Carter, Reagan became the favorite to receive the Republican nomination in 1980.

During the next four years Reagan campaigned for Republican candidates and raised money for his 1980 campaign. He was upset in the Iowa caucuses by George Bush but recovered with a win in the New Hampshire primary. Reagan went on to win all but four of the remaining Republican primaries. He then defeated incumbent Jimmy Carter in the general election, 489 electoral votes to 49.

Presidency

On March 30, 1981, less than three months after he became president, Reagan was shot as he was leaving the Washington Hilton Hotel, where he had spoken to a group of union officials. The assailant, John Hinckley Jr., fired six shots at Reagan with a .22-caliber pistol. One bullet struck Reagan in the chest and lodged in his left lung. A police officer, a Secret Service agent, and presidential press secretary James Brady were also wounded in the shooting. Reagan was rushed to a nearby hospital, where surgeons removed the bullet. Reagan became the first incumbent president to be wounded by an assailant and survive. Hinckley, who declared he shot the president to impress Jodie Foster, a Hollywood actress, was found not guilty by reason of insanity and confined at St. Elizabeth's Hospital in Washington, D.C.

During 1981 the Reagan administration focused on economic policy. The president pushed a large tax cut through Congress, along with increases in the defense budget and decreases in funding for many domestic programs. Reagan claimed that the tax cut would produce an economic boom that would lower unemployment while ultimately increasing tax revenues that would balance the federal budget. A severe recession that began in late 1981, however, increased unemployment to postdepression highs. In early 1983 the economy began to recover. Unlike economic recoveries during the 1970s, however, the expansion was not accompanied by high inflation.

In the 1984 presidential election, with the economy prospering, Reagan overwhelmed his Democratic challenger, former vice president Walter F. Mondale, 525–13 in the electoral college. The economic expansion continued through the end of Reagan's term.

Although most Americans were satisfied with the economic recovery, critics charged that it was flawed because low-income groups had fared poorly during the Reagan years, the U.S. trade position had deteriorated, and the federal government had built up huge budget deficits. The last of these problems was particularly troublesome to Reagan, because he had promised in his 1980 campaign to balance the federal budget. Instead, Reagan's military buildup and tax cut had exacerbated the nation's budget deficit problem. In 1981 when Reagan entered office, the budget deficit was $78.9 billion. Two years later it had more than doubled to $207.8 billion, and in 1986 it stood at $221.2 billion. The national debt had risen from a little over one trillion dollars in 1981 to more than two trillion dollars in 1986. Reagan and the Democratic Congress addressed the debt problem by enacting the Gramm-Rudman-Hollings amendment in 1985. The measure mandated across-the-board spending cuts if the president and Congress could not agree on budget reductions that would reduce the deficit to specified yearly targets.

In foreign affairs, the first five years of Reagan's presidency were characterized by hard-line anticommunist rhetoric and efforts to block communist expansion and even overturn procommunist governments in the developing world. Reagan supported military funding to the anticommunist Nicaraguan rebels known as the "contras," who were fighting to overthrow the Marxist regime in their country. He also supported aid to anticommunist guerrillas fighting in Angola and Cambodia, and Afghan rebels fighting Soviet forces that had invaded Afghanistan in 1979. In 1983 Reagan dispatched U.S. troops to Grenada to overthrow the Marxist government and bring stability to the tiny Caribbean island.

With the rise of Mikhail Gorbachev as the leader of the Soviet Union in 1985, however, the president softened his anticommunist rhetoric and began developing a working relationship with the Soviet leader. During his last three years in office, Reagan held five summits with Gorbachev and signed a treaty banning intermediate nuclear missiles in Europe.

The Reagan administration also took actions to strike back at terrorists in the Middle East, including a 1986 bombing raid on Libya in retaliation for alleged Libyan support for a terrorist bombing of a Berlin nightclub. Reagan's tough antiterrorist posture was undercut late in 1986 when the administration disclosed that the president had approved arms sales to Iran that appeared to be aimed at securing the release of American hostages in Lebanon held by pro-Iranian extremists. Reagan denied that the sale was an arms-for-hostages swap, which would have contradicted his policy of not negotiating with terrorists, but the evidence suggested otherwise.

Investigations revealed that members of the president's National Security Council staff had used the arms sales profits to aid the contras, despite a congressional prohibition then in force against U.S. aid to the contras. Although investigators found no evidence that Reagan had been aware of the diversion of funds to the contras, the scandal led to the resignation of several administration officials. The Tower Commission, appointed by the president to investigate the Iran-contra affair, issued a report in 1987 that criticized the president's detached style of management, which allowed his subordinates to operate without his knowledge.

Despite the Iran-contra affair, Reagan remained one of the most popular presidents of the twentieth century. After Vice President George H. W. Bush won the Republican presidential nomination in 1988, Reagan campaigned hard for him. Bush easily defeated Gov. Michael Dukakis of Massachusetts in the November election.

When Reagan's term ended, he returned to his home in Bel Air, California, and maintained a low public profile. In November 1994 Reagan announced in a handwritten note that he had been diagnosed with Alzheimer's disease, which causes progressive mental and physical deterioration. He said that he wanted his announcement to help raise awareness about the disease. Reagan and his wife Nancy received the Congressional Gold Medal in May 2002.

Reagan's long illness came to an end on June 5, 2004, when he died at his home. His death led to a week of funeral ceremonies that stretched from coast to coast. Reagan's body was flown across the country to lie in state in the Capitol Rotunda; President George W. Bush called for a national day of mourning to take place on June 11. That day, a memorial service was held at the National Cathedral in Washington, after which Reagan's body was flown back to California for a sunset burial service at his presidential library in Simi Valley.

Reagan married Jane Wyman, an actress, on January 24, 1940. The couple had one daughter and adopted a son before divorcing in 1948. Reagan then married another actress, Nancy Davis, on March 4, 1952. They had one daughter and one son.

George H. W. Bush

Born: June 12, 1924; Milton, Massachusetts
Party: Republican
Term: January 20, 1989–January 20, 1993
Vice President: Dan Quayle

George Herbert Walker Bush was the second of the five children of Prescott and Dorothy Bush. George's father was a wealthy Wall Street banker who represented Connecticut in the U.S. Senate from 1952 to 1963.

George grew up in Greenwich, Connecticut, where he attended a private elementary school before enrolling in the Phillips Academy in Andover, Massachusetts. At this exclusive prep school he excelled in athletics and academics and was elected president of his senior class. He graduat-

ed in 1942 and joined the navy, becoming the youngest bomber pilot in that branch of the service.

On September 22, 1944, while flying a mission from the light aircraft carrier *San Jacinto,* Bush was shot down near the Japanese-held island of Chichi Jima. He parachuted safely into the Pacific Ocean and after four hours was rescued by a submarine. Bush received the Distinguished Flying Cross. In December 1944 he was reassigned as a naval flight instructor in Virginia, where he remained until his discharge in September 1945.

After the war Bush enrolled in Yale University and majored in economics. He was also captain of Yale's baseball team. He graduated Phi Beta Kappa in 1948. Bush then moved to Texas, where he gradually made a small fortune in the oil business. He ran for the Senate in 1964 against incumbent Ralph Yarborough, a Democrat. Although he received 200,000 more votes in Texas than Republican presidential nominee Barry Goldwater, Bush lost the election.

Political Career

In 1966 when reapportionment gave Houston another House seat, Bush ran for it and won. He served on the Ways and Means Committee and became an outspoken supporter of Richard Nixon. Bush was reelected to the House in 1968 when Nixon captured the presidency. Two years later Bush followed Nixon's advice and abandoned his safe House seat to run for the Senate. He was defeated by conservative Democrat Lloyd Bentsen, who would be the Democratic vice-presidential nominee in 1988 on the ticket opposing Bush.

After the 1970 election Nixon appointed Bush ambassador to the United Nations. When Nixon was reelected in 1972, he asked Bush to leave the UN to take over as chair of the Republican National Committee. Bush served in that post during the difficult days of the Watergate scandal. At first he vigorously defended President Nixon. In 1974, however, as the evidence against Nixon mounted, he privately expressed doubts about the president's innocence. Nevertheless, Bush avoided public criticism of the president and concentrated on maintaining Republican Party strength despite the president's troubles. On August 7, 1974, Bush wrote a letter asking Nixon to resign, which the president did two days later.

When Vice President Gerald R. Ford succeeded to the presidency upon Nixon's resignation, Bush was a leading candidate to fill the vice-presidential vacancy. Bush wanted the job, but he was bypassed in favor of Gov. Nelson A. Rockefeller of New York. Ford offered Bush the ambassadorship to Britain or France. Bush chose, however, to take the post of chief of the U.S. Liaison Office in the People's Republic of China.

In 1975 Ford called Bush back to the United States to become director of the Central Intelligence Agency. As CIA chief, Bush's primary goal was restoring the reputation of the agency, which had been damaged by revelations of its illegal and unauthorized activities during the 1970s, including assassination plots against foreign officials and spying on members of the domestic antiwar movement. Bush won bipartisan praise for his efforts to repair the agency's morale and integrity. After being replaced as CIA director when Democrat Jimmy Carter became president in 1977, Bush returned to Houston to become chairman of First International Bank. He stayed active in politics by campaigning for Republican candidates before the 1978 midterm election. On January 5, 1979, he declared his intention to seek the presidency. Bush campaigned full-time during 1979 and established himself as the leading challenger to Republican front-runner Ronald Reagan when he won the Iowa caucuses on January 21, 1980. During the primary campaign Bush attacked Reagan as an ultraconservative and called his economic proposals "voodoo economics." Reagan, however, prevailed in the primaries and secured enough delegates for the nomination before the Republican National Convention in Detroit in July 1980.

At the convention Reagan's team approached former president Ford about running for vice president. When Ford declined, they asked Bush to be the vice-presidential nominee in an attempt to unify the party. Bush accepted, and the Republican ticket defeated President Jimmy Carter and Vice President Walter F. Mondale in a landslide.

Despite Bush's differences with Reagan during the campaign, as vice president he was extremely loyal to the president. When Reagan was wounded by an assailant in 1981, Bush emphasized that Reagan was still president and exerted leadership over the administration in the president's absence. Bush was frequently called upon to make diplomatic trips overseas. While vice president he visited more than seventy countries. His frequent attendance at state funerals led him to joke that his motto was "I'm George Bush. You die, I fly." Reagan and Bush won

a second term in 1984 by easily defeating the Democratic ticket of Walter F. Mondale and Geraldine Ferraro.

Late in Reagan's second term Bush launched his campaign for the presidency. Despite his status as a two-term vice president, he was challenged for the nomination by Senate Minority Leader Robert Dole of Kansas and several other candidates. Dole defeated Bush in the Iowa caucuses, as Bush had defeated Reagan eight years before. In the first primary, in New Hampshire, however, Bush scored a decisive victory and secured the nomination before the end of the primary season.

Bush faced Gov. Michael S. Dukakis of Massachusetts in the general election. Bush attacked his opponent for liberal policies and promised to continue Ronald Reagan's diplomacy with the Soviet Union. Despite the presence of massive budget deficits, Bush also pledged not to raise taxes. Bush overcame speculation about his role in the Reagan administration's Iran-contra affair and criticism of Dan Quayle, his vice-presidential choice, to defeat Dukakis. Bush won the election decisively in the electoral college, 426–112.

Presidency

Bush had pledged to carry on the conservative legacy of Ronald Reagan. However, he had also promised to preside over a "kinder, gentler America," implying that partisanship had gone too far during the Reagan period. Nevertheless, partisan battles with the Democratic Congress would characterize much of Bush's presidency. In November 1990, after months of partisan negotiation and posturing, Bush signed a budget bill that aimed to trim about $500 billion off the deficit over five years. Congressional Democrats forced Bush to accept a tax increase as part of the deal. Many Americans saw Bush's acquiescence to the tax increase as a betrayal of his campaign pledge.

The previous August, events in the Persian Gulf region had intruded on Bush's other priorities and provided a troubling backdrop to the budget negotiations. On August 2 Iraqi forces invaded and quickly occupied the small, oil-rich nation of Kuwait. Bush responded by rallying international opposition against Iraq and sending hundreds of thousands of American troops to join the coalition assembling in the region. The administration argued that this aggression by Iraqi leader Saddam Hussein had to be reversed because it threatened the stability of world oil markets and set a dangerous precedent that could encourage other acts of aggression. Bush also was concerned about mounting evidence that Iraq was engaged in an ambitious nuclear weapons program.

On January 17, 1991, Bush ordered a devastating bombing campaign against Iraqi military forces. On February 24, after thirty-eight days of sustained bombing, coalition ground forces attacked the Iraqi troops, routing them from Kuwait. The ground war lasted just one hundred hours before Bush gave the cease-fire order. The stunning success of the operation and the low casualty figures boosted the president's popularity to a high of 89 percent immediately following the war. Commentators speculated that Bush's victory in the Gulf might make him unbeatable for reelection in 1992, and several prominent Democrats declined to enter the race because of Bush's standing. But his popularity did not last. After the war, the American people turned their attention back to domestic matters. The nation had entered a recession in the summer of 1990. As wages stagnated and unemployment continued to rise after the war, Bush was perceived as having no answers to domestic problems. He also was seen as spending too much time on foreign affairs, the area of policy in which he had the most expertise and success.

Bush's reelection chances were further damaged when he was challenged for the Republican nomination by conservative political commentator Pat Buchanan. Although Buchanan did not seriously threaten Bush's nomination, the challenger's attacks from the right weakened enthusiasm for Bush among conservatives and forced the president to defend himself instead of preparing for the fall election.

Democrats nominated Gov. Bill Clinton of Arkansas to face Bush. Billionaire Ross Perot mounted a self-financed independent candidacy that also drew significant attention. Clinton won the election with 43 percent of the popular vote and 370 electoral votes. Bush finished second with 37 percent of the popular vote and 168 electoral votes. Perot did not win any states, but finished with 19 percent of the popular vote. Clinton capitalized on Bush's inattention to domestic matters by promising to focus "like a laser beam" on the economy.

Bush left office declaring that he would spend time in retirement with his grandchildren. In 1993 he made a trip to Kuwait, where he was greeted as a liberator. Intelligence findings that Iraqi agents had plotted to assassinate Bush during the trip led President Clinton to launch a missile attack against Iraq on June 26, 1993. In 1994 two of Bush's sons, George W. and John Ellis ("Jeb"), ran for the governorships of Texas and Florida, respectively. George W. won in Texas, but Jeb lost a close election, then won the post in the 1998 race. George W. won the White House himself in 2000, marking the second time that a son of a president was elected to the presidency. Bush kept a relatively low profile during his son's first years as president but campaigned around the country for George W.'s reelection in 2004.

Bush married nineteen-year-old Barbara Pierce, the daughter of a prominent magazine publisher, on January 6, 1945. They had four sons and two daughters. Their daughter Robin died of leukemia in 1953.

Bill Clinton

Born: August 19, 1946; Hope, Arkansas
Party: Democratic
Term: January 20, 1993–January 20, 2001
Vice President: Al Gore

Bill Clinton was the only child of William Jefferson Blythe III and Virginia Cassidy Blythe. Bill originally was named William Jefferson Blythe, after his father. But the senior Blythe died in an automobile accident before his son was born. When Bill was four, his mother married Roger Clinton, a car salesman who legally adopted Bill. Bill's stepfather was an emotionally and physically abusive alcoholic who frequently quarreled with his mother.

Clinton grew up in Hot Springs, Arkansas, where he excelled in public schools and played saxophone in the band. In 1968 he graduated from Georgetown University in Washington, D.C., with a degree in international affairs. He earned a Rhodes Scholarship and attended Oxford University for two years. He returned to the United States in 1970 and entered Yale University Law School, earning his law degree in 1973.

Political Career

Politics has been Clinton's lifelong ambition. In 1972 he managed the Texas campaign of Democratic presidential nominee George McGovern. After a brief stint as a staff member of the House Judiciary Committee, he began teaching law at the University of Arkansas in 1973. The next year, he ran unsuccessfully for a House seat. Although he lost, his strong showing established his position in Arkansas politics.

In 1976 Clinton was elected attorney general of Arkansas. Then in 1978, at thirty-two, he defeated a crowded field of Democratic contenders for the gubernatorial nomination and easily won the general election. Two years later, however, Clinton was defeated for reelection. His popularity had been weakened by rioting among eighteen thousand Cuban refugees housed at Fort Chaffee, Arkansas. He also was attacked by his opponent for raising taxes and licensing fees to pay for road construction projects. In addition, many voters resented Clinton's broader political ambitions, which he did not hide.

After his defeat Clinton went to work for the Little Rock law firm Wright, Lindsay, and Jennings but spent much of his time preparing for another run. During the 1982 campaign he declared that his tax increases had been a mistake. He won and was reelected in 1984 to a two-year term and in 1986 and 1990 to four-year terms.

At the 1988 Democratic National Convention, Clinton delivered an overlong nominating speech for Michael Dukakis that was widely criticized. Nevertheless, during the late 1980s and early 1990s Clinton achieved national prominence as a reform governor and was often mentioned as a future presidential candidate. He served two terms as chair of the National Governors Association. In 1990 and 1991 he also headed the Democratic Leadership Council, a national organization of Democrats who favored the party's realignment to more moderate positions.

On October 3, 1991, despite an earlier promise to serve his full term as governor, Clinton announced he would seek the Democratic presidential nomination. He quickly emerged as one of the front-runners. The campaign was placed in jeopardy, however, by allegations of his marital infidelity and avoidance of military service during the Vietnam War. Without denying either charge, Clinton and his wife, Hillary, appealed for understanding in a notable television appearance on "60 Minutes." Clinton outlasted rivals Paul Tsongas and Jerry Brown to win the nomination.

In the general election Clinton faced incumbent George Bush and billionaire populist Ross Perot, who ran as an independent. Bush's support had been weakened by a stagnant economy and a widespread belief that he had little interest in domestic policy. Clinton promised to make economic policy and the middle class his top priorities, promoting himself as a fiscally conscientious agent of change who would reform the country's health care, welfare, and education systems. He chose Sen. Al Gore of Tennessee as his running mate. The two young southern Democrats (each then in his mid-forties) projected a youthful energy that appealed to many younger voters. Clinton won the election with 43 percent of the popular vote and 370 electoral votes. Bush finished second with 37 percent and 168 electoral votes. Perot won nearly twenty million votes, almost half of Bush's total.

Presidency

Clinton's first hundred days in office were a mixed bag of successes and setbacks. His first two choices

for attorney general were forced to withdraw after revelations that they had employed illegal immigrants as nannies; he was forced to compromise on his campaign pledge to lift the ban on gays in the military; and his economic stimulus bill was defeated by a Republican filibuster in the Senate. But Clinton succeeded in passing family leave legislation and a long-stalled motor-voter bill.

During the second half of 1993 Clinton scored three major victories. His aggressive lobbying led to the passage of a budget plan that was projected to reduce the anticipated deficit by about $500 billion over five years. On strict party-line votes, the House on August 5 passed the budget 218–216; the next day the Senate passed it 51–50, with Vice President Gore casting the tie-breaking vote. Later in the year, Clinton scored major legislative successes with the North American Free Trade Agreement, primarily on the strength of Republican votes, and the Brady bill, which mandated a five-day waiting period for the purchase of a handgun, the first major gun control legislation to pass Congress since 1968.

In 1994, however, Clinton was less successful. With First Lady Hillary Clinton serving as the head of Clinton's task force on health care, the administration attempted to advance a comprehensive reform plan. Republicans attacked it as overly complex, expensive, and bureaucratic. By early fall, lacking sufficient congressional, industry, or public support, the bill was withdrawn without coming to a final vote in either house. Clinton's disappointment was tempered somewhat by passage of a major crime bill and revisions to the General Agreement on Tariffs and Trade.

The 1994 congressional elections stunningly realigned Washington. With many Republican candidates campaigning against Clinton's policies, Republicans gained control of both houses of Congress for the first time in four decades. Clinton suddenly faced an aggressive, conservative, Republican-controlled Congress intent on rolling back years of

Democratic legislation. The highly partisan Congress also reinvigorated a lingering ethics investigation arising from investments Clinton and his wife had made in an Arkansas land development deal known as "Whitewater" during his time as governor, establishing a charged political climate in Washington that would later lead to Clinton's impeachment and trial.

During 1995 Clinton blocked many Republican priorities with adept use of the veto, a weapon he did not use during his first two years in office. Most notably, Clinton vetoed Republican legislation to balance the budget in seven years, terming the proposed cuts in health care, education, environment, and welfare as draconian. The vetoes led to two shutdowns of government services and bitter partisan accusations as the two parties sought political advantage. With the polls showing strong support for his position, Clinton was able to keep a firm hand in the budget negotiations. His stubborn style proved successful by April 1996, as the final 1996 fiscal spending bill reflected his priorities, not the deeper cuts sought by the congressional Republicans.

As he had promised during his campaign, Clinton deemphasized foreign policy to focus on domestic problems, but world events soon altered this approach. Clinton actively promoted a broadening of the accord signed earlier between Israel and the Palestine Liberation Organization on achieving peace, and he advanced negotiations between warring factions in Ireland. Clinton also expanded the humanitarian mission in Somalia that had been launched during the Bush administration. But when U.S. military units began experiencing casualties, Clinton withdrew American troops. In 1994 Clinton also sent American forces to Haiti to reestablish the deposed government of Jean-Bertrand Aristide.

But Clinton's largest foreign policy endeavor during his first term was in the Balkans. In 1995 he sent twenty thousand U.S. troops to a NATO peace-keeping mission in war-torn Bosnia. The deployment followed the signing of a complex U.S.-brokered peace agreement in Dayton, Ohio. Critics charged that the United States had no vital interests in Bosnia, that the troops would be targets, and that the factions would resume fighting when the NATO force eventually withdrew. But Clinton followed through with his previous commitment to deploy American peacekeepers if a peace agreement was signed.

During the second half of 1996, Clinton moved to the political center, a policy called "triangulation," in preparation for his November reelection bid. He signed, despite opposition from liberal Democrats, a landmark welfare reform bill pushed by the Republican Congress. Clinton also signed Republican bills to phase out most farm subsidies and establish a presidential line-item veto (later found unconstitutional by the Supreme Court), and Democratic bills to increase the minimum wage and provide for health insurance portability.

Clinton faced former Senate majority leader Bob Dole in the 1996 presidential election. Despite several embarrassing White House ethics questions and the ongoing inquiries into the Whitewater affair, Clinton led Dole in the polls throughout the campaign. He benefited from a strong economy, low inflation and unemployment, and the perception of many voters that congressional Republicans had been too strident in pursuit of their conservative agenda. Clinton received 49 percent of the popular vote and defeated Dole 379 to 159 in the electoral college.

In 1997 Clinton and the Republican majority in Congress struck a historic agreement to balance the federal budget in five years. However, with a strong economy boosting federal tax receipts, a $70 billion surplus—the first government surplus in twenty-nine years—was attained just a year later. The debate in Washington quickly turned from how to balance the budget to how to spend the surplus.

In December 1998 years of rancorous animosity toward Clinton from conservatives in and out of Washington culminated in the president's impeachment by the House of Representatives. The impeachment grew out of an investigation by Independent Counsel Kenneth Starr into reports that Clinton had covered up a sexual relationship with a one-time White House intern, Monica Lewinsky. The relationship had come to light because of a sexual harassment suit brought against Clinton by a former Arkansas state employee, Paula Corbin Jones, and Clinton's efforts to conceal his relationship with Lewinsky from Jones's attorneys, some of whose legal fees were paid by anti-Clinton conservatives.

Clinton acknowledged "an inappropriate relationship" with Lewinsky in a televised address on August 17, 1998, and Starr, on September 9, turned over to the House what he termed was "substantial and credible information that may constitute grounds" for impeaching the president.

Despite his televised admission, Clinton's standing in public opinion polls held strong; the majority of those polled indicated a distrust of Republican motives. In the elections on November 3, the GOP lost five House seats, marking the first time in sixty-four years that the party holding the presidency registered such a gain in a midterm election. Still the House leadership went forward with the impeachment process. Through the last two months of 1998 the House Judiciary Committee heard testimony and then voted virtually on party lines to impeach Clinton on four counts. On December 19 the full House, again almost on strict party lines, voted for two articles of impeachment (charging Clinton with giving false and misleading testimony and obstructing justice). Clinton thus became the second president in U.S. history to be impeached.

Beginning on January 7, 1999, Chief Justice William H. Rehnquist presided over Clinton's trial in the Senate. Senate leaders set ground rules in which no witnesses were called but House managers and White House lawyers were allowed to assert their cases and did so with fervor. The trial's outcome, however, was never in doubt as the Republicans held only fifty-five seats and a two-thirds vote of members (or sixty-seven votes) were needed for conviction. On February 12 the Senate found the president not guilty on both counts, with the votes following party lines. Not a single Democrat voted against the president on either count, and five Republicans broke ranks to vote against the obstruction of justice charge.

In foreign policy during his second term Clinton increased U.S. involvement in the turbulent Balkans after reports of widespread atrocities in Serbia's "ethnic cleansing" campaign against ethnic Albanians, many of whom were Muslims, in the Serbian province of Kosovo. After the failure of negotiations with Serbian president Slobodan Milosevic in 1999, NATO nations led by U.S. warplanes began an extensive bombing campaign against Milosevic's Yugoslavia, flying over thirty-five thousand sorties and inflicting devastating damage on that nation's infrastructure. After eleven weeks of bombing, Milosevic finally pulled out of Kosovo, allowing NATO peacekeepers in and giving Clinton a foreign policy triumph.

Relations between the United States, the People's Republic of China, and Russia, however, frayed during this period. China's embassy in Belgrade was accidentally struck by bombs from a U.S. jet. Moscow, supporting its traditional Serbian ally, raised tensions when it unilaterally took over control of an important airport, and a confrontation with NATO troops was averted at the last moment. Nearly eight thousand U.S. soldiers joined a fifty-thousand-member NATO force in Kosovo to try and keep the peace; they remained there as Clinton's term in office ended.

Clinton spent part of his last year in office trying to broker a historic peace agreement between Israel and the Palestinians. Despite encouraging progress, discord over the status of Jerusalem and the eruption of violence in the Middle East in September 2000 brought the talks to a halt.

Clinton remained embroiled in scandal through his last days in office. Just hours before leaving the White House Clinton pardoned more than 130 people, including his brother Roger, publishing heiress Patty Hearst, and billionaire financier Marc Rich. Rich's pardon was particularly controversial—he had been indicted for tax evasion, fraud, and participating in illegal oil deals and had been a fugitive in Switzerland for twenty years.

Clinton has spent his time out of office traveling the globe and giving speeches. He also published his best-selling memoirs, titled *My Life,* in 2004 and embarked on a book tour that summer. He planned to spend the fall of 2004 campaigning for Democratic candidates, including Sen. John Kerry, the party's presidential nominee. But, after suffering chest pains, Clinton underwent successful quadruple heart bypass surgery on September 6, 2004. While he recovered well, the operation kept him from making more than a few campaign appearances.

Clinton married Hillary Rodham on October 11, 1975. The couple met while students at Yale University Law School. They have one daughter, Chelsea, who was born in 1980. Mrs. Clinton won election to the U.S. Senate from New York in 2000, the first first lady to seek elective office.

George W. Bush

Born: July 6, 1946; New Haven, Connecticut
Party: Republican
Term: January 20, 2001–
Vice President: Richard Cheney

George Walker Bush, the eldest child of former president George Herbert Walker Bush and Barbara Pierce Bush, was born in New Haven, Connecticut, while his father was finishing his undergraduate studies at Yale University after serving as a navy bomber pilot in World War II. When George Bush finished school, the family moved to Midland, Texas, where George W. grew up in a modest ranch house. Midland is considered the center of the Permian Basin, one of the United States' richest oil fields, and George Bush soon became successful in the oil business.

George W. attended public schools in Midland (he and his future wife Laura Welch were in the same seventh-grade class), but when the family moved to Briarwood, a Houston suburb, he was sent east to attend Phillips Academy in Andover, Massachusetts, where his father and grandfather (Prescott Bush, who was a U.S. senator representing Connecticut after a successful career as a Wall Street banker) had preceded him. George W. was not an exceptional student, but he quickly became a familiar figure at the exclusive all-male school, noted for his gregariousness and quick-witted (and sometimes sarcastic) nature. He would become the school's head cheerleader and also gained fame for being the organizer of an intramural stick ball league during his senior year.

After graduation Bush moved south to New Haven, Connecticut, where he attended Yale University, as his father, his father's three brothers, and his grandfather (by now a Yale trustee) had before him. At Yale he was tapped for the secretive Skull and Bones society (again, like his father) and was elected president of the Delta Kappa Epsilon fraternity, which had a reputation as a group that threw parties more than it studied. Bush was arrested twice while an undergraduate, both times for fraternity-related pranks. He graduated in 1968, but in later years he would downplay his Ivy League roots.

While a senior at Yale, Bush had been accepted into the Texas National Guard. The move seemed likely to limit the chance that he would be sent to fight in the Vietnam War, and some critics have charged that Bush and other sons of prominent Texas families received preferential treatment from Guard leaders. Bush moved to Texas and spent his first summer there in basic training, then began learning to fly F-102 jets, becoming a pilot as his father had been before him. His service hitch lasted from 1968 to 1973 and took him to Georgia, Alabama, and Ellington Air Force Base near Houston.

After completing his military duty, Bush worked in Houston for a friend of his father and took up residence in an apartment complex called the Chateau Dijon, then considered the "in spot" among Houston's ambitious young strivers. In 1970 his father, then a representative for the area, ran for the U.S. Senate against Lloyd Bentsen, whose son also lived in the exclusive complex. While his father lost this election, Bush took an active role as campaign chairman for the three-hundred-unit apartment complex. He also joined the Master's Club, an elite group of one hundred young bachelors drawn

from the cream of Houston society. He has confessed to continuing some of his fraternal partying ways during these early years in Houston and would later, at age forty, become a born-again Christian and give up drinking at the urging of his family.

In May 1972 Bush traveled to Alabama to help in the unsuccessful senatorial campaign of a former member of the Nixon cabinet, Winton M. Blount, against the entrenched and powerful incumbent, Democrat John J. Sparkman. After returning to Houston in late 1972, he went to work for an inner-city youth program called Professional United Leadership League (PULL), run by a former professional athlete who was a friend of his father. PULL's objective was to have professional athletes act as mentors for disadvantaged children from Houston's poor Third Ward, and Bush did his best to convince members of the Houston Astros baseball team to work with the children.

About this time Bush, who admittedly had been "drifting," decided to go back to school. In 1974 he graduated from Harvard University Business School with a master's in business administration and returned to Midland to start up an oil company, Arbusto Energy (later, Bush Exploration). His personal net worth at the time was about $50,000. But, despite his less-than-successful experiences with oil-well drilling and a drastic fall-off in crude prices, Bush would leave Midland in the late 1980s with a net worth of more than $1 million. In a financial analysis of Bush's wildcatting days, the *New York Times* reported that while Bush raised $4.67 million from the limited partners in Arbusto, he returned only $1.55 million in distributions; the partners and Bush took sizable tax write-offs.

In 1977 Bush married Laura Welch, a Midland native whom he had known briefly in elementary school. The next year, breaking his promise to her that she would never have to make a political speech, Bush decided to run for Congress. For a thirty-one-year-old with little or no political experience, Bush got some substantial financial support from non-Texans including William Ford of Ford Motor Company; Donald Kendall, chairman of Pepsico; and A. W. Clausen, chairman of the Bank of America among others. In the general election, Democrat Kent Hance played incessantly on Bush as a carpet-bagger, Bush's elitist roots in the East, and the fact that nearly half of Bush's campaign contributions came from out of the district. Hance won the election 53 percent to 47 percent.

Bush left the oil business in 1986 when his failing company was acquired by a larger oil company that employed him for a while as a consultant. In 1987 Bush went to Washington and spent eighteen months immersed in his father's successful presidential campaign. He took little interest in policy questions and positions but served more as the family watchdog over the professional campaign staffers. He learned the nuts and bolts of running a campaign, from budgeting to scheduling, and would be his father's political alter ego to smaller campaign venues.

After George Bush's victory, George W. was named a member of the transition team but reportedly soon grew impatient in the job and returned to Texas. In 1989, with $600,000 he borrowed, he bought a two percent stake in the Texas Rangers baseball team from another old friend of his father and became the team's managing general partner. He supervised construction of a new stadium for the team and traveled widely to promote the team. Bush and his aides gradually built the team into a contender that won the American League's Western Division title in 1994, which was Bush's last year with the Rangers. He sold his share for some $15 million.

Political Career

When his father lost the 1992 presidential election to Bill Clinton, Bush decided to run on his own for the Texas governorship in 1994. With high name recognition and well-known for his work with the Texas Rangers, Bush was well placed to mount a challenge to Democratic incumbent Ann Richards, who had been elected in 1990. Richards had gained a measure of national fame and reportedly incurred the private wrath of the Bush family when, in a keynote address to the 1988 Democratic National Convention, she quipped that George Bush (known for his occasional malapropism) was "born with a silver foot in his mouth." She was equally disdainful of George W., calling him "Shrub." Bush, in contrast, always referred to Richards respectfully. Bush campaigned on educational reform and school accountability, and he pulled out an upset win, taking 53 percent of the vote to Richards's 46 percent.

The Texas constitution makes the governorship one of the weakest among the fifty states with other elected officials holding more appointive and regulative power. Since the legislature meets for just about four and one-half months every other year, much of the day-to-day function of government devolves to the Speaker of the House and the lieutenant governor, who leads the Senate. In his first public office, Bush chose to work with these leaders, both Democrats, and achieved success in getting much of his program enacted into law. Among the measures were tort reform and a reworking of the state's welfare program, which limited the payment of benefits and mandated job training for recipients.

Bush also pushed his education agenda, which included state-run testing of public school students and tougher accountability standards for education officials. He opposed gun control measures and during his first term signed into law a bill that allowed Texans to carry concealed weapons. He also sided with industry on environmental measures, even as pollution problems in some of the state's larger cities mounted.

Bush was easily reelected in 1998 with 68 percent of the vote, becoming the first Republican governor of Texas to be reelected to a second term.

He also worked hard statewide for the entire Republican slate but refused to actively campaign against Democrats who had backed his programs in the legislature. In 1999 Bush tried to push through a property tax reform by cutting that levy by 40 percent and making up revenues with increases in sales and business taxes, but he could not get the measure through the legislature.

His margin of victory, high popularity ratings, and name recognition made Bush a leading contender for the 2000 Republican presidential nomination. Anti-Clinton sentiment among some Republicans was so strong that Bush quickly raised a record sum of more than $60 million to finance his primary campaigns; he then had to spend most of it fending off a strong challenge from maverick Republican John McCain, Arizona's senior senator, who defeated Bush in several of the early races. Bush was never seriously challenged thereafter and was chosen the party's nominee at its Philadelphia convention in August.

Bush chose Richard Cheney, a former representative from Wyoming and defense secretary during the presidential administration of his father, as his running mate.

Bush called himself a "compassionate conservative," attempting to put a kindly face on an image tarnished somewhat by the hard-line conservatives elected to Congress in the Republican upset that won the party control of both Houses in 1994. Bush proposed a $1.3 trillion income tax cut if elected and said he favored a Social Security reform allowing private accounts. On the environment, he favored voluntary cleanups instead of mandated action by the Environmental Protection Agency. Most importantly for the party faithful and others disenchanted with the Clinton administration, he vowed that he and Cheney would restore "honor and decency" to the White House.

In one of the closest presidential races in history, with the election results from Florida hotly disputed, Bush won the White House by narrowly defeating the Democratic ticket of Vice President Al Gore and his running mate Sen. Joseph Lieberman of Connecticut. The outcome of the cliff-hanger race was not known until five weeks after the election. Although the vote in Oregon and New Mexico was so close that absentee ballots had to be counted over several days before the winner of those states could be determined, Florida's twenty-five electoral votes were key to Bush's victory. His brother Jeb was Florida's governor. Both campaigns raised numerous legal challenges in state and federal court on the legitimacy of Florida's final tally, especially in regards to manual recounts of disputed votes. The election outcome was finally resolved when a deeply divided U.S. Supreme Court in a 5–4 decision halted a statewide recount, effectively giving Bush the presidency.

Although Bush won the electoral vote, he lost the popular vote by half a million. Only three times in U.S. history had a presidential candidate lost the popular vote but won the electoral vote. The last time was in 1888 when Benjamin Harrison defeated Grover Cleveland.

The terrorist attacks on the World Trade Center and Pentagon on September 11, 2001, shaped Bush's first term into one focused on homeland security and a "War on Terrorism." The Bush administration quickly undertook a war in Afghanistan, overthrowing the Taliban government and installing new leadership. In late 2002 Bush won approval from Congress and the United Nations for the possible use of force against Iraq, and on March 19, 2003, Bush told the nation that the military operation against Iraq had begun. While the war succeeded in rapidly toppling Iraqi leader Saddam Hussein, the aftermath of the conflict proved bloody, with attacks continuing into late 2004.

Back at home, Bush, after first opposing it, agreed to the creation of a new Department of Homeland Security, which merged security-related functions from other government agencies. The department, under Secretary Tom Ridge, began operations on March 1, 2003, with responsibilities over the Secret Service, the Coast Guard, and the Customs Service, among other agencies.

On the domestic side, Bush's first term was perhaps best known for its tax cuts. The administration pushed through a $1.35 trillion tax cut in its first year and followed with three more tax cuts in the next three years. Other major pieces of legislation included a bipartisan education reform bill, signed into law in January 2002, and a Medicare reform bill, signed in December 2003.

Bush campaigned hard in the 2002 midterm elections, stumping for congressional candidates around the country. In the end, the Republican Party picked up additional House seats and won control of the narrowly divided Senate—a rare midterm success for the party of an incumbent president.

Bush's Democratic opponent in the 2004 presidential election was Sen. John Kerry of Massachusetts. The campaign's key issues included the war in Iraq, the economy, and both men's military service during the Vietnam era. Kerry, who had supported giving Bush the authority to use force in Iraq, attacked Bush's Iraq policy, charging that the administration did not have a plan for the war's aftermath and that Kerry could do a better job of enlisting allies into the effort. In addition, documents released after the war's end concluded that Iraq had no weapons of mass destruction at the time of the invasion, which had been a key rationale used by the administration to justify the war. Bush responded that Kerry had no consistent position on the war and that he could not be trusted as commander in chief in an era marked by terrorism. Bush and Kerry also sparred over the state of the economy, with Bush citing improvements under his watch and Kerry pledging to roll back the part of Bush's tax cut applying to those making more than $200,000 a year. In addition, Bush supporters scrutinized Kerry's Vietnam service and attacked his decision to oppose the war after his return. Kerry's backers, meanwhile, questioned apparent gaps in Bush's National Guard record.

The election was expected to be close, with polls indicating a neck-and-neck race for much of the period leading to election day. Bush suffered a setback in the first of three presidential debates, where he appeared to be scowling and grimacing during Kerry's answers. But he rebounded in the second debate, which was viewed as a draw; the third debate was seen as a Kerry victory. In the end, Bush captured 51 percent of the popular vote to Kerry's 48 percent, with an electoral college majority of 286–252.

Bush married Laura Welch, an elementary school librarian and a native of Midland, Texas, on November 6, 1977. They had twin girls, Barbara and Jenna, in 1981.

On January 6, 2005, Congress formally counted the electoral votes as follows: 286 for George W. Bush, 251 for John Kerry, and 1 for John Edwards.

Biographies of the First Ladies

By Stephen L. Robertson

As the president's wife, the first lady holds no official position and earns no salary. The Constitution does not mention her, yet she is one of the most prominent women in the country. Most importantly the first lady can, and often does, influence the president's political decisions and shape public perception of his administration.

Many first ladies have had little to distinguish them except the position they have held by marriage, but others have achieved distinction on their own. Particularly since 1900 the first lady has been increasingly active politically and visible to the public. She is now among the best-known figures in American politics, better known in fact than members of Congress and cabinet secretaries, and often even the vice president.

The term *first lady* was not applied to the president's wife until after the Civil War. In its early days, the Republic, uncertain of how much respect was due its leader's wife, tried several titles without success. Among them were Lady Washington, Mrs. President, presidentress, and republican or democratic queen. Sometimes no title was used at all. Julia Grant was the first presidential spouse to be called the "first lady," in 1870, but the title did not gain wide acceptance until Lucy Hayes held the position from 1877 to 1881.[1]

In the early days of the Republic, the first lady fulfilled public expectations if she was a gracious hostess and ran the White House efficiently. Although she still oversees the daily domestic affairs of the presidential residence and acts as hostess at social functions, a modern first lady is expected to be a public figure as well. To succeed, she must seem articulate, well informed, and self-assured.

EARLY FIRST LADIES

If the first ladies of the eighteenth and early nineteenth centuries had political views and ambitions, most were careful to keep them under wraps. In those days, women were expected to conform to an ideal of passive purity that did not include participation in the sordid world of politics. For most of these first ladies, life in the White House was very restricting, for it was imperative that the president's wife display only "proper" behavior. Martha Washington declared herself to be a virtual prisoner as first lady.

The limits on first ladies were most clearly evident during the tenure of Abigail Adams, the nation's second first lady and a pioneering feminist. She took an active role in politics and occasionally expressed her views openly, for which she was widely criticized as unladylike. Her well-known influence as a political adviser to her husband, John Adams, was viewed with suspicion and alarm.

Dolley Madison, another memorable first lady, avoided politics and instead poured her considerable intelligence and energy into entertaining. Her social grace and charm helped to offset the public aloofness of James Madison. But while she excelled as a hostess, she was also tough: During the War of 1812 when British soldiers marched on Washington and burned the White House, she stayed behind until the last possible moment to supervise the removal of documents and valuables. Thanks to her presence of mind, a full-length portrait of George Washington painted by Gilbert Stuart was saved from the fire and hangs in the current White House.

Julia Tyler, second wife of John Tyler, followed Dolley Madison's tradition. During her brief stay in the White House in 1844, she entertained lavishly, received guests while seated on a raised platform, and hired her own press agent. Mary Todd Lincoln also caused a stir, but for negative reasons. President Abraham Lincoln called her his "child wife" because of her emotional instability. Her compulsive shopping and other erratic behavior drew widespread public attention and hurt Lincoln's image during the difficult times of the Civil War.

In the second half of the nineteenth century, public interest in first ladies grew as the spread of mass-circulation newspapers and magazines (and the leisure time to read them) steadily increased. First ladies became celebrities on a par with actresses, sports figures, and society women. At the same time, the image of women in general as passive, delicate creatures was fading fast as the women's suffrage movement arose. Women would not win the right to vote until 1920, however.

Julia Grant was the first president's wife to become a truly national figure and the first to be called "first lady of the land." During Ulysses S. Grant's two terms in the post–Civil War period, Julia redecorated the White House at great expense and entertained regally. And the public loved her flamboyance. The elegant Frances Folsom, who married Grover Cleveland in a well-publicized White House wedding in 1886, attained even greater public celebrity. Her hairstyle and clothing became national fads and her White House parties and receptions had great social cachet.

TWENTIETH-CENTURY FIRST LADIES

Edith Roosevelt, second wife of Theodore Roosevelt, was first lady at the start of the twentieth century, and her handling of the job was, in keeping with the start of the new millennium, distinctly modern. For the first time, a first lady hired her own staff to answer mail and reporters' questions instead of relying on the president's staff. She displayed a new sophistication in her dealings with the press, carefully managing news about her boisterous family of six children so as to project a positive image. And while she was not a political activist, it is well known that she gave political advice to her husband and that he listened to and heeded it. Unlike Abigail Adams, she was not criticized for her influence.

Successors to Edith Roosevelt found other new possibilities in the role. It was widely believed that William Howard Taft would not have become president without the driving ambition of Helen Taft, who was an energetic participant in her husband's political life and who had little patience with social events. President Woodrow Wilson's first wife, Ellen, became the first first lady to publicly support social legislation pending before Congress when she openly campaigned for a bill to improve housing in the poor neighborhoods of the capital city.

Wilson's second wife, Edith Wilson, showed little interest in politics until her husband suffered a stroke in 1919. She then took on many of his responsibilities and was believed by many to be running the government while he recovered. Lou Hoover, wife of President Herbert Hoover, was a serious intellectual who spoke five languages. As first lady, she commented frequently on social issues.

THE MODERN FIRST LADY

Eleanor Roosevelt, wife of President Franklin D. Roosevelt, is judged by many to have been the most remarkable first lady in the nation's history. She held the position from 1933 to 1945 and set a daunting example for others to follow. A woman of great energy and intellect, she traveled extensively and fought openly for a variety of liberal issues, chief among them women's rights and an end to racial discrimination. During World War II, she visited soldiers at the front and served as deputy director of the Office of Civilian Defense. And while other first ladies had settled for behind-the-scenes influence, Mrs. Roosevelt stood as an independent political force, holding regular press conferences (to which only women reporters were invited), giving lectures, making regular radio broadcasts, and writing a daily syndicated newspaper column. Her activism made enemies as well as friends and she was sometimes ridiculed in the press, but she broadened her husband's political and social outlook, increasing his base of support, and she earned a place in history alongside him.

When Mrs. Roosevelt left the White House, she had changed the role and the public's expectation of the first lady drastically and permanently; after her, Americans would begin to look for an active, involved woman in the White House. The passive, retiring first lady came to be considered a historical relic.

In sharp contrast to Mrs. Roosevelt, however, her next two successors as first lady, Bess Truman and Mamie Eisenhower, chose to remain in the background. Although Mrs. Truman shrank from publicity and refused to grant interviews, it was well known that she was very influential with her husband and gave him considerable, if general, political advice. Despite her weak heart and chronic inner ear problems, Mrs. Eisenhower was more visible than Mrs. Truman. Her political involvement was negligible, but she was widely admired by women across the country for her dress and coiffure.

Jacqueline Kennedy's ascension to the first lady role raised it to a glamorous high. Although in many ways the most private of people, she succeeded in transforming the White House into a grand public stage where elegance and cultural entertainment drew the nation's fond attention and admiration. Her cultured charm and poise, seen best in her televised tour of the White House in 1962, left her successors with a high-profile position to fill.

Lady Bird Johnson may have lacked some of Mrs. Kennedy's style, but she resurrected the political possibilities of the first lady. Mrs. Johnson helped her husband win the 1964 election by setting the precedent of campaigning for him on her own in the South; Lyndon Johnson, at the time, faced serious opposition there because of his support for civil rights legislation. Lady Bird was able to win over voters who might have shunned her husband and thus pioneered what has become a familiar role for subsequent first ladies, that of political surrogate. Mrs. Johnson also traveled thousands of miles across the country to support her beautification program and lobbied Congress in behalf of the Highway Beautification Act of 1965.

Pat Nixon was not as publicly prominent as her immediate predecessors or successors. By nature reserved in public, she dutifully made the necessary appearances. Because she also tried to avoid publicity whenever possible, many people did not know that she was one of the most widely traveled first ladies, that she visited a hospital at the front lines in

Vietnam, and that she was the first first lady to represent the president abroad in peacetime.

Unlike Pat Nixon, Betty Ford was active in a variety of social causes, and she encouraged the fine arts whenever possible. She worked in behalf of the poor, the elderly, and the handicapped, and became perhaps the nation's most visible spokesperson for women's rights in general and the Equal Rights Amendment (ERA) in particular. She also proved to be one of the most candid of first ladies; she was willing to discuss almost everything, including controversial issues, such as abortion and premarital sex, and personal difficulties, such as her own breast cancer.

Rosalynn Carter campaigned extensively on her own for her husband and became one of the most active and influential first ladies since Eleanor Roosevelt. She spoke and lobbied avidly on behalf of her own interests, which included better care of the mentally ill and elderly, passage of the Equal Rights Amendment to the Constitution for women, and for improving the plight of refugees. She regularly sat in on cabinet meetings and occasionally represented the president on trips abroad. The extent of her involvement in the Carter administration tested the limits of the first lady's role and provoked considerable public criticism.

Nancy Reagan pulled back from the extreme exposure of Mrs. Carter. Her public political activity was slight; she exercised her influence behind the scenes. After a Carter administration that had been viewed as "austere," she was interested in restoring "elegance" to the White House. The public no longer accepted such a limited social role for the first lady, however, and Mrs. Reagan's public image suffered. She did not begin to gain wide public favor until she began to travel widely and host conferences aimed at reducing drug abuse among young people in the United States. She also promoted the Foster Grandparents Program.

Barbara Bush focused her public activity as first lady on eliminating illiteracy. In keeping with her husband's "Thousand Points of Light" theme, she also encouraged voluntarism and community service. She was not publicly prominent in political affairs, and in her memoirs Mrs. Bush described her own political judgment as poor and denied any influence on policy matters. Yet some observers felt that she had extensive influence with President Bush, who publicly acknowledged that he respected and valued her opinions.

Hillary Rodham Clinton's impact during her husband's two terms in office also has been likened to Mrs. Roosevelt's. An intelligent and well-educated wife, mother, and a highly successful attorney, to many she epitomized the modern woman. Where several of the first ladies who had recently preceded her—Pat Nixon, Nancy Reagan, and Barbara Bush—acted as more traditional first ladies, staying behind the scenes, acting as supportive spouses, and taking on as their "causes" relatively uncontroversial topics, Mrs. Clinton moved to the political fore with an active role in her husband's administration. She assumed leadership of the president's task force on health care reform—a major legislative undertaking that ultimately failed in the face of strong opposition. She also registered some other firsts, becoming the first sitting first lady to be subpoenaed by and to testify before a grand jury in connection with the Whitewater investigation. Her greatest personal triumph, however, occurred in 2000 when she became the first first lady to run for and win public office. Her election to the U.S. Senate from New York raised the bar for high-profile activism on the part of first ladies.

Laura Bush, Barbara Bush's daughter-in-law, took a more traditional, quieter approach to the role of first lady than had Hillary Clinton. A former librarian and teacher, Laura Bush focused on education and reading. In 2001 she organized what became an annual event during her husband's White House tenure, the National Book Festival in Washington, D.C. She testified twice on Capitol

Hill in 2002, on education issues. After the September 11, 2001, terrorist attacks on the United States, she appeared regularly on television, trying to reassure children; she became known as the "comforter in chief." Mrs. Bush, who had higher popularity ratings than her husband in 2004, campaigned hard for his reelection.

The modern first lady, then, is part of her husband's team. In one sense, this always has been true. Every first lady has had at least a social role to play; the success with which she has filled it has been important to the success of her husband's administration. Yet over the years the position has expanded beyond simply "hostess" as first ladies have enlarged their roles. Today the first lady takes positions, works for causes, makes public appearances and speeches, and often is an important figure in her own right. First ladies now may take a much more active role in electoral politics as well. At one time, the idea of a woman campaigning was inconceivable, and even the otherwise irrepressible Eleanor Roosevelt did not campaign separately for her husband. This, however, has changed. Today the first lady campaigns for the White House nearly as extensively as her husband.

Another change in recent years has been the increasing emergence of "second ladies," or vice presidents' wives. Joan Mondale, wife of Vice President Walter Mondale, testified several times on Capitol Hill about art, her field of expertise, in 1979 and 1980. Marilyn Quayle, an attorney, the wife of Vice President Dan Quayle, testified twice in 1990 about health-related issues. Tipper Gore, wife of Vice President Al Gore, appeared before a Senate committee to discuss mental health issues. Tipper Gore had been well known for her advocacy against X-rated song lyrics even before her husband became vice president. Lynne Cheney, who headed the National Endowment for the Humanities from 1986–1993, also was prominent before her husband, Richard Cheney, became vice president. Lynne Cheney was a fellow at the American Enterprise Institute and an author.

Martha Washington

Born: June 21, 1731;[2] New Kent County, Virginia
Parents: Col. John and Frances Jones Dandridge
Spouses: Col. Daniel Parke Custis (June 1749; New Kent County); George Washington (January 6, 1759; New Kent County)
Children: By Daniel Parke Custis: John Parke (1754–1781); Martha "Patsy" Parke (1756–1773)
Died: May 22, 1802; Mount Vernon, Virginia

The early years of Martha Dandridge Custis Washington are not well documented. Her father was a small plantation owner, who, although not well-to-do, was part of the Virginia aristocracy. Martha was well trained in the social graces but apparently had little schooling, as her erratic spelling attests.

In 1749 Martha met and married Col. Daniel Parke Custis, son of a wealthy Virginia plantation owner. Custis, by whom Martha had four children (two died in infancy), was twice her age. Daniel's father left his son his considerable estate when he died in November 1749. Thus when Daniel himself died of heart failure on July 8, 1757, the estate passed on to Martha, making her a very wealthy widow at the age of twenty-six.

George Washington probably had met Martha before her husband's death, and shortly afterward he came to pay his respects to the widow. Courtship followed, and although many historians have argued that Martha was not Washington's first love, the pair married in 1759. The addition of Martha's estate to George's plantation, Mount Vernon, where the Washingtons lived, made the couple wealthy, and the years until 1775 were spent tending to the plantation. But this period was punctuated by two

Martha Washington

sorrows: the Washingtons' failure to have more children and the 1773 death of Martha's daughter, Patsy, from an epileptic seizure.

With the onset of the American Revolution in 1775, George left Mount Vernon to lead the American army. Martha spent the summers of the war at Mount Vernon, but each winter, when the armies paused in their struggle, she joined her husband in camp, endeavoring to cheer him and his troops. When the war drew to a successful conclusion in 1781, Martha looked forward to a quiet retirement with George, but instead he became the nation's first president on April 30, 1789.

Martha did not join George in New York, the temporary capital of the new nation, until May 1789. She found being first lady (although not called such then) to be somewhat restrictive: "I live a very dull life here. . . . I am more like a state prisoner than anything else." Martha may not have been well read, but she was a pleasant and engaging hostess who generally enjoyed entertaining; her Mount Vernon home rarely had been empty. As the nation's first first

lady, she established practices that were followed by her successors, such as the regular Friday afternoon parties for ladies and the custom of opening the White House to all visitors on New Year's Day. The latter custom remained in effect until 1931, when it was discontinued by the Hoovers.

George and Martha retired to Mount Vernon in 1797. The time left was not easy; financial worries nagged them, for the plantation had not been very profitable in recent years, and Martha's health had begun to deteriorate. "Lady Washington" lived quietly at her home until her death in 1802. She was buried on the plantation grounds next to George, who had died two years earlier.

Abigail Adams

Born: November 11, 1744; Weymouth, Massachusetts
Parents: Rev. William and Elizabeth Quincy Smith
Spouse: John Adams (October 25, 1764; Weymouth)
Children: Abigail Amelia (1765–1813); John Quincy (1767–1848); Susanna (1768–1770); Charles (1770–1800); Thomas Boylston (1772–1832)
Died: October 28, 1818; Quincy, Massachusetts

Outspoken Abigail Smith Adams was the second of four children born to a New England minister and his wife. Abigail was sickly as a child, and she had no formal schooling, yet she acquired a considerable education in the private library of her family. Her intelligence, sharp wit, and willingness to speak out impressed those people who knew her.

One such person was John Adams, who made his first reference to Abigail in his diary when she was only fourteen. After overcoming the objections of her parents, who did not consider him to be in her social class, John and Abigail married in 1764. Abigail quickly proved to be an adept manager of their household. She ran their family farm efficiently, prosperously, and largely on her own while John was pursuing his legal and political careers and serving as an American diplomat abroad. She also helped to educate their children, teaching them Latin after first teaching herself.

In 1784, after a six-year separation, she sailed to London and rejoined John, who was then the first American minister to England. She spent four years in London and Paris, not entirely approving of the customs there, before returning to the United States in 1789 when John became vice president. Abigail became first lady when John was elected president in 1796. In many ways the four years that she spent as first lady were difficult for her. The expense of entertaining was a strain on the president's $25,000 salary, and the demands on her left her with almost no time of her own. Although she managed to save some money and find some private time, she complained bitterly (but privately) about both problems. Moreover, John was not a popular president and was subjected to constant vilification in the press, which angered Abigail greatly.

In 1800 Abigail supervised the move from Philadelphia, the temporary capital, to the new presidential mansion in Washington. Unfortunately, the mansion was far from finished when she arrived; only a few rooms were habitable and many facilities were lacking. But as a practical New Englander, she made do and hung her laundry in the East Room. The nation's new capital was in no better condition, with mud roads and half-built buildings, and Abigail was privately unhappy at having left Philadelphia for it. Nevertheless, she spent her time there laying the foundations of a proper social life for the new capital.

Abigail was a prolific letter writer (more than two thousand of her letters still exist) and from them it is clear that, unlike most other first ladies for years to come, she took an active interest in politics and did not hesitate to express her views on the issues and personalities of the day. For example, in 1775

Abigal Adams

Abigail had urged John to support American independence and later to back more education for women and the abolition of slavery. As a pioneering feminist, Abigail repeatedly urged her husband to "remember the ladies" in forming the new government. She attacked his political enemies such as Alexander Hamilton, who opposed Adams's nomination for a second term and whom she called "the very devil." Her husband had a very high regard for her judgment and intelligence, and her influence and political involvement were clear to her contemporaries. Many of them, however, took exception to both as unbecoming a woman. The extent of her political activism, while perhaps not as great as that of some modern first ladies, would be unmatched for years to come.

Roundly disliked by Federalists for refusing to go to war with France and by the Republicans for being a "monarchist," John Adams served only one term as president before retiring to Massachusetts. Abigail lived there for seventeen years, her health gradually deteriorating but her mind remaining

WIVES WHO DIED BEFORE THEIR HUSBAND'S PRESIDENCY

Often overlooked in discussions of first ladies are the four women who died before their husbands reached the White House: Martha Jefferson, Rachel Jackson, Hannah Van Buren, and Ellen Arthur.

Martha Jefferson

Martha Wayles Skelton Jefferson was born October 19, 1748, in Charles City County, Virginia. Her parents were John and Martha Eppes Wayles. When she was seventeen, Martha married Bathhurst Skelton, a lawyer and landowner, by whom she had one son. Skelton died in 1768, and four years later, on January 1, 1772, she married Thomas Jefferson. She and Jefferson had six more children, but only two—daughters Martha "Patsy" Washington (1772–1836) and Mary "Polly" (1778–1804)—lived more than two years.

Relatively little is known of Martha Jefferson. Few references to her remain, and none of her correspondence still exists. Although there are no portraits of her, she was apparently a very attractive woman who had considerable talent on the piano and harpsichord, as well as the practical ability to keep accounts for the Jeffersons' Virginia plantation, Monticello. Moreover, her inheritance made her fairly wealthy.

Never very strong, Martha's health was weakened by the repeated burdens of childbearing and a flight through the snow and freezing weather from British troops in 1780. The birth of her last child, in May 1782, proved too much for her, and she died on September 6, 1782, at Monticello. Jefferson was so distraught at her death that he refused to leave his room for three weeks. He never remarried.

Rachel Jackson

Rachel Donelson Robards Jackson hailed from a pioneering family. Her parents, John and Rachel Stockley Donelson, were among the first settlers of Nashville, Tennessee. Rachel was born on June 15, 1767, in Halifax County, Virginia; she moved with her family to Tennessee in 1780. She had little formal education.

In 1784 Rachel married Lewis Robards, a Kentucky landowner, and moved to Kentucky with him. Robards, however, proved to be insanely jealous and abusive. Fearing physical harm, Rachel fled back to Nashville. She returned once to Robards but shortly afterward left again in the company of Andrew Jackson, who had been sent to her aid by her family. To protect her from Robards, Jackson brought her to Natchez, Mississippi.

In 1791, on receiving word that Robards had been granted a divorce, Andrew and Rachel married. But the information was wrong: Robards only had been given permission to seek the divorce in Kentucky, and the actual divorce did not occur until 1793. When the Jacksons were informed, they immediately remarried on January 17, 1794, but the damage was done. The fact that Rachel was technically an adulteress would haunt her for the rest of her life, and Andrew fought several duels to protect her honor.

Rachel stayed at the Hermitage, the Jackson estate in Nashville, for much of her married life. She wanted only to remain quietly at home with her husband, but his ambition frequently took him away for long intervals. Although she moved to Washington after he became a senator, she was generally reclusive. Short, stout, and interested only in friends, family, and church, she favorably impressed some visitors with her unassuming ways, but others thought her to be detrimental to Jackson's career. Rachel accepted Jackson's election to the presidency in 1828 with great reluctance, saying that she "would rather be a doorkeeper in the house of God than live in that palace in Washington." She feared that she was unsuited to be first lady.

During the 1828 campaign, Jackson's opponents had viciously resurrected the story of Rachel's "adultery." The details, however, were kept from her until she overheard some women discussing them disparagingly. Friends found her weeping hysterically. Rachel suffered a heart attack a few days later and died on December 22, 1828, at the Hermitage. Jackson never remarried.

Hannah Van Buren

The first president's wife to be born an American citizen, Hannah Hoes Van Buren entered the world on March 8, 1783, at Kinderhook, New York. Her parents, Johannes and Maria Quackenboss Hoes, were Dutch, and Hannah grew up speaking that language. She knew Martin Van Buren as a child, and by age eighteen the couple was engaged. Because Martin wanted to study law and gain admittance to the bar before they wed, the wedding did not take place until February 21, 1807, in Catskill, New York.

Shortly after their marriage, Martin began his political career. He was a New York state senator from 1812 to 1820 and state attorney general from 1816 to 1819. From 1808 to 1817, Hannah spent much of her time in their home in Hudson, New York, raising their new family. They had four children: Abraham (1807–1873), John (1810–1866), Martin (1812–1855), and Smith (1817–1876). In 1817 she moved the family to Albany, where the weather proved bad for her health. She contracted

tuberculosis and gradually declined. She never left her home after September 1818 and died on February 5, 1819, at the age of thirty-five.

Very little is written about Hannah Van Buren. She left no correspondence or writing of her own, and her husband's autobiograph says virtually nothing about his wife of twelve years. Apparently she was an attractive although shy woman who was religious and very concerned with the poor and the needy. Though Hannah was originally buried in Albany, Martin later had her reburied in Kinderhook. He never remarried.

Ellen Arthur

Ellen Lewis Herndon Arthur, the daughter of William and Frances Hansbrough Herndon, was born on August 30, 1837, at Fredericksburg, Virginia. After her father, a naval officer, died at sea in 1857, she and her mother moved to New York City. There she met Chester A. Arthur, a young lawyer, in 1858, and they married on October 25, 1859. Chester's law practice proved very successful, and he entered New York State politics. The Arthurs continued to live in New York City, where Ellen cared for their three children: Billy (1860–1863), Chester Jr. (1864–1937), and Ellen (1871–1915).

A gifted singer, Ellen was active in the Mendelssohn Glee Club and performed publicly several times. She also was active in charity work. Her musical and charitable work helped Chester's developing political career. In early January 1880 Ellen became ill after waiting outside in the cold for a carriage. Her illness was not considered serious at first, but she worsened abruptly and died of pneumonia on January 12. She was buried in Albany. Chester never remarried; he placed flowers before her portrait every day and kept her room in their home as she had left it.

alert, before she died of typhoid fever at the age of seventy-four. She was buried in Quincy. John, who outlived her by six years, was buried next to her. Shortly before his death, John wrote of the love and admiration that he always had had for his wife and spoke of his gratitude for her "never-failing support" during his political career.

Dolley Madison

Born: May 20, 1768; New Garden, North Carolina
Parents: John and Mary Coles Payne
Spouses: John Todd (January 7, 1790; Philadelphia); James Madison (September 15, 1794; Harewood, Virginia)
Children: By John Todd: John Payne (1792–1852); William Temple (1793)
Died: July 12, 1849; Washington, D.C.

Dolley Madison

Perhaps the most popular of the early first ladies, the elegant Dorothea "Dolley" Payne Todd Madison was born into a Quaker family of nine children.[3] Her family lived on a Virginia plantation until she was five, when her father freed their slaves and moved his family to Philadelphia. There, in 1789, Dolley met a young Quaker lawyer, John Todd, whom she married a year later. They had been married for three years when a yellow fever epidemic struck Philadelphia and claimed Dolley's husband and younger son.

Shortly after Todd's death, Dolley met James Madison and within a year married him. For the indiscretion of marrying outside her faith (James was Episcopalian), she was expelled from the Friends, but this only seemed to allow her true self to shine through. She discarded her plain gray Quaker garments for bright clothing and elegant turbans. Moreover, she found that she loved entertaining and delighted in giving large, formal dinner parties. In fact, she was greatly admired as a hostess, particularly because of her memory for names and her

remarkable ability to put everyone at ease. In this, she was an asset to Madison's political career, for he was generally withdrawn and cool around crowds.

With Dolley as first lady the White House became a festive place. Although she occasionally had served as hostess for the widowed Thomas Jefferson, Dolley came into her own when Madison was elected president in 1808. Her weekly receptions always were lively and gay. And she paid all the expected social calls, knowing that to do so would help her husband. So popular was Dolley that even her habit of taking snuff, which was considered very unladylike, was overlooked. Although Dolley greatly loved social life and company, she was not one dimensional. As a Quaker, she was a well-educated woman for her time, and her managerial skills were good as well. But she downplayed her intelligence and strong will to help her husband.

During the War of 1812 when the British threatened Washington, she displayed her courage by staying behind in the White House to supervise the removal of documents. When she finally was forced to leave the mansion, she took with her the portrait of George Washington by American portraitist Gilbert Stuart. (Contrary to popular legend, the painting was not cut out of its frame. Dolley had its frame broken, and it was rolled up.)

When Madison's second term expired in 1817, he and Dolley retired to their Virginia estate, Montpelier. Life was not easy in retirement; Dolley still entertained, but financial woes plagued them, aggravated by the wastefulness of her son, John Payne. After Madison died in 1836, Dolley was reduced to near poverty and had to sell first James's papers on the Constitutional Convention and then Montpelier itself to pay her debts. Finally, she returned to Washington and spent the rest of her life there.

Even as she grew older, she remained the center of Washington society, admired by every president through James K. Polk. She was even granted a lifetime seat on the floor of the House of Representatives. In 1849 her funeral was attended by every dignitary in the capital. She was buried in Washington but later was removed to rest beside Madison at Montpelier.

Elizabeth Monroe

Born: July 30, 1768; New York City
Parents: Capt. Lawrence and Hannah Aspinwall Kortright
Spouse: James Monroe (February 16, 1786; New York City)
Children: Eliza Kortright (1786–1835); James Spence (1799–1801); Maria Hester (1803–1850)
Died: September 23, 1830; Oak Hill, Virginia

Elizabeth Kortright Monroe, who brought a new touch of aristocracy to the White House, was born into one of New York's premier families. Not much is known of her younger years. She met James Mon-

Elizabeth Monroe

roe in 1785, and although her family and friends disapproved of both his politics and his social status, she married him the next year.

The Monroes moved from New York to Virginia in 1789. James was elected to the U.S. Senate in 1790, and from 1794 to 1796 he served as ambassador to France. While in France, Elizabeth, on learning that the wife of the Marquis de Lafayette (America's friend in the Revolutionary War) was facing execution, boldly drove to the prison to speak with her publicly. The gesture earned Madame Lafayette's release. James later served on other diplomatic missions to Europe (1803–1807), and Elizabeth spent much of that time in Paris, where she found the environment convivial.

While in Europe, the Monroes adopted European formality, believing that it helped them to deal with Europeans. That formality was carried into the White House when James became president in 1817, for the Monroes believed it to be appropriate to the presidential office. The contrast between the haughty Elizabeth Monroe and her predecessor, the warm, friendly Dolley Madison, was dramatic and, so far as social Washington was concerned, very unfavorable for Elizabeth. Quiet and somewhat aloof, she refused to follow the accepted Washington custom of paying social calls. Her many critics decried her as too aristocratic and French, and for a time they boycotted her receptions. Her elder daughter, Eliza, angered many with her arrogant behavior, and Elizabeth angered them further when she refused to extend mass invitations to younger daughter Maria's wedding, the first in the White House.

Bothered by chronically weak health and disliking much of her role as first lady, Elizabeth nonetheless continued her entertaining until she left the White House in 1825. Her last years were spent at the Monroe mansion, Oak Hill, in Virginia, but they were clouded by financial difficulties. She died in 1830 and was buried at Oak Hill. Monroe died in New York a year later and was buried next to her.

Louisa Adams

Louisa Adams

Born: February 12, 1775; London, England
Parents: Joshua and Catherine Nuth Johnson
Spouse: John Quincy Adams (July 26, 1797; London)
Children: George Washington (1801–1829); John (1803–1834); Charles Francis (1807–1886); Louisa Catherine (1811–1812)
Died: May 15, 1852; Washington, D.C.

Louisa Catherine Johnson Adams did not see the United States until she was twenty-six. She was born in 1775 in England, where her father represented an American tobacco firm, but her family moved shortly to France and lived there until 1790. In 1790 they returned to England. There, in 1795, she met John Quincy Adams, who was on a diplo-

matic mission for the United States. Two years later they married. The early years of their marriage were somewhat strained because their personalities were quite different in many ways—she was outgoing, sensitive, and forgiving; he was stern, dogmatic, and demanding. They grew much closer in later years, however.

Louisa's time abroad has led some to call her "the most traveled woman of her time." From England she went to Berlin, where John Quincy was the American minister to Prussia during the administration of his father, John Adams (1797–1801). When Jefferson became president in 1801, John Quincy was recalled, bringing Louisa to the United States for the first time. There she finally met her in-laws, who received her with reservations. (Abigail Adams, in particular, questioned Louisa's foreign childhood, her associations with British royalty, and whether the younger woman was good enough for Abigail's favorite son.) From 1803 to 1808, Louisa lived in Massachusetts while John Quincy served in the U.S. Senate.

In 1809 President James Madison appointed him minister to Russia. Concerned about the expenses of living abroad, John Quincy forced Louisa to leave her two oldest sons—George, eight, and John, six— behind with their grandmother. The time in Russia was difficult for Louisa. The harsh weather adversely affected her health, and her only daughter died after living less than a year. Moreover, Louisa was frequently lonely, particularly after John Quincy left for Belgium in 1814 to negotiate the treaty ending the War of 1812. Early in 1815 he sent word to her that his mission in Russia was finished and that she should join him in France. After packing their goods and disposing of their property in St. Petersburg, she set out with her young son in the dead of the Russian winter for Paris; only her courage and resourcefulness got them through the perilous two thousand-mile journey.

An intelligent and talented woman, Louisa spoke French fluently and enjoyed sketching and playing the harp and piano. Yet she seems to have had virtually no effect on John Quincy's political career. By her own admission, "no woman certainly had interfered less in [politics] than I have." For his part, John Quincy deliberately shared none of his professional life with her.

President James Monroe appointed John Quincy secretary of state in 1817, and in 1825 he became president. Louisa's time as first lady was not a pleasant one, however. She held regular, well-attended receptions, but they were rather lackluster and placed a strain on her. She suffered from poor health in the form of recurrent migraine headaches and fainting spells, and she was hurt by the vicious criticism that was aimed at her husband, particularly after his controversial victory over Andrew Jackson in 1824. No doubt she was pleased to return to Massachusetts in 1829 when his term expired.

Louisa came back to Washington when John Quincy was elected to the House of Representatives in 1830. There she lived quietly the rest of her life,

generally apart from Washington society. In 1848 John Quincy suffered a stroke on the floor of the House and died without regaining consciousness. Despite the strains their marriage had endured in earlier times, Louisa's letters indicate her anguish at losing her husband of fifty years so abruptly. She died four years later and was buried next to him in Quincy, Massachusetts.

Anna Harrison

Born: July 25, 1775; Walpack Township, New Jersey
Parents: John and Anna Tuthill Symmes
Spouse: William Henry Harrison (November 25, 1795; North Bend, Ohio)
Children: Elizabeth Bassett (1796–1846); John Cleves Symmes (1798–1830); Lucy Singleton (1800–1826); William Henry Jr. (1802–1838); John Scott (1804–1878); Benjamin (1806–1840); Mary Symmes (1809–1842); Carter Bassett (1811–1839); Anna Tuthill (1813–1845); James Findlay (1814–1817)
Died: February 25, 1864; North Bend

Almost a footnote in White House history, Anna Symmes Harrison never saw the executive mansion that she was supposed to run. Anna's father was a New Jersey farmer and an army officer. She was educated at some of the better schools for girls in the young nation and is the first first lady for whom there is a definite record of her schooling. In 1795 Anna's father took her to the new Ohio settlement of North Bend, where she met William Henry Harrison, a military officer who was stationed there. The two eloped the same year over the objections of Anna's father, who did not believe that an army man could adequately support his daughter. The life Anna adopted was that of an army officer's wife. She traveled with her husband until her family

WHITE HOUSE HOSTESSES SERVING WIDOWER OR BACHELOR PRESIDENTS

Six presidents had no wife to act as first lady during part or all of their tenure in office: four presidents (Jefferson, Jackson, Van Buren, and Arthur) entered the White House as widowers, and two others (Buchanan and Cleveland) were bachelors; Cleveland married while in office. The following are the women who acted as surrogate first ladies while serving widower or bachelor presidents.

Martha Jefferson Randolph

The need for a surrogate first lady first occurred during the term of Thomas Jefferson, who had been a widower for eighteen years when he became president in 1801. Although Jefferson did less formal entertaining than his predecessor John Adams, the White House was still the center of much social activity. Dolley Madison, wife of Secretary of State James Madison, and Jefferson's daughter, Martha Jefferson Randolph, frequently acted as hostess for Jefferson.

Martha Randolph was the eldest of Jefferson's six children and one of only two to live to maturity. She was born in 1772 at Monticello, her family's home in Virginia. After her mother died in 1782, Martha went to a boarding school in Philadelphia. In 1784, when Jefferson became U.S. minister to France, Martha went with him. She attended an elite convent school in Paris for five years, until her decision to become a nun prompted her father to remove her from the school and hire tutors instead. Martha's girlhood letters indicate a great interest in her studies and her personal habits and appearance.

After returning to the United States in 1789, Martha married her cousin, Thomas Mann Randolph, in 1790 and had the first of her five children in 1791. The demands of her family prevented her from acting regularly as White House hostess. Her only extended stays at the mansion were during the winters of 1802–1803 and 1805–1806. An intelligent and very practical woman, Martha skillfully managed the White House and later Monticello. After the deaths of her father in 1826 and her husband in 1828, Martha was forced to sell the Virginia estate to settle debts. Her last appearance in Washington society was during Andrew Jackson's administration when Secretary of State Martin Van Buren, needing a hostess for a state dinner, turned to Martha. She died of apoplexy in 1836.

Emily Donelson

Andrew Jackson came to the presidency in 1829 newly widowed; his wife, Rachel, died in the interval between his election and the inauguration. For much of his time in office the role of first lady was played by his niece, Emily Donelson, who was born in 1808 in Davidson County, Tennessee. Emily was educated at the Old Academy in Nashville and at age sixteen married a cousin who served as Jackson's secretary. She had four children.

After the election and before her death, Rachel Jackson, who was uncomfortable in Washington society, had asked Emily to handle many of the social functions of the White House. Despite her relative lack of sophistication and education, Emily was charming, gracious, and very popular in Washington society. She remained a hostess there until shortly before her death in 1836 from tuberculosis.

Angelica Singleton Van Buren

Martin Van Buren's wife, Hannah, died nineteen years before he reached the White House in 1837. His daughter-in-law, Angelica Singleton Van Buren, served as the mansion's hostess during his administration. The daughter of a wealthy South Carolina planter, Angelica was related to several powerful southern families and was a distant relative of Dolley Madison. She met President Van Buren's eldest son, Abraham, at a state dinner in March 1838 and married him eight months later. President Van Buren, who until that time had had no White House hostess and had done little entertaining, asked Angelica to take charge of the mansion's social life. For the remainder of Van Buren's term in office, Angelica enlivened the White House.

Harriet Lane

Because James Buchanan never married, his niece, Harriet Lane, served as hostess during his administration (1857–1861). Born in 1831, Harriet was orphaned at age nine, and her guardianship passed to Buchanan. He found homes with relatives for her siblings but chose to raise Harriet as his own daughter. She was sent to the best schools, concluding with two years at an elite Georgetown convent school.

Few women have come to the White House as well prepared for their social duties as the lively and attractive Harriet Lane. In fact, Buchanan's term was judged by many contemporaries to be the "gayest administration" because of her skill as a hostess. As with other immensely popular first ladies, fashions changed in response to her preferences, and the lower necklines she favored suddenly became the rage.

Yet Harriet was more than just a capable hostess. Having been exposed for years to political discussions at Buchanan's table, she was well informed, and it is likely that the president listened to her opinions on many questions. She also was seen as an intermediary by those with problems and therefore received many appeals for help from the general public.

In 1866 Harriet married Henry Johnston and had two sons, neither of whom lived beyond age fourteen. When Buchanan died in 1869, he left his Pennsylvania estate to Harriet, and she lived there until her husband died in 1884. Harriet's remaining years were spent in Washington and abroad. Her extensive art collection formed the basis of the collection of the National Gallery of Art, which was opened to the public in 1941. She died in 1903.

Rose Cleveland

Grover Cleveland (1885–1889) was the second bachelor president to reside in the White House. He eventually married while president, but until then his sister Rose served as White House hostess. The youngest child in the family, Rose Cleveland was born in Fayetteville, New York, in 1846. An intelligent and well-educated woman, she taught at Houghton Seminary and gained a favorable reputation as a lecturer. She knew several languages and published scholarly studies on literature. Although a sparkling conversationalist and a gracious hostess, she sometimes intimidated visitors with her intellect. At times, she was bored with her social duties. Finding receiving lines dull, Rose would occupy herself by silently conjugating Greek verbs. After Cleveland married Frances Folsom in 1886, Rose returned to her scholarly work and lived in Europe until her death in 1918.

Anna Harrison

reception in Washington. When William Henry left for the capital in February 1841, Anna was too ill to accompany him; she decided to wait for spring before going herself. But Harrison died after only a month in office, and Anna never left Ohio.

Anna Harrison lived for nearly twenty-three more years in North Bend. In fact, she outlived all but one of her children. After her home burned down, she spent her final years in the home of her last surviving son, John, and there she died in 1864. Despite being the wife of one president and the grandmother of another (Benjamin Harrison), Anna never saw Washington. She was buried next to her husband and her father in North Bend.

became too large. The couple lived primarily in a substantial log cabin in North Bend during their marriage, but they did spend a few years in Vincennes when Harrison was governor of the Indiana Territory. There Anna managed to care for her large family, frequently without any help from her absent husband.

Anna was intelligent and much better educated than most frontier women, and she was a devout Presbyterian. The years on the frontier were hard on her health, however. Moreover, the Harrisons rarely had any excess money, particularly after they were forced to assume the debts of their eldest son, who owed the government $12,000 when he died.

When the country went wild over the "Tippecanoe and Tyler Too" campaign in 1840 ("Tippecanoe" was Harrison's nickname), Anna was far less enthusiastic. Her husband had been content in retirement, and she thought he should stay there. She was concerned about her ability to be a satisfactory hostess—although she had proved able to entertain capably when necessary—and about her

Letitia Tyler

Born: November 12, 1790; Cedar Grove, New Kent County, Virginia
Parents: Col. Robert and Mary Brown Christian
Spouse: John Tyler (March 29, 1813; Cedar Grove)
Children: Mary (1815–1848); Robert (1816–1877); John Jr. (1819–1896); Letitia (1821–1907); Elizabeth (1823–1850); Anne Contesse (1825); Alice (1827–1854); Tazewell (1830–1874)
Died: September 10, 1842; Washington, D.C.

Letitia Christian Tyler was born into a wealthy Virginia plantation family; her father was a friend of President George Washington. Although Letitia apparently had no formal education, she learned at home the skills needed to be the mistress of a southern plantation. Modest and reserved, she had many friends.

Letitia met John Tyler in 1808, and after a five-year courtship in part imposed by her parents, they married. Letitia's skills as a manager were needed quickly, for John's law practice and budding political career—he had been elected to the Virginia House

Letitia Tylor

of Delegates in 1811—kept him away from home frequently. Apparently, Letitia was an excellent manager and ran the growing Tyler plantation very effectively. She refused to go to Washington when John was elected senator from Virginia in 1826, both because she was needed on the plantation and because she disliked the unpleasant conditions then found in the capital. She also was a quiet woman who was devoted to her family and preferred to remain in her husband's shadow.

By the time John became president after William Henry Harrison's death in 1841, Letitia's health had deteriorated dramatically. She had suffered a serious stroke in 1839 and had only partially recovered. Although she could still oversee the plantation, she was largely homebound. Letitia finally came to the White House, but she took no part in the mansion's public life. During her time as first lady, her daughter Letitia managed the White House, and her daughter-in-law Priscilla served as hostess. Her only public appearance was at daughter Elizabeth's White House wedding in January 1842. Otherwise, she

remained out of sight, a semi-invalid, content to read her Bible and prayer book.

On September 9, 1842, Letitia suffered another stroke. She died one day later, becoming the first president's wife to die in the White House. The depressed president ordered the White House hung in black for an extended period of mourning. Letitia was buried in Virginia on her father's estate, Cedar Grove.

Julia Tyler

Born: May 4, 1820; Gardiners Island, New York
Parents: David and Juliana McLachlan Gardiner
Spouse: John Tyler (June 26, 1844; New York City)
Children: David Gardiner (1846–1927); John Alexander (1848–1883); Julia Gardiner (1849–1871); Lachlan (1851–1902); Lyon Gardiner (1853–1935); Robert Fitzwalter (1856–1927); Pearl (1860–1947)
Died: July 10, 1889; Richmond, Virginia

Vivacious Julia Gardiner Tyler, who brought cheer back to the Tyler White House, was a dark-haired beauty from a wealthy New York family. She was educated at an elite New York finishing school, and she was very popular in New York society. Somewhat impetuous and daring, at age nineteen Julia scandalized her family by posing for a department store advertisement, which polite ladies did not do in 1839. Her family promptly took her to Europe to avoid more embarrassments.

Julia first met President Tyler at a reception in 1842 while her family was visiting Washington, but he did not take much notice of her until after the death of his wife, Letitia. Julia refused his first marriage proposal in early February 1843, but she changed her mind after her father was killed in an accident on board a U.S. Navy frigate a year later. In

Julia Tyler

little money. Moreover, she was plagued by legal battles over her property and her share of her mother's estate, contested by estranged members of her family. When she petitioned Congress for a pension, the pleas of the widow of the traitor Tyler were not favorably received for some years. Much of what she did have was lost in an economic panic in the early 1870s. Not until the late 1870s was Julia able to begin rebuilding her estate.

In 1882 Congress included her in a pension it extended to widowed ex–first ladies, enabling her to be more comfortable in her last years. In July 1889 Julia Tyler died of a stroke in the same Richmond hotel in which John had died twenty-seven years earlier. She was buried next to him in Richmond.

June 1844 the couple was wed in a secret ceremony in New York. The wedding was so secret in fact that even Tyler's children were not told in advance. As a result, relations between several of them and Julia were strained for years. Julia produced seven additional Tyler offspring during her marriage, the youngest when John was seventy.

The energetic Julia's time in the White House was brief, but she enjoyed it enormously. She established her own "court," despite the ridicule of the press, and entertained lavishly. She was the first first lady to have her own press agent (although she hardly needed one), and she initiated the custom of playing "Hail to the Chief" for the president. The Tylers left the White House in 1845 for their Virginia plantation. Conservative and defensive of her husband's politics, Julia became increasingly pro-southern, and by the time of the Civil War, both she and John wholeheartedly supported the Confederacy.

The years after John's death in 1862 were very difficult for her. The Civil War and Reconstruction destroyed most of the Tyler estate, and Julia had very

Sarah Polk

Born: September 4, 1803; Murfreesboro, Tennessee
Parents: Capt. Joel and Elizabeth Whitsitt Childress
Spouse: James K. Polk (January 1, 1824;
    Murfreesboro)
Children: None
Died: August 14, 1891; Nashville, Tennessee

One of the most politically minded of the first ladies, Sarah Childress Polk was born on her father's plantation in Rutherford County, Tennessee. She was educated at a private school in Nashville and spent one year at the Moravian Female Academy in North Carolina, one of the best schools of its kind in the South, before her father's death forced her to return home. In 1819 she began a courtship with James K. Polk, who was a clerk in the Tennessee Senate. They married in 1824.

Intelligent and strong-willed, Sarah began to play an important role in her husband's career. Far from being a reluctant partner, she shared and actively encouraged his political ambitions, and, unlike other

Sarah Polk

1849, and for the rest of her life Sarah always wore a bit of black. Showing great business skill, she operated profitably the Mississippi plantation that James had acquired while president until—perhaps anticipating the changes coming to the South—she sold it in 1860. She continued to live alone at Polk Place in Nashville until her death in 1891. The southern woman who said that she belonged to the entire nation remained respected and admired by all, even during the turmoil of the Civil War. She and James are buried on the grounds of the Tennessee capital building in Nashville.

politicians' wives in those days, she routinely assisted her husband in his political activities. For example, she served as his personal secretary, marking papers important for him to read, and kept him informed about political matters when he was absent and provided advice on questions of the day. Her high profile led many observers to conclude that Polk was under her thumb, but she insisted that she was helping because of his delicate health.

During the presidential campaign of 1844, Sarah let it be known that she had no intention of churning butter and keeping house if she became first lady, and she kept her word. Impatient with social functions, she preferred to spend time with her husband on political matters and often did so until late at night. The Polks worked together without a vacation for four years. While she dutifully carried out her social responsibilities as first lady, Sarah, a devout Presbyterian, dismayed Washington society by banning drinking and dancing at the White House.

Worn out by his exertions in the White House, James died a few months after his term ended in

Margaret Taylor★

Born: September 21, 1788; Calvert County, Maryland
Parents: Walter and Ann Mackall Smith
Spouse: Zachary Taylor (June 21, 1810; Jefferson County, Kentucky)
Children: Ann Mackall (1811–1875); Sarah Knox (1814–1835); Octavia Pannel (1816–1820); Margaret Smith (1819–1820); Mary Elizabeth "Betty" (1824–1909); Richard (1826–1879)
Died: August 18, 1852; Pascagoula, Mississippi

One of the most obscure of first ladies, Margaret Mackall Smith Taylor was born into a prosperous Maryland family, but very little record of her early years has survived. It is known, however, that she attended a New York finishing school and that she met Zachary Taylor in 1809 while visiting her sister in Kentucky. She and Taylor married a year later.

For the better part of the next thirty years, Margaret led the life of a military wife, following her husband to various posts from Wisconsin and Minnesota to Louisiana and throughout the South. She

---

★No portrait known.

was unable to make a truly permanent home until 1840, when Zachary became southwestern commander and was assigned to Baton Rouge, Louisiana. Even then, he had to leave her to fight in the Mexican War. The constant moving took a toll on Margaret's health and that of her family. A malaria outbreak in Louisiana in 1820 claimed two of her daughters and almost killed her.

By 1848 Margaret Taylor was a semi-invalid who wanted only to live peacefully with her husband. She was appalled at Zachary's nomination and election to the presidency in that year, regarding it as a plot to deprive her of his company. Thus she came to Washington very reluctantly, and once there she completely abdicated her duties as first lady in favor of her youngest daughter, Betty. Because her time in the White House was spent upstairs as a semirecluse, wild rumors soon spread through Washington that she was a pipe-smoking simpleton. But in fact she was quite articulate with the few old friends she saw, and tobacco smoke made her acutely ill. So withdrawn was she that many people did not know until Zachary died that there even was a Mrs. Taylor.

Devastated by President Taylor's sudden death in July 1850, Margaret left the White House and went to live with family in Mississippi. Two years later she died there without ever referring to her days as first lady. Only one photograph of her is known to exist, and her obituary in the *New York Times* failed to give her Christian name. She was buried next to Zachary near Louisville, Kentucky.

Abigail Fillmore

Born: March 13, 1798; Stillwater, New York
Parents: Rev. Lemuel and Abigail Newland Powers
Spouse: Millard Fillmore (February 5, 1826; Moravia, New York)
Children: Millard Powers (1828–1889); Mary Abigail (1832–1854)
Died: March 30, 1853; Washington, D.C.

Abigail Fillmore

Growing up on the frontier, Abigail Powers Fillmore had little formal education. Yet she was able to educate herself well from the large library left by her father, who died when she was two. By sixteen, Abigail was a teacher in New Hope, New York, where she met Millard Fillmore, who was one of her students, although only two years younger than she. After a seven-year romance, the couple overcame the objections of her family, who found him beneath her socially, and married.

For the first two years of their marriage Abigail continued to teach, which was unusual at a time when married women rarely worked. She did not cease working until Millard's election to the New York state legislature in 1828. She continued to educate herself, however, learning to speak French and to play the piano.

Intelligent and well informed, Abigail took an active interest in her husband's political career and often joined in political discussions with friends. Her political sense was keen, and she advised Millard frequently throughout his career. He acknowledged that he consulted her on any important matter. Yet despite her private importance in Millard's life, she felt a public role for herself was inappropriate and refused public speaking opportunities.

Abigail remained in New York when Millard became vice president in 1849 and did not arrive in Washington until October 1850, after he had become president upon the death of Zachary Taylor. As first lady, Abigail turned much of the formal entertaining over to her daughter, Mary, generally limiting herself to more casual evening receptions and musicales. In part this was because of an old ankle injury that made prolonged standing difficult for her, but she also had little interest in Washington social life. She preferred a quiet evening with a book to a party and thought that social Washington would find her dull. Appalled at finding few books in the White House, Abigail sought and received a congressional appropriation to start the mansion's first library.

In March 1853 Abigail insisted on attending the outdoor inauguration of Millard's successor, Franklin Pierce, despite her poor health and the bad weather. A chill turned into pneumonia, and Abigail Fillmore died less than a month later in Washington. She and Millard, who died twenty-one years later, were buried in Buffalo.

Jane Pierce

Born: March 12, 1806; Hampton, New Hampshire
Parents: Rev. Jesse and Elizabeth Means Appleton
Spouse: Franklin Pierce (November 19, 1834; Amherst, Massachusetts)
Children: Franklin (1836); Frank Robert (1839–1843); Benjamin (1841–1853)
Died: December 2, 1863; Andover, Massachusetts

Jane Means Appleton Pierce was born in 1806 to a Congregationalist minister and his wife, who hailed from a wealthy New England family. Jane's father,

Jane Pierce

the excessively hard-working president of Bowdoin College in Brunswick, Maine, died in 1819. Under her parents' strict Calvinist influence, Jane became a very religious yet almost morbid young woman, possessed of delicate health and a fragile beauty that she hid in her simple dress. Although she had little formal schooling, it is likely that she gained a reasonable education from her father and various tutors.

Jane met Franklin Pierce, a graduate of Bowdoin, at her widowed mother's house in Amherst around 1826. Because of resistance from Jane's family, who looked unfavorably on Franklin's political ambitions, they did not marry until 1834. After their marriage they moved to Washington, D.C., as Franklin was then a member of Congress from New Hampshire. Jane, however, passionately hated Washington and politics. Thus she stayed away from the capital as much as possible and tried to convince Franklin to leave politics for his law practice. In 1842 he surrendered to her pleas and resigned his seat in the U.S. Senate.

But the quiet, happy life that Jane wanted in

OTHER SURROGATE FIRST LADIES

Over the course of the American presidency, particularly between 1828 and 1868, several presidents' wives refused or were unable, usually for health reasons, to fulfill the social duties of first lady. When these situations arose, other family members stepped in as surrogate to carry out the social responsibilities of the first lady.

Jane Irwin Harrison

The first of these presidents was William Henry Harrison, whose widowed daughter-in-law, Jane Irwin Harrison, agreed to assist as White House hostess. Harrison's term lasted only a month after his inauguration in 1841, however, and thus Jane was left as a footnote in White House history.

Priscilla Cooper Tyler

When John Tyler succeeded Harrison in 1841, his first wife, Letitia, who had suffered a stroke, was a semi-invalid. She died in 1842. His daughter-in-law, Priscilla Cooper Tyler, acted as his hostess. Born in 1816, Priscilla was one of the nine children of actor Robert Cooper. She performed on stage herself for a time as a young woman, but she lived in severe financial straits. In 1837 she met Tyler's son Robert after he saw her perform as Desdemona in Shakespeare's *Othello*. They were married in September 1839.

Priscilla served as hostess until Tyler's marriage to Julia Gardiner in 1844. Her letters convey both her devotion to the president and her wonder at being acting first lady. She died in 1889 in Montgomery, Alabama.

Mary Elizabeth Taylor

When Zachary Taylor came to the White House in 1849, his wife, Margaret, lacked the health or the desire to act as first lady. That role was played by her youngest daughter, Mary Elizabeth "Betty." Betty Taylor was born in 1824 in Jefferson County, Kentucky. Although her father had little formal education, he was concerned with that of his children, and Betty was sent to boarding school in Philadelphia. She married Maj. William Bliss, her father's adjutant, in 1848. After his death, she married Philip Pendleton Dandridge in 1858. Contemporaries have noted that she was charming, gracious, and lovely, and a popular hostess while in the White House, particularly in contrast to the more austere Sarah Polk, her predecessor. Betty died in 1909 in Winchester, Virginia.

Mary Abigail Fillmore

Abigail Fillmore, who followed Margaret Taylor into the White House, also lacked the interest or

---

New Hampshire was not to be. Her first child lived only three days; her second died of typhoid fever at the age of four. These tragedies accentuated her tendency toward depression and nervous tension so much that Franklin refused an appointment as U.S. attorney general. He did, however, volunteer for the Mexican War. He also maneuvered himself into the

Democratic presidential nomination in 1852, despite assuring Jane he would not do so. When Jane discovered his deception, her trust in him was shattered. She prayed for his defeat in the presidential election of 1852 and was greatly depressed when he was elected.

In January 1853 the Pierce family was involved

health to be hostess and so let her daughter take her place. Mary Abigail Fillmore was born in 1832 in Buffalo, New York, and was educated in schools in Massachusetts and New York. She taught school for a time before coming to Washington in 1850 when her father became president. A talented young woman, Mary spoke five languages and played the guitar, piano, and harp. At age twenty-two, less than two years after Millard Fillmore left the presidency, she contracted cholera and died in Aurora, New York.

Abby Kent Means

For the first two years of Franklin Pierce's presidency (1853–1857) his wife, Jane, crushed by the tragic death of her only remaining child, refused to participate in White House society. Mrs. Abby Kent Means, a longtime friend of Jane Pierce and the second wife of Jane's uncle, thus filled in as first lady. With the help of Varina Davis, wife of Secretary of War Jefferson Davis, Abby attempted to maintain pleasantness in a melancholy White House and held receptions twice a week. But despite her efforts, the White House was a gloomy place, even after Jane Pierce assumed her duties.

Martha Johnson Patterson

Andrew Johnson's wife, Eliza, suffered from tuberculosis when she became first lady, and her daughter, Martha Johnson Patterson, became hostess instead. Martha was born in Greeneville, Tennessee, in 1828 and married David Patterson in 1855. When her father became president in 1865, she was both White House hostess and wife of a U.S. senator. Proclaiming herself to be "plain folks from Tennessee," Martha put cows on the White House lawn to provide milk and butter. Her simplicity and calm dignity earned her respect and admiration during the turbulent Johnson years. She died in Greeneville in 1901.

Mary Arthur McElroy

When Chester A. Arthur succeeded James A. Garfield as president in 1881, his wife, Ellen, had been dead for about eighteen months. Although Arthur personally took a great interest in White House entertainment, the official hostess in his administration was his younger sister, Mary Arthur McElroy. Mary was born in Greenwich, New York, in 1842 and was educated in private schools, concluding with Mrs. Willard's Female Seminary in Troy, New York. She married John McElroy in 1861. While White House hostess, Mary continued to live in Albany, New York, traveling to Washington for the social season each year. Although Mary was popular as a hostess, she also was careful to protect the privacy of both the president and her family. She died in 1917.

---

in a train wreck in Massachusetts. Franklin and Jane were unhurt, but their remaining son, Bennie, was killed before his mother's eyes. Jane never recovered from this disaster. She believed Bennie's death to be some sort of divine judgment of Franklin's election. She did not come to Washington until after the inauguration of her husband, and when she did

arrive, she stayed upstairs in the White House and wrote letters to her dead son. She did not make an appearance as first lady until New Year's Day 1855. Her sense of duty led her to carry out her social responsibilities for the rest of Franklin's term, but she had no enthusiasm for them. Throughout her stay in Washington she was considered an invalid, and the White House was regarded as a gloomy place.

An admittedly sick woman by 1857, Jane left the White House to travel abroad in the West Indies and Europe for her health. The cure was ineffective, however, and she returned to Massachusetts depressed and ill. She died of tuberculosis in 1863 and was buried beside her children (and eventually her husband) in Concord, New Hampshire.

Mary Lincoln

Born: December 13, 1818; Lexington, Kentucky
Parents: Robert and Elizabeth Parker Todd
Spouse: Abraham Lincoln (November 4, 1842; Springfield, Illinois)
Children: Robert Todd (1843–1926); Edward Baker (1846–1850); William Wallace (1850–1862); Thomas "Tad" (1853–1871)
Died: July 16, 1882; Springfield

Perhaps the most controversial of the first ladies, Mary Todd Lincoln was one of fifteen children born to a prominent Lexington, Kentucky, businessman and his wife. Her parents provided her with a good education; Mary spoke French and studied dance and music. By age twenty-one she had gone to live with a sister in Springfield, Illinois. Mary was attractive, intelligent, and witty, but she was troubled by severe insecurity and a mercurial temperament that worsened as she grew older.

While in Springfield, she met Abraham Lincoln, whom she married when she was twenty-four. The motive for her decision to marry Lincoln, as with so many of Mary's actions, is not clear. Some scholars believe that she claimed to see a future president in the man she chose above other suitors, but the early years of their marriage were hardly presidential. They lived in near poverty for the first year, and, although circumstances improved as Abraham

Mary Lincoln

served in Congress and then was a Springfield lawyer, Mary still lacked the luxury she had known as a girl.

Mary's belief in her husband was justified when he was elected president in 1860, but her dream of being first lady was to become a nightmare. The difficulties of her young married life, including the death of her son Edward at age four, had combined with her moody temperament to leave her emotionally unstable. Abraham called her his "child wife," and often he had to treat her as one. By the time she became first lady, she was extremely nervous and prone to blinding headaches. Her moods swung erratically and violently, making her extremely impetuous and unpredictable. Her insecurity often showed as well, frequently in displays of irrational jealousy. Her instability made her a burden on a president trying to deal with war.

During Mary's stay at the White House, she was the target of unceasing criticism. With the Civil War on, she fought with Congress for more money to renovate the White House. Her family's ties to the

Confederacy led many to call her a traitor, and she was even investigated by a congressional committee. When she held White House receptions, she was criticized for her inappropriate frivolity during a national crisis. If she chose not to host social functions, she was attacked for "adding to the gloom" of the day. When her son Willie died of typhoid in 1862, her unrestrained grief was condemned as excessive in a time of national tragedy. Her grief at Willie's death was indeed "uncontrolled"; Abraham had to treat her like a "sick child." She refused ever again to enter the rooms where the boy died and was embalmed. She also banned flowers and music from the White House (for which she was criticized as well) and conducted séances with his spirit.

The constant pressure and criticism intensified Mary's emotional problems, and her behavior became even more extreme. Driven by her insecurity and the pressures of living in the White House, Mary compulsively bought clothes without Abraham's knowledge, and her clothing bills soon exceeded his yearly salary. She fearfully awaited the returns of the 1864 elections, knowing that a loss would force her to face creditors she could not pay. When Abraham won, she bought more clothes.

Mary was forty-seven when her husband was assassinated in 1865. She did not attend his funeral and stayed in mourning in the White House for five weeks. Her behavior after leaving the White House became increasingly erratic. Among other things, she developed an obsession that she was impoverished—although Abraham's estate left her $35,000 after settling debts. Mary petitioned Congress for a pension, but she was so clumsy in her appeals that she alienated most members of Congress as well as the public.

To escape the criticism, she went with her favorite son, Tad, to Europe and did not return until Congress gave her a small pension in 1870. When Tad died of typhoid in 1871 she developed symptoms of paranoia and kept her money and securities sewed into her coat. Her behavior became so erratic that in May 1875 her remaining son, Robert, had her committed to a mental hospital. After one of her sisters arranged her release from the sanitarium a few months later, Mary moved to France and lived there alone until she fell and badly injured her back in 1879.

Sick and unhappy, estranged from her only remaining son, and largely forgotten, Mary went back to Springfield and died there of a stroke in 1882. She was buried next to her husband and children in Springfield.

Eliza Johnson

Born: October 4, 1810; Leesburg, Tennessee
Parents: John and Sarah Phillips McCardle
Spouse: Andrew Johnson (May 17, 1827; Greeneville, Tennessee)
Children: Martha (1828–1901); Charles (1830–1863); Mary (1832–1883); Robert (1834–1869); Andrew Jr. (1852–1879)
Died: January 15, 1876; Greeneville

Eliza McCardle Johnson was born a few miles from Greeneville in east Tennessee. Her father was a shoemaker who died when she was still very young, but her mother was able to support herself and her daughter by weaving, and Eliza managed to acquire a basic education. She met Andrew Johnson, a tailor newly arrived in Greeneville, in 1826. Within a year they married. While the Johnsons lived frugally on Andrew's income as a tailor, Eliza taught him to read and write and otherwise improved his education.

In 1828, two years after arriving in Greeneville, Andrew's political career began when he was elected town alderman. That career would take him to the U.S. House of Representatives, the Tennessee governorship, the U.S. Senate, and the vice presidency. Throughout his career, however, Eliza shunned

Eliza Johnson

the attendant social life, preferring instead to focus on the efficient operation of her home.

With Andrew's work and Eliza's management, the family prospered, but Eliza's health did not. She suffered from a form of tuberculosis, and by 1853 the disease already had progressed so far that she felt unable to move to Nashville when Andrew became governor. During the Civil War, Eliza was forced from her east Tennessee home by the Confederate army, but she returned when the troops left and stayed there even when Andrew was elected vice president in 1864. Lincoln's assassination in April 1865, which elevated Andrew to the presidency, changed her plans, and she arrived in Washington in August of that year.

Although Eliza lived in the White House during her husband's turbulent administration, she took very little part in it. By then largely an invalid, she usually stayed in an upstairs room overlooking the front lawn, making only two public appearances during her time as first lady. Her daughter Martha

served as White House hostess and supervised the renovation of the mansion after the Civil War. Although Eliza had no influence on Andrew's politics, her support for him never wavered. When told of his acquittal on impeachment charges, she said that she had known he would be vindicated.

With the expiration of Johnson's term in March 1869, Eliza returned to east Tennessee, where she lived for the next seven years. She died at the age of sixty-five, six months after her husband's death, and was buried next to him in Greeneville.

Julia Grant

Born: January 26, 1826; St. Louis, Missouri
Parents: Col. Frederick and Ellen Wrenshall Dent
Spouse: Ulysses S. Grant (August 22, 1848; St. Louis)
Children: Frederick Dent (1850–1912); Ulysses Simpson Jr. (1852–1929); Ellen "Nellie" Wrenshall (1855–1922); Jesse Root (1858–1934)
Died: December 14, 1902; Washington, D.C.

Julia Boggs Dent Grant was born at White Haven, her father's large farm about five miles west of St. Louis, Missouri. From ages ten to seventeen she attended a private school in St. Louis. In 1843 she met Ulysses S. Grant, an army officer stationed in St. Louis, who had been a classmate of her brother at the U.S. Military Academy. The pair soon decided to marry, but opposition from Julia's father and the outbreak of the Mexican War delayed them for five years.

The first twelve years of their marriage were not always easy ones for Julia. Ulysses's army career led to several moves and then a long separation when he was transferred to the Pacific coast. In 1854 he left the army and returned to civilian life, but his attempts at farming and business were failures. Julia,

Julia Grant

but Grant's memoirs, written while he was dying of cancer, brought Julia an adequate income. She lived for seventeen years after his death in 1885 and wrote her own autobiography—the first president's wife to do so. It remained unpublished, however, until 1975. The woman who was the first to be called the "first lady of the land" died in Washington, D.C., and was buried next to her husband in New York City.

who had been brought up in a slave-owning family, struggled to raise four children and manage her household largely on her own and with very little income. She also had to deal with Ulysses's tendency to drink excessively. The Civil War gave Ulysses the chance to escape oblivion. By its end, his battlefield success had made him the most popular man in the United States, except perhaps for President Lincoln, and he was easily elected president in 1868.

As first lady, the engaging Julia was a striking contrast to her immediate predecessors. At great expense she refurbished the White House, and she entertained lavishly—formal banquets had as many as twenty-nine courses. The country loved her style and her lively family. Politics was of no interest to her, but no one expected it to be; her society was sufficient. She was so prominent that, according to one historian, she was the first first lady to become a truly "national" figure.

After eight years in the White House, the Grants toured the world and then settled in New York City. Another bad business deal left them penniless,

Lucy Hayes

Born: August 28, 1831; Chillicothe, Ohio
Parents: Dr. James and Maria Cook Webb
Spouse: Rutherford B. Hayes (December 30, 1852; Cincinnati, Ohio)
Children: Birchard Austin (1853–1926); James Webb Cook (1856–1934); Rutherford Platt (1858–1927); Joseph Thompson (1861–1863); George Crook (1864–1866); Fanny (1867–1950); Scott Russell (1871–1923); Manning Force (1873–1874)
Died: June 25, 1889; Fremont, Ohio

Lucy Ware Webb Hayes was the daughter of an Ohio doctor, who died in 1833 while on a trip to Kentucky to free his family's slaves. From her parents Lucy acquired a strong opposition to slavery. She was educated in private schools in Chillicothe and graduated from Wesleyan Women's College in Cincinnati in 1850, the first first lady to have a college degree.

Lucy met Rutherford B. Hayes in 1847, before entering college. He later set up a law practice in Cincinnati and eventually proposed to her, in 1851. Lucy was a serious, intelligent woman, who took an active interest in her husband's military and political careers. During his service in the Civil War, she traveled regularly to the camps where he stayed, and

Lucy Hayes

help and advice. She initiated the custom of the children's Easter egg roll on the White House lawn.

After one term as president, Hayes retired to Fremont, Ohio, in 1881. Lucy spent the next few years busy with her family and various charitable activities. On June 21, 1889, she suffered a severe stroke and died four days later. She was buried in Fremont, where Rutherford was laid to rest in 1893.

Lucretia Garfield

Born: April 19, 1832; Hiram, Ohio
Parents: Zebulon and Arabella Mason Rudolph
Spouse: James A. Garfield (November 11, 1858; Hiram)
Children: Elizabeth Arabella (1860–1863); Harry Augustus (1863–1942); James Rudolph (1865–1950); Mary "Molly" (1867–1947); Irvin McDowell (1870–1951); Abram (1872–1958); Edward (1874–1876)
Died: March 14, 1918; South Pasadena, California

once brought him to Ohio to recuperate after being wounded. She was very interested in politics and kept abreast of the issues of the day. It was Lucy's persuasion that helped to turn Rutherford against slavery, and at least in her early days she displayed feminist leanings. Her compassion for people showed in her kindness toward wounded soldiers and her concern for orphans and the poor while Rutherford was governor of Ohio.

Lucy became first lady in 1877. Her simplicity and frugality marked a dramatic change from the extravagance characteristic of the Grant administration. Devoutly religious and a teetotaler, Lucy instituted daily morning worship in the White House and banned alcohol from White House functions. The latter act, which earned her the derisive nickname of "Lemonade Lucy," was in fact as much a political as a moral gesture, for temperance was a burning issue of the day. Beyond this issue, however, she displayed no political leanings while first lady. She was a popular national figure who received letters from women throughout the country asking for

Lucretia Rudolph Garfield was born to parents who strongly believed in education. Her father was one of the founders of what became known as Hiram College in Hiram, Ohio. With the encouragement of her parents, Lucretia grew into a studious, thoughtful young woman, who attended the school her father had founded. There her intelligence impressed many.

While at Hiram, Lucretia came to know James A. Garfield, who was both a student and a teacher at the school. Although James admired Lucretia's intellect, he initially found her "dull." The romance that developed between them was an off-and-on affair that lasted nine years before their marriage, in part because Lucretia was reluctant to surrender her independence and in part because James mistrusted what he saw as her feminist leanings. Initially, their

Lucretia Garfield

country. Unlike any previous first lady, she both organized his funeral and appeared publicly at it.

Lucretia Garfield lived for thirty-six more years, avoiding publicity while living briefly in Europe and then in Ohio. She died at her winter home in California and was buried next to James in Cleveland, Ohio.

Frances Cleveland

Born: July 21, 1864; Buffalo, New York
Parents: Oscar and Emma Harmon Folsom
SPOUSES: Grover Cleveland (June 2, 1886; Washington, D.C.); Thomas J. Preston Jr. (February 10, 1913; Princeton, New Jersey)
Children: Ruth (1891–1904); Esther (1893–1980); Marion (1895–1977); Richard Folsom (1897–1974); Francis Grover (1903)
Died: October 29, 1947; Baltimore, Maryland

marriage was a strained one, aggravated by frequent separations during its first four years. A close bond did not begin to develop between them until after the death of their first child in 1863. By then, James was on his way to Congress.

As the wife of a member of Congress, Lucretia had little impact on Washington society. She preferred to spend time at the Library of Congress, which was near her home, and joined the Washington Literary Society. She also took a hand in her children's education in the classics and advised her husband when asked. She had become a political wife.

James became president in 1881, but Lucretia's time as first lady was very brief. She was making plans to redecorate the White House in a historical manner and undertaking research for accuracy when she was stricken with malaria in May 1881. She then left Washington to recuperate. James was on his way to visit her when he was shot in July; he died on September 19. Lucretia's stoic courage through his ordeal won her the admiration of the

Frances Folsom Cleveland, the daughter of a Buffalo, New York, attorney, was born in 1864. One of the first people to see the infant Frances was her father's close friend Grover Cleveland, who became her de facto guardian after her father, Oscar Folsom, was killed in an accident in 1875. Frances was educated in public schools in Buffalo and attended Wells College in Aurora, New York. She grew into a lively and attractive young woman, who maintained close ties with her friend Grover Cleveland.

In 1884 Cleveland became the first bachelor elected to the presidency since James Buchanan. For two years rumors about potential romances surrounded him—including one linking him with Frances's mother—until the White House announced his engagement to Frances in May 1886. Their wedding, the first of a president to be held in the White House, was small and yet a public sensation.

Frances Cleveland

publicly. Her picture eventually appeared on Democratic campaign posters, the first time a politician's wife had been used in that way. When Frances returned to the White House in 1893, she reduced her social schedule to accommodate her growing family. Her second daughter, Esther, was the first child to be born in the White House.

In 1897 the Clevelands retired to Princeton, New Jersey. Eleven years later Grover died. Frances remained in Princeton and eventually married Thomas J. Preston Jr., an archaeology professor who later taught at Princeton University. She remained active in social and charity work and was a key figure in distributing clothes to the poor during the depression. On October 29, 1947, Frances died suddenly while visiting her son Richard in Baltimore. She was buried in Princeton next to Grover.

Frances Cleveland was admired widely. Her hairstyle and clothing became national fads, and her picture was used without her permission in various advertisements. Numerous causes solicited her endorsement without success. She held public receptions at the White House on evenings and Saturdays so that working women could come, and thousands did so. At one such reception nine thousand people came through her receiving line, and Frances's arms had to be massaged afterward. Her formal parties were just as popular. Frances's charm and beauty served as a valuable contrast to Grover, who could be rude and boorish. In fact, the public curiosity about her was so great that the Clevelands rented a second residence in Washington to use as living quarters, and Grover commuted to the White House.

Frances's six years as first lady were interrupted by the term of Benjamin Harrison (1889–1893). During the campaign of 1888, she became a campaign issue as the Republicans accused the president of beating his wife; Frances had to refute the charges

Caroline Harrison

Born: October 1, 1832; Oxford, Ohio

Parents: Rev. John and Mary Neal Scott

Spouse: Benjamin Harrison (October 20, 1853; Oxford)

Children: Russell Benjamin (1854–1936); Mary Scott (1858–1930)

Died: October 25, 1892; Washington, D.C.

Caroline Lavinia Scott Harrison was the second of three children born to one of the "most illustrious educators of the early West." Because her parents believed in education for women, Caroline was well taught; she displayed outstanding artistic and musical talents as well.

Caroline first met Benjamin Harrison in 1848 while he was a student at Farmer's College in Cincinnati, Ohio, where the Reverend Scott was teaching. In 1849 the Reverend Scott took his family back to Oxford, Ohio, Caroline's birthplace, to establish the Oxford Female Institute, and in 1850

Benjamin transferred to Miami University in Oxford. Both Benjamin and Caroline were serious and intelligent and soon were attracted to one another; in 1853 they married. Within a year they settled in Indianapolis, Indiana, where they made their home until 1881.

Benjamin became a successful lawyer, and in 1881 he was elected by the Indiana legislature to the U.S. Senate. For her part, Caroline never completely developed her artistic abilities. Spurred perhaps by the needs of her husband's career, she concentrated on civic work and was active in her church. In contrast to her aloof husband, Caroline was a lively, cheerful person who made guests welcome and spent much time teaching art, music, and needlepoint.

Benjamin was elected president in 1888. Caroline came to the White House with the hope of not just refurbishing the mansion but also structurally changing or rebuilding it. She had three different plans for major changes drawn up. Congress refused to approve any of them, however, and she was left with a more modest remodeling that included repairing the furniture, redoing the floors and plumbing, repainting, exterminating the mice and insects, and adding bathrooms (an important consideration since the Harrisons had several relatives staying with them). Electricity also was installed in the White House while Caroline was first lady, but she was so fearful of it that she would never touch the switches. Caroline designed her own china pattern and started the White House china collection by gathering pieces from previous administrations. Outside the White House she played an important role in making the new Johns Hopkins medical school coeducational.

Caroline's health became a problem as her term as first lady wore on. She had been seriously ill in 1883 and in 1886, but she had recovered. By 1892, however, she was so sick with tuberculosis that Benjamin refused to appear publicly in his reelection bid

Caroline Harrison

(his opponent, Grover Cleveland, also refrained from campaigning). Caroline continued to deteriorate through the summer and died two weeks before the election that turned her husband out of the White House. She was buried in Indianapolis, where Benjamin was buried as well nine years later.

Ida McKinley

Born: June 8, 1847; Canton, Ohio
Parents: James and Catherine Dewalt Saxton
Spouse: William McKinley (January 25, 1871; Canton)
Children: Katherine (1871–1875); Ida (1873)
Died: May 26, 1907; Canton

Ida Saxton McKinley was one of three children born to a wealthy Canton, Ohio, banker from a prominent family. Active and headstrong as a young woman, she attended Brook Hall Seminary in

Ida McKinley

Media, Pennsylvania, and worked in her father's bank for the pleasure of it, something rare for a woman in the 1860s. While working, she met William McKinley, a Civil War veteran and Canton lawyer, whom she married within a year.

For a brief time things went well for Ida. The family lived comfortably in Canton, and their first child was born within a year of their marriage. Then in early 1873 Ida's mother died. Shortly thereafter her second daughter was born, but the sickly infant lived only a few months. Less than two years later the McKinleys' other child, Katy, also died. Ida never recovered physically or emotionally from these successive shocks. She developed a form of epilepsy and was subject to frequent seizures. She also suffered from severe headaches and phlebitis and was frequently depressed and irritable. For the rest of her life Ida remained an invalid who made extreme demands on the time and patience of her husband. Yet William remained devoted to her, tending carefully to her needs despite his flourishing political career, which led him to the presiden-

cy in 1896. Ida returned his devotion with a love that was almost worship.

Unlike previous first ladies who had been ill, Ida refused to remain in the background. She insisted on playing her role as White House hostess, and on attending all the social functions, despite the difficulties caused by her health. Special arrangements had to be made for every event to deal with the possibility of her becoming acutely ill. The president even changed the seating at formal dinners to place Ida next to him. If a minor seizure struck in the presence of guests, he would calmly cover her face with his handkerchief until it had passed and she could rejoin the conversation. Quick exits followed a major seizure. She also insisted on traveling with him, even though she was often too weak to do more than just be seen. William developed a reputation as a saint for his care of his wife, and his foremost concern upon being shot in 1901 was for her. Ida, however, displayed surprising strength during his decline, death, and funeral, despite the anguish recorded in her diary.

She returned to Canton to live, sick and lonely, for six more years. At first, she prayed daily to die, but later she decided that she wanted to live until completion of the McKinley mausoleum. She died four days before its dedication and was buried in Canton next to William and her two long-dead daughters.

Edith Roosevelt

Born: August 6, 1861; Norwich, Connecticut
Parents: Charles and Gertrude Tyler Carow
Spouse: Theodore Roosevelt (December 2, 1886; London, England)
Children: Theodore Jr. (1887–1944); Kermit (1889–1943); Ethel Carow (1891–1977); Archibald Bulloch (1894–1979); Quentin (1897–1918)
Died: September 30, 1948; Oyster Bay, New York

Edith Roosevelt

Edith Kermit Carow Roosevelt was a childhood acquaintance of her future husband. They grew up in the same neighborhood, where she was a close friend of Theodore's younger sister. Although Edith did not attend college, she was a voracious reader and was considered well educated. Edith was not Theodore's first love; his first wife had died in 1884 after a four-year marriage. A year later Theodore renewed his long association with Edith, and in 1886 they married.

Edith was intelligent and serious, and she possessed a detached serenity that served her well in managing the boisterous Roosevelt household. She had five children of her own, a stepdaughter, Alice, from Theodore's first marriage, and Theodore himself, whom she often seemed to regard as another child.

Because she also was politically astute, Theodore, who respected her intelligence, frequently looked to her for advice. Her stepdaughter, Alice, noted

that the afternoon walks that Edith and Theodore took regularly seemed to have a "calming" effect on him.

Edith's organizational skills were valuable to her as first lady. To eliminate friction and control expenses, she held weekly meetings of cabinet wives to coordinate entertainment. And in running the White House, she used caterers for formal entertaining and a personal secretary to help handle correspondence.

Edith introduced other innovations as well. She began carrying bouquets of flowers to avoid having to shake hundreds of hands during receptions, and she initiated a portrait gallery so that there would be a permanent memorial to each first lady. A music lover, Edith replaced the customary White House socials with musicales.

Edith also worked to ensure that her family had some measure of privacy in the fishbowl of the White House. Realizing that public curiosity about the president's family would have to be satisfied, she released posed photographs and managed stories to produce more, instead of less, privacy. To the same end, when the White House was remodeled in 1902, she arranged to have the first family's living quarters separated from the White House offices and placed off limits. She also controlled the publicity surrounding Alice's elaborate White House wedding in 1906.

Public opinion was very favorable about Edith when she left the White House in 1909 to retire with Theodore to Oyster Bay. After his death in 1919, Edith traveled widely throughout the world, engaged in charity work, and continued her ties with the Republican Party—she actively opposed Franklin Roosevelt's presidential bid in 1932. Her last years were spent quietly at Oyster Bay, and, after her death in 1948, she was buried there next to Theodore.

Helen Taft

Helen Taft

Born: June 2, 1861; Cincinnati, Ohio

Parents: John and Harriet Collins Herron

Spouse: William Howard Taft (June 19, 1886; Cincinnati)

Children: Robert Alphonso (1889–1953); Helen Herron (1891–1987); Charles Phelps (1897–1983)

Died: May 22, 1943; Washington, D.C.

Helen Herron Taft was the eldest daughter of the eleven children born to a Cincinnati judge and his wife. During a quiet childhood, she attended private schools and became a skilled pianist. Later she taught school for a few years and was part of a group of the city's young people who met frequently to discuss ideas. Although the Herrons knew the Tafts well, Helen did not meet William Howard until she was eighteen. During the next seven years a romance gradually developed between the two, and they married in 1886.

Ambitious and discontented with a quiet life in Ohio, Helen prodded her less-driven husband in his career, which he had begun as a lawyer. She had visited the White House in 1888 and greatly wanted to return to it as its mistress. Although Taft was content with a place on the federal bench in Ohio, Helen pushed him to accept nationally important positions, first as U.S. solicitor general, then as governor of the Philippines (1901–1904), and finally as Theodore Roosevelt's secretary of war. Her objections twice led him to refuse a possible appointment to the U.S. Supreme Court during the Roosevelt administration. In 1908, despite his reluctance, Helen encouraged him to run for the presidency. It was widely known that without her push, he never would have made the effort.

In the inaugural parade of 1909, Helen broke precedent by riding next to her husband. The symbolism was appropriate, for she was intimately involved in his political decisions and frequently assisted and advised him on political matters. Her influence over him was obvious. She had little patience for social events and tried to downplay them as much as possible to remain where important things happened. She even complained that when traveling with the president, she was often shunted to some idle social frivolity while he was engaged in important meetings.

But Helen's drive for William's success strained her health. During her stay in the Philippines, she had been forced to go to Europe for treatment for nervous exhaustion. After two months as first lady she suffered a severe stroke that temporarily impaired her speech and took her out of the public eye for more than eighteen months. Typically, she found the forced absence from the political councils far more aggravating than missed social duties.

Taft served only one term as president, and Helen left the White House bitter toward Roosevelt, whom she believed had ruined her husband's chance at reelection. The Tafts then moved to New

Haven, Connecticut, where William taught at Yale Law School. In 1921 they returned to Washington when he was appointed chief justice of the Supreme Court. No longer politically active, Helen remained in Washington after William's death in 1930, until her own death in 1943. She was the first first lady to be buried in Arlington National Cemetery. Helen Taft left at least one enduring legacy: Washington's famed cherry trees were planted at her request.

Ellen Wilson

Born: May 15, 1860; Savannah, Georgia
Parents: Rev. Samuel and Margaret Hoyt Axson
Spouse: Woodrow Wilson (June 24, 1885; Savannah)
Children: Margaret Woodrow (1886–1944); Jessie Woodrow (1887–1933); Eleanor Randolph (1889–1967)
Died: August 6, 1914; Washington, D.C.

Ellen Louise Axson Wilson was born into a family of Presbyterian ministers. She was an intelligent woman who, according to her father, was "entirely too much inclined" to make her own decisions. She attended Rome Female College in Georgia, and, as a talented artist, she spent a year taking art classes in New York City. Ellen continued to paint throughout her life and maintained a studio on the third floor of the White House while she was first lady. She was a member of what is now the National Association of Women Artists, and her work was publicly displayed at a one-woman exhibition in 1913.

In 1883, while still at home in Georgia, she met Woodrow Wilson, who was visiting Rome on legal business. He was immediately attracted to her and proposed within five months. Ellen returned his affection, but their marriage had to wait for two years; because her mother was dead and her father was emotionally unstable, Ellen felt that she had to

Ellen Wilson

remain at home to care for her younger siblings. Her father's sudden death in 1884 provided her with the freedom and money to pursue her interest in art and then to marry Woodrow.

Woodrow's academic career took the Wilsons to Bryn Mawr College in Pennsylvania, Wesleyan University in Connecticut, and Princeton University in New Jersey, where he became the university's president. Ellen was an immense asset to him. By tending to the daily household details he disliked, Ellen freed Woodrow for his work. More facile in language than he, she learned German to help translate materials he needed. Her calm disposition provided stability for her intense husband. When Woodrow left Princeton to become governor of New Jersey in 1910, Ellen again proved invaluable; her incisive intellect and her intuitive understanding of people and politics made her one of his most trusted advisers.

Throughout their years together the Wilsons maintained a special relationship. Although there is no evidence that Woodrow ever had an affair, he did prefer the company of attractive women, yet Ellen never displayed any jealousy. Because the Wilsons were frequently apart for various reasons, they maintained a constant correspondence that eventually totaled about fourteen hundred letters. In those letters their devotion to each other is obvious.

As first lady, Ellen maintained a hectic schedule of entertainment and social concerns. Perhaps because of her three career-oriented daughters, two of whom had White House weddings, Ellen became interested in women's suffrage. She supported the vote for women long before Woodrow did but never advocated it publicly. Instead, she took an interest in charitable work; for example, the revenue from her 1913 art exhibition went to a school for the underprivileged. After the problem of substandard housing in Washington came to her attention, she toured the capital's ghettos and then openly pushed for legislation to improve the decrepit African American neighborhoods. When a housing bill eventually passed in 1914, it was popularly known as "Ellen Wilson's bill." (The Supreme Court later declared the law unconstitutional, however.)

But Ellen Wilson did not live to enjoy her legislative success. She was terminally ill with Bright's disease, a kidney ailment, and her health began failing rapidly in late 1913. She was on her deathbed when her legislation was passed. Ellen died a few days before World War I began in Europe and was buried in Rome, Georgia, next to her parents.

Edith Wilson

Born: October 15, 1872; Wytheville, Virginia

Parents: William and Sallie White Bolling

Spouses: Norman Galt (1896; Washington, D.C.);
Woodrow Wilson (December 18, 1915;
Washington, D.C.)

Children: None

Died: December 28, 1961; Washington, D.C.

Edith Wilson

Born into a family of eleven children, Edith Bolling Galt Wilson received most of her education at home and had only a few years of formal schooling. At age twenty-four she married Norman Galt, an older man who was a Washington, D.C., jeweler. But in 1908 Galt died suddenly and left his store to his wife. Edith continued to manage the business, and she lived well, dressing fashionably and often making trips to Europe.

In March 1915 Edith was introduced to Woodrow Wilson by Wilson's cousin, Helen Bones, who was helping him to manage the White House after Ellen Wilson's death. Edith and Woodrow were immediately attracted to one another, and a romance developed rapidly. After hesitating briefly because of the possible political consequences of Woodrow marrying too soon after Ellen's death, they wed quietly at Edith's home. Despite the fears of his aides, Wilson suffered no political fallout, and he was reelected president in 1916.

Self-assured and decisive, the new Mrs. Wilson brought life and entertainment back to the White

House. She also proved to be an important assistant to the president, working as his personal secretary and helping with his papers. Her primary interest was her husband; she was not particularly interested in politics and denounced the women's suffrage movement as "unladylike." When the United States entered World War I, Edith tried to set an example for the country by observing the various meatless and gasless days, sewing items for the Red Cross, curtailing entertainment, and using sheep to keep the White House lawn trimmed (she donated their wool to the war effort).

While battling the Senate for ratification of the Treaty of Versailles after the war, Wilson's health broke down. By October 1919 a stroke had largely paralyzed him. Edith immediately stepped in to protect and shield her husband. She screened all papers, business, and visitors, keeping as much as possible away from him while he recovered. For a time, almost no one saw Wilson except his wife. Exactly how much power she wielded and how long she held it have never been determined conclusively. Critics then and now have argued that she was actually the acting president and essentially ran the country for the balance of Wilson's term. Edith herself claimed that her "regency" lasted but a few weeks and that Woodrow always made the important political decisions; however, by her own admission, she alone decided what was important and what was not.

Woodrow Wilson never really recovered from his illness and lived only three years, a broken and disillusioned man, after leaving the White House. Edith survived him by almost thirty-eight years. During that time she traveled widely, participated in Democratic politics, wrote her memoirs, and served as a director of the Woodrow Wilson Foundation. She died of heart disease in 1961 and was buried with Woodrow in the nave of Washington's National Cathedral. Their house on S Street in Washington is now a museum.

Florence Harding

Florence Harding

Born: August 15, 1860; Marion, Ohio

Parents: Amos and Louisa Bouton Kling

Spouses: Henry A. DeWolfe (1880; Marion); Warren G. Harding (July 8, 1891; Marion)

Children: By Henry DeWolfe: Eugene Marshall (1880–1915)

Died: November 21, 1924; Marion

Florence Kling DeWolfe Harding was born into one of the wealthiest families in Marion, Ohio. She was educated at the local schools and then attended the Cincinnati Conservatory of Music. Willful and tenacious, Florence fought repeatedly with her domineering father. In 1880 she eloped with Henry DeWolfe, the son of a local coal dealer, and six months later had her only child. A man who liked to drink and hated to work, DeWolfe proved unreliable and abandoned Florence in 1882; she divorced him in 1886. She then allowed her parents to adopt her son, and she eked out a living giving piano lessons.

In 1890 she met Warren G. Harding, then a Marion newspaperman, and married him a year later over the violent objections of her father. Strong and demanding where Warren was weak and pliable, Florence quickly became the dominant force in the Harding household. She took charge of his newspaper, the *Marion Star,* and made it into an effective business, thereby freeing him for politics. She also pushed his political career, helping him into the U.S. Senate in 1914 and into the presidency in 1920. A believer in astrology, Florence at first hesitated to urge Warren to seek the presidency because a fortune-teller had predicted that although Warren would win the office, he also would die there.

Florence's personal life was not so successful. Health problems deprived her of the limited beauty she had enjoyed, and she knew that Warren, who was quite handsome, was having affairs. Her shrill voice and domineering manner led to further difficulties between them. Unflatteringly, Warren once had nicknamed her "Duchess." Their relationship continued to be strained during his presidency.

As first lady, Florence showed no interest in running the White House; she preferred to meet people. She entertained constantly, if not lavishly, opened the White House to the public, and shook hands for hours. She frequently visited wounded war veterans. She also tried to control the news coming from the White House, partly to conceal the continued indiscretions of Warren and their unhappy marriage, and partly to downplay his unsteady health. Her own health was poor; the one kidney she had (the other had been lost in 1905) was frequently infected. In fact, she almost died in 1922. Nevertheless, assertive and demanding, Florence continued to strongly influence her husband, but she later destroyed most of the papers that could have indicated her exact role.

As scandals began to break over the Harding administration in 1923, the president traveled to the West Coast, where he died suddenly on August 2.

His death was so unexpected—the true state of his weak health had been well hidden—that rumors circulated that Florence had poisoned him. The night before his state funeral she sat for hours with his body, speaking to it as a mother would speak to a child.

Florence then returned to Marion, where Warren was buried. Based again on astrological forecasts, she believed that she had only a short time left to live. In fact, her diseased kidney continued to weaken, and she died fifteen months after leaving the White House. Ironically, one of the songs sung at her funeral was "The End of a Perfect Day." She was buried next to her husband.

Grace Coolidge

Born: January 3, 1879; Burlington, Vermont
Parents: Andrew and Lemira Barrett Goodhue
Spouse: Calvin Coolidge (October 4, 1905; Burlington)
Children: John (1906–2000); Calvin Jr. (1908–1924)
Died: July 8, 1957; Northampton, Vermont

An only child, Grace Anna Goodhue Coolidge was born to parents from old New England families. She attended public high school and graduated from the University of Vermont in 1902, making her the first president's wife to have attended a coeducational university. After graduation from college, she spent three years teaching at the Clarke Institute for the Deaf in Northampton, Vermont. She remained interested in the hearing impaired throughout her life.

In 1903, while teaching at Clarke, Grace met Calvin Coolidge. Looking up from her gardening one morning, she noticed a man standing by the

Grace Coolidge

made her extremely popular. Many thought that her cheerful vitality epitomized the 1920s. She was charming, friendly, and colorful, and was seen frequently with children or her pet animals. Her passion for baseball made her popular with men. Moreover, she loved music and the theater and brought notables in both fields to entertain at the White House. When the White House was renovated in 1927, Grace campaigned to have authentic period furniture donated to the mansion, but few people gave. Grace's stay at the White House was marred by one tragedy: the death of her younger son in 1924 from blood poisoning contracted from a blister on his toe.

Calvin Coolidge died four years after leaving the White House, but Grace lived and remained active for twenty-four more years. As first lady, she had helped to raise $2 million for the Clarke School, and she spent much of her retirement trying to help meet the needs of the hearing impaired. During World War II, she worked with the Red Cross and civil defense programs. In her last years her health slowly failed, and she died in 1957. Grace was buried next to her husband and younger son in Plymouth Notch, Vermont.

window shaving while wearing only a felt hat and his underwear. The sight struck her as ludicrous, and she burst out laughing. The man was Coolidge, who heard her laughter and arranged to meet her. A romance developed between the two (which many friends, then and later, found hard to understand because Grace and Calvin seemed so different), and they married two years later.

Calvin's political career led him to the White House after Warren G. Harding's death in 1923; he was elected to the presidency in his own right in 1924. Along the way Grace was a great asset to her husband. She was never involved politically (Calvin refused to allow it, nor would he permit her to be interviewed), and there is no indication she ever gave him any political advice; she learned that he was not running for reelection in 1928 from reporters. But her outgoing personality and her remarkable memory for names and faces were a great contrast to tight-lipped Calvin's dour disposition, and she often won friends for him.

As first lady, Grace's good-natured cheerfulness

Lou Hoover

Born: March 29, 1874; Waterloo, Iowa
Parents: Charles and Florence Weed Henry
Spouse: Herbert Hoover (February 10, 1899; Monterey, California)
Children: Herbert Clark Jr. (1903–1969); Allan Henry (1907–1993)
Died: January 7, 1944; New York City

One of the best educated of the first ladies, Lou Henry Hoover was born in 1874 about one hundred miles from the birthplace of Herbert C.

Lou Hoover

Hoover, West Branch, Iowa. She lived in Waterloo, Iowa, attending public schools until 1884, when, because of Mrs. Henry's poor health, her family moved to California. A public lecture on geology that she heard in Pacific Grove, California, led her to enroll at Stanford University in 1894; she was the first woman to major in geology there. Lou was an intelligent woman who learned to speak five languages (she later would converse with her husband in Mandarin when they wanted to speak privately in public). She also translated a sixteenth-century mining treatise from Latin into English.

In 1894 Lou met Herbert Hoover, also a Stanford geology student; four years later, she graduated from Stanford and accepted a marriage proposal from Herbert, who wired it from his job site in Australia. In 1899 he returned to California to marry her, and a week later they set out for China, where he had accepted a position with a mining firm. Thus began a global odyssey that would make Lou Hoover the most-traveled first lady in a century.

In China the Hoovers found themselves in the middle of the Boxer Rebellion, and Lou tried to assist people wounded in the conflict. From China they went to Great Britain and were there when World War I began in 1914. Lou helped Herbert's relief efforts, working with the poor in England and traveling in the United States and abroad in search of donations of food, clothes, and money to aid war victims. For her work Belgium's King Leopold awarded her the Cross of Chevalier, one of the country's highest honors.

In 1929 Lou Hoover became first lady. As first lady, Lou preferred a more active public role than earlier cabinet wives and recent first ladies. She supported social causes, advocated better social status for women, and was national president of the Girl Scouts of America. She made radio broadcasts from the White House. When Lou became mistress of the White House, she found it drab and spent some of her private funds to refurbish it. Also at her own expense, she had a photographic record made of the mansion's furnishings.

The Hoover administration was barely eight months old when the collapse of the stock market triggered the Great Depression. Touched by the suffering of the poor, Lou donated generously to charity and publicly urged others to do the same. She put the White House on a tight budget, using her own money to supplement the public funds. Almost all of her generosity, however, was kept from public view. This, combined with the Hoovers' formal and reserved manner and Herbert's inability to resolve the crisis, led to the perception that the Hoovers were cold and uncaring. Even the White House staff, which was kept at arm's length (staff members were instructed to stay out of sight when the president or first lady passed), shared this feeling. The staff also was bothered by the frequent and often impulsive entertainment carried out in the Hoover White House.

Overwhelmed by the depression, Herbert Hoover was defeated for reelection in 1932. Lou remained active in social causes after leaving the White House, particularly the Girl Scouts. With the outbreak of World War II, she began organizing efforts to provide necessities for war refugees. She was still at work when she suffered a heart attack and died in her New York apartment in 1944. So carefully had she guarded her privacy that even her husband did not realize how many people she had helped until he examined her papers after her death. In her desk drawer was a stack of uncashed checks from people who had tried to repay her generosity; she had kept them as souvenirs.

Lou Hoover was buried in Palo Alto, California; her body was later moved to West Branch, Iowa, and placed next to Herbert's.

Eleanor Roosevelt

Eleanor Roosevelt

Born: October 11, 1884; New York City

Parents: Elliott and Anna Hall Roosevelt

Spouse: Franklin D. Roosevelt (March 17, 1905; New York City)

Children: Anna Eleanor (1906–1975); James (1907–1991); Franklin (1909); Elliott (1910–1990); Franklin Delano Jr. (1914–1988); John Aspinwall (1916–1981)

Died: November 7, 1962; New York City

Anna Eleanor Roosevelt Roosevelt, perhaps the most dynamic of all the first ladies, was born into a distinguished New York family. Her mother died of diphtheria when she was eight; her father, of whom she was very fond, was an alcoholic who died when she was ten. An unhappy girl, Eleanor was raised by a strict great aunt and taught by tutors. Her formal education consisted of three years at Allenwood School in London between the ages of fifteen and eighteen. In 1902 Eleanor met Franklin D. Roosevelt, a distant cousin, and married him two years later. Their wedding date was set for the conven-

ience of Eleanor's uncle, President Theodore Roosevelt, who gave the bride away.

Ironically, Eleanor, who became one of the most prominent first ladies, was very shy and insecure as a youngster. She was a plain girl, in contrast to her beautiful mother, and she felt the difference keenly. So serious was her disposition that her own mother nicknamed her "Granny." Things only grew worse when she married. Franklin's witty and urbane friends made her feel inadequate, and her mother-in-law, Sara Delano Roosevelt, was a domineering personality who largely ran Eleanor's household. Eleanor was even intimidated by the nursemaids who looked after her children.

Not until she was in her thirties did she begin to emerge from her shell. A series of events—including a move away from Sara to Washington; exposure to the capital's politics; the discovery of her husband's affair with her social secretary, Lucy Page Mercer; and finally Franklin's polio attack in 1921—combined to bring her into public life. Knowing that Franklin's political career depended on having an active wife, she learned to make public appearances and to participate in New York politics even before he assumed the governorship in 1928. Her new energy spilled over into other aspects of her life. She began teaching history, English, and drama at Todhunter, a private school for girls; she wrote and lectured; and she even opened a furniture factory with two other women.

Her whirlwind of activity continued when she became first lady in 1933. Although she had to give up her teaching job, she made it clear that she did not intend to surrender any of her other activities. She continued to earn her own income from her writing, primarily for the satisfaction of doing so, but she donated most of her money to various charities.

As President Roosevelt's eyes and ears, she was everywhere. She traveled throughout the country, visiting coal mines and impoverished Appalachian farms. During World War II, she regularly traveled abroad to cheer American troops. She was the first first lady to fly and advocated air travel when most Americans were afraid of it.

Refusing to be a quiet helpmate as first lady, Eleanor adopted a variety of causes and fought openly for them all. She called for programs to assist the young and the rural poor. An advocate of women's rights (although not of an equal rights amendment), she was influential in the selection of the first female cabinet member, Secretary of Labor Frances Perkins, and helped to expand government employment opportunities for women. She was an outspoken critic of racial discrimination, symbolized in her public resignation from the Daughters of the American Revolution because of the group's racist policies, and she pushed for better job opportunities for African Americans.

Her activism made many criticize her harshly, but only her concern with Franklin's reelection kept her from being more vocal than she was. Although she publicly denied influencing the president, privately she regularly, and often passionately, discussed her views on policy and legislation with him and clearly was an important factor in many decisions.

No first lady has been more visible than Eleanor Roosevelt. She was active in the National Youth Administration and acted as deputy director of the Office of Civilian Defense. In addition to her travels and political activism, she held regular news conferences (as Franklin did), but she invited only women reporters because only men attended his. She made frequent radio broadcasts, continued writing magazine articles and giving public lectures, and began her own daily newspaper column. She also kept up a steady correspondence, personally answering most of the thousands of letters she received, and she did it all with only a tiny staff to help her. Her tremendous energy allowed her to work eighteen-hour days regularly.

Eleanor's time as first lady ended abruptly when Franklin Roosevelt died on April 12, 1945, but she did not fade away. Named as a delegate to the infant United Nations in 1946, she was instrumental in writing the Universal Declaration of Human Rights.

She actively supported Adlai E. Stevenson's presidential bids in 1952 and 1956 and continued to speak and write in favor of more equality in American society. Her last public appointment came at the age of seventy-seven when in 1961 she was selected by John F. Kennedy to chair the President's Commission on the Status of Women.

Seriously ill with bone marrow tuberculosis, Eleanor Roosevelt failed rapidly during the summer and autumn of 1962. The woman who was called "first lady of the world" died in November 1962 at her New York home. She was buried next to her husband on their Hyde Park estate.

Bess Truman

Bess Truman

Born: February 13, 1885; Independence, Missouri

Parents: David and Madge Gates Wallace

Spouse: Harry S. Truman (June 28, 1919; Independence)

Children: Mary Margaret (1924–)

Died: October 18, 1982; Independence

Elizabeth Virginia "Bess" Wallace Truman was one of four children born into a prominent family in Independence, Missouri. Besides attending school, Bess was something of a tomboy, who enjoyed baseball, basketball, tennis, and fencing, as well as throwing the shot put. Her father committed suicide when she was eighteen, leaving her to help her mother with her younger siblings. The trauma of this event, according to her daughter, Margaret, largely led to her later insistence on privacy for her own family.

Her relationship with Harry S. Truman, whom she had known since childhood, developed slowly for some eighteen years before they were married in

1919 after he returned from World War I. As her husband went into the very public career of politics, Bess, who argued that publicity was unbecoming to a lady, carefully remained in the background. She was far from insignificant in Harry's career, however. A calm and practical woman, she exerted an enormous influence over Harry. She was essentially his partner, reviewing his speeches, working on his correspondence and papers, and moderating his hot temper. She was so important to Harry that he put her on his Senate staff, arguing that "I need her there. . . . I never make a report or deliver a speech without her editing it."

The same pattern held when Bess became first lady in 1945, for she was determined not to be changed by the White House and actually became annoyed if old acquaintances treated her differently than before. Harry consulted her on many problems, including major ones such as the Marshall Plan and the Korean intervention, claiming that "her judgment [is] always good." She continued to restrain Harry's impulsive anger, and her admonishing "you didn't have to say that" was legendary among the White House staff. She insisted on remaining private, generally refusing to take stands on issues or make public statements, except for appeals for charities or on the question of repairing the White House (which by then badly needed it). Unlike Eleanor Roosevelt, Bess did not hold regular press conferences; in fact she spoke with the press very reluctantly. So successful was she at remaining in the background that, despite her importance in Harry's decisions, she was a virtual unknown. In 1949 the news media dubbed her a "riddle," and many of the "facts" reported about her were wrong. Throughout the Trumans remained one of the closest families ever to occupy the White House.

Harry and Bess retired to Independence in 1953. Although he had been unpopular when he left Washington, Harry gradually acquired a reputation as a sort of folk hero, while Bess was considered one of the grand ladies of America. She went on living as quietly as ever, however, until her death from heart failure at the age of ninety-seven. She was buried next to Harry, who had died a decade earlier, in Independence.

Mamie Eisenhower

Born: November 14, 1896; Boone, Iowa
Parents: John and Elivera Carlson Doud
Spouse: Dwight D. Eisenhower (July 1, 1916; Denver, Colorado)
Children: Doud Dwight (1917–1921); John Sheldon Doud (1922–)
Died: November 1, 1979; Washington, D.C.

Mamie Eisenhower

Marie "Mamie" Geneva Doud Eisenhower, the last first lady born in the nineteenth century, was raised in Iowa by well-to-do Scandinavian parents. When Mamie was seven her mother's poor health prompted the family to move to Colorado, where Mamie attended high school and finishing school. The Douds later bought a winter home in San Antonio, Texas. There, in 1915, Mamie met Dwight D. Eisenhower, an army officer assigned to a nearby base. They married less than a year later.

For the next thirty-five years Mamie moved constantly as Dwight went from one military assignment to another. They moved in fact twenty-eight times, and they did not have a permanent home until they bought a farm in Gettysburg, Pennsylvania, in 1950. The longest time spent in one place before retirement was the Eisenhowers' eight-year occupancy of the White House.

Throughout these years, Mamie suffered from poor health, becoming critically ill in 1937. She was bothered by a weak heart, which apparently was a hereditary problem that had killed her sister as a

young woman. She also suffered from Ménière's disease, a chronic inner ear condition that interfered with her balance and often caused her to stumble and bump into things. This condition led to groundless rumors that she was an alcoholic. Because of another illness, she was unable to care for her first son when he contracted scarlet fever in 1921; his death from the disease was a devastating blow to the Eisenhowers and led to a temporary but serious strain on their marriage.

As first lady, Mamie brought frills and lace to the White House and became the nation's model for femininity. Although more visible than her predecessor Bess Truman, she took no interest at all in politics, preferring to concentrate on her managerial and social duties. She claimed to enjoy entertaining, and she worked diligently at being a good hostess. Mamie became very popular all over the country. Women copied her clothes, her bangs (a hairstyle she adopted to please her husband), and even her recipe for fudge. Her health continued to be a problem, however, and many of her friends feared she would not survive a second Eisenhower term. Yet despite her apparent delicacy, she was a strong and demanding woman who ran the White House with a firm hand, often conducting white-glove inspections.

The Eisenhowers left the White House and retired to Gettysburg in 1961. When Dwight suffered a series of heart attacks in 1968–1969, he spent almost eleven months in the hospital with Mamie at his side. She lived quietly after his death in 1969, until she had a stroke in September 1979. She never recovered and died two months later; she was buried in Abilene, Kansas. Her birthplace in Iowa is now a national museum. Abigail Adams is the only other first lady so honored.

Jacqueline Kennedy

Jacqueline Kennedy

Born: July 28, 1929; Southampton, New York

Parents: John and Janet Lee Bouvier III

SPOUSES: John F. Kennedy (September 12, 1953; Newport, Rhode Island); Aristotle Onassis (October 20, 1968; Skorpios, Greece)

Children: Caroline Bouvier (1957–); John Fitzgerald Jr. (1960–1999); Patrick Bouvier (1963)

Died: May 19, 1994; New York City

The embodiment of "Camelot" and one of the most glamorous of the first ladies, Jacqueline Lee Bouvier Kennedy was the daughter of a New York stockbroker. Her parents divorced in 1940, however, and her mother later married the very wealthy Hugh Auchincloss.

Intelligent and strikingly attractive, Jacqueline grew up in high social circles. In fact, she was noted in the society columns at age two. She attended private schools and then Vassar, the Sorbonne (Paris), and George Washington University, graduating in 1951 with a degree in art. She worked as a writer for a time on the *Washington Times-Herald* and became its "Inquiring Camera Girl" and columnist.

Jacqueline met Sen. John F. Kennedy at a dinner party in 1951 and, after an off-and-on romance, married him two years later. But she found being a political wife sometimes trying, for she had little interest in politics and had to learn to temper her wit for public consumption. With her beauty, intelligence, and youth—she was thirty-one when John became president in 1961—Jacqueline cut a much higher profile as first lady than her immediate predecessors. She made the White House a center for promoting culture and the arts, and she worked to obtain authentic antiques to furnish the mansion. As part of these efforts, she led a televised tour of the White House in February 1962, which enhanced her popularity. Women throughout the country found "Jackie" glamorous and began copying her fashions (particularly her fondness for pillbox hats) and hairstyle, much as they had done with Mamie Eisenhower. Citing the needs of her small children, she stubbornly insisted on a restricted social schedule. Her independent streak also showed when she took vacations separately from the president.

Despite its fairy tale appearance, life was not always easy for Jacqueline. For several reasons, her marriage was strained; she and John often seemed to be distant and formal with one another, frequently traveling and vacationing separately. Moreover, shadowing her marriage were the extramarital affairs of her husband, which were hushed up at the time. Childbirth proved traumatic: her first child was stillborn, the next two were difficult Caesarean births, and her last, Patrick, died after only two days. The anguish of Patrick's death drew John and Jackie closer, and a deeper bond began developing between them. Finally, later in 1963, on one of the infrequent political trips that she took with John, he was assassinated as she rode next to him through the streets of Dallas, Texas. En route to Washington later the same day, she witnessed the swearing-in of Vice President Lyndon B. Johnson while still wearing a pink suit stained with her husband's blood. Back in Washington, she largely planned her husband's funeral.

After leaving the White House Jacqueline tried to maintain a more private life, despite constant pressure by inquisitive outsiders. In 1968 she married Aristotle Onassis, a wealthy Greek shipping tycoon, but his death in 1975 left her a widow for a second time. Her interest in the arts then led her to pursue a career in publishing beginning in 1975, and she accepted a position as a senior editor for Viking Press and then Doubleday. She also became involved in historical preservation.

In February 1994 the former first lady revealed that she was suffering from non-Hodgkin lymphatic cancer. The disease quickly spread to her brain and liver and proved untreatable. After contracting pneumonia, she abruptly worsened and died on May 19 in her New York apartment. She was buried next to President Kennedy in Arlington National Cemetery.

Lady Bird Johnson

Lady Bird Johnson

Born: December 22, 1912; Karnack, Texas
Parents: Thomas and Minnie Pattillo Taylor
Spouse: Lyndon B. Johnson (November 17, 1934; San Antonio, Texas)
Children: Lynda Bird (1944–); Luci (originally Lucy) Baines (1947–)

Her given name was Claudia Alta Taylor, but a nursemaid nicknamed her "Lady Bird" while she was still an infant. Her father was a successful farmer and merchant, but her mother, who suffered from health problems, died from a fall when Lady Bird was five. Thus the young Texan was raised mostly by a maternal aunt.

Lady Bird graduated from high school in Marshall County, Texas, at age fifteen, and spent two years at St. Mary's School for Girls in Dallas. From there she attended the University of Texas, where she finished in the top ten of her class with degrees in liberal arts and journalism. She earned a teaching certificate as well.

In 1934 she met Lyndon B. Johnson, then a secretary to a member of Congress, and married him after a courtship of only two months. A skillful and frugal homemaker, Lady Bird handled all of the family's financial and domestic matters. She also proved to be an astute businesswoman. In 1942 she borrowed from her inheritance to purchase a nearly bankrupt Austin radio station. Under her supervision, the station expanded into a multimillion-dollar broadcasting empire known as the Texas Broadcasting Corporation. Although the extent of her active management of the corporation varied over the years, she always maintained some involvement in its operation.

Lady Bird had virtually no experience in politics, but she quickly became a capable political wife. She learned to entertain numerous guests on short notice and became adept at remembering names, faces, and places. She borrowed from her inheritance to provide money for Lyndon's first race for Congress in 1937, and when he volunteered for active duty at the beginning of World War II, she ran his congressional office by herself for a few months. She was so capable that, according to some observers, she could have won elected office herself, although she never showed any interest in doing so. During her time as the vice president's wife (1961–1963), she substituted for the first lady at several formal events when Jacqueline Kennedy, who zealously guarded her time, refused to appear.

Lady Bird became first lady when President John F. Kennedy was assassinated in 1963. When her husband sought election to the presidency in 1964, he faced serious opposition in the South because of his support for civil rights legislation. To shore up his support among southerners, the likable Lady Bird hit the campaign trail, where she made forty-seven speeches and gained votes from people who would

have refused to listen to the president himself.

With Lyndon elected, she turned her attention to her national "beautification" project, which she saw as symbolic for improving the quality of life in both urban and rural areas. She and her staff rallied public and private support for her program. Lady Bird also traveled 200,000 miles to make speeches in its behalf and personally lobbied Congress for passage of the Highway Beautification Act of 1965. She took an interest in education policy as well. In all, despite her attempt to avoid controversial policy issues such as the Vietnam War, she was the most active first lady since Eleanor Roosevelt. She also was an excellent manager. Observers have claimed that she ran her wing of the White House much better than the president ran his.

President Johnson's decision not to run for reelection in 1968—which was as much of a surprise to Lady Bird as everyone else—led to their retirement to their Texas ranch. After Lyndon's death in 1973 Lady Bird largely withdrew from public life. She continued to manage her business interests successfully and pursue her interests in natural resources, including publishing in 1988 the book *Wildflowers Across America*. In May 2002 Lady Bird suffered a small stroke and was hospitalized briefly.

Pat Nixon

Born: March 16, 1912; Ely, Nevada
Parents: William and Katharine Bender Ryan
Spouse: Richard Nixon (June 21, 1940; Riverside, California)
Children: Patricia (1946–); Julie (1948–)
Died: June 22, 1993; San Clemente, California

Thelma Catherine Ryan Nixon was the daughter of an Irish miner, who nicknamed her "Pat" because

Pat Nixon

her birthday was so close to St. Patrick's Day. Her father took up farming in Artesia, California, when she was two. In 1925 her mother died, leaving Pat to take care of the house. When her father died four years later after a lengthy illness, she went to New York to work.

In 1932 Pat returned to California and entered the University of Southern California. After graduating cum laude she took a teaching job in Whittier and there met Richard M. Nixon at a local theater production in which both were playing. He proposed to her on the night of their first meeting. Startled, Pat at first refused, but she eventually changed her mind and they married two years later. Richard became successful as a small-town lawyer, but he sought more and entered politics after World War II.

For Pat, the decision proved to be a trying one, one that—as she once acknowledged—she never would have made herself. She did not relish the constant public exposure, and as Richard sought higher offices and the campaigns became more intense and vicious, she came to dislike politics. In September

1952 rumors about financial misconduct forced Richard to make his famed Checkers speech in a successful effort to save his vice-presidential candidacy. Although for him it was a great triumph, for Pat it was a public humiliation as the family finances became common knowledge.

As early as 1950 she extracted a pledge from Richard not to seek office again, but he broke it repeatedly. Dutifully, Pat learned to be a proper political wife, but her lively personality was replaced, at least in public, by the stiff, formal, almost "doll-like" demeanor that earned her the unkind nickname of "Plastic Pat." The years between 1960 and 1968 were spent in private life, much to Pat's satisfaction, but then Richard Nixon became president in 1969.

As first lady, Pat gathered more than five hundred authentic antiques and original paintings to refurnish the White House, more than any other first lady. She also tried to make the mansion more accessible to the public: she initiated Christmas candlelight tours and seasonal garden tours, introduced multilingual guidebooks, and made the mansion more accessible to the disabled. The most traveled of first ladies, Pat visited eighty-three countries. Because she knew that public expectations of first ladies had changed and required more social activism, Pat attempted to embrace various social projects, promoting education and voluntarism, but her efforts were largely ineffective. Of the modern first ladies, she was one of the least active. This stemmed in part from her own difficulties in dealing with the public and in part from the White House staff's insistence that she maintain a low profile. She seemed to have little influence on her husband's political business and was left out of many important decisions, including his decision to run for president in 1968. As the Watergate scandal broke over Richard Nixon in 1973, Pat urged him to destroy the White House tapes, arguing that they were a private diary and not public fare. Her husband chose to ignore her warning, however. He resigned from the presidency in 1974.

Freed at last from the burden of politics, Pat withdrew from all but family and close friends. In 1976, while at home in California, she suffered a stroke and had to undergo several months of physical therapy; she had a second but milder stroke in 1983. Battling emphysema and chronic lung infections, her health deteriorated steadily over her last years. She died of lung cancer in 1993, on the day after her fifty-third wedding anniversary.

Betty Ford

Born: April 8, 1918; Chicago, Illinois
Parents: William and Hortense Neahr Bloomer
Spouses: William C. Warren (1942; Grand Rapids, Michigan); Gerald R. Ford (October 15, 1948; Grand Rapids)
Children: Michael Gerald (1950–); John Gardner (1952–); Steven Meigs (1956–); Susan Elizabeth (1957–)

Betty Ford

Elizabeth "Betty" Bloomer Warren Ford was the daughter of a Chicago salesman who moved to Grand Rapids, Michigan, when she was three. As a young girl, Betty decided to become a dancer. Thus in 1935 she graduated from the Calla Travis Dance Studio and then spent time at the Bennington School of Dance in Bennington, Vermont. From 1939 to 1941 she worked in New York City as a dancer and model. After returning to Grand Rapids, she married William C. Warren, a local salesman, in 1942, but their marriage ended after five years.

Betty met Gerald R. Ford in 1947 and married him the next year. Three weeks after their wedding Gerald was elected to Congress for the first time, and Betty took on the role of political wife. She joined the organizations expected of the wife of a rising member of Congress, and, because her husband frequently was away on speaking trips or campaigning for fellow House Republicans, she took a major role in raising their four children. But the demands on her were great, and the strain finally forced her to seek psychiatric counseling in 1970. In 1973, just as she was learning stress management and had fixed a date with Gerald for his retirement from politics, he was named Richard Nixon's vice president, replacing Spiro T. Agnew, who had resigned.

When Nixon resigned from the presidency on August 9, 1974, Betty Ford found herself first lady. Her outspoken honesty quickly brought her considerable attention. She strongly endorsed the Equal Rights Amendment, which was faltering in its drive for ratification, and personally lobbied state legislators for its passage. Although the ratification effort eventually failed, she worked to increase the number of women in high government positions and pushed unsuccessfully for a woman on the Supreme Court. She also supported more assistance for the arts, the handicapped, and the mentally disabled.

FIRST AND SECOND LADIES ON THE HILL

Formal appearances by first ladies on Capitol Hill have been rare. Before 1940, no first lady had testified before any congressional committee. But since then, four first ladies and three second ladies have appeared before Congress. Of these appearances, the most important has been that of Hillary Rodham Clinton, who spent a week testifying extensively about a proposed major social reform.

December 10, 1940: Eleanor Roosevelt testifies before the House Select Committee to Investigate the Interstate Migration of Destitute Citizens about people forced by the Great Depression to wander the nation looking for work.

January 14, 1942: Mrs. Roosevelt appears before the House Select Committee Investigating National Defense Migration about the problems caused by people moving to industrial centers to find defense work.

February 7, 1979: Rosalynn Carter testifies before the Senate Labor and Human Resources Committee in support of more federal funding for mental health programs.

April 30, 1979: Mrs. Carter appears before an oversight hearing by the House Science and Technology Committee.

June 26, 1979: Joan Mondale, wife of Vice President Walter F. Mondale, testifies before the Senate Labor and Human Resources Committee on the Arts, Humanities and Museum Services Act of 1979.

September 25, 1979: Mrs. Mondale testifies before the Senate Governmental Affairs Committee on the subjects of art and architecture.

Some of her statements proved to be controversial, however. Her endorsement of the Supreme Court's abortion decision, discussion of a hypothetical affair by her daughter, and comments on her children's experimentation with drugs all created a storm of protest. The courage and openness she displayed in her bout with breast cancer, which ended in a radical mastectomy, won her admirers and helped to focus public attention on that health problem. Her influence on President Ford was considerable. He acknowledged the value he placed on her opinions, while she referred to the importance of the "pillow talk" she had with him over issues.

Betty Ford left the White House in 1977 and retired with Gerald to Palm Springs, California. By the time she left she had become one of the most outspoken, and one of the more popular and respected, of the first ladies. She was praised when she publicly acknowledged her dependency on drugs and alcohol (caused by pain from an inoperable pinched nerve and arthritis, together with the emotional stress of being a political wife) and told of her struggle to overcome it. She received awards for her work in behalf of women's rights and against cancer, and she helped establish the Betty Ford Center for Drug and Alcohol Rehabilitation in Rancho Mirage, California. In 2003 she published the book *Healing and Hope,* which told the stories of six women who had been to the Betty Ford Center.

February 7, 1980: Mrs. Mondale appears before the House Select Committee on Aging to discuss senior citizens and art.

March 3, 1980: Mrs. Mondale testifies before the House Education and Labor Committee during hearings on the reauthorization of both the 1965 National Foundation for the Arts and the Humanities Act and the 1976 Museum Services Act.

April 23, 1990: Marilyn Quayle, wife of Vice President Dan Quayle, appears before the House Committee on Energy and Commerce to discuss women's health issues.

May 16, 1990: Mrs. Quayle testifies before the House Select Committee on Aging on breast cancer.

May 13, 1993: Tipper Gore, wife of Vice President Al Gore, appears before the Senate Labor and Human Resources Committee to discuss mental health care.

September 27–31, 1993: Hillary Rodham Clinton appears before five different committees—House Ways and Means Committee, House Education and Labor Committee, House Energy and Commerce Committee, Senate Finance and Labor Committee, and Senate Human Resources Committee—to explain and defend the president's health care reform proposal.

January 24, 2002: Laura Bush testifies before the Senate Committee on Health, Education, Labor and Pensions on programs to improve early childhood education.

March 14, 2002: Mrs. Bush appears before the House Education and the Workforce Committee in support of the administration's education legislation.

Sources: Thomas H. Moore, "First Ladies on the Hill," *Congressional Quarterly Weekly Report,* October 2, 1993, 2641; www.whitehouse.gov/firstlady (accessed November 16, 2004).

Rosalynn Carter

Born: August 18, 1927; Plains, Georgia
Parents: Wilburn and Frances "Allie" Murray Smith
Spouse: Jimmy Carter (July 7, 1946; Plains)
Children: John William (1947–); James Earl "Chip" III (1950–); Donnel Jeffrey (1952–); Amy Lynn (1967–)

Rosalynn Smith Carter was born and grew up about three miles from the Plains, Georgia, home of her future husband, Jimmy Carter. Her father died of leukemia when she was thirteen, leaving her to help her mother with the family. After serving as valedictorian of her high school class, Rosalynn attended Georgia Southwestern Junior College in Americus so that she could remain near home. She had known Jimmy for some time, but her first date with him was not until she was seventeen; she married him a year later.

Jimmy was a naval officer at the time of their marriage, and for the first time Rosalynn moved away from Plains, spending time in California, Pennsylvania, Hawaii, Virginia, and Connecticut. She enjoyed her new independence and the opportunities it offered. When her father-in-law died in 1953 and Jimmy decided to resign his commission to run the family peanut business, Rosalynn reluctantly returned to Plains.

Despite her initial resistance, she soon began to

like her life in Plains. She helped with the business and became active in local organizations.

Rosalynn overcame an acute fear of public speaking so that she could help Jimmy when he entered politics; she traveled the state when he ran unsuccessfully for governor of Georgia in 1966, and again in 1970, when he was elected. When he decided to run for the presidency in 1976, Rosalynn again set off alone to campaign for him, traveling thousands of miles to give speeches on his behalf.

Few first ladies have achieved the prominence that Rosalynn Carter attained between 1977 and 1981. She frequently was compared to Eleanor Roosevelt, even by her husband—she was always on the go. It has been noted that "in her first two years as first lady, she made 248 speeches or public comments, gave 154 press interviews, attended 641 briefings, and visited 36 foreign countries." She fought for better treatment of the mentally ill and appeared before congressional subcommittees to support her views. Problems of the aged and equality for women were causes she supported.

Rosalynn also traveled abroad on the president's behalf, most notably to Latin America in 1977. She frequently sat in on cabinet meetings and even participated in President Carter's Camp David negotiations between Egyptian president Anwar Sadat and Israeli prime minister Menachem Begin. Rosalynn was thus Jimmy's alter ego; she discussed policy matters and appointments with him daily. Their partnership in policy making was so openly equal that Rosalynn Carter has been called one of the most influential of all the first ladies. In fact, in a poll of historians she was rated much more effective as first lady than her husband was as president.

Burdened by an economic downturn and his failure to obtain the release of American diplomats being held hostage in Iran, Jimmy Carter was defeated in his bid for reelection in 1980. He and

Rosalynn Carter

Rosalynn retired to Plains where they wrote separate accounts of their years in the White House. She also worked with Jimmy to establish the Carter Center, a foundation in Atlanta devoted to promoting human rights and peace around the world, and she was active in Habitat for Humanity and other charitable organizations.

In 1987 she and Jimmy coauthored *Everything to Gain: Making the Most of the Rest of Your Life,* which described their activities and lifestyle since leaving the White House. Out of her concern for the problems of the aged, the mentally ill, and those who care for them, she has coauthored the books *Helping Someone with Mental Illness: A Compassionate Guide for Family, Friends, and Caregivers*, and *Helping Yourself Help Others: A Caregivers Guide.* In 2002 she was inducted into the National Women's Hall of Fame.

Nancy Reagan

Nancy Reagan

Born: July 6, 1923;[4] New York City
Parents: Kenneth and Edith Luckett Robbins
Spouse: Ronald Reagan (March 4, 1952; Riverside, California)
Children: Patricia Ann (1952–); Ronald Prescott (1958–)

Nancy Reagan was the daughter of an auto sales-man and a stage actress. Her father left the family shortly after she was born, and her mother, deter-mined to pursue a stage career, left young Nancy with relatives. Born Anne Frances Robbins, Nancy, as she was nicknamed, lived until age six with an aunt in Washington, D.C.

In 1929 her mother married a Chicago physi-cian, and Nancy went to live with them. She was legally adopted at age fourteen and became Nancy Davis. Later, Nancy attended a private high school in Chicago and Smith College in Massachusetts. While attending Smith, she had a brief romance with a Princeton student, who was accidentally struck by a train and killed.

Similar to her mother, Nancy decided to pursue an acting career. She had been in theatrical produc-tions in high school and had majored in drama at Smith. In 1943 Nancy began her stage career, and in 1949 she moved to Hollywood to break into movies. There she met Ronald Reagan, then president of the Screen Actors Guild, who cleared her of a baseless charge of communist associations. After the couple married in 1952, Nancy largely abandoned her act-ing career to be a homemaker, returning to the screen only for very brief intervals when financially necessary. She made her last movie in 1954.

She returned to the public eye, however, when Ronald entered politics and became governor of California in 1966 and president in 1980. Initially as first lady, Nancy argued that her only concern was taking care of her husband. She thus attempted to remain out of sight. Her first two years in the White House were stormy ones, however. She was criti-cized sharply for her fashionable wardrobe, her rich friends, and the general image of luxury that she projected while the president cut spending on pro-grams for the poor. Particularly attacked were her $900,000 remodeling of the White House and the $200,000 china set she ordered (although most of the money used for both was from private dona-tions).

By 1982 Nancy was making determined efforts to improve her public image and to establish better rela-tions with the news media. Among other things, she became active in drug abuse programs, a longtime concern, and supported antidrug efforts, both domes-tically and internationally. By 1985 Nancy had gone from being one of the most disliked first ladies to being more popular than the president. Beyond these efforts, she also was a great influence on the president himself. Moreover, she displayed an iron will in pro-tecting the interests of the more easy-going Ronald. Nancy kept abreast of current events, but she was more interested in personalities. Even the president acknowledged that she was very perceptive in personnel matters. Her behind-the-scenes influence, particularly on personnel, was strong. Several White House insiders attested to her power to remove people she thought a liability to her husband.

In 1989, after two terms in the White House, the Reagans retired to Los Angeles, California. In retirement, Nancy devoted most of her time to caring for her beloved husband, who suffered from progressive Alzheimer's disease and had to have a hip replacement after a fall in 2001. Her public appearances were few; she addressed the Republican National Convention in 1996 and was honored by the National Center on Addiction and Substance Abuse at Columbia University in 1997. The only first lady to publish an autobiography before entering the White House, she later wrote a memoir of her years there, *My Turn: The Memoirs of Nancy Reagan.* Nancy emerged briefly into the national spotlight during the week of mourning following her husband's death in June 2004; Ronald Reagan lay in state in the Capitol Rotunda, and services were held at the National Cathedral in Washington and at the Reagan Presidential Library in California.

Barbara Bush

Barbara Bush

Born: June 8, 1925; Rye, New York
Parents: Marvin and Pauline Robinson Pierce
Spouse: George Bush (January 6, 1945; Rye)
Children: George Walker (1946–); Pauline Robinson "Robin" (1949–1953); John Ellis "Jeb" (1953–); Neil Mellon (1955–); Marvin Pierce (1956–); Dorothy Walker (1959–)

A distant relative of President Franklin Pierce, Barbara Pierce Bush was born in Rye, New York, a sub-

urb of New York City. Her father was the publisher of *McCall's* magazine; her mother was the daughter of an Ohio Supreme Court justice. Her family was wealthy, and she attended school at prestigious Ashley Hall in South Carolina.

She met George Bush at a Christmas dance in 1942 and became engaged to him a year later. Their marriage was delayed, however, while George served in the U.S. Navy. In 1945 Barbara dropped out of school after two years at Smith College to marry him. After George graduated from Yale University in 1948, the Bushes moved to Odessa, Texas, where George entered the oil business. That was the beginning of an odyssey that included twenty-eight homes in seventeen cities.

After succeeding in oil, George became active in politics, serving as a member of Congress from Texas, U.S. ambassador to the United Nations, chair of the Republican National Committee, U.S. representative to China, director of the Central Intelligence Agency, and finally vice president and president. In the midst of traveling around the country and the world, Barbara had six children, the second of whom, Robin, died of leukemia just before her fourth birthday.

A strong believer in voluntarism, Barbara donated much of her time before becoming first lady to helping the less fortunate. She was honorary chair of the Leukemia Society of America and won the Distinguished American Woman Award in 1987. Her primary concern was illiteracy in the United States, and she was actively involved in programs to improve literacy.

These concerns continued for Barbara when she became first lady. She started the Barbara Bush Foundation for Family Literacy and donated the entire proceeds from her best-selling book, *Millie's Book,* to it. (Revenues from her earlier book, *C. Fred's Story,* also had been given to literacy groups.) Remembering her deceased daughter, she often visited chronically ill children in the hospital; a widely circulated photograph of her holding an AIDS-infected baby helped to reduce prejudice against victims of the disease. And she spoke out in behalf of the homeless and of poor and single parents.

Mrs. Bush also traveled widely as first lady, visiting sixty-eight countries, and she was very active in her social duties, hosting almost twelve hundred events while attending more than eleven hundred others in her four years. These efforts, with her grandmotherly appearance and self-deprecating wit, made her immensely popular, so much so, in fact, that *Good Housekeeping* named her to its list of most admired Americans for four straight years, and another poll declared her to be the world's most popular woman. She still rates as one of the most popular first ladies.

Finally, she was a close if informal adviser to President Bush, reviewing papers and discussing policy with him. Although she downplayed her own political instincts, others regarded her as a "key element" in the Bush presidency.

After George lost his reelection bid in 1992, the Bushes retired to Houston, Texas. Barbara continued to travel and to enjoy reading, needlepoint, gardening, and spending time with her family, which included eleven grandchildren. Her autobiography, *Barbara Bush: A Memoir,* was published in 1994. When her oldest son, George W., decided to seek the presidency in 2000, she played an active role in his campaign, making public appearances and speeches, writing letters and taping telephone messages, and raising money. In 2001 she became the second woman (after Abigail Adams) to be both the wife and the mother of a president. Barbara published another memoir, *Reflections: Life After the White House,* in 2003. She again hit the campaign trail in 2004 for George W.'s reelection bid.

Hillary Rodham Clinton

Born: October 26, 1947; Chicago, Illinois
Parents: Hugh and Dorothy Rodham
Spouse: Bill Clinton (October 11, 1975; Fayetteville, Arkansas)
Children: Chelsea Victoria (1980–)

Hillary Rodham Clinton was raised in the Chicago suburb of Park Ridge by parents whose strong support for education and self-reliance were important factors in her growth and development. She attended public high school in Chicago and then went to Wellesley College, where her intelligence and skills as a mediator won praise and her political views became more liberal. She delivered her class commencement address, punctuating it with an attack on the day's guest speaker, Sen. Edward Brooke (R-Mass.), as a representative of establishment politics. The verbal fireworks earned her national publicity in *Life* magazine.

After graduating from Wellesley, Hillary attended Yale Law School. There she became interested in

Hillary Rodham Clinton

children's rights issues, joined the Yale Child Study Center, and assisted in the preparation of two books on child development. She also met and began dating Bill Clinton, a fellow law student.

After her graduation from Yale in 1973, Hillary worked at the Children's Defense Fund for a brief time and then, in January 1974, joined the U.S. House of Representatives Judiciary Committee's Impeachment Inquiry staff, which was grappling with legal questions surrounding the possible impeachment of President Richard M. Nixon. Her work with the committee led to several prestigious job offers after Nixon's resignation, but she decided to join Bill in Arkansas. She taught law at the University of Arkansas in Fayetteville and married Bill in a house he had purchased there for them.

In 1976 Bill was elected attorney general of Arkansas, and the Clintons moved to Little Rock, where Hillary joined a prominent law firm, working in family law, commercial litigation, and criminal law. She quickly established herself as one of the city's best lawyers. Two years later, Bill became gov-

ernor. During this time, Hillary founded the Arkansas Advocates for Children and Families, was appointed by President Jimmy Carter to chair the Legal Services Corporation, and served on the board of the Children's Defense Fund. But as first lady of Arkansas, Hillary's high profile, outspokenness, and "liberal" ideas—such as continuing to use her maiden name—made her a lightning rod for criticism and contributed to Bill's reelection defeat in 1980.

In 1982 Bill rebounded to be reelected governor of Arkansas; he held the office for the next decade. Finally adjusting to Arkansas realities, Hillary changed her image while remaining prominent and became one of the state's more popular first ladies. In the meantime, she spearheaded education reform by serving as the chair of the Arkansas Education Standards Committee. And, not least, she served as an adviser to her husband, evincing political skills good enough to earn her mention as a gubernatorial candidate in her own right. Her law practice and her reputation also grew, and by 1989 the *National Law Journal* had cited her as one of the nation's "100 Most Powerful Lawyers."

In the 1992 presidential campaign, her intelligence and proven abilities, which sometimes led the campaign to claim the public would be getting "two for the price of one" in a Clinton presidency, proved to be a double-edged sword. It won many supporters, some of whom thought her better qualified than her husband to be president; but it also left her open to attacks from political opponents, particularly the Republican right, who claimed that she had too much influence with her husband and that her views were "antifamily."

Once the Clintons were in the White House, Hillary quickly became the most high-profile and openly powerful first lady ever. She maintained an office in the West Wing, which no first lady had previously done, and chaired staff meetings herself. She publicly served as one of her husband's most important advisers on almost every topic; "Ask Hillary" was the watchword in the White House. Most significantly, President Clinton appointed her to head a task force established to create a health care reform program. When after eight months the commission produced a plan, Hillary became its foremost advocate, lobbying behind the scenes and testifying before five different congressional committees to explain and defend it. As one commentator noted, she was unique because she had a "strong separate source of power inside the administration with a mandate of authority from the president and an operational base from which to carry it out." Some described her essentially as a copresident.

But as in Arkansas, Hillary's prominence led to controversy among a public unprepared for such an unconventional first lady, and she became a target for criticism. Legal and ethical questions arose about her role in the 1993 firing of the White House Travel Office staff and in the handling of the Clintons' Whitewater real estate venture. In the latter case, she responded to questions from a Senate investigation committee and, in February 1996, became the first sitting first lady to be subpoenaed by, and to testify before, a grand jury. In March 2002 the final special prosecutor's report found insufficient evidence to charge her with any wrongdoing in the case. After the health care reform bill she had championed failed, at least in part because opponents successfully attacked the bill by attacking her, observers both inside and outside the administration agreed that giving her such a visible and important role had been a mistake. By 1996 opinion polls indicated that more than 50 percent of the public disapproved of her and thought that she made the president look weak. She had become a public relations liability for the administration.

In response, as in Arkansas, Hillary remade her public image. She scaled back her overt political involvement (while privately remaining as influential as ever); the "copresidency" disappeared, and she publicly concentrated on issues that were closer to the more traditional first lady's concerns. Hillary was involved with the White House Conference on Early Childhood Development and Learning, the Reach Out and Read program, and the White House Conference on Child Care. She was instrumental in passing the Adoption and Safe Families Act of 1997. Her public role was no less visible than before: She made more than nine hundred public appearances at more than five hundred events; she traveled to eighty-three countries on more than forty overseas trips. The most noteworthy of these was her address to the United Nations Conference on Women in Beijing, China, in 1995. In all her appearances abroad, she tried to meet with local women and to promote women's issues; she became "the administration's most forceful human rights advocate." She also wrote a weekly newspaper column and published a book, *It Takes a Village,* which dealt with family life and childrearing.

Revelations in January 1998 about President Clinton's extramarital relationship with a White House intern created a political and personal crisis for Hillary. As the details about Bill's affair and his attempts to deny it became known, Mrs. Clinton was forced to endure a public humiliation that dragged on for months. In private, fearing the destruction of everything she had worked for, she organized a spirited defense of the embattled Clinton presidency, especially during the ensuing impeachment and acquittal of the president. Her stoic and dignified public handling of her ordeal won her sympathy as the wronged wife and the respect of many. Her approval ratings rose to their highest level, and for the first time she was more popular than her husband. The president's affair put a tremendous strain on the Clintons and led some observers to argue that she should leave him; however, friends had often noted that a deep bond existed between Bill and Hillary, and with time it seemed to draw them back together.

Although always involved in politics, she had never held an elected office. As the Clinton administration drew to a close, she decided to seek the New York Senate seat being vacated by Democrat Daniel Patrick Moynihan. In 1999 the Clintons bought a house in Chappaqua, New York, to establish residency in the state. Hillary entered the Senate race and handily won the election in 2000. The Clintons' roles had reversed: she was the candidate, he was the supporter. In January 2001 Mrs. Clinton was sworn in as a U.S. senator, becoming the only first lady to be elected to public office.

Hillary Clinton was an unusual freshman senator; she already was extremely well-known and was seen as a possible candidate for national office. But the former first lady succeeded in learning the ropes and forging alliances while maintaining a lower profile than some had expected. During her first year in the Senate, she fought for money for New York in the wake of the terrorist attacks of September 11, 2001; the state received $20 billion in emergency aid.

In the 108th Congress, Hillary took on a leadership role as chair of the Steering and Coordination Committee, which coordinates between Senate Democrats and other Democratic political leaders around the nation. As the 2004 presidential election drew closer, Hillary remained in the spotlight as a potential White House aspirant. She chose not to run for president that year, and the eventual nominee, Sen. John Kerry of Massachusetts, selected Sen. John Edwards of North Carolina as his running mate. Some saw Hillary and Edwards as potential opponents in a future presidential primary four or eight years down the line. At the 2004 Democratic National Convention in Boston, Hillary spoke on the first night, introducing her husband. As one of the best-known Democrats in the country, she campaigned for the Kerry-Edwards ticket, as did Bill Clinton, although he was temporarily sidelined after undergoing heart bypass surgery in September 2004.

Her Senate committee assignments included Armed Services, Environment and Public Works, and Health, Education, Labor and Pensions.

Laura Bush

Laura Bush

Born: November 4, 1946; Midland, Texas
Parents: Harold and Jenna Louise Hawkins Welch
Spouse: George W. Bush (November 5, 1977; Midland)
Children: Barbara (1981–); Jenna (1981–)

Laura Welch Bush was the only child born to a successful Midland, Texas, real estate developer and his wife. Her earliest memory was of sitting in her mother's lap while listening to her mother read to her, which kindled a passion for reading and books in Laura. (Her favorite pastime is still reading, preferably stretched out on her bed; her favorite piece of literature is "The Parable of the Grand Inquisitor" from Dostoyevsky's *The Brothers Karamazov*). By the age of seven, she wanted to be a teacher; she would line up dolls as in a classroom and give lessons to them. Laura was an outstanding student in high school, taking honors courses and working on the school yearbook. She was a Girl Scout and worked as a camp counselor, which encouraged an interest in outdoor activities such as whitewater rafting. In general, her childhood was the ideal of small-town America in the 1940s and 1950s. But her idyllic adolescence was tragically marred on November 6, 1963, when she failed to see a stop sign and struck another car that was driven by a close friend. While she was uninjured and no charges were filed against her, her friend died at the scene.

After graduating from high school, she enrolled at Southern Methodist University in Dallas, where she majored in elementary education. Graduating with distinction, she taught briefly in Dallas and then Houston. She entered the graduate school at the University of Texas in 1970 and received a masters in library science there in 1972. She worked in the Houston Public Library for a short time and then, in 1974, became a school librarian in Austin, where she worked for the next three years.

In late summer of 1977 mutual friends introduced Laura to George W. Bush at a cookout in Midland. Although the Welches and Bushes had once lived only a few blocks apart in Midland, and Laura and George had lived on opposite ends of the same apartment complex in Houston, they had not previously met. They seemed to be total opposites: he—energetic, party-going, political; she—reserved, serious, with absolutely no interest in politics (in fact, she had avoided meeting him previously because of her lack of interest in politics). Despite that, when they finally met, they got along at once, and within three months they were married. Laura would prove to be a settling influence on him.

At the time of their wedding, George was in a campaign for Congress; immediately after their wedding, he resumed campaigning. Laura quickly became a political wife. Although he had promised her that she would not have to give speeches, with-

in two months Laura had delivered her first campaign speech. She would become a polished speaker and used her skill to help her husband's later political campaigns. She also learned to heed her mother-in-law's advice to never criticize George's speeches. Once, when returning from an appearance during the first campaign, he asked her how the day's speech had gone. When she told him it was lousy, he was so startled that he drove the car into the side of the house.

After his bid for Congress proved unsuccessful, George entered the oil business. Laura did not resume her career as a librarian and instead settled down as a housewife in Midland. The couple briefly considered adopting children before Laura learned that she was pregnant in March 1981. Her pregnancy proved a difficult one, complicated by toxemia, which eventually forced the premature birth by Caesarian section of her daughters. Fraternal twins Barbara and Jenna were born in November 1981 in Dallas.

After several successful business ventures, George was elected governor of Texas in 1994. As first lady of Texas, Laura worked to promote her lifelong interest in reading. At her husband's inauguration as governor, she arranged for several Texas writers to give public readings as part of the ceremonies. In 1996 she helped initiate the annual Texas Book Festival, which over the years raised more than a million dollars for the benefit of libraries in Texas. She was a strong supporter of the arts in general. In 1998 she helped launch an initiative encouraging family literacy and preparing young children for reading when they entered school. She helped to establish Rainbow Rooms, which assist abused and neglected children, throughout Texas. She also worked to promote women's health issues, especially breast cancer prevention and treatment.

When Governor Bush became President Bush in January 2001, Laura brought these same concerns to Washington. In July 2001 she led the White House

Summit on Early Childhood Cognitive Development, a conference focusing on childhood learning issues. She promoted the Ready to Read, Ready to Learn initiative, which included programs to increase awareness by parents of the importance of reading, to improve early childhood educational development, and to attract and retain more quality teachers. On September 8, 2001, she hosted the first National Book Festival in Washington, D.C.; in conjunction with the festival, she announced the formation of the Laura Bush Foundation for America's Libraries, created to help improve school libraries throughout the United States. The book festival became an annual event during her husband's presidency. Laura even traveled to Moscow to join Russian president Vladimir Putin's wife, Ludmila, at the Russian Book Festival in 2003.

In January 2002 Laura became the fourth first lady to testify before Congress, advocating to a Senate committee programs to improve early childhood education. She testified again, about the administration's education legislation, before a House committee in March 2002.

In the wake of the 2001 terrorist attacks in New York, Virginia, and Pennsylvania, Mrs. Bush made numerous public appearances, including on television shows such as *Oprah, 60 Minutes,* and *Good Morning America,* in an attempt to reassure children and to remind parents of the need to help their children cope with the tragic events. Some called her the "comforter in chief." On November 17, 2001, she became the first first lady to deliver the entire weekly presidential radio address. In March 2002 she spoke before the U.N. Commission on the Status of Women, discussing her support for Afghan women on International Women's Day.

When her husband sought reelection in 2004, Laura Bush, whose popularity ratings were higher than those of her husband at that point, made numerous campaign appearances around the country on his behalf. She spoke in support of her husband at the 2004 Republican National Convention in New York. The Bushes' daughters, who recently had graduated from college—Barbara from Yale and Jenna from the University of Texas—made their political debut during their father's reelection bid and proved to be popular draws on the campaign trail as well.

Notes

1. Betty Boyd Caroli, *First Ladies* (New York: Oxford University Press, 1987), xv.
2. Scholars disagree about Martha Washington's actual birth date. June 21, 1731, is the date most commonly used, but several others also have been mentioned.
3. Dolley Madison's given name is not clear. Some scholars have declared that "Dorothea" was her given name and "Dolley" a nickname. Others have insisted that Dolley was her real name.
4. The birth records for Nancy Reagan have been lost, but school records indicate that she was born in 1921. Mrs. Reagan claims that she was born in 1923.

Biographies of the Vice Presidents

By Daniel C. Diller

Almost since its creation, the vice presidency has been ridiculed as an insignificant office. Benjamin Franklin quipped that the vice president should be addressed as "Your Superfluous Excellency." Even some vice presidents have poked fun at the office. Thomas R. Marshall, who occupied the vice presidency during Woodrow Wilson's two terms as president, said that the vice president is like "a man in a cataleptic fit; he cannot speak; he cannot move; he suffers no pain; he is perfectly conscious of all that goes on, but has no part in it." John Nance Garner was a fairly active vice president during the first two terms of Franklin D. Roosevelt's administration, but his pithy assessment of the office is probably the most frequently quoted of all: "The vice presidency isn't worth a pitcher of warm spit."

Nevertheless, the importance of the vice presidency is evident when its occupant is called upon to succeed the president. Nine vice presidents, one-fifth of those who served in the office up to the year 2000, became president when the incumbent chief executive died or resigned. "I am vice president," said John Adams, the first person to hold the office. "In this I am nothing, but I may be everything."

Adams, though, found a lot of "nothing" in the office. Midway through his tenure he lamented to his wife, Abigail, that "my country has in its wisdom contrived for me the most insignificant office that ever the invention of man contrived or his imagination conceived." Little did Adams realize that the vice presidency was at a peak of influence during the period he served. The vice president's chief constitutional function was to preside over the Senate. Because the Senate was small and still relatively unorganized at the time, he was able to cast twenty-nine tie-breaking votes (still the record), guide the upper house's agenda, and intervene in debate.

The election of the nation's second vice president, Thomas Jefferson, revealed an unexpected complication to the setup of the office. The original Constitution provided that the vice presidency be awarded to the person who received the second highest number of electoral votes for president. Unforeseen by the Constitution was the development of political parties. Jefferson, as leader of Democratic-Republicans, worked behind-the-scenes in Congress in opposition to President Adams and the Federalists.

The enactment of the Twelfth Amendment, which established separate elections for president and vice president, effectively prevented this type of partisan split, but it also weakened the already constitutionally weak vice presidency. Party leaders, not presidential candidates, now chose the nominees for vice president. One criterion for vice-presidential selection was that the nominee placate the region or faction of the party that had been most dissatisfied with the presidential selection, which lead to numerous New York–Virginia, North–South, conservative–liberal, and other such pairings.

Many national leaders were unwilling to accept the second spot in this type of ticket balancing. Daniel Webster, declining a vice-presidential spot on the Whig Party ticket in 1848, said, "I do not propose to be buried until I am dead." Those who did and were elected vice presidents found that fresh political problems four years after their nomination invariably led party leaders to balance the ticket differently; no first-term vice president in the nineteenth century was renominated for a second term by a party convention. Nor, after Vice President Martin Van Buren in 1836, was any nineteenth-century vice president elected or even nominated for president.

Not surprisingly, then, the nineteenth-century vice presidents make up a virtual rogues' gallery of personal and political failures. Because the office was so unappealing, an unusual number of the politicians who could be enticed to run for vice president were old and in bad health. Six died in office, all of natural causes. A few vice presidents became embroiled in financial or personal scandals.

The rise of national news media, a new style of active presidential campaigning, and alterations in the vice-presidential nominating process enhanced the status of the vice presidency during the first half of the twentieth century. In 1900 Theodore Roosevelt became the first vice-presidential candidate to campaign vigorously nationwide. In the decades that followed more able and experienced political leaders accepted the post, including Charles Dawes, who had served in three administrations and won a Nobel Peace Prize; Charles Curtis, the Senate majority leader; and John Nance Garner, the Speaker of the House.

A turning point in the vice presidency came when Vice President Harry S. Truman became president upon the death of Franklin D. Roosevelt at the close of World War II. Truman's lack of preparation for the task of running the country at war, along with the subsequent development of an ongoing cold war between the United States and the Soviet Union and the proliferation of intercontinental ballistic missiles armed with nuclear warheads, heightened public concern that the vice president should be a leader who was not just willing but also ready and able to step into the presidency at a moment's notice if the need for a successor should arise.

To meet the new public expectations about vice-presidential quality, most modern presidential candidates have paid considerable attention in selecting their running mates. Winning votes on election day is as much the goal as in the old-style ticket balancing, but presidential nominees realize that voters now care more about competence and loyalty—a vice-presidential candidate's ability to succeed to the presidency ably and to carry on the departed president's policies faithfully—than they do about having all regions of the county or factions of the party represented on the ticket.

During the past four decades the office itself has become increasingly larger and more complex than in the past (the vice president's staff, for example, has grown from twenty in 1960 to around seventy today). Additionally, certain kinds of vice-presidential activities now are taken for granted. These include regular private meetings with the president, attendance at many important presidential meetings, membership on the National Security Council, full national security briefings, frequent diplomatic missions, public advocacy of the president's leadership and programs, and party leadership.

One of the most influential modern vice presidents was Walter Mondale, who during the administration of President Jimmy Carter attained additional status as a general adviser to the president.

Subsequent vice presidents, to a varying degree, have also functioned as top advisers, if only in certain policy areas. Al Gore elevated the visibility of the vice presidency further with his undertaking of numerous high-profile assignments within the administration of President Bill Clinton. Gore was also one of the three or four people whose advice Clinton sought on virtually every important matter of presidential politics and policy. If anything, the position of vice president became even more important during the Bush-Cheney administration. Dick Cheney's years of experience in the federal government—including his service as defense secretary to President George W. Bush's father—allowed him to function as a key adviser, especially in the wake of the terrorist attacks of September 11, 2001.

Besides its long-standing role as presidential successor, the vice presidency also has become an important electoral springboard to the presidency. Five vice presidents have been elected to the presidency in their own right—two since 1968. The modern vice president has become not only a presumptive candidate for president but the presumptive front-runner as well. Seventeen of twenty-one vice presidents in the twentieth century went on to seek the presidency.

The biographies of all forty-six vice presidents follow. Those fourteen vice presidents who have gone on to the presidency have an abbreviated biography here; their full biographies are found in Biographies of the Presidents.

John Adams

Born: October 30, 1735; Braintree (now Quincy), Massachusetts
Party: Federalist
Term: April 30, 1789–March 3, 1797
President: George Washington
Died: July 4, 1826; Quincy, Massachusetts
Buried: Quincy

(See full biography, p. 33.)

An outspoken advocate of independence from Britain, John Adams was a delegate to the First Continental Congress and served on the committee assigned to draft a declaration of independence. He served in a number of diplomatic posts in Europe and signed the armistice ending war with the British in 1783. In 1789, after finishing second to George Washington in the nation's first presidential election, he became the first vice president and was a strong influence as presiding officer of the Senate. Still today he holds the record for casting the deciding vote whenever the Senate is tied. After serving as vice president for eight years, he won the presidency in the 1796 election.

Thomas Jefferson

Born: April 13, 1743; Goochland (now Albemarle) County, Virginia
Party: Democratic-Republican
Term: March 4, 1797–March 3, 1801
President: John Adams
Died: July 4, 1826, Charlottesville, Virginia
Buried: Charlottesville

(See full biography, p. 36.)

Gifted as a writer, Jefferson, at thirty-three, was chosen by his peers in the First Continental Congress to draft the Declaration of Independence. Named ambassador to France, Jefferson witnessed the French Revolution in 1789 and missed the drafting of the Constitution. On his return home Jefferson was named the first secretary of state. Disagreements with Alexander Hamilton, the Treasury secretary, led to Jefferson's resigning his post and forming the Democratic-Republican Party, which opposed Hamilton's Federalists.

He ran for president in 1800 and was voted into office by the House of Representatives after receiving the same number of votes as his opponent, Aaron Burr.

Aaron Burr

Aaron Burr

Born: February 6, 1756; Newark, New Jersey
Party: Democratic-Republican
Term: March 4, 1801–March 4, 1805
President: Thomas Jefferson
Died: September 14, 1836; Staten Island, New York
Buried: Princeton, New Jersey

Aaron Burr was born into a family of prominent ministers, headed by his grandfather, the famous theologian and preacher Jonathan Edwards. Burr's father, Rev. Aaron Burr, was the cofounder and second president of Princeton University. His uncle, Timothy Edwards, was a clergyman as well. Shortly after Aaron's birth his parents died, and he and his sister were left in the custody of his uncle.

Burr was only thirteen when he entered Princeton University as a sophomore. He graduated with honors three years later in 1772 and briefly studied theology before abandoning it for a law career. But he had barely begun his legal studies when he received a commission in the army in 1775. Burr joined Gen. George Washington's army at Cam-

bridge, Massachusetts, and served as a captain in Gen. Benedict Arnold's force, which failed to capture Quebec. He then became a member of General Washington's staff until the mutual dislike of the two men resulted in Burr's transfer to the staff of Gen. Israel Putnam. After Burr's promotion to lieutenant colonel he commanded a regiment that fought in the battle of Monmouth (New Jersey) in 1778. The following year he resigned his commission because of illness.

Burr studied law in Albany, New York, until 1782, when he was admitted to the bar. After practicing law in New York City, he was elected to the New York State legislature in 1784. New York governor George Clinton appointed Burr the state's attorney general in 1789, and two years later Burr was elected to the U.S. Senate.

Burr served in the Senate until 1797, then returned to New York. He won a seat in the New York legislature a year later and helped the Democratic-Republican Party take control of that body through his organizational work. Burr's reputation for political intrigue and romantic affairs had made him a controversial figure, but his intelligence, charm, and service to the Democratic-Republicans led to his nomination for vice president by that party in 1800.

The electoral procedure in effect through the 1800 election dictated that the candidate who received the second highest number of electoral votes for president became vice president. Each elector voted for two candidates, with no distinction made between a vote for president and a vote for vice president. Although the parties distinguished between their presidential and vice-presidential candidates, nothing prevented a vice-presidential candidate from being elected president if that candidate received more electoral votes than his presidential running mate.

In the election of 1800 this voting procedure resulted in a tie between the Democratic-Republican presidential candidate, Thomas Jefferson, and Burr, his vice-presidential running mate. Both men received seventy-three electoral votes, and Burr refused to concede the election. The responsibility for selecting a president then fell to the House of Representatives, where the Federalists had a majority. After a week and thirty-six ballots, the weary representatives elected Jefferson president. (The confusion of the 1800 election led to the Twelfth Amendment to the Constitution, which was ratified in 1804; it separated the voting for president and vice president.) Predictably, Jefferson did not include Burr in the deliberations of his administration.

Because of Alexander Hamilton's historic reputation as one of the most important Founders of the United States, the romantic mystique that surrounds the antiquated practice of dueling, and the incomprehensibility of a vice president committing murder while in office, Burr will always be remembered as the man who shot and killed Hamilton in a duel on July 11, 1804, at Weehawken, New Jersey. The duel occurred when Burr challenged Hamilton for

making derogatory remarks about him during the 1804 New York gubernatorial campaign, which Burr lost to Hamilton's candidate. After Burr mortally wounded Hamilton he fled south to avoid the warrants that had been issued for his arrest in New York and New Jersey. Because federal law did not yet provide for the extradition of criminals from the District of Columbia, Burr returned to the capital. Incredibly, he resumed his duties as presiding officer of the Senate as if nothing had happened.

Even before he left office in 1805 Burr had begun to formulate a treasonous conspiracy. Although the details of Burr's plot are unclear, it is known that he hoped to incite a rebellion in the western regions of the United States, conquer Mexico, and then establish a vast western empire with New Orleans as its capital. While vice president he had proposed to the British ambassador in Washington that he lead a revolt in the western United States in return for $110,000. The offer was rejected, but Burr raised money through other means. He assembled a small force in the summer of 1806 and was preparing to move against Mexico when one of his co-conspirators, James Wilkinson, exposed the plot. Burr eventually was arrested and tried for treason in 1807 with Chief Justice John Marshall personally presiding over the case. President Jefferson pushed for a conviction, but, despite evidence that he had planned the conspiracy, Burr was acquitted because he had not yet committed an overt act of treason.

Even after his trial Burr continued to plot ways to gain an empire. In Europe he tried unsuccessfully to convince Napoleon to help him conquer Florida. After living in Europe for four years he returned to the United States in 1812 to be with his only daughter, Theodosia, who was married to Joseph Alston, the governor of South Carolina. She sailed from South Carolina to meet him in New York, but her ship was lost at sea. Burr then settled in New York City and spent the rest of his years practicing law.

Burr had married Theodosia's mother, Theodosia Prevost, in 1782; she died in 1794. In 1833 Burr married Eliza Jumel, a wealthy widow twenty years his junior. She was granted a divorce the day Burr died.

George Clinton

Born: July 26, 1739; Little Britain, New York
Party: Democratic-Republican
Term: March 4, 1805–April 20, 1812
Presidents: Thomas Jefferson; James Madison
Died: April 20, 1812; Washington, D.C.
Buried: Kingston, New York

George Clinton

Unlike the majority of his contemporaries who reached high office, George Clinton did not have the advantage of being born into a wealthy family. His father was a poor Irish immigrant who could not afford to send George to college. Thus, George went to sea when he was eighteen but returned home after a year. He then fought in the French and Indian War as a lieutenant and gained combat experience during the campaign of 1760 in which the British and their colonial allies captured Montreal.

After the war Clinton studied law in New York City and eventually was admitted to the bar. He then practiced law in his native Ulster County, New York, and in 1765 became district attorney. In 1768 Clinton began his rise in politics when he was elected to the New York Assembly. He served in that body until 1775, when he was elected to the Second Continental Congress.

As a prominent public figure with military experience, Clinton was appointed a brigadier general in the New York militia. Gen. George Washington then ordered him to lead his troops in defense of New York in the summer of 1776. Consequently, he was absent from the Continental Congress when the Declaration of Independence was signed, but he had advocated independence before his departure.

Although Clinton's forces were unable to defend Fort Montgomery in the highlands of the Hudson River from advancing British forces under Sir Henry Clinton, the stiff resistance shown by the New York militia enhanced George Clinton's reputation despite his mediocre military skills. In March 1777 Congress granted him the rank of brigadier general in the Continental army to go along with his generalship in the New York militia. He gave up his commissions, however, when he was chosen governor of New York. He assumed the office on July 30, 1777, and served six successive terms until 1795. During the Revolutionary War Governor Clinton became known for his harsh treatment of New York's loyalists.

Clinton's power within his home state made him a natural opponent of the new federal Constitution, which, if approved, would limit state sovereignty and slice into his personal power. As the presiding officer at New York's ratifying convention, he did his best to prevent ratification, but the Constitution won approval, 30–27.

Clinton's preeminence in New York gubernatorial elections was not challenged until 1792, when he narrowly defeated John Jay only after he had the votes of three counties invalidated on a technicality. Clinton recognized that his popularity in New York had slipped, and he declined to run for reelection in 1795. Six years later, however, he won another three-year term as governor with the support of his powerful nephew DeWitt Clinton, who manipulated his aging uncle during his last term in office.

Clinton's nomination as the candidate of the Democratic-Republican Party for vice president in 1804 stemmed from the new Twelfth Amendment, which linked the fates of a party's presidential and vice-presidential candidates. Vice-presidential nominees were chosen according to their ability to attract votes for their running mates. Although at age sixty-five Clinton's physical and mental capacities were declining, he could still deliver many votes for the Democratic-Republicans in his native New York. As a northerner he also would provide geographic balance to the ticket with Virginian Thomas Jefferson. After Aaron Burr the Democratic-Republicans desired a noncontroversial figure like Clinton for the number two spot. Clinton, who had designs on the presidency, accepted the vice-presidential nomination in the hope that it would be a steppingstone to the higher office. The Jefferson-Clinton ticket won easily over Federalists Charles Cotesworth Pinckney and Rufus King.

Clinton was regarded unanimously as a poor presiding officer of the Senate. His forgetfulness and inattention to detail caused much parliamentary confusion. He complained that his duties were tiresome, and he spent an increasing proportion of his time at his home in New York rather than at the capital.

Clinton still desired the presidency in 1808, but he was widely regarded as senile. Thus, he had little chance of beating out Jefferson's chosen successor, James Madison, for the Democratic-Republican nomination. Even though Clinton declared his availability for the presidency, the party caucus, as expected, selected Madison as its nominee, and Clinton bitterly accepted the consolation of yet another vice-presidential nomination. Madison and Clinton were easily elected, but the victory did not soften the vice president's hard feelings. He refused to attend Madison's inauguration and openly opposed the president's policies.

In 1811 Clinton got his chance to strike a blow against Madison and other Democratic-Republican leaders whom he believed had denied him the presidential nomination that he deserved. When the vote on the bill to recharter the Bank of the United States, which Madison favored, was tied in the Senate, Clinton, as vice president, cast the deciding vote against rechartering the bank. On April 20, 1812, at the age of seventy-two, Clinton became the first vice president to die in office.

Clinton married Cornelia Tappan, who was a member of a politically powerful family in New York's Ulster County, on February 7, 1770. They had six children. Cornelia died in 1800, before her husband became vice president.

Elbridge Gerry

Born: July 17, 1744; Marblehead, Massachusetts
Party: Democratic-Republican
Term: March 4, 1813–November 23, 1814
President: James Madison
Died: November 23, 1814; Washington, D.C.
Buried: Washington, D.C.

Elbridge Gerry was the son of a prosperous Massachusetts merchant. Upon graduating from Harvard in 1752, he entered his father's lucrative importing and shipping business. His resentment of British efforts to tax American commerce drew him into revolutionary circles. Gerry was elected to the General Court of Massachusetts in 1772 and subse-

Elbridge Gerry

quently the Massachusetts Provincial Congress. From his position in this body he managed supply procurement operations for his state's patriot forces in the early days of the American Revolution.

From 1776 to 1781 Gerry served in the Continental Congress. An influential member of its treasury committee, he put his supply procurement experience to use in the service of the Continental army. He also represented Massachusetts in Congress under the Articles of Confederation from 1783 to 1785. Gerry signed both the Declaration of Independence and the Articles of Confederation. At the Constitutional Convention he advocated strengthening the federal government. He refused, however, to endorse the document that the convention eventually produced because he thought it gave the federal government too much power over the states. After the Constitution was adopted by Massachusetts, Gerry put his reservations aside and supported the document. He was elected to two terms in the House of Representatives (1789–1793).

In 1797 President Adams sent Gerry, along with John Marshall and Charles C. Pinckney, to France to negotiate a treaty that would head off war between France and the United States. The talks were abandoned by the American side when the French representatives demanded as preconditions to negotiations a bribe for Foreign Minister Talleyrand, a loan for the French government, and an apology for Adams's recent criticisms. Marshall and Pinckney, who were known to be unsympathetic toward France, left for home. But Gerry stayed in Paris until the following year in the vain hope that his pro-French reputation might create an opening with the French that could lead to a treaty. A bribery incident, which came to be known as the "XYZ affair," after the French representatives who were referred to as "X, Y, and Z" in documents released by Adams, outraged the American public and ushered in several years of undeclared naval warfare with France. Gerry's Federalist opponents accused him of conducting an accommodating diplomacy with an enemy nation, but his reports of France's desire to avoid war contributed to Adams's decision to send another negotiating team to France in 1799.

When Gerry returned to the United States, he ran for the governorship of Massachusetts four consecutive years (1800–1803) without winning. His prospects for election were hampered by his position as a Democratic-Republican in a traditionally Federalist state. Finally, in 1810 and 1811, Gerry was elected to consecutive terms as governor.

Before the Massachusetts elections of 1812, Gerry left his most indelible mark on U.S. political culture. He signed a bill that restructured the senatorial districts of his state so that his party, the Democratic-Republicans, would be likely to win more seats than their actual numbers warranted. Because the map of the new districts was perceived to resemble the outline of a salamander, the redistricting tactic was dubbed a "gerrymander." Gerry had not sponsored the bill, but Federalists were quick to blame him for it. That year he failed to win reelection to his third term as governor.

Despite Gerry's advanced age and his defeat in his home state, his political career was not over. In 1812 the Democratic-Republicans were searching for a northerner to balance their ticket with President James Madison. After DeWitt Clinton of New York and John Langdon of New Hampshire refused the second spot, the party turned to Gerry. He and Madison defeated DeWitt Clinton and Jared Ingersoll, who had formed a coalition of Federalists and maverick Democratic-Republicans.

Gerry fulfilled his constitutional duty of presiding over the Senate despite his weakening health. During his vice presidency he was an outspoken proponent of the War of 1812. He narrowly missed becoming president in 1813 when Madison was stricken by a severe fever. Madison recovered and lived twenty-three years longer, but Gerry died in 1814 while still in office.

Gerry married Ann Thompson, the twenty-year-old daughter of a New York merchant, on January 12, 1786. The couple had ten children. Because of Ann's poor health, she did not move to Washington, D.C., with her husband when he became vice president, but, ironically, she lived thirty-five years after his death.

Daniel D. Tompkins

Born: June 21, 1774; Fox Meadows (now Scarsdale), New York

Party: Democratic-Republican

Term: March 4, 1817–March 4, 1825

President: James Monroe

Died: June 11, 1825; Tompkinsville, Staten Island, New York

Buried: New York City

Daniel D. Tompkins

Daniel D. Tompkins was born into a family of wealthy farmers in Westchester County, New York. His parents did not give him a middle name, but he added a middle initial to distinguish himself from another boy with the same name. He graduated from Columbia College in 1795 and was admitted to the bar two years later.

Tompkins enjoyed a brilliant early career in New York State politics that was sponsored by New York political boss DeWitt Clinton; Clinton eventually became his political enemy, however. In 1803 Tompkins won a seat in the New York State Assembly. The following year he was elected to the U.S. House of Representatives, but he resigned after he was appointed to the New York Supreme Court. He occupied that post until he was elected governor in 1807. He remained New York's chief executive until his rise to the vice presidency in 1817.

As governor, Tompkins was one of the few political leaders in the Northeast who supported the War of 1812. He borrowed millions of dollars and oversaw the disbursement of funds to pay troops and buy supplies. During his ten years as New York's chief executive, Tompkins also worked for prison reform, better treatment of Native Americans, and the abolition of slavery in his state. Following his lead, the state legislature passed a bill in 1817 that outlawed slavery as of 1827. In 1814 President James Madison offered Tompkins the post of secretary of state, but he declined the appointment to remain governor of New York.

Tompkins sought the presidential nomination in 1816, but he was forced to settle for the vice presidency because Madison supported James Monroe and Tompkins was not well known outside New York. Like his predecessors, George Clinton and Elbridge Gerry, Tompkins provided the Democratic-Republican ticket with geographic balance. Unlike Clinton and Gerry, however, Tompkins had the advantage of being a youthful forty-two years old.

Tompkins's term as vice president was dominated by his fight against charges that he had mismanaged New York finances while he was governor during the war. Tompkins had indeed failed to keep accurate, detailed records of wartime expenditures and had mixed his personal finances with those of the state. Accounts showed that he owed New York $120,000. In April 1819 the state legislature voted to cancel the vice president's debt by granting him a commission on money he had raised during the war, but Tompkins insisted on a higher commission that would have required the state to pay him a sum in addition to forgiving the debt. His influence in the New York legislature, however, had been damaged by his decision to run for governor against DeWitt Clinton in 1820. Tompkins lost the election and incurred the enmity of Clinton, who snuffed out a movement in the Assembly to give Tompkins the money he claimed. Under Clinton's direction the state filed a suit against the vice president to recover the debt.

Despite the financial scandal, Tompkins was again chosen by the Democratic-Republican Party as its candidate for vice president in 1820. Monroe and Tompkins won easily, with only one electoral college vote cast against them. Throughout his second term Tompkins remained preoccupied with his debt problem and devoted little time to the duties of his office. He declined to travel to the capital for the inauguration and was instead given the oath of office in a private ceremony in New York. In 1823, at Tompkins's request, the Senate chose a president pro tempore to preside over its deliberations; Tompkins never again led that body. When his term ended in 1825, he made no attempt to run for another national or state office. Instead, he continued to work to exonerate himself. Weakened by the stress of the scandal and his heavy drinking, he died a year later.

After Tompkins's death, audits finally revealed that New York actually owed him money. His descendants were paid $92,000. In 1827 the law abolishing slavery that had been signed by Tompkins ten years before went into effect. To honor the governor for his efforts to end slavery in the state, a square in New York City was renamed after him.

Tompkins married Hannah Minthorne, a member of a prominent New York family, around 1797. They had eight children.

John C. Calhoun

Born: March 18, 1782; Abbeville District, South Carolina
Party: Democratic-Republican
Term: March 4, 1825–December 28, 1832
Presidents: John Quincy Adams; Andrew Jackson
Died: March 31, 1850; Washington, D.C.
Buried: Charleston, South Carolina

John Caldwell Calhoun hailed from a family of wealthy and prestigious South Carolina planters. He received his early education at a school in Georgia

John C. Calhoun

and entered Yale University in 1802. After graduating in 1804 he studied law in Litchfield, Connecticut, and Abbeville, South Carolina. He was admitted to the South Carolina bar in 1807 and opened a law office in Abbeville. The following year he won a seat in the state legislature, and in 1811 he was elected to the U.S. House of Representatives as a Jeffersonian Democrat.

During the War of 1812 Calhoun gained national fame as a leader of the War Hawks, a group of expansionist members of Congress who helped push the United States toward war with the British. He served three terms in the House and chaired the Foreign Relations Committee. In 1817 President James Monroe appointed Calhoun secretary of war, a post that he held throughout Monroe's presidency.

Calhoun sought the presidency in 1824, but he received less support for the office than either John Quincy Adams or Andrew Jackson. Thus, he gave up his immediate presidential aspirations and maneuvered for the vice presidency. He courted Jackson and Adams and received the support of both men

for his vice-presidential candidacy. Adams was elected president by the House of Representatives after neither he nor Jackson received a majority of electoral votes; Calhoun's fence-straddling strategy thus paid off.

Calhoun's quest for the vice presidency was not motivated primarily by his ambition to serve in that office. He saw the post as a steppingstone to the presidency. Nevertheless, the talented former House member devoted himself to his duties as the presiding officer of the Senate. In this capacity he worked to foil the programs of President Adams, with whom he shared few political goals. The two men vented their antagonism toward one another through letters published in newspapers under pseudonyms.

Calhoun endured a political scandal during his first term as vice president. It was discovered that, while Calhoun had served as secretary of war under James Monroe, an assistant had awarded a $450,000 military construction contract to the assistant's brother-in-law. Calhoun was accused of receiving a cut of the profits from the deal. After declaring his innocence, the vice president asked the House of Representatives to investigate the matter, and he took a temporary leave of absence while a seven-member committee examined the charges. Six weeks later the committee exonerated Calhoun of any misconduct. The vice president confidently resumed his duties, but the scandal had damaged his reputation.

By 1828 Calhoun's break with John Quincy Adams was complete. The vice president threw his support behind Democratic presidential candidate Andrew Jackson, who in turn backed Calhoun's nomination for a second vice-presidential term. The Jackson-Calhoun ticket easily defeated Adams and Richard Rush of Pennsylvania.

Like John Quincy Adams, Jackson soon became disaffected with his vice president. The split between the two men was first opened in early 1829 not by a political dispute, but by the refusal of Calhoun's wife to accept the wife of Secretary of War John H. Eaton into Washington society. Eaton had met his wife, Peggy O'Neale Timberlake, while he was living in a tavern owned by Peggy and her first husband. Eaton had carried on an affair with Mrs. Timberlake, and, after Mr. Timberlake's death at sea, Eaton followed the advice of his close friend Andrew Jackson and married her. When the wives of prominent politicians in Washington, led by Calhoun's wife, Floride, refused to accept Mrs. Eaton as an equal, Jackson blamed his vice president.

The Eaton affair was a small matter compared to Calhoun's increasingly radical opinions on states' rights. During his early career Calhoun had been known as a nationalist. He had not only called for war with the British in 1812, but also supported the National Bank, internal improvements, and a high tariff that many of his fellow southerners opposed. By 1827, however, Calhoun had begun to believe that the southern states needed protection from the high tariffs being imposed by the federal government and the growing antislavery movement in the North. He even wrote anonymously in support of nullification, a concept that allowed a state to nullify within its borders a federal law that it believed was against its interests. Andrew Jackson rejected nullification as an illegal usurpation of national sovereignty by the states.

On April 13, 1830, at a Jefferson Day dinner, Jackson resolved to find out whether his vice president's first loyalties were to his country or to his state. The president stared directly at Calhoun as he delivered the toast: "Our Union—it must be preserved." When the vice president replied, "The Union, next to our liberties, most dear," he finally committed himself to South Carolina and the South. As a result, Calhoun no longer had much influence with Jackson, and he lost any chance of eventually attaining the presidency.

In 1832 the Nullification Crisis occurred when South Carolina declared that federal tariffs had no force in the state. But South Carolina leaders agreed to a compromise tariff after Andrew Jackson threatened to send 200,000 troops to that state to enforce the law. Two months before his term was to expire Calhoun resigned the vice presidency in response to Jackson's actions and accepted an appointment to a vacant Senate seat from South Carolina. He remained in that office until 1844, when he resigned to become secretary of state during John Tyler's last year in office. He returned to the Senate in 1845 and served there until his death in 1850.

After he left the vice presidency Calhoun did not try to conceal his southern partisanship. He was celebrated in the South for his eloquent advocacy of slavery and states' rights.

Calhoun married Floride Bonneau Calhoun, a wealthy cousin, in January 1811. They had nine children.

Martin Van Buren

Born: December 5, 1782; Kinderhook, New York
Party: Democratic
Term: March 4, 1833–March 3, 1837
President: Andrew Jackson
Died: July 4, 1862; Kinderhook
Buried: Kinderhook

(See full biography, p. 51.)

As secretary of state, Martin Van Buren was the most influential member of President Andrew Jackson's cabinet and Jackson's most powerful supporter from the northeastern states. At political odds with Jackson's first vice president John C. Calhoun, Van Buren resigned his cabinet post and later was rejected by Calhoun's tie-breaking vote in the Senate as ambassador to Great Britain. Jackson replaced Calhoun with Van Buren as his running mate in the 1832 election and the team won easily. With Jackson's strong support, Van Buren was elected president in 1836.

Richard M. Johnson

Born: October 17, 1780; Floyd's Station, Kentucky
Party: Democratic
Term: March 4, 1837–March 4, 1841
President: Martin Van Buren
Died: November 19, 1850; Frankfort, Kentucky
Buried: Frankfort, Kentucky

Richard M. Johnson

The son of a wealthy Kentucky landowner, Richard Mentor Johnson studied law at Transylvania University in Lexington, Kentucky, and was admitted to the bar in 1802. After briefly practicing law, Johnson began his political career at the age of twenty-four when he was elected to the Kentucky legislature. Two years later, in 1806, he was elected to the U.S. House of Representatives, where he served until 1819.

Before the War of 1812 Johnson joined with other War Hawks from the South and West in calling for war with Great Britain. When the fighting began, he left the capital without resigning his seat in Congress to become a colonel in command of a regiment of his fellow Kentuckians. In 1813 he led his troops skillfully at the battle of the Thames, where U.S. forces defeated the British and their Indian allies. Johnson, who was seriously wounded in the battle, gained national fame for allegedly killing the Indian chief Tecumseh.

When his wounds healed, Johnson returned to Congress, where he worked to secure military pensions for veterans. In 1816 he authored a bill that granted members of Congress a $1,500 salary instead of a daily allowance for expenses. Although Johnson had justified the salary as a way to encourage Congress to expedite legislative business, the public saw only greed in the law. Johnson respond-

ed by supporting the repeal of his own bill. In 1819 he retired from the House and returned to Kentucky, where the state legislature promptly elected him to an unexpired Senate seat. He served in that body until 1829, when he was again elected to the House after losing reelection to the Senate.

In 1824 Johnson backed Henry Clay's presidential bid but switched to Andrew Jackson when Clay threw his support behind John Quincy Adams. Because no candidate had received a majority of electoral votes, the election was decided by the House, which elected Adams. Thereafter, Johnson developed a close political association with Andrew Jackson, who became president in 1829. As a member of Congress, Johnson voted for the president's tariff policies and supported Jackson's stands against the Second Bank of the United States and the use of public funds for internal improvements.

Before the 1836 presidential election Andrew Jackson designated Martin Van Buren as the Democratic Party's presidential nominee and pushed for Johnson to be Van Buren's running mate. Jackson probably wanted to reward the Kentuckian for his political loyalty, but the outgoing president also may have believed that Johnson would strengthen Van Buren's candidacy. The Kentuckian gave the ticket geographical balance and a more heroic image. The lore surrounding Johnson's Indian-fighting exploits helped to offset the popularity of William Henry Harrison, one of the Whig candidates, who also had a reputation as an Indian fighter and had been Johnson's commanding general at the battle of the Thames.

Despite these contributions to the winning ticket, the scandals surrounding Johnson's personal life would have prevented his nomination had he not had the support of Jackson, who was still the most powerful and popular political figure in the United States. Johnson was reviled by his fellow politicians for keeping a succession of black mistresses. He had two daughters by his first mistress, Julia Chinn, a mulatto slave he had inherited from his father. The vice president's attempts to introduce his daughters into society as equals offended many powerful southern slaveowners. His vulgar manners and shabby appearance also lost him support.

When it came time to select Van Buren's running mate in 1840, the Democratic Party initially ignored Johnson. Even Andrew Jackson denounced Johnson's candidacy, saying it would cost "thousands of votes." Thus, rather than renominate Johnson, the Democratic convention chose to allow individual states to nominate vice-presidential candidates. Enough states nominated Johnson, however, to get his name on the ballot. Van Buren and Johnson tried to repeat their success of 1836, but they faced a better-organized Whig Party, which had coalesced behind Harrison, who was running once again. The economic depression that had plagued Van Buren's presidency and a shrewd Whig campaign that relied on catchy slogans and generous quantities of hard cider brought Harrison victory.

After leaving the vice presidency in 1841 Johnson returned to Kentucky, where he again served in the state legislature until 1842. Two years later he sought the Democratic presidential nomination at the Baltimore national convention, but his favorite-son candidacy received little support. In 1850 the ailing sixty-nine-year-old was elected to the Kentucky legislature for the final time; however, he died of a stroke without ever taking up his legislative duties.

John Tyler

Born: March 29, 1790; Charles City County, Virginia
Party: Whig
Term: March 4, 1841–April 4, 1841
President: William Henry Harrison
Died: January 18, 1862; Richmond, Virginia
Buried: Richmond

(See full biography, p. 55.)

Although John Tyler was not supposed to play a leading role in the administration of William Henry Harrison, he was thrust onto center stage when Harrison died within a month of taking the oath of office. The Constitution did not specify whether a vice president was to become president upon the death of an incumbent or merely assume the powers and duties of the office. Many members of Congress and other national leaders sought to limit Tyler's power, but he ignored them and assumed not only the duties of the presidency but also its title and all of its power, the first vice president to succeed to the presidency. No vice president served with him.

George M. Dallas

George M. Dallas

Born: July 10, 1792; Philadelphia, Pennsylvania
Party: Democratic
Term: March 4, 1845–March 4, 1849
President: James K. Polk
Died: December 31, 1864; Philadelphia
Buried: Philadelphia

George Mifflin Dallas was born into a wealthy Philadelphia family. His father, Alexander Dallas, had served as secretary of the Treasury under James Madison. George was groomed for college by Philadelphia's best tutors. After graduating from Princeton University in 1810, he went to work in his father's law office. He was admitted to the bar in 1813. That year he traveled to Russia to serve as a private secretary to Albert Gallatin, the U.S. minister in St. Petersburg. When he returned in 1814, he worked for his father in the Treasury Department and later on the legal staff of the Second Bank of the United States. During the 1820s Dallas became

increasingly active in politics. He supported the presidential candidacy of John C. Calhoun in 1824. After Andrew Jackson's strong showing in that election, however, Dallas became a Jacksonian Democrat.

Dallas began his own political career in 1828 when he was elected mayor of Philadelphia. In 1829 he accepted an appointment as U.S. district attorney for eastern Pennsylvania. Two years later his state legislature sent him to the U.S. Senate, where he served out an unexpired term. Although Dallas remained personally loyal to President Jackson, he favored the rechartering of the National Bank, which Jackson successfully opposed. When his senatorial term expired in 1833, Dallas returned to Pennsylvania, where he served as state attorney general until 1835. Martin Van Buren appointed him minister to Russia in 1837, but he resigned the post in 1839, claiming there was little work for a U.S. minister to do there. Upon his return to Pennsylvania, he reestablished his law practice while remaining active in state politics.

In 1844 the Democratic National Convention, meeting in Baltimore, Maryland, chose Sen. Silas Wright of New York as James K. Polk's running mate. Wright, who was in Washington, D.C., refused to accept the nomination because his close political associate, Martin Van Buren, had been denied the top spot on the ticket. Wright had received the news of his nomination by telegraph and had wired his answer back to the convention. Democratic leaders, however, wanted to make sure the new invention had not made a mistake and sent a messenger to Washington. By the time the confirmation of Wright's refusal reached Baltimore, many of the delegates had gone home.

Those delegates still in Baltimore gathered early the next morning to select another candidate. On the second ballot they nominated Dallas to balance the ticket with Polk, who was from Tennessee. Polk and Dallas defeated Whigs Henry Clay and Theodore Frelinghuysen by 170–105 in the electoral college, with Pennsylvania's twenty-six votes contributing to the margin of victory.

Dallas believed that a vice president should support the administration's policies even when in disagreement with them. In 1846 he demonstrated his devotion to this principle by breaking a tie vote in the Senate on a low-tariff bill supported by Polk, in spite of his state's strong protectionist sentiment. The vice president's action was attacked so bitterly in Pennsylvania that he arranged to move his family to Washington, D.C., because he feared for their safety.

By voting for the low-tariff bill, Dallas had hoped to win support in the South and West for his own presidential candidacy in 1848. At the Democratic National Convention that year he received only a handful of votes on the first ballot; Democrats were skeptical of a candidate who probably could not even win his home state. The convention chose instead Sen. Lewis Cass of Michigan, and Dallas retired from politics. In 1856 President Franklin Pierce appointed Dallas minister to Great Britain, a post he retained under James Buchanan. In 1861 he returned to Philadelphia, where he lived until he died suddenly on the last day of 1864.

Dallas married Sophia Nicklin in Philadelphia on May 23, 1816. The couple, who took their family with them on diplomatic missions to Europe, had eight children. Dallas, Texas, is named after George Dallas, who was vice president when Texas was admitted to the Union on December 29, 1845.

Millard Fillmore

Born: January 7, 1800; Cayuga County, New York
Party: Whig
Term: March 5, 1849–July 9, 1850
President: Zachary Taylor
Died: March 8, 1874; Buffalo, New York
Buried: Buffalo

(See full biography, p. 61.)

Millard Fillmore was the second vice president to rise to the presidency through a president's death. Running on the Whig ticket with Zachary Taylor in the 1848 election as a political balance to the slave-owning Taylor, Fillmore as vice president was largely excluded from policymaking in the administration. When Taylor died suddenly after some seventeen months, the antislavery Fillmore took his place and under his administration the Compromise of 1850 was passed, which set an important precedent of allowing the federal government to pass legislation on slavery rather than leaving the issue to the states.

William R. King

Born: April 7, 1786; Sampson County, North
    Carolina
Party: Democratic
Term: March 24, 1853–April 18, 1853
President: Franklin Pierce
Died: April 18, 1853; Dallas County, Alabama
Buried: Selma, Alabama

William Rufus Devane King was the son of well-to-do North Carolina planters William and Margaret King. Young William graduated from the University of North Carolina in 1803. After studying law in Fayetteville, North Carolina, he was admitted to the bar in 1806.

King entered politics in 1807 at the age of twenty-one when he won a two-year term in the North Carolina House of Commons. In 1810 he was elected to the U.S. House of Representatives, where he sided with the War Hawks, who supported the War of 1812 with Great Britain. He resigned from the House in 1816, however, to undertake a diplomatic mission to Italy and Russia.

William R. King

When he returned to the United States in 1818, King moved to Alabama and bought a plantation. He was a delegate to the convention that established Alabama's state government, and he was elected to the U.S. Senate in 1820 as one of Alabama's first senators. During his long career in the Senate King was a strong supporter of Andrew Jackson's policies. He served as president pro tempore of the Senate from 1836 to 1841.

In 1844 King left the Senate after twenty-four years when President John Tyler appointed him minister to France. While in Paris he helped secure French acquiescence to the U.S. annexation of Texas.

He returned to Alabama in 1846 and was defeated for reelection to the Senate. Two years later, however, King was appointed by the governor of Alabama to fill an unexpired Senate seat. He served as chairman of the Senate Foreign Relations Committee, and, when Millard Fillmore became president following the death of Zachary Taylor in 1850, the Senate selected King to take over Fillmore's duties as presiding officer of the Senate.

During King's time in Washington, D.C., he was surrounded by an air of personal scandal. His lack of a wife and his intimate friendship with James Buchanan, with whom he shared an apartment while the two men served in the Senate, led to speculation that he was a homosexual. King also was ridiculed for his fastidious dressing habits and his insistence on wearing a wig long after they had gone out of style. Andrew Jackson referred to King as "Miss Nancy." Like Richard M. Johnson, however, King overcame the gossip about his private life to obtain the vice presidency.

In 1852 the Democrats chose King to balance the ticket with their dark-horse presidential candidate, Franklin Pierce of New Hampshire. The choice of King was also intended to satisfy supporters of James Buchanan, who had sought the presidential nomination. King, however, was already ill with tuberculosis when he received the nomination. His condition deteriorated rapidly before the election, and he was not able to campaign. King's condition did not raise much concern among voters, however, as the Pierce-King team defeated Whigs Winfield Scott and William Alexander Graham by an electoral college vote of 254–42.

After the election King traveled to Cuba in the hope that the Caribbean climate would heal him. There on March 24, 1853, with the special permission of Congress, he became the only executive officer of the United States to take the oath of office on foreign soil. King realized that he was weakening and asked the U.S. government for a ship to take him back to the United States to die. The U.S. Navy steamship *Fulton* transported him to Mobile, Alabama. He reached his plantation, King's Bend, on April 17 and died the next day. King served just twenty-five days of his term, fewer than any other vice president.

John C. Breckinridge

John C. Breckinridge

Born: January 21, 1821; Lexington, Kentucky
Party: Democratic
Term: March 4, 1857–March 4, 1861
President: James Buchanan
Died: May 17, 1875; Lexington
Buried: Lexington

John Cabell Breckinridge was born into a prominent Kentucky family. His grandfather, John Breckinridge, had represented Kentucky in the Senate and had served as attorney general under Thomas Jefferson. His father, Joseph Cabell Breckinridge, was an influential lawyer and politician.

Breckinridge attended Centre College in Danville, Kentucky, graduating in 1839. After studying law at the College of New Jersey (later Princeton University) and Transylvania College in Lexington, Kentucky, he was admitted to the bar in 1841. He opened a law practice in Burlington, Iowa, but returned to Kentucky after two years. By

1845 he had established a successful law partnership in Lexington.

In 1846 he declined to fight in the Mexican War. The following year, however, after delivering a moving speech honoring the state's war dead in front of thousands of people, he was given a commission as a major and sent to Mexico. Although he arrived after most of the fighting was over, he was able to add military experience to his political credentials.

In 1849 Breckinridge was elected to the Kentucky legislature as a Democrat. Two years later he upset the Whig candidate for a seat in the U.S. House of Representatives from Henry Clay's former district. In 1855, after two terms, Breckinridge left Congress to resume his law practice in Kentucky and improve his finances. That year he also turned down President Franklin Pierce's offer of the ambassadorship to Spain.

The 1856 Democratic National Convention nominated Pennsylvanian James Buchanan for president and Breckinridge for vice president. Buchanan easily defeated John C. Fremont of the new Republican Party, whose election many Americans feared would bring civil war. Breckinridge was a capable presiding officer of the Senate. The handsome and eloquent vice president was so popular in his home state that, sixteen months before his vice-presidential term was to expire, he was elected to a term in the U.S. Senate, which was to begin when he left the vice presidency.

In 1860 southern Democrats nominated Breckinridge for the presidency, while Illinois senator Stephen A. Douglas was nominated by Democrats in the North. Breckinridge had not encouraged this split in his party, but he accepted the nomination. He declared that he favored preserving the Union and that it could be saved if slavery were not prohibited in the territories. Breckinridge finished second with seventy-two electoral votes from eleven southern states. Abraham Lincoln received less than 40 percent of the popular vote, but with three other candidates splitting the vote—Breckinridge, Douglas, and John Bell of the Constitutional Union Party—Lincoln won 180 electoral votes and the presidency.

As a lame-duck vice president, Breckinridge worked with Democratic leaders who searched vainly for a compromise that would prevent civil war. After Lincoln's inauguration Breckinridge returned to Kentucky, whose leaders were debating the future of their state. Breckinridge was in favor of secession, but he accepted the state's declaration of neutrality. When Congress reconvened on July 4, 1861, he took his seat in the Senate. Throughout the summer he defended the right of southern states to secede and opposed Lincoln's efforts to raise an army to put down the insurrection.

In September Union and Confederate armies invaded Kentucky. When the Union army won control of the state, Breckinridge offered his services to the South and was indicted for treason by the federal government. He joined the Confederate army and was commissioned as a brigadier general. After serving at the battle of Shiloh in April 1862, he was promoted to major general. He led troops at the battles of Vicksburg, Murfreesboro, Chickamauga, Chattanooga, and Cold Harbor. In February 1865 Confederate president Jefferson Davis appointed Breckinridge secretary of war.

When the South surrendered in April 1865, Breckinridge feared that he would be captured and prosecuted as a traitor. He and his small party eluded federal troops for two months as they made their way through the South and across the water to Cuba. For three and a half years Breckinridge lived in Europe and Canada while he waited for the treason charge against him to be dropped. On Christmas Day 1868 President Andrew Johnson declared an amnesty for all who had participated in the insurrection. The following March Breckinridge returned to Kentucky, where crowds greeted him as a hero. He settled in Lexington and resumed his law prac-

tice. He died at the age of fifty-four after undergoing his second unsuccessful liver operation.

Breckinridge married Mary Burch of Lexington, Kentucky, on December 12, 1843. They had five children. Although Mary suffered through several periods of poor health during her lifetime, she lived for thirty-two years after her husband's death.

Hannibal Hamlin

Born: August 27, 1809; Paris Hill, Maine
Party: Republican
Term: March 4, 1861–March 4, 1865
President: Abraham Lincoln
Died: July 4, 1891; Bangor, Maine
Buried: Bangor

Hannibal Hamlin's ancestors were among the first settlers in Maine. His father, Cyrus, was a Harvard-educated doctor who also dabbled in farming and small-town politics. Hannibal's parents intended to send him to college and even gave him a prep school education, but family financial troubles forced him to abandon his college plans. He worked as a surveyor, printer, schoolteacher, and farmer before deciding to study law.

In Portland, Maine, Hamlin studied law in the office of Samuel C. Fessenden, the leading antislavery activist in the state. Hamlin was admitted to the bar in 1833 and established a lucrative law practice in Hampden, Maine. In 1836 he was elected as a Democrat to the Maine House of Representatives. During his five years in that body he served three one-year terms as Speaker.

In 1843 Hamlin was elected to the U.S. House of Representatives, where he served two terms. Then in 1847, after a brief stint back in the Maine legislature, that body elected him to the U.S. Senate. While in the Senate, Hamlin became an outspoken opponent of slavery. He supported Democrat Franklin

Hannibal Hamlin

Pierce in the 1852 presidential election, but in 1856 his abolitionist sentiments caused him to defect to the new Republican Party. He was elected governor of Maine in 1857 but resigned after serving only a few weeks when he once again was elected to the Senate.

The 1860 Republican National Convention nominated Abraham Lincoln of Illinois for president. Republican leaders correctly saw that Lincoln had little chance to win electoral votes in the South, even if a southerner were nominated for the vice presidency. Consequently, giving the ticket geographic balance meant choosing a northeasterner for vice president. Republican leaders were also looking for a candidate who would satisfy William H. Seward, the powerful New York senator who had hoped to be the presidential nominee. The convention settled on Hamlin, who met both requirements and had the proper antislavery credentials. Lincoln and Hamlin faced a divided Democratic Party and won the election with less than 40 percent of the popular vote.

Hamlin, who criticized the president's circumspect approach to emancipation, had little influence within the Lincoln administration. Hamlin disliked the vice presidency, not only because of his lack of power, but also because the office did not allow him to dispense any patronage, which for Hamlin had been the foremost reward of political success. Although well qualified to preside over the Senate, Hamlin spent little time in this capacity. Routinely, he presided over a new session of the Senate only until it chose a president pro tempore, after which he returned to Maine.

Despite Hamlin's misgivings about the vice presidency, he wanted a second term. Lincoln, however, believed that Hamlin's view toward the South had become too radical and did not support his candidacy. The 1864 National Union Convention, a coalition of Republicans and pro-Union Democrats, nominated Tennessee Democrat Andrew Johnson to run with Lincoln. Republican leaders hoped Johnson would be better able than Hamlin to attract votes in border states and among northern Democrats.

After retiring from the vice presidency Hamlin served for a year as collector of the port of Boston and two years as president of a railroad company. In 1868 Maine again elected him to the Senate. He served two terms during which he was associated with the Radical Republicans who advocated harsh Reconstruction policies. Hamlin retired from politics in 1881 but secured an appointment as minister to Spain. During his year and a half in Europe he and his wife traveled widely on the Continent, occasionally showing up in Madrid to perform the minimum duties of his post.

In late 1882 Hamlin returned to Maine, where he enjoyed a quiet retirement. He died of heart failure on July 4, 1891, at the age of eighty-one.

Hamlin married Sarah Emery on December 10, 1833, in Paris Hill, Maine. The couple had four children before she died in 1855. On September 25, 1856, Hamlin married Ellen Vesta Emery, a younger half-sister of his first wife. They had two sons; the younger was born while Hamlin was vice president.

Andrew Johnson

Born: December 29, 1808; Raleigh, North Carolina
Party: Democratic
Term: March 4, 1865–April 15, 1865
President: Abraham Lincoln
Died: July 31, 1875; Carter's Station, Tennessee
Buried: Greeneville, Tennessee

(See full biography, p. 70.)

An antislavery southerner and a Democrat, Andrew Johnson was rewarded for his political courage with the vice-presidential nomination by Republican Abraham Lincoln in the 1864 election. Together they made up the Union Party ticket in hope of bringing the nation together. After Lincoln's assassination on April 15, 1965, Johnson assumed the office after serving as vice president for only six weeks. His opposition as president to the harsh Reconstruction policies put forth by vengeful Republicans in Congress contributed to his impeachment by the House of Representatives in 1867. He was acquitted in his Senate trial by one vote.

Schuyler Colfax

Born: March 23, 1823; New York City
Party: Republican
Term: March 4, 1869–March 4, 1873
President: Ulysses S. Grant
Died: January 13, 1885; Mankato, Minnesota
Buried: South Bend, Indiana

Schuyler Colfax was the son of Schuyler and Hannah Colfax. His father died in 1822, and his mother

Schuyler Colfax

married George Matthews in 1832. Schuyler attended public schools in New York City until he was ten. In 1836 he moved with his family to New Carlisle, Indiana, where he studied law but never passed the bar. His interest in politics stemmed from his writing for newspapers, which he began at age sixteen. In 1841 Schuyler's stepfather, who was county auditor, appointed his stepson deputy auditor, a post Schuyler then occupied for eight years.

Colfax became active in state politics in 1842 when he began a two-year term as enrolling clerk of the Indiana Senate. In 1845 Colfax became part owner of the *South Bend Free Press*. He changed its name to the *St. Joseph Valley Register* and used it to support Whig candidates and issues. Colfax attended several state and national Whig conventions and ran unsuccessfully for the U.S. House of Representatives in 1851.

When the Republican Party was formed, Colfax became a member and helped build a Republican organization in Indiana. In 1855 he was elected to the U.S. House of Representatives, where he served for the next fourteen years until he became vice president in 1869. During his last five and a half years in the House, he held the office of Speaker.

At the 1868 Republican National Convention Colfax actively sought the vice presidency. He hoped the Republican presidential nominee, Ulysses S. Grant, would serve only one four-year term, thereby setting the stage for his own nomination for president in 1872. Colfax emerged from a crowd of favorite-son candidates to receive the vice-presidential nomination on the fifth ballot despite being from Indiana, a state contiguous to Grant's home state of Illinois. Grant, however, was the most celebrated hero of the Civil War, and a geographically balanced ticket was not necessary for victory. He and Colfax easily defeated Democrats Horatio Seymour and Francis P. Blair Jr. 214–80 in the electoral college. Like most nineteenth-century vice presidents, Colfax did not play a significant role in his running mate's administration.

During Colfax's rise in government he had gained a reputation for political intrigue. He was known as the "Smiler" and "Great Joiner" for his propensity to join any club or organization that would accept him. Abraham Lincoln had called Colfax a "friendly rascal." Events would show, however, that Colfax was not just an opportunistic and manipulative politician; he was also corrupt.

A September 1872 newspaper exposé implicated Colfax in the Crédit Mobilier scandal. In 1867 Congress had appropriated funds for the construction of the Union Pacific Railroad. The director of the railroad, Oakes Ames (R-Mass.), who was also a House member, set up a holding company, Crédit Mobilier of America, in which he deposited millions of dollars of money appropriated for the railroad. He proceeded to bribe other members of Congress not to expose his corruption and to support legislation favorable to the railroad by selling them shares of stock in the holding company at bargain prices.

While Speaker of the House, Colfax had received twenty shares of Crédit Mobilier stock and substantial dividends from those shares. His defense of his actions was unconvincing, and he fell back on the argument that his mistakes while in Congress should not affect his tenure as vice president. Some members of Congress considered impeaching him, but, because his term was about to expire, they dropped the matter. Colfax then claimed he had been exonerated, but his political reputation was ruined.

When Colfax left office, he made a good living by touring the country delivering lectures. During a lecture tour of Minnesota in 1885 he died of a stroke after changing trains in subzero weather.

Colfax married Evelyn Clark on October 10, 1844. His wife, who had no children, died in 1863 while he was Speaker of the House. On November 18, 1868, he married Ellen Wade, a niece of Sen. Benjamin F. Wade (R-Ohio), who had been Colfax's primary rival for the 1868 vice-presidential nomination. The couple had one child, Schuyler Colfax III. Colfax's grandfather, William Colfax, had been the commander of George Washington's bodyguard during the Revolutionary War.

Henry Wilson

Born: February 16, 1812; Farmington, New Hampshire

Party: Republican

Term: March 4, 1873–November 22, 1875

President: Ulysses S. Grant

Died: November 22, 1875; Washington, D.C.

Buried: Natick, Massachusetts

Henry Wilson was born Jeremiah Jones Colbath, the son of Abigail and Winthrop Colbath, a poor New Hampshire sawmill worker. When Jeremiah was ten, he was indentured to a farmer, for whom he labored for over ten years for room and board. During his

Henry Wilson

free hours he educated himself by reading hundreds of borrowed books. On his twenty-first birthday Jeremiah was given his freedom as well as six sheep and a pair of oxen. He broke with the hard life he had led by selling the livestock for eighty-five dollars and legally changing his name to Henry Wilson.

Wilson then walked over one hundred miles to Natick, Massachusetts, where he apprenticed himself to a shoemaker. He learned the trade within a month, bought his freedom from his master, and went into business for himself. By the time he was twenty-seven Wilson owned a shoe factory that employed as many as one hundred people. Although Wilson was accumulating a modest fortune, his political ambitions were stronger than his desire for wealth. He continued to read voraciously and developed his speaking skills at the Natick Debating Society. In 1840 Wilson was elected as a Whig to the Massachusetts legislature, where he served for most of the next twelve years.

Wilson left the Whig Party in 1848 because of its indecisiveness on the slavery issue. He helped form the Free Soil Party and edited the *Boston Republican*, a party organ, from 1848 to 1851. He joined the ultraconservative American (Know-Nothing) Party in 1854 but walked out of its 1855 convention when it too failed to take a strong stand against slavery.

Earlier in 1855 Wilson had been elected to the U.S. Senate by the Massachusetts legislature to fill an unexpired term. He served in the Senate until 1873, when he became vice president. Wilson joined the Republican Party after his rejection of the Know-Nothings. He made many enemies among southern members of Congress for his harsh attacks in the Senate against slavery. His fear of assassination led him to carry a pistol and make plans for his family to be provided for in the event of his death. In addition to his activism against slavery, Wilson also established himself as an advocate of the rights of factory workers.

During the Civil War Wilson served as chairman of the Senate Committee on Military Affairs. In this capacity he earned praise from military and political leaders for his effective legislative leadership in raising and supporting the huge Union army. After the war he supported the harsh Reconstruction program of the radical Republicans and voted for Andrew Johnson's impeachment in 1868. Wilson's Reconstruction views softened late in his Senate career after he toured the South and West extensively.

Wilson was nominated to be President Ulysses S. Grant's vice-presidential running mate at the 1872 Republican National Convention in Philadelphia. Like his vice-presidential predecessor, Schuyler Colfax, Wilson had been involved in the Crédit Mobilier scandal. A few weeks before the 1872 presidential election the *New York Sun* broke the story that several members of Congress, including Wilson, were involved in the bribery scheme. Wilson, however, claimed that he had returned the twenty Crédit Mobilier shares he had purchased before he reaped any profit from them. Although Wilson was not exonerated by the congressional committees investigating the scandal until several months after the election, his troubles did not affect the election's outcome. The highly popular president Grant easily defeated Democrat Horace Greeley 286–66 in the electoral college.

Shortly after the election Wilson suffered a stroke. When he recovered, he claimed to be in good health, but he was a poor presiding officer of the Senate. In 1875 he died from a second stroke with a year and a half left in his term.

Wilson married sixteen-year-old Harriet Malvina Howe on October 28, 1840. She died of cancer on May 28, 1870. They had one son, Henry Hamilton Wilson, who distinguished himself as a Union officer during the Civil War. He died in 1866 while still in the army.

William A. Wheeler

William A. Wheeler

Born: June 30, 1819; Malone, New York
Party: Republican
Term: March 4, 1877–March 4, 1881
President: Rutherford B. Hayes
Died: June 4, 1887; Malone
Buried: Malone

William Almon Wheeler was the second of the two children of Eliza and Almon Wheeler. Although William's father was a lawyer, he left virtually no estate when he died in 1827. William worked his way through a preparatory academy, and in 1838 he enrolled in the University of Vermont, where he led a spartan existence. He had so little money that at one point he lived on bread and water for several weeks. After two years these financial problems forced Wheeler to drop out of college before graduating.

He returned to his home in Malone, New York, where he studied law with a local lawyer. He was admitted to the New York bar in 1845 and served as district attorney of Franklin County from 1846 to 1849. In 1850 he was elected to the New York State legislature as a Whig. Upon leaving the assembly in 1851 he took over the management of a Malone bank, and two years later he became a trustee for the mortgage holders of the Northern Railway. Like many northern Whigs, Wheeler switched his loyalty to the Republican Party in the mid-1850s. From 1858 to 1860 he served in the New York State Senate, where as president pro tempore he gained experience presiding over a legislature.

In 1861 Wheeler was elected to the U.S. House of Representatives, his first national office. He served only one term but remained active in New York politics. In 1867 he was chosen to preside over the New York constitutional convention because he was on good terms with the New York Republican machine while retaining his independence. He was reelected to the U.S. House in 1869 and served there until he became vice president in 1877.

Wheeler was best known not for his legislative skill or political acumen but for his scrupulous honesty. He demonstrated this quality during the "Salary Grab" of 1873, in which Congress voted itself a 50 percent pay raise and back pay of $5,000. Wheeler voted against the measure, and, when it was passed, he returned the back pay. His most notable accomplishment during his time in the House was his service on a congressional committee that investigated an election dispute in Louisiana in 1874. He developed a compromise known as the "Wheeler adjustment" that resolved the dispute and ended the threat of civil unrest.

When Wheeler's name was put into contention for the vice presidency at the 1876 Republican National Convention, he was virtually unknown. Earlier in the year when someone had suggested a Hayes-Wheeler ticket, Hayes commented in a letter to his wife, "Who is Wheeler?" Despite his lack of prominence, Wheeler received the vice-presidential nomination because he was from New York, he had a spotless reputation, and the convention delegates were anxious to go home.

The election of 1876 involved the uncontroversial Wheeler in one of the most intense political controversies in American history. Although the Hayes-Wheeler ticket received a minority of the popular vote and their Democratic opponents appeared to win the electoral college, Republican leaders challenged the election results in several southern states. After months of political maneuvers and backroom deals, a congressionally appointed electoral commission ruled in favor of Hayes and Wheeler.

Wheeler was a conscientious presiding officer of the Senate, but he had little enthusiasm for his office. He frequently referred to Benjamin Franklin's comment that the vice presidency was so insignificant that its occupant should be called "Your Superfluous Excellency."

Wheeler welcomed the end of his term as vice president. He quietly retired to Malone, where he lived the last six years of his life. He had married Mary King on September 17, 1845. She died in

March 1876, three months before he was nominated for the vice presidency. The couple had no children, and, when Wheeler's sister died shortly after his wife, he was left without any immediate family. Although Hayes had never met Wheeler before 1876, they became close friends during their time in office. The widowed vice president spent many evenings at the White House with Hayes and his wife, Lucy.

Chester A. Arthur

Born: October 5, 1830; Fairfield, Vermont
Party: Republican
Term: March 4, 1881–September 19, 1881
President: James A. Garfield
Died: November 18, 1886; New York City
Buried: Albany, New York

(See full biography, p. 80.)

Chester Alan Arthur, a Republican Party loyalist, had never held elective office before being nominated, on the thirty-seventh ballot, by a badly divided Republican convention. Arthur assumed office when President James Garfield died of an assassin's bullet some seven months after being sworn in. Despite his opposition to civil service reform and preference for the patronage system, Arthur signed the Pendleton Civil Service Reform Act of 1883.

Thomas A. Hendricks

Born: September 7, 1819; near Zanesville, Ohio
Party: Democratic
Term: March 4, 1885–November 25, 1885
President: Grover Cleveland
Died: November 25, 1885; Indianapolis, Indiana
Buried: Indianapolis

Thomas A. Hendricks

Thomas Andrews Hendricks was born in Ohio, the son of John and Jane Hendricks. In 1820, when Thomas was a baby, the family moved to Indiana, where Thomas grew up working on the family farm in Shelby County. He attended local schools before enrolling in Hanover College near Madison, Indiana. After his graduation in 1841, Thomas began to study law in Shelbyville, Indiana. In 1843 he traveled to Chambersburg, Pennsylvania, to study law under an uncle who was a judge. He returned to Shelbyville the following year, passed the bar, and established a successful law practice.

Hendricks entered politics in 1848 when he was elected to the Indiana legislature. In 1850 he served as a delegate to the convention called to revise the Indiana constitution. At the convention he supported a proposal to prohibit African Americans from entering the state. He was elected to the U.S. House of Representatives in 1851 and again in 1852 when the state constitution mandated that House elections be held in even-numbered years. While in the House, Hendricks aligned himself with the policies

of Democratic senator Stephen A. Douglas of Illinois. Hendricks was a strong supporter of Douglas's Kansas-Nebraska Act, which permitted Kansas to decide for itself whether it would be a slave state or free state and precipitated a bloody war in that territory. Hendricks lost reelection to the House in 1854, but President Franklin Pierce appointed him commissioner of the general land office, a post he occupied until 1859.

In 1860 Hendricks ran for governor of Indiana but was defeated by Republican Henry S. Lane. When the Democratic Party gained control of the Indiana legislature in 1863, Hendricks was elected to the U.S. Senate. During his single term he was a leading critic of Lincoln's leadership during the war. Hendricks supported appropriations to pay for troops, weapons, and supplies, but he opposed the Emancipation Proclamation, the draft, and many other wartime measures. After the war he backed President Andrew Johnson's magnanimous Reconstruction plan and worked against the Thirteenth Amendment, which abolished slavery, and the Fourteenth Amendment, which gave African Americans the rights of U.S. citizens. Hendricks claimed that the black slave was "inferior and no good would come from his freedom."

In 1868 Hendricks again was nominated as his party's candidate for governor of Indiana, but he lost the election. The following year, when his Senate term expired, he retired to Indianapolis, where he resumed his law practice. In 1872, however, he ran for governor for the third time and was finally elected by a narrow 1,148-vote margin.

In 1872 the national prominence attained by Hendricks was demonstrated when he received forty-two of the sixty-two electoral votes for president won by fellow Democrat Horace Greeley, who had died between the election and the electoral college vote. Four years later the Democrats nominated Hendricks as Samuel J. Tilden's vice-presidential running mate. The presence of Hendricks on the ticket helped Tilden carry Indiana and seemingly the election. The Republicans, however, disputed the election results in several southern states, and an election commission that favored the Republicans ruled in favor of the Republican presidential candidate, Rutherford B. Hayes.

Hendricks was nominated again for vice president in 1884 to balance the ticket with New Yorker Grover Cleveland. Like eight years before, his popularity helped the Democrats carry Indiana, but this time they won the election. Cleveland and Hendricks defeated Republicans James G. Blaine and John A. Logan 219–182 in the electoral college and by just sixty thousand votes in the popular balloting.

As vice president, Hendricks presided over only a one-month session of the Senate called to consider President Cleveland's cabinet nominations. Hendricks died in his home in Indianapolis two weeks before the Senate was scheduled to resume its business in December. The vice president had served less than nine months of his term.

Hendricks married Eliza C. Morgan of North Bend, Ohio, on September 26, 1845. They had one child, Morgan, who died when he was three years old. Eliza died at the age of eighty in 1903.

Levi P. Morton

Born: May 16, 1824; Shoreham, Vermont
Party: Republican
Term: March 4, 1889–March 4, 1893
President: Benjamin Harrison
Died: May 16, 1920; Rhinebeck, New York
Buried: Rhinebeck

Levi Parsons Morton was the son of Lucretia and Daniel Morton, an Episcopalian minister. His ancestors arrived in New England before 1650. He received a modest education as a boy and never attended college.

Levi P. Morton

Morton began his climb in the business world as a clerk in a Hanover, New Hampshire, store. He later worked in Boston for an import company and by 1855 owned a wholesale business in New York City. He suffered a financial setback in 1861 because the Civil War debts owed to him by southerners went unpaid. He was able to pay his creditors, however, and in 1863 established a Wall Street banking firm. Over the next thirteen years he accumulated a large personal fortune and developed his firm, Morton, Bliss & Company, into one of the most powerful financial institutions in the United States.

In 1876 Morton decided to try his hand at politics. He ran unsuccessfully for a seat in the U.S. House of Representatives from Manhattan's wealthy Eleventh District but won the seat two years later. Morton was reelected to Congress in 1880, but he resigned his House seat when President James A. Garfield appointed him minister to France.

The 1880 Republican National Convention nominated dark horse James A. Garfield of Ohio as president instead of former president Ulysses S.

Grant, who was allied with Morton's political mentor, Republican senator Roscoe Conkling of New York. As a gesture to the Conkling faction, Garfield offered the vice-presidential nomination to Morton, who refused on the instructions of Conkling. Instead, the nomination went to another Conkling ally, Chester A. Arthur, who accepted the nomination against Conkling's wishes.

Had Grant been nominated and elected, Morton would have likely been nominated Treasury secretary, a post that the New York banker coveted. After Garfield won the election, however, he sought to limit the influence of the Conkling faction and chose William Windom of Minnesota to be Treasury secretary. Morton's fund-raising efforts on behalf of Garfield were rewarded by an appointment as minister to France, where for four years Morton lived in splendor and threw lavish parties for European royalty. Morton, who had relinquished his House seat to go to France, returned to the United States in 1885 hopeful of winning a Senate seat, but his election campaigns for the Senate in 1885 and 1887 were unsuccessful.

In 1888 Morton was offered the vice-presidential slot on the Republican ticket with Indianan Benjamin Harrison. Having seen Chester Arthur succeed to the presidency when Garfield was killed by an assassin in 1881, Morton did not refuse the nomination a second time. During the 1888 campaign Morton concentrated on doing what he knew best—raising money. Although Harrison and Morton lost the popular election by ten thousand votes to President Grover Cleveland and Allen G. Thurman, they won in the electoral college 233–168.

Morton fulfilled his duties as presiding officer of the Senate conscientiously. During one Democratic filibuster in late 1890 and early 1891, Morton opposed the position of his party and refused to cooperate with Republican attempts to end the filibuster. The Democrats stopped the legislation, however, and Morton's standing in the Republican Party

was damaged. He was willing to accept a second vice-presidential term, but Republican Party leaders dropped him for fellow New Yorker Whitelaw Reid.

In 1895 Morton ran successfully for governor of New York with the support of Sen. Thomas C. Platt (R–N.Y.), the most powerful figure in New York politics. Morton, however, displayed the same independence that he had shown as vice president and refused to be part of Platt's machine. In particular, he angered his machine supporters by advocating civil service reform. Morton hoped to be his party's presidential nominee in 1896 (his name was entered as a favorite-son candidate), but William McKinley was the clear choice of the party bosses and the convention. When Morton's term as governor ended in January 1897, he retired from politics to manage his business interests. He formed the Morton Trust Company in 1899 and merged it with the Guaranty Trust Company in 1909.

Morton spent much of his retirement traveling or at Ellerslie, his thousand-acre estate in Rhinebeck, New York. He died there in 1920 on his ninety-sixth birthday.

On October 15, 1856, Morton married Lucy Young Kimball, who died in 1871 before her husband entered politics. They had one daughter, who died in infancy. Morton then married Anna Livingson Street on February 12, 1873, and the couple had five daughters. Anna died at Ellerslie in 1918, two years before her husband.

Adlai E. Stevenson

Born: October 25, 1835; Christian County, Kentucky
Party: Democratic
Term: March 4, 1893–March 4, 1897
President: Grover Cleveland
Died: June 14, 1914; Chicago, Illinois
Buried: Bloomington, Illinois

Adlai E. Stevenson

Adlai Ewing Stevenson was the second of the seven children of Eliza and John Stevenson, a slave-owning Kentucky planter. As a boy, Adlai worked on the farm and obtained an elementary education at local schools.

When Adlai was sixteen his family moved to Bloomington, Illinois, where he taught school and attended briefly Illinois Wesleyan University. He then enrolled in Centre College in Danville, Kentucky. In 1857, after two years of study, he left Centre without a degree when the death of his father forced him to resume teaching to supplement his family's income. While teaching, Adlai studied law and was admitted to the bar in 1858.

That same year Stevenson opened a law office in Metamora, Illinois. He also became a Democrat and a follower of Illinois senator Stephen A. Douglas. In 1864 Stevenson won his first elective office, state's attorney for the Metamora judicial district. After four years in the post Stevenson moved back to Bloomington and resumed his successful career as a lawyer.

In 1874 Stevenson was elected to the U.S. House of Representatives. He was defeated for reelection in 1876 but won his seat back in 1878. After his term expired in 1881 he returned to private life.

In 1885 President Grover Cleveland appointed Stevenson first assistant postmaster. In this office Stevenson was in charge of firing postmasters appointed by the previous Republican administrations. Cleveland believed that, despite the traditional practice, government employees should not be fired simply because they belonged to the party out of power. But Cleveland's fellow Democrats were not as magnanimous. They demanded that Cleveland replace Republicans with loyal Democrats. Stevenson agreed and wrote a letter to the *New York World,* a Democratic paper, supporting patronage. Under pressure from his party, Cleveland relented and gave Stevenson permission to proceed with the mass removal of Republican postmasters.

Although Stevenson was known for his tact and amiability, he made many enemies in the process of firing tens of thousands of people and earned the nickname the "Headsman." Cleveland appointed Stevenson to the Supreme Court in 1889, but the Republican majority in the Senate refused to confirm the nomination of a man who had just fired tens of thousands of their fellow party members.

Stevenson went to the 1892 Democratic National Convention as the chairman of the Illinois delegation. There he received the party's nomination for vice president. By choosing Stevenson, the Democrats improved their chances of winning Illinois, a large, traditionally Republican state. Stevenson's support of bimetallism, the coinage of money based on both gold and silver, also appealed to many citizens in the South and West who believed that having more money in circulation would increase their buying power and the country's economic health.

With Stevenson on the ticket, Illinois voted for a Democratic presidential candidate for the first time since 1856. Cleveland and Stevenson defeated Republican incumbent Benjamin Harrison and vice-presidential candidate Whitelaw Reid 277–145 in the electoral college.

As vice president, Stevenson made many friends in the Senate, where he was regarded as a good presiding officer. And, although he was on friendly terms with President Cleveland, Stevenson was not a regular participant in policymaking. In July 1893, when Cleveland secretly underwent surgery for mouth cancer, Stevenson was not even informed.

In 1900 Stevenson again received the Democratic nomination for vice president on a ticket with William Jennings Bryan, but they were defeated by incumbent William McKinley and vice-presidential nominee Theodore Roosevelt. In 1908 the Illinois Democratic Party honored the aging Stevenson with its nomination for governor. He lost, however, to Republican Charles Deneen in a close election. After this defeat Stevenson retired from politics. His book, *Something of Men I Have Known,* a collection of speeches and political anecdotes, was published in 1909. In 1914 Stevenson died of heart failure following prostate surgery.

On December 20, 1866, Stevenson married Letitia Green, whom he had met while attending Centre College, where her father served as president. They did not marry, however, until they met again nearly a decade later after she had moved to Illinois. Letitia died on Christmas Day in 1913, a few months before her husband. The Stevensons had three girls and a boy. Their son, Lewis, managed his father's vice-presidential campaign in 1892 and served as his father's private secretary while he was in office. Lewis was the father of Adlai Stevenson II, who was the Democratic nominee for president in 1952 and 1956.

Garret A. Hobart

Born: June 3, 1844; Long Branch, New Jersey
Party: Republican
Term: March 4, 1897–November 21, 1899
President: William McKinley
Died: November 21, 1899; Paterson, New Jersey
Buried: Paterson

Garret Augustus Hobart was the eldest son of Addison and Sophia Hobart, who owned a store and a small farm. When Garret was sixteen, he enrolled in Rutgers College in New Jersey. There he majored in math and English and graduated with honors in 1863. Garret then taught school briefly before moving to Paterson, New Jersey, to work in the law office of Socrates Tuttle, a close friend of his father. Garret was admitted to the bar in 1869.

After serving on the Paterson city council in 1871, Hobart entered state politics and in 1872 was elected to the state assembly. He became speaker in 1874 at the age of thirty. Two years later he won election to the state senate, where he served two three-year terms. Hobart left the state senate in 1882 but continued to be a leading figure in New Jersey politics. From 1880 to 1891 he was chairman of the state Republican committee. Although Hobart was not a well-known figure outside of New Jersey, he had become a member of the Republican National Committee in 1884 and was acquainted with the leading Republicans around the country, including Ohio boss Mark Hanna.

Although Hobart was enthusiastic about his political career, he considered it a hobby. Most of his energies went into his legal and business career. He served as president of the Passaic, New Jersey, water company and was director of several banks. By the time he entered national politics, he had amassed a fortune.

In 1896 the Republican Party was confident of recapturing the White House. Grover Cleveland and

Garret A. Hobart

The last vice president of the nineteenth century proved to be one of the most able and influential. Despite never having held national office, Hobart understood national political issues and became one of McKinley's closest friends and advisers. The press often referred to Hobart as the "Assistant President." He also was credited with presiding over the Senate with energy and fairness.

Hobart became ill in the spring of 1899. He left the capital to recuperate in New Jersey, but he died at his home in Paterson in November. Hobart received stirring eulogies in the nation's newspapers, and his funeral was attended by President McKinley and many other top government officials. Paterson erected a bronze statue of Hobart in front of its city hall next to a statue of Alexander Hamilton.

Hobart married Jennie Tuttle on July 21, 1869. While vice president, they entertained lavishly at their rented mansion on Lafayette Square near the White House. The couple had two children, Garret Jr. and his older sister Fannie, who died in 1895 from diphtheria while in Europe with her family.

Mrs. Hobart died on January 8, 1941, at the age of ninety-one. She wrote two books about her experiences, *Memories,* published in 1930, and *Second Lady,* published in 1933.

the Democrats had received much of the blame for the economic and labor troubles of the previous four years. The Democrats nominated William Jennings Bryan as president and Arthur Sewall as vice president. The Republicans countered with William McKinley of Ohio and a conservative platform that advocated the gold standard. Republican Party leaders wanted a gold supporter from the East as the vice-presidential candidate to balance the ticket and reinforce their commitment to hard money. They found their candidate in Hobart, who was an outspoken advocate of the gold standard. In his acceptance speech at the Republican National Convention in St. Louis, Hobart uttered one of the most famous quotes of his era: "An honest dollar, worth 100 cents everywhere, cannot be coined out of fifty-three cents of silver, plus a legislative fiat."

Despite Bryan's stirring campaign speeches, the Republicans won the 1896 election 271–176 in the electoral college. Hobart's presence on the ticket helped the Republicans win New Jersey for the first time since Ulysses S. Grant's success there in 1872.

Theodore Roosevelt

Born: October 27, 1858; New York City
Party: Republican
Term: March 4, 1901–September 14, 1901
President: William McKinley
Died: January 6, 1919; Oyster Bay, New York
Buried: Oyster Bay

(See full biography, p. 89.)

Theodore Roosevelt had served as assistant secretary of the navy in William McKinley's first term as president and made a name for himself by overstepping the bounds of his authority and ordering Commodore George Dewey to attack the Spanish fleet in Manila Bay. Dewey's victory and Roosevelt's resignation from the navy to lead the so-called "Rough Riders" in Cuba cemented Roosevelt's national reputation for daring and courage. Elected governor of New York in 1898, he was the popular choice for the Republican vice-presidential nomination in 1900. When McKinley died of an assassin's bullet on September 14, 1901, Roosevelt became, at forty-two, the youngest person ever to serve as president and one of the most active, overseeing a vigorous antitrust program and acquiring land for the Panama Canal. In winning the 1904 election, he became the first successor president to win the White House on his own.

Charles W. Fairbanks

Charles W. Fairbanks

Born: May 11, 1852; near Unionville Center, Ohio
Party: Republican
Term: March 4, 1905–March 4, 1909
President: Theodore Roosevelt
Died: June 4, 1918; Indianapolis, Indiana
Buried: Indianapolis

Charles Warren Fairbanks was born in a one-room log cabin on a farm in Ohio. His parents, Loriston and Mary Fairbanks, were Methodist abolitionists who helped runaway slaves before the Civil War. As a child, Charles worked on the family farm and attended a district school. Despite his humble background, he enrolled in Ohio Wesleyan University in Delaware, Ohio, at the age of fifteen. He worked his way through college and graduated in 1872.

He was admitted to the bar in 1874 and moved to Indianapolis. He quickly built a reputation as an attorney specializing in railroad litigation. While accumulating a fortune from his law practice, Fair-

banks became involved in politics. He supported various Republican candidates, including fellow Indianan Benjamin Harrison. By 1896 he was one of the state's leading Republicans, although he had never held public office. That year his keynote address at the Republican National Convention brought him national acclaim. In 1897 he was elected to the U.S. Senate.

In the Senate Fairbanks was one of President William McKinley's most consistent supporters. Republican leaders considered Fairbanks for the vice-presidential nomination in 1900, but he decided to remain in the Senate. For Fairbanks, who had presidential ambitions, the decision was a bad one; Theodore Roosevelt was nominated instead.

Fairbanks had planned to run for the presidency after McKinley served out his second term, but McKinley's assassination in 1901 eliminated any chance of his nomination for the presidency in 1904. Theodore Roosevelt assumed the presidency and became so popular that he was the inevitable choice of his party for a second term.

In 1904 Fairbanks settled for the vice-presidential nomination. Roosevelt would have preferred someone else, but he accepted Fairbanks, who was the choice of the party's conservative wing. While Roosevelt remained aloof in Washington, Fairbanks campaigned vigorously across the country. Roosevelt and Fairbanks easily defeated Democrats Alton B. Parker and Henry G. Davis.

While serving as McKinley's vice president, Theodore Roosevelt had advocated a greater role for the occupant of the nation's second highest office. As president, however, Roosevelt made no effort to involve Fairbanks in his administration. He had a low opinion of Fairbanks and was disdainful of Fairbanks's persistent maneuverings to set himself up as the Republican nominee in 1908. Roosevelt's endorsement of Secretary of War William Howard Taft ensured that Fairbanks would not get the nomination.

After finishing his vice-presidential term, Fairbanks never again held public office, but he remained a powerful figure in national and state politics. His fellow Indiana Republicans supported his bid for the presidential nomination in 1916, but his favorite-son candidacy was unsuccessful. He asked that his name not be placed in nomination for the vice presidency that year, but, when it was, he accepted. The election was extremely close and remained in doubt until the day after the voting. Fairbanks, responding to erroneous news reports that the Republican ticket had won, even sent a congratulatory telegram to his presidential running mate, Charles Evans Hughes. Woodrow Wilson and Thomas Marshall, however, won in the electoral college 277–254.

After the defeat Fairbanks retired from politics. When World War I began, he was appointed to the Indiana State Council of Defense. He died in 1918 at the age of sixty-six after a speaking tour supporting the war effort.

In 1874 Fairbanks married Cornelia Cole, whom he had met at Ohio Wesleyan University, where they coedited the college newspaper. The couple had five children. Cornelia died on October 24, 1913. The second largest city in Alaska is named after Fairbanks, who sat on a senatorial commission on Alaskan affairs.

James S. Sherman

Born: October 24, 1855; Utica, New York
Party: Republican
Term: March 4, 1909–October 30, 1912
President: William Howard Taft
Died: October 30, 1912; Utica
Buried: Utica

James Schoolcraft Sherman was the son of Richard and Mary Sherman. James's father was a newspaper editor and a Democratic politician who held minor offices at the state and national levels. After attending both public and private schools, James enrolled at Hamilton College in Clinton, New York, where he earned a bachelor's degree in 1878 and a law degree in 1879. He then moved back to Utica, where he joined his brother-in-law's law firm.

Despite his family's Democratic affiliation, Sherman chose to enter politics as a Republican. In 1884 he was elected mayor of Utica, an office once held by his brother, who was a Democrat. Two years later Sherman won a seat in the U.S. House of Representatives, where he served from 1887 to 1891 and 1893 to 1909. As a member of Congress, Sherman was known best for his amiability and his parliamentary skills. He became close friends with Republican leaders Thomas B. Reed (R–Maine) and Joseph G. Cannon (R–Ill.), both of whom served as Speaker during Sherman's tenure in the House. Reed and Cannon frequently called on Sherman to preside over House debates.

In 1908 Theodore Roosevelt had pushed

James S. Sherman

Republican Party leaders to nominate William Howard Taft as his successor to the presidency, but Roosevelt did not express a strong preference for a vice-presidential candidate. When congressional Republicans led by Cannon backed Sherman's nomination for vice president, Taft and Roosevelt agreed. Sherman, like Taft, was nominated on the first ballot at the Republican National Convention in Chicago.

During the 1908 campaign Sherman was accused of misconduct. Edmund Burke, a California lawyer, claimed that he and Sherman had obtained tens of thousands of acres of Native American land in New Mexico at bargain prices through bribery and Sherman's influence as chairman of the House Committee on Indian Affairs. The Democrats, however, did not press the scandal issue, and the Republicans denounced the unproven charges as an attempt to slander their candidate. Taft and Sherman easily defeated William Jennings Bryan and John W. Kern 321–162 in the electoral college.

As vice president, Sherman got to do what he did

best—preside over a legislative body. He won praise from both parties for his handling of the Senate. Sherman was not a close confidant of Taft, who did not like his vice president's ties to New York Republican machine politicians, but early in their term the two shared a regular golf game together and became more friendly.

Even before becoming vice president, Sherman suffered from Bright's disease, a kidney ailment. He became seriously ill in the spring of 1908 but recovered in time to accept the vice-presidential nomination. During his vice presidency he experienced occasional periods of illness that prevented him from presiding over the Senate. Nevertheless, he was renominated in 1912 along with Taft. In the fall he became very ill, and on October 30, 1912, he died of complications caused by his kidney condition. He was the only vice president who died before election day after having been nominated for a second term.

Because the election was just six days away, the Republican Party did not have time to choose a replacement for Sherman. His death, however, did not affect the outcome of the election. Democrat Woodrow Wilson swept to victory when Theodore Roosevelt's third-party candidacy split the Republican vote.

Sherman married Carrie Babcock on January 26, 1881, while he practiced law in Utica; they had three sons. Sherman's wife died in 1931 in Utica at the age of seventy-four.

Thomas R. Marshall

Born: March 14, 1854; North Manchester, Indiana
Party: Democratic
Term: March 4, 1913–March 4, 1921
President: Woodrow Wilson
Died: June 1, 1925; Washington, D.C.
Buried: Indianapolis, Indiana

Thomas R. Marshall

Thomas Riley Marshall was the son of Martha and Daniel Marshall, a country doctor. Thomas was born in Indiana, but as a boy he lived in Illinois, Kansas, and Missouri before his family resettled in Indiana. He was educated at public schools and attended Wabash College in Crawfordsville, Indiana. He graduated in 1873 and was selected for membership in Phi Beta Kappa, a national honor society.

After college Marshall studied law and was admitted to the bar in 1875. He then embarked on a successful legal career in Columbia City, Indiana. Although Marshall became friends with many prominent Democratic politicians, he never ran for office until he was nominated for governor of the state in 1908 at the age of fifty-four.

Marshall's candidacy seemed a long shot, since Indiana had not had a Democratic governor since 1892. Nevertheless, he won the election by more than ten thousand votes, overcoming the coattails of Republican presidential nominee William Howard Taft, who carried Indiana by fifteen thousand votes.

As governor, Marshall opposed capital punishment (he issued many pardons), Prohibition, and voting rights for women. Because Indiana barred a governor from seeking two consecutive terms, Marshall planned to return to Columbia City when his four-year term expired.

In 1912, however, Indiana Democratic Party leader Thomas Taggart backed Marshall for vice president. Marshall received the number two slot on the Democratic ticket with Woodrow Wilson. Wilson and Marshall faced a Republican Party divided by Theodore Roosevelt's third-party candidacy. The Democrats received less than 42 percent of the popular vote but won 435 electoral votes to Roosevelt's 88 votes and President William Howard Taft's 8 votes.

While serving as vice president, Marshall gained a national reputation for his dry humor. After listening to Sen. Joseph L. Bristow (R-Kan.) deliver a long speech on the needs of the country, he remarked in a voice loud enough for many in the Senate chamber to overhear, "What this country needs is a really good five-cent cigar." This line was reported in newspapers and immediately became his most famous utterance. During his political career he declined to run for Congress on the grounds that he "might be elected."

The vice presidency was among the targets of Marshall's wit. He told a story about two brothers: "One ran away to sea; the other was elected vice president. And nothing was ever heard of either of them again." He also likened his position to "a man in a cataleptic fit; he cannot speak; he cannot move; he suffers no pain; he is perfectly conscious of all that goes on, but has no part in it."

Both President Wilson and Vice President Marshall were renominated for a second term. In the 1916 election, however, they were opposed by a Republican Party united behind Charles Evans Hughes and former vice president Charles W. Fairbanks. Wilson and Marshall narrowly defeated

Hughes and Fairbanks 277–254 in the electoral college.

Marshall's most significant action as vice president may have been something he did not do. When President Wilson returned to the United States after negotiating the Versailles treaty, he encountered strong Senate opposition to U.S. entry into the League of Nations that was to be created by the treaty. In response, Wilson toured the country trying to build support for ratification. The stress of the tour caused Wilson to suffer a nervous breakdown and a stroke.

With Wilson paralyzed, many people advised Marshall to assume the presidency. At that time, however, there was no provision in the Constitution for the removal of an incapacitated president by the vice president. Marshall refused to make any move to replace Wilson because he believed such a move would set a bad precedent and might divide the government and the nation. Marshall merely took over many of Wilson's ceremonial duties to lighten the weakened president's workload.

When Marshall's second term expired in 1921 he retired to Indianapolis. He was the first vice president since Daniel D. Tompkins to serve two full terms. Marshall occupied his time by writing syndicated articles, delivering lectures, and traveling. Just before his death at the age of seventy-one, he finished writing *Recollections,* a book containing many of his humorous stories and witticisms.

Marshall married twenty-three-year-old Lois Kimsey on October 2, 1895. The couple had no children but took care of a foster child for a period while they lived in Washington. It is said that the couple spent only two nights of their twenty-nine-year marriage apart.

Calvin Coolidge

Born: July 4, 1872; Plymouth Notch, Vermont
Party: Republican
Term: March 4, 1921–August 2, 1923
President: Warren G. Harding
Died: January 5, 1933; Northampton, Massachusetts
Buried: Plymouth, Vermont

(See full biography, p. 101.)

Calvin Coolidge was serving as a popular governor of Massachusetts when the 1920 Republican convention unexpectedly nominated him as the party's vice-presidential candidate under Warren G. Harding of Ohio. The slate handily won the general election. In 1923 Coolidge was elevated to the presidency following Harding's sudden death and dutifully prosecuted those in Harding's administration who were involved in several notorious scandals.

He won reelection in 1924 and took a hands-off approach to business, deferring needed reforms in the financial sector and thus encouraging the overspeculation that eventually contributed to the 1929 stock market collapse and the subsequent Depression.

Charles G. Dawes

Born: August 27, 1865; Marietta, Ohio
Party: Republican
Term: March 4, 1925–March 4, 1929
President: Calvin Coolidge
Died: April 23, 1951; Evanston, Illinois
Buried: Chicago, Illinois

Charles Gates Dawes was the son of Mary and Rufus Dawes, a Civil War general who served one term in the House of Representatives. Charles's great-great-grandfather was William Dawes, who rode with Paul

Charles G. Dawes

Revere to alert the people near Boston that British troops were approaching on April 18, 1775.

Dawes attended Marietta College in Marietta, Ohio, graduating in 1884. He earned his law degree from Cincinnati Law School in 1886 and joined a Lincoln, Nebraska, law firm the following year. His practice grew as he became known for his expertise on banking issues and his opposition to discriminatory railway freight rates.

In 1894 Dawes bought gas and light companies in Evanston, Illinois, and LaCrosse, Wisconsin. He moved to Chicago to oversee his new business ventures. He soon expanded his profitable utility operations and was joined in business by his three brothers.

Since his days in Lincoln, Dawes had been active in the Republican Party. He directed William McKinley's early 1896 presidential campaign in Illinois and became the campaign finance director after McKinley won the nomination. After McKinley became president in 1897, he appointed Dawes comptroller of the currency. In 1902 Dawes resigned

and ran unsuccessfully for the Senate in Illinois. He returned to Chicago, where he organized the Central Trust Company of Illinois and became its president. The bank's success made him one of the leading financiers in the nation.

When the United States entered World War I, Dawes asked for a commission and was made a major in the Seventeenth Engineers. Soon after, his close friend, Gen. John J. Pershing, commander of the American Expeditionary Force in Europe, appointed him chief purchasing agent for the American army. Dawes oversaw the purchase and transportation of millions of tons of supplies for the troops in Europe. He retired from the army in 1919 with the rank of brigadier general. He became a popular figure after the war when he answered a petty congressional inquiry into his wartime purchasing records by exclaiming, "Hell and Maria, we weren't trying to keep a set of books, we were trying to win the war!"

President Warren G. Harding offered to appoint Dawes secretary of the Treasury in 1921, but Dawes chose instead a one-year assignment as director of the new Bureau of the Budget. In 1923 Dawes was appointed chairman of the Allied Reparations Commission, formed to study Germany's budget and make recommendations on restructuring payments of its World War I reparations. He helped to develop the "Dawes Plan," adopted in August 1924, which reduced German reparation payments and provided for a foreign loan to stimulate the German economy. For his efforts Dawes was awarded the Nobel Peace Prize in 1925.

In 1924 the Republican Party nominated Gov. Frank Lowden of Illinois as the vice-presidential candidate on the ticket with President Calvin Coolidge. When Lowden turned down the nomination, the convention turned to Dawes, who accepted. Coolidge and Dawes defeated Democrats John W. Davis and Charles W. Bryan 382–136 in the electoral college.

On inauguration day Dawes stole some of the limelight from President Coolidge when he demanded in his inaugural speech that the Senate pass new rules limiting filibusters. As vice president, Dawes became active in Senate politics, where he worked behind the scenes for naval appropriations, banking reforms, and farm relief programs. When President Coolidge announced he would not run for another term, Dawes also declared he would not seek reelection.

After leaving the vice presidency, Dawes was appointed ambassador to Great Britain in 1929 by President Herbert Hoover. He served there until January 1932, when Hoover appointed him director of the Reconstruction Finance Corporation (RFC), a government agency charged with making loans to banks and businesses in financial trouble. He resigned after several months to return to Chicago to reorganize his old bank into the City National Bank and Trust Company. He was criticized for securing an RFC loan for the bank shortly after resigning as the agency's director, but the loan helped return his bank to financial stability and it was properly repaid.

Dawes married Caro Blymer on January 24, 1889. When Dawes died in 1951 at the age of eighty-five, they had been married sixty-two years. Mrs. Dawes died on October 3, 1957. The couple had two children and later adopted two more. Dawes was a talented amateur composer, whose "Melody in a Major" was published in 1911. The piece became a popular song in 1951, when it was set to lyrics and retitled, "It's All in the Game."

Charles Curtis

Born: January 25, 1860; North Topeka, Kansas
Party: Republican
Term: March 4, 1929–March 4, 1933
President: Herbert Hoover
Died: February 8, 1936; Washington, D.C.
Buried: Topeka, Kansas

Charles Curtis

Charles Curtis was the older of the two children of Oren and Ellen Curtis. Charles's father was a drifter who had two sons by a previous marriage, which had ended in divorce. When Ellen Curtis died in 1863, Oren left Charles and his sister in the care of their two grandmothers and joined the Union cavalry. He remained in the cavalry after the war and seldom saw his children. His daughter by a third marriage would develop a close relationship with Charles.

After living with his paternal grandmother, Permelia Curtis, from 1863 to 1866, Charles spent three years with his maternal grandmother, Julie Pappan. Mrs. Pappan, who was half Kaw Indian, lived on a Native American reservation in Kansas. During this period Charles became such a skilled horseman that he was able to supplement his income as a teenager by riding racehorses at county fairs.

After 1869 Charles again lived with Permelia Curtis in North Topeka, Kansas. He had attended a mission school on the reservation, but he had fallen behind his classmates in North Topeka. Nevertheless, he graduated from a public high school in 1879.

He then clerked for a Topeka lawyer and was admitted to the bar in 1881.

Curtis practiced law in Topeka for several years before being elected county attorney in 1885. His vigorous prosecution of Prohibition violators brought him statewide recognition. He returned to his law practice in 1889 but stayed active in local politics.

In 1892 Curtis was elected to the U.S. House of Representatives. His greatest strength as a politician was staying in contact with his constituents. He kept information about persons throughout his district so he would be able to answer their mail with a personal touch and call them by name on campaign trips. This attention to detail helped Curtis win seven consecutive terms.

In 1907 Curtis shifted from the House to the Senate when he was elected by the Kansas legislature to fill several months of an unexpired term. The legislature elected him to a term of his own that year, and he served until 1913, when he was defeated for reelection. In 1914, however, he was elected to the Senate in the first election in which senators were chosen by popular vote according to the new Seventeenth Amendment.

Curtis served in the Senate until 1929. He supported Prohibition, voting rights for women, and bills benefiting farmers and Native Americans. He rarely introduced bills or made speeches, preferring to influence legislation through personal consultations and backroom meetings with other senators. He became Republican whip in 1915 and Senate majority leader in 1924.

Curtis wanted the Republican presidential nomination in 1928, and his name was placed in nomination at the Republican National Convention in Kansas City, Missouri, along with several other candidates. Herbert Hoover, however, was nominated on the first ballot. Party leaders chose Curtis for vice president because he was a political conservative from a farm state who could balance the ticket with Hoover, a liberal Californian. With the nation enjoying prosperity after eight years of Republican presidential leadership, Hoover and Curtis had little trouble defeating Democrats Alfred E. Smith and Joseph T. Robinson.

As vice president, Curtis faithfully supported Republican policies. Although he had served thirty-four years in Congress, he considered the vice presidency to be an office with higher status and asked colleagues who had called him "Charley" for decades to address him as "Mr. Vice President."

Hoover and Curtis were renominated in 1932, but the Great Depression had turned voters against the Republicans. They were defeated by Franklin D. Roosevelt and John Nance Garner 472–59 in the electoral college. After leaving the vice presidency, Curtis practiced law in Washington, D.C. He died of a heart attack in 1936.

On November 27, 1884, Curtis married Anna E. Baird, whom he had met in high school. They had three children. Anna died in 1924, five years before Curtis became vice president. The vice president's half-sister, Dolly Gann, who worked as his secretary during his years in Congress, served as his official hostess.

John Nance Garner

Born: November 22, 1868; near Detroit, Texas
Party: Democratic
Term: March 4, 1933–January 20, 1941
President: Franklin D. Roosevelt
Died: November 7, 1967; Uvalde, Texas
Buried: Uvalde

John Nance Garner was the oldest of the six children of Sarah and John Garner, a former soldier in the Confederate cavalry. Young John attended a Texas country school until the fourth grade, when he stopped going because of poor health. Thereafter he was tutored by a maiden aunt.

Garner enrolled at Vanderbilt University in Nashville, Tennessee, when he was eighteen, but he

John Nance Garner

returned to Texas in less than a month, considering himself scholastically unprepared for college. Rather than go back to school, he studied law under local attorneys. He was admitted to the bar in 1890 and opened a law practice in the northeast Texas city of Clarksville, about fifteen miles from where he was born.

While Garner was in Clarksville, doctors tentatively diagnosed him as having tuberculosis and advised him to move to a drier climate. He took their advice and in 1892 relocated to Uvalde, Texas, a town of about 2,500 people. He joined a local law firm and regained his health. Through shrewd investing, he gradually acquired thousands of acres of land, three banks, and numerous businesses that made him a millionaire.

Garner was elected a judge of Uvalde County in 1893. He served until 1896, when he returned to his law practice. Two years later he was elected to the Texas House of Representatives. After two terms there, he won a seat in the U.S. House in 1902. When Woodrow Wilson was elected president in

1913, Garner gained a seat on the powerful Ways and Means Committee and soon developed into one of Wilson's most important congressional allies. Garner served in the House continuously until 1933, becoming minority leader in 1928 and Speaker on December 7, 1931.

In 1932 Garner ran for the Democratic presidential nomination. In the early balloting at the party's national convention in Chicago, he was a distant third place behind front-runner Franklin D. Roosevelt and the 1928 Democratic presidential candidate, Alfred E. Smith. After the third ballot the convention appeared to be headed for a deadlock. More than half the delegates favored Roosevelt, but he could not secure the two-thirds needed for nomination. Rather than see the party divided, Garner agreed to release his ninety delegates from Texas and California. The addition of Garner's delegates gave Roosevelt enough votes for the nomination. Roosevelt then supported Garner for the vice-presidential nomination, which the Texas representative received on the first ballot. The Roosevelt and Garner camps claimed they had not traded Garner's delegates for his nomination, but they convinced few political observers. Roosevelt and Garner were swept into office by a landslide victory over President Herbert Hoover and Vice President Charles Curtis.

Garner had reservations about taking the vice presidency because he had long aspired to the speakership of the House and had attained his goal less than a year before being nominated for vice president. Indeed, during his vice presidency, Garner would remark that his office "isn't worth a pitcher of warm spit." Garner, however, had wanted the party to be united for the 1932 election and believed that holding the vice presidency increased his chances of eventually becoming president.

Unlike many previous vice presidents, Garner remained active. He attended cabinet meetings and used his congressional contacts and experience to help push Franklin Roosevelt's New Deal legislation through Congress in 1933. Roosevelt and Garner were reelected in 1936, but during their second term a split developed between them. Garner was alarmed by the enhancement of executive power under Roosevelt and opposed the president's plan to increase the number of Supreme Court justices in 1937. The vice president also thought that deficit spending on Roosevelt's New Deal social programs should be cut back. In response, the president excluded Garner from many important White House meetings.

In December 1939 Garner announced he was a candidate for president, but Roosevelt chose to break precedent and seek a third term. Garner denounced the president's action, but Roosevelt was nominated by acclamation in 1940, with Garner receiving only a handful of votes at the Democratic National Convention in Chicago. After this disappointment, Garner quit politics and retired to Uvalde. He died in 1967, two weeks before his ninety-ninth birthday. He lived longer than any other vice president or president.

Garner married Mariette Rheiner on November 25, 1895. They had met on a train after he moved to Uvalde. Their one son, Tully, was born in 1896.

Henry A. Wallace

Born: October 7, 1888; Adair County, Iowa
Party: Democratic
Term: January 20, 1941–January 20, 1945
President: Franklin D. Roosevelt
Died: November 18, 1965; Danbury, Connecticut
Buried: Des Moines, Iowa

Henry Agard Wallace was the son of May and Henry C. Wallace, a magazine editor and secretary of agriculture under Warren G. Harding and Calvin Coolidge. Henry attended public school in central

Henry A. Wallace

Iowa and graduated in 1910 from Iowa State University in Ames with a degree in animal husbandry.

After college Wallace worked as a writer and editor on his father's magazine, *Wallaces' Farmer,* one of the most influential agricultural journals in the United States. He also conducted plant breeding experiments and farmed a small plot of land. He became associate editor of the magazine in 1916 and editor in 1924.

Despite his father's Republicanism, Wallace left the party during the late 1920s because he believed the high tariffs advocated by the Republicans hurt farmers, and he supported farm export bills that President Calvin Coolidge had vetoed. Wallace backed Democrat Alfred E. Smith for president in 1928 and Franklin D. Roosevelt in 1932.

In 1933 Wallace entered public service when President Roosevelt appointed him secretary of agriculture. Wallace traveled to all forty-eight states during his first year in office to survey the plight of the farmers, who had endured low commodity prices since the 1920s. Armed with the Agriculture

Adjustment Act of 1933, a measure giving the secretary of agriculture broad powers to address the farm crisis, Wallace began subsidy payments to farmers who took fields out of production, authorized the slaughter of millions of hogs to raise prices, and introduced systematic controls to prevent overproduction. He also supported Secretary of State Cordell Hull's efforts to negotiate with foreign nations tariff reductions that increased world trade and opened up markets for U.S. agricultural products.

In 1940 a rift between Roosevelt and Vice President John Nance Garner caused Democratic leaders to look for a new vice-presidential candidate. During Wallace's two terms as agriculture secretary, he had supported virtually all of the president's programs, including his unpopular attempt to increase the number of Supreme Court justices in 1937. This loyalty and Wallace's popularity in farm states led Roosevelt to support him as Garner's replacement. Many Democrats, however, did not want Wallace. Not only did they consider him to be too liberal, they were suspicious of his unconventional personal philosophy, which was influenced by Eastern religions and mysticism. Nevertheless, when Roosevelt insisted that he would not run for a third term without Wallace as his running mate, the 1940 Democratic National Convention in Chicago gave Wallace the nomination on the first ballot. Roosevelt and Wallace easily defeated Republicans Wendell Willkie and Charles L. McNary 449–82 in the electoral college. The vice presidency was the only office to which Wallace was ever elected.

Wallace was an active vice president. He made goodwill tours of Latin America, China, and Soviet Asia. He also became an outspoken advocate of an internationalist post–World War II foreign policy in which the United States would cooperate closely with the Soviet Union and provide economic and technical assistance to underdeveloped nations.

By 1944 Wallace's liberal views had alienated many Democratic leaders, who urged Roosevelt to drop him from the ticket. Roosevelt said he wanted to keep Wallace, but that he would also accept either Supreme Court Justice William O. Douglas or Sen. Harry Truman of Missouri. This weak endorsement ended Wallace's chances for a second term, and Truman was nominated. Roosevelt and Truman then defeated Thomas E. Dewey and John W. Bricker in the general election.

Even after being dropped from the ticket, Wallace campaigned hard for Roosevelt and Truman. Roosevelt rewarded him by naming him secretary of commerce in 1945. After Roosevelt died in April of that month, Wallace became concerned that President Truman would abandon Roosevelt's policy of friendship toward the Soviet Union. In July 1946 he wrote to the president, urging him to recognize Soviet security interests that Wallace believed were legitimate. When Wallace spoke out against Truman's tough policy toward the Soviets in September 1946, Truman fired him.

While the people of the United States were becoming increasingly alarmed by the threat of communist expansion and subversion, Wallace continued to speak out in favor of cooperation between the superpowers. On December 29, 1947, he announced his intention to run for the presidency as the candidate of the Progressive Party. Wallace's candidacy hurt Truman's chances of being elected in 1948, especially since southern Democrats had also formed a separate party and nominated Sen. Strom Thurmond of South Carolina to run for president. The endorsement of Wallace by the American Communist Party, however, reinforced perceptions that he was at best a naive dreamer and at worst a communist. Wallace received barely more than 2 percent of the vote and won no states. Truman overcame the divisions within his party to win the election.

After his defeat, Wallace retired to his farm in South Salem, New York. By 1952 Wallace's attitudes toward the Soviet Union had undergone a transformation. He published *Why I Was Wrong,* a book that explained his newfound distrust of the Soviet Union.

Wallace married Ilo Browne on May 30, 1914. They had two sons and a daughter. Before his death in 1965, Wallace spent much of his retirement conducting agricultural experiments.

Harry S. Truman

Born: May 8, 1884; Lamar, Missouri
Party: Democratic
Term: January 20, 1945–April 12, 1945
President: Franklin D. Roosevelt
Died: December 26, 1972; Kansas City, Missouri
Buried: Independence, Missouri

(See full biography, p. 109.)

After Democratic leaders spurned Vice President Henry Wallace for renomination at the 1944 Democratic convention, Sen. Harry S. Truman was tapped on the second ballot to be Franklin D. Roosevelt's running mate. Roosevelt and Truman went on to an easy victory over the Republican ticket composed of Gov. Thomas E. Dewey of New York and Gov. John Bricker of Ohio. Truman—Roosevelt's third vice president—served just eighty-two days in office before FDR died. Truman entered the office of the presidency at a precarious moment— as the nation was engaged in World War II. He authorized atomic attacks on two Japanese cities, hastening the end of the war. Truman would preside over the beginning of the cold war, the rebuilding of Europe with Marshall Plan aid, and a continuation of FDR's New Deal—which Truman called the Fair Deal. He won a close and surprising reelection victory in 1948.

Alben W. Barkley

Alben W. Barkley

Born: November 24, 1877; Lowes, Kentucky
Party: Democratic
Term: January 20, 1949–January 20, 1953
President: Harry S. Truman
Died: April 30, 1956; Lexington, Virginia
Buried: Paducah, Kentucky

Alben William Barkley was the son of Electra and John Barkley, a poor tobacco farmer and railroad worker. Alben, who was born in a log cabin, worked on his father's farm and attended country schools.

At age fourteen he entered Marvin College in Clinton, Kentucky. He paid his tuition by working as a janitor at the college. After graduating in 1897, he studied law for a year at Emory University in Oxford, Georgia. He then moved to Paducah, Kentucky, and got a job in a law office. He was admitted to the bar in 1901 and attended the University of Virginia Law School in 1902 to sharpen his legal skills.

Entering Democratic politics, Barkley won his first election in 1905, becoming prosecuting attorney of McCracken County, Kentucky. In 1909 he was elected county judge, an administrative rather than a judicial position that was primarily responsible for building and maintaining public roads. Barkley ran for the U.S. House of Representatives in 1912 and won a seat he held continuously until he became a senator in 1927.

In Congress Barkley was a staunch supporter of President Woodrow Wilson. He backed Wilson's decision to enter World War I and voted for the Versailles treaty. Although he supported most liberal causes, he gained a reputation as a political compromiser who would make political deals when it was in the interests of his constituents. He also was renowned for his speaking ability, which combined a bombastic style with homespun humor and wisdom. He delivered the keynote addresses at the 1932, 1936, and 1948 Democratic National Conventions.

After Barkley was reelected to the Senate in 1932, Democratic majority leader Joseph Robinson of Arkansas appointed him assistant majority leader. In 1937, with the support of the White House, Barkley was elected majority leader when Robinson died. Barkley supported both Roosevelt's New Deal social programs and his aid to Britain and its allies before World War II. He remained majority leader until 1946, when the Republicans gained control of the Senate and he became minority leader.

In 1948 Truman's first choice for vice president was Supreme Court Justice William O. Douglas, but Douglas turned him down. Barkley had long wanted to be president, but Franklin Roosevelt's four-term grip on the Democratic presidential nomination prevented him from running. Now, at the age of seventy, Barkley was unwilling to challenge an incumbent Democratic president for the nomination, but he decided that he wanted to be vice president. He telephoned Truman during the convention to tell him he would accept a nomination as his

running mate. Truman agreed to support his candidacy, and the convention nominated him by acclamation. Although opinion polls indicated that the Democrats would lose, Truman and Barkley campaigned tirelessly around the country and defeated Republicans Thomas E. Dewey and Earl Warren.

Although Barkley, at seventy-one, was the oldest vice president ever to take office, he had an active term. He lobbied Congress to support administration programs and made many ceremonial appearances. His grandson called him the "Veep," a title that stuck with the office of vice president even after Barkley had left.

In 1952 Barkley announced his interest in the presidential nomination, but he received little support because of his age. He retired briefly but was elected to the Senate in 1954 by the voters of Kentucky. He died in 1956 from a heart attack suffered during a speaking engagement at Washington and Lee College in Lexington, Virginia.

Barkley married Dorothy Brower on June 23, 1903. They had four children. Dorothy died in 1947 after a long illness. Barkley became the only incumbent vice president ever to marry, when he wed Jane Rucker Hadley, a thirty-eight-year-old St. Louis widow, on November 18, 1949.

Richard Nixon

Born: January 9, 1913; Yorba Linda, California
Party: Republican
Term: January 20, 1953–January 20, 1961
President: Dwight D. Eisenhower
Died: April 22, 1994; New York City
Buried: Yorba Linda, California

(See full biography, p. 120.)

Richard Nixon brought a reputation for dubious campaign tactics and anticommunist fervor to the

1952 Republican presidential campaign, but the heroic image of Dwight D. Eisenhower carried the pair into the White House. Nixon, a former representative and senator, was an active vice president, chairing several domestic policy committees and frequently traveling overseas on diplomatic missions. During a 1959 visit to the Soviet Union, he and Premier Nikita Khrushchev engaged in a famous spontaneous debate on the merits of capitalism and communism. Nixon was defeated for president in 1960 by Democrat John F. Kennedy but won the White House in 1968. As president, Nixon moved beyond his early anticommunist stances and significantly improved relations with both the Soviet Union and mainland China.

The Watergate scandal, erupting shortly after his 1972 reelection, eventually would force Nixon to resign before what appeared to be a certain vote in the House of Representatives to impeach him. On August 9, 1974, he became the first president ever to resign his office.

Lyndon B. Johnson

Born: August 27, 1908; Stonewall, Texas
Party: Democratic
Term: January 20, 1961–November 22, 1963
President: John F. Kennedy
Died: January 22, 1973; San Antonio, Texas
Buried: Johnson City, Texas

(See full biography, p. 118.)

As Senate majority leader, Lyndon B. Johnson was one of the most powerful men in Washington, and he wanted to be president. He lost the 1960 Democratic nomination to John F. Kennedy and surprised many by accepting second spot on the ticket. The slate won a narrow victory that many credit to Johnson's appeal in some southern states. Johnson was a

valuable counsel to Kennedy on legislative matters and undertook many diplomatic missions for the president. When Kennedy was slain by an assassin in Dallas, Texas, on November 22, 1963, Johnson took the oath of office aboard *Air Force One* as he returned to Washington. Using the memory of the dead president, Johnson pushed many of Kennedy's legislative proposals through Congress, including the important Civil Rights Act of 1964. Johnson won the presidency on his own in 1964. By 1968, facing massive discontent over his Vietnam policy among the public and even within his own party, Johnson declared that he would not run again for president.

Hubert H. Humphrey

Born: May 27, 1911; Wallace, South Dakota
Party: Democratic
Term: January 20, 1965–January 20, 1969
President: Lyndon B. Johnson
Died: January 13, 1978; Waverly, Minnesota
Buried: Minneapolis, Minnesota

Hubert Horatio Humphrey Jr. was the second of the four children of Hubert and Christine Humphrey. His father was a druggist and his mother was a Norwegian immigrant who had come to the United States in her teens. Hubert Jr. was born above the family drugstore in Wallace, South Dakota. When he was four, the Humphreys moved to Doland, South Dakota, where his father ran another drugstore. Hubert attended public schools in Doland and was the valedictorian of his high school class.

Humphrey enrolled in the University of Minnesota in 1929, but he left the following year because of family financial troubles caused by the Great Depression. He helped his father run a drugstore in Huron, South Dakota, where his family had moved. In 1932 Humphrey entered the Denver

Hubert H. Humphrey

School of Pharmacy and was licensed as a registered pharmacist in 1933. Humphrey managed the family drugstore when his father, who had been active in local politics as a Democrat, won a seat in the South Dakota state legislature.

In 1937 Humphrey returned to the University of Minnesota. He graduated magna cum laude in 1939 with a degree in political science and was elected to the Phi Beta Kappa honor society. He then enrolled in graduate school at Louisiana State University, where he had received a teaching assistantship. After earning his master's degree in 1940, he again returned to the University of Minnesota, hoping to earn a doctorate, but financial problems forced him to withdraw after less than a year.

Color blindness and a double hernia disqualified Humphrey from military service during World War II. Instead, he served as state director for war production training and later became assistant director of the state War Manpower Administration. While serving in these administrative posts, he made many political contacts, especially among labor organizations.

In 1943 Humphrey ran for mayor of Minneapolis on the Democratic ticket. He had the support of labor unions and intellectuals at the University of Minnesota, but he lost by a close vote. Two years later, after helping to forge an alliance between the Minnesota Democratic and Farmer Labor Parties, he was elected mayor in his second try. He gained a reputation as a hard-working reformer and easily won a second term as mayor in 1947.

In 1948 Humphrey ran for the Senate. His advocacy of a civil rights platform at the 1948 Democratic convention in Philadelphia won him national recognition and helped him defeat his Republican opponent, Sen. Joseph Ball. In the Senate, Humphrey became a leading supporter of legislation promoting civil rights and welfare programs. He was easily reelected in 1954 and 1960.

Humphrey announced his candidacy for his party's presidential nomination in January 1960, but he withdrew after doing poorly against John F. Kennedy in the primaries. In 1961 Humphrey became Senate majority whip and helped guide several of President Kennedy's legislative proposals, including the nuclear test ban treaty and the Civil Rights Act of 1964, to approval.

In 1964 President Lyndon Johnson chose Humphrey as his running mate after securing a promise from the senator that he would remain loyal to the administration even if he disagreed with specific policies. Johnson and Humphrey defeated Republicans Barry M. Goldwater and William E. Miller by more than sixteen million popular votes.

As vice president, Humphrey was not a member of Johnson's inner circle of advisers. Nevertheless, he worked hard to help push Johnson's Great Society social programs through Congress and made several goodwill tours of foreign nations, including two trips to Vietnam.

After Johnson announced on March 31, 1968, that he would not seek another term, Humphrey entered the race. His nomination was secure when his main rival, Sen. Robert F. Kennedy of New York, was assassinated in Los Angeles on June 5. Humphrey's campaign was burdened by the unpopularity of the Vietnam War and the unfavorable media attention given violent protests at the Democratic National Convention in Chicago. He was defeated 301–191 in the electoral college but received only a half million fewer votes than Richard Nixon out of more than sixty-three million cast.

After leaving the vice presidency in 1969 Humphrey taught at Macalester College in St. Paul, Minnesota. In 1970 he returned to the Senate after winning the seat vacated by retiring Democrat Eugene J. McCarthy. Humphrey entered the race for the 1972 Democratic presidential nomination after the campaign of Sen. Edmund S. Muskie, his 1968 vice-presidential running mate, sputtered. The nomination, however, went to Sen. George McGovern of South Dakota. Humphrey considered running for the presidency again in 1976, but he announced in April of that year that he would not be a candidate.

In August 1976 doctors detected an advanced cancer in Humphrey's prostate and bladder. Surgery failed to arrest the cancer. Despite his illness, the voters of Minnesota reelected him to the Senate in 1976. The Senate honored him by electing him deputy president pro tempore, a post created especially for him. Humphrey's fortitude and high spirits during the year preceding his death won him admiration around the country. He died at his Waverly, Minnesota, home on January 13, 1978.

Humphrey married Muriel Buck on September 3, 1936. They had one daughter and three sons. Muriel Humphrey was appointed to her husband's Senate seat after his death and served until January 3, 1979.

Spiro T. Agnew

Spiro T. Agnew

Born: November 9, 1918; Baltimore, Maryland
Party: Republican
Term: January 20, 1969–October 10, 1973
President: Richard Nixon
Died: September 17, 1996; Berlin, Maryland
Buried: Timonium, Maryland

Spiro Theodore Agnew was the son of Theofrastos and Margaret Agnew. Spiro's father, whose original name was Anagnostopoulos, immigrated to the United States from Greece in 1897. He settled in Baltimore, Maryland, where he became the owner of a successful restaurant. Spiro's Greek ancestry was not a major factor in his childhood. He was raised in his mother's Episcopalian church, attended public schools, and preferred to be called "Ted."

Agnew enrolled in Johns Hopkins University in Baltimore in 1937 with the intention of studying chemistry, but he dropped out after two years. He then took classes at the Baltimore Law School at night, while holding a succession of jobs during the day, including supermarket manager and insurance claims adjuster.

In 1941 Agnew was drafted into the army and assigned to officer candidate school at Fort Knox, Kentucky. He was commissioned as a lieutenant in 1942. While serving with the Tenth Armored Division during World War II, he saw combat in France and Germany.

Agnew returned to the Baltimore Law School after the war and earned his law degree in 1947. He then opened a law office in Towson, Maryland, a Baltimore suburb. Agnew had been a Democrat, but he switched to the Republican Party in the late 1940s and actively supported local Republican candidates. In 1957 he was appointed to the Zoning Board of Appeals of Baltimore County. In 1962 he ran for executive of the county, a post with responsibilities similar to those of a mayor. He won the election, becoming the first Republican in the twentieth century to be elected executive of Baltimore County.

Agnew ran for governor of Maryland in 1966. During the campaign he acquired a reputation as a liberal, in part because his Democratic opponent, George Mahoney, was a segregationist, while Agnew took a strong stand on civil rights. Substantial support from blacks and liberal Democrats helped Agnew defeat Mahoney decisively, despite the Democratic Party's three-to-one advantage over the Republicans among Maryland's registered voters.

Agnew fulfilled many of his campaign promises in his first year as governor. With the cooperation of the Maryland legislature he reformed the state's tax code, increased aid to the poor, passed an open housing law, repealed the ban on racial intermarriage, liberalized the abortion law, and enacted strict regulations to reduce water pollution. In 1968, however, Agnew appeared to shift to the right. In particular, his uncompromising response to race riots in Baltimore after the assassination of civil rights leader

Martin Luther King Jr. in April 1968 caused observers to question his liberal image. Agnew called out the National Guard and had thousands of blacks arrested. He then met with black leaders and scolded them for failing to control the rioting, even though many of the leaders had made an earnest effort to stop the riots.

On August 7, 1968, Agnew placed Richard Nixon's name in nomination for president at the Republican National Convention in Miami. The following morning, after Nixon had secured the nomination, he surprised many observers by announcing that he had chosen Agnew as his running mate. Agnew was virtually unknown outside of Maryland, but Nixon hoped that his new running mate would appeal to southern voters who might be drawn to the third-party candidacy of former Alabama governor George C. Wallace.

During the 1968 campaign, Agnew made several political blunders that betrayed his lack of national political experience. His claim that Democratic presidential candidate Hubert H. Humphrey was "squishy soft on communism" rekindled memories of Nixon's extreme anticommunist rhetoric during the 1940s and 1950s. Agnew also used the derogatory term "Polack" in a statement referring to a person of Polish ancestry and remarked in an interview that "If you've seen one city slum, you've seen them all." Nixon and Agnew overcame these mistakes to defeat Democrats Hubert H. Humphrey and Edmund S. Muskie 301–191 in the electoral college.

As vice president, Agnew had little influence on policy decisions, but he became the administration's hard-line spokesperson against liberal members of the news media, Vietnam war protesters, and other Nixon opponents. In 1972 Nixon and Agnew were reelected in a landslide. Early in 1973 Agnew's noninvolvement in the Watergate scandal made him a potential contender for his party's presidential nomination in 1976.

In August 1973, however, the U.S. attorney in

Baltimore disclosed that Agnew was under investigation for receiving bribes from contractors during his years as Baltimore County executive and governor of Maryland. Agnew claimed he was innocent, but his lawyers worked out a plea bargain in which the vice president agreed to resign, plead "no contest" to income tax evasion, and pay a $10,000 fine and $150,000 in back taxes. In return, the Justice Department agreed not to prosecute Agnew for taking bribes. Agnew resigned the vice presidency on October 10, 1973. Two days later Nixon nominated Gerald R. Ford to replace him.

Early in 1974 Agnew was disbarred. He decided to write a novel to pay his debts, and in 1976 he published *The Canfield Decision,* a story about a U.S. vice president who becomes involved with Iranian militants. Agnew also opened Pathlite Inc., a profitable consulting service for firms doing business in the Middle East. In 1980 he published his autobiography, *Go Quietly . . . or Else,* in which he claims he was innocent of the crimes that forced his resignation.

In April 1994 Agnew made a rare public appearance when he attended the funeral of Richard Nixon. Agnew disclosed that he had not spoken with Nixon since he resigned from the vice presidency. After a short hospitalization, Agnew died on September 17, 1996, of acute leukemia.

Agnew married Elinor "Judy" Judefind on May 27, 1942. The couple had met while Agnew worked in an insurance office. They had four children.

Gerald R. Ford

Born: July 14, 1913; Omaha, Nebraska
Party: Republican
Term: December 6, 1973–August 9, 1974
President: Richard Nixon

(See full biography, p. 123.)

When Richard Nixon's first vice president, Spiro T. Agnew, was forced to resign because of tax evasion charges, Nixon needed to nominate a person of unquestioned integrity. He turned to Gerald Ford, Republican minority leader in the House of Representatives. Under the provisions of the Twenty-fifth Amendment, this nomination had to be approved by both houses of Congress, and Ford became the first unelected vice president chosen by this method. He succeeded to the presidency upon Nixon's resignation on August 9, 1974, becoming the first unelected president. A month later he gave Nixon a controversial unconditional pardon. In 1976 Ford and running mate Robert Dole lost the presidential election to Democrats Jimmy Carter and Walter Mondale.

Nelson A. Rockefeller

Born: July 8, 1908; Bar Harbor, Maine
Party: Republican
Term: December 19, 1974–January 20, 1977
President: Gerald R. Ford
Died: January 26, 1979; New York City
Buried: North Tarrytown, New York

Nelson Aldrich Rockefeller was the second of the six children of Abby and John D. Rockefeller Jr. Nelson's paternal grandfather was John D. Rockefeller, the billionaire philanthropist who founded Standard Oil. Nelson's maternal grandfather was Nelson W. Aldrich, a senator from Rhode Island.

After attending private schools in New York City, Nelson enrolled in Dartmouth College in 1926. Although hindered by dyslexia, he graduated with a degree in economics in 1930 and was named to the Phi Beta Kappa honor fraternity. Rockefeller then helped manage the numerous holdings of the Rockefeller family, including real estate properties in New York City. From 1935 to 1940 he served as director of the Standard Oil subsidiary in Venezuela. During

Nelson A. Rockefeller

this period he developed an intense interest in Latin American affairs.

In 1940 Rockefeller entered public service when President Franklin D. Roosevelt appointed him coordinator of a new agency, the Office for Coordination of Commercial and Cultural Relations between the American Republics. During World War II the agency was renamed the Office of Inter-American Affairs. In 1944 Roosevelt transferred Rockefeller to the State Department, where he became assistant secretary for Latin American affairs. After clashing with other State Department officials in 1945, Rockefeller was asked by incoming secretary James F. Byrnes to resign. In 1950 Rockefeller returned to government when President Harry Truman appointed him to chair the Advisory Board on International Development. When the president did not commit himself to acting on the board's recommendations, Rockefeller resigned in 1951.

Rockefeller supported Dwight Eisenhower's successful bid for the presidency in 1952, and in 1953 Eisenhower appointed him under secretary of the newly created Department of Health, Education, and Welfare. In 1954 Rockefeller became special assistant to the president for foreign affairs, but he resigned in 1955 after conflicts with Secretary of State John Foster Dulles. From 1953 to 1958 Rockefeller also chaired Eisenhower's Advisory Committee on Government Organization, which studied ways to reorganize the government.

Rockefeller was elected governor of New York as a Republican in 1958. In this office he supported civil rights legislation and urban renewal and oversaw the expansion of New York's state university system. He was reelected governor in 1962, 1966, and 1970. In September 1971, after inmates had taken hostages at the state prison in Attica, Rockefeller ordered more than a thousand policemen to storm the cellblock. This controversial action culminated in the deaths of thirty-four prisoners and nine hostages.

Rockefeller also pushed for and won stringently punitive laws regarding those convicted of narcotics violations. These laws came under public attack in New York thirty years later in 2000 for their arbitrary nature.

Rockefeller wanted to be president and unsuccessfully sought the Republican nomination before all three presidential elections during the 1960s. He was a leading candidate for the nomination in 1964, but he lost it to Sen. Barry M. Goldwater of Arizona. Rockefeller suffered from an image problem. Although he was conservative on many issues, including law enforcement, military spending, and superpower relations, he was seen as an urbane liberal by the conservatives who dominated his party during the 1960s.

Rockefeller resigned from the governorship on December 18, 1973, to establish the National Commission on Critical Choices for Americans, an organization devoted to developing new national policy options.

On August 20, 1974, President Gerald R. Ford, who had succeeded to the presidency from the vice presidency after the resignation of President Richard Nixon, nominated Rockefeller for vice president. The sixty-six-year-old Rockefeller had considered another run for the presidency in 1976, but knowing his chances of being elected were small, he accepted the nomination.

Under the Twenty-fifth Amendment, Rockefeller's appointment had to be approved by a majority of both houses of Congress. The confirmation hearings lasted throughout the fall as committees examined the nominee's vast financial holdings for potential conflicts of interest. Finally, on December 19, 1974, he was sworn in as the forty-first vice president.

Rockefeller chaired several boards and commissions as vice president, including a commission set up by the president to investigate the CIA. At Ford's request, Rockefeller announced on November 3, 1975, that he would not accept the Republican nomination for vice president. Ford believed he could attract more votes in the Republican primaries without Rockefeller. Nevertheless, the vice president remained loyal to Ford. He delivered the speech nominating Sen. Robert J. Dole of Kansas as the Republican vice-presidential nominee and campaigned for the Ford-Dole ticket.

After leaving the vice presidency in 1977, Rockefeller returned to New York to manage various family business and philanthropic enterprises. In 1979 he died of a heart attack in his Manhattan townhouse while in the company of Megan Marshack, a twenty-six-year-old assistant.

Rockefeller married Mary Todhunter "Tod" Clark, a member of a prominent Philadelphia family, on June 23, 1930. They had three sons and two daughters. The couple became estranged during Rockefeller's first term as governor and divorced in 1962. In May 1963 he married Margaretta "Happy" Murphy, with whom he had two sons.

Walter F. Mondale

Walter F. Mondale

Born: January 5, 1928; Ceylon, Minnesota
Party: Democratic
Term: January 20, 1977–January 20, 1981
President: Jimmy Carter

Walter Frederick Mondale was the second of the three sons of Claribel and Theodore Mondale, a Methodist minister who served as pastor of a succession of churches in southern Minnesota. Theodore married Claribel in 1925 after the death of his first wife, with whom he also had three sons. In 1946 Walter, who was nicknamed "Fritz," graduated from Elmore (Minnesota) High School, where he excelled in athletics and music.

Mondale then entered Macalester College in St. Paul. He dropped out in 1949 when his father died, but he resumed his education at the University of Minnesota the following year. After graduating with honors in 1951, he enlisted in the army. He was discharged with the rank of corporal after serving two years at Fort Knox, Kentucky. Mondale then returned to the University of Minnesota, where he earned his law degree in 1956. That year he was admitted to the Minnesota bar and began practicing law.

Since Mondale's college years he had been active in the Minnesota Democratic Party. He became a follower of Hubert H. Humphrey in 1946 when Humphrey was mayor of Minneapolis. In 1948, when Humphrey ran successfully for the Senate, Mondale managed Humphrey's campaign in Minnesota's Second Congressional District. Mondale also worked on the campaign of Orville Freeman, who was elected governor of Minnesota in 1954, and served as Freeman's campaign chairman in his successful bid for reelection in 1958.

That year Freeman appointed Mondale special assistant to Minnesota's attorney general. When the attorney general resigned in 1960, Freeman appointed Mondale to serve out the remaining eight months of the term. Mondale was elected to the post in 1960 and reelected in 1962. As attorney general, he won praise for his enforcement of civil rights, antitrust, and consumer protection laws.

When Humphrey resigned from the Senate in 1964 after being elected vice president, Minnesota governor Karl Rolvaag appointed Mondale to Humphrey's seat. Mondale was elected to a term of his own in 1966 and reelected in 1972. In the Senate Mondale compiled a consistently liberal voting record on domestic issues. He became a leading advocate of civil rights legislation, Lyndon Johnson's Great Society social programs, and bills benefiting farm workers, Native Americans, children, and the elderly. In foreign policy he was less consistent. He supported U.S. participation in the Vietnam War until 1968. He then sided with those members of Congress who sought to limit U.S. military involvement in Southeast Asia.

In 1974 Mondale took time off from his Senate duties to campaign across the country for the 1976 Democratic presidential nomination. He abandoned

his candidacy after several months when he failed to attract significant support. Jimmy Carter, the eventual Democratic presidential nominee, however, selected Mondale to be his vice-presidential running mate. Carter said he chose Mondale because the Minnesota senator was qualified to assume the presidency, had substantial Washington experience that would complement Carter's "outsider" image, and gave the ticket geographic balance. On October 15, 1976, Mondale engaged the Republican vice-presidential candidate, Robert J. Dole, in the first televised debate between vice-presidential candidates in U.S. election history. Most observers believed Mondale won the debate. Carter and Mondale defeated President Gerald R. Ford and Dole 297–240 in the electoral college.

Mondale was deeply involved in Carter administration policymaking. He helped choose cabinet officers and draft policy proposals. He also met with Carter alone at least once a week and had an open invitation to attend any White House meeting. During Carter's first week in office he demonstrated Mondale's importance by sending him as a personal emissary to Western Europe and Japan. In 1980 Carter and Mondale were renominated, but a sagging economy and the Iran hostage crisis weakened their chances for reelection. They were easily defeated by Republicans Ronald Reagan and George Bush.

In 1984 Mondale was the front-runner of a pack of Democrats seeking the party's presidential nomination. Mondale overcame early primary successes by Sen. Gary Hart of Colorado to win the nomination. Mondale made history by choosing Rep. Geraldine Ferraro of New York as his running mate. She was the first woman to be nominated as vice president by a major political party. Mondale and Ferraro, however, faced President Ronald Reagan and Vice President George Bush, who were running for reelection during a period of economic prosperity. The Democrats won only Minnesota and the

District of Columbia as they were buried in a forty-nine-state Republican landslide. After the election, Mondale retired from politics and returned to Minnesota.

On July 30, 1993, Mondale was confirmed by the Senate as U.S. ambassador to Japan, after being nominated by President Bill Clinton. The appointment of a former vice president to this post was intended to signal the importance of U.S.-Japanese relations. He resigned from the posting in 1998 and returned to private life. In the fall of 2002 Mondale briefly reemerged into politics when he agreed to step into Minnesota's Senate race at the last minute, filling the place of the late Sen. Paul Wellstone, a Democrat who had died in an October 25 plane crash. Mondale lost to Republican Norm Coleman, the former mayor of St. Paul.

Mondale married Joan Adams, the daughter of a Presbyterian minister, on December 27, 1955. They had two sons and a daughter.

George H. W. Bush

Born: June 12, 1924; Milton, Massachusetts
Party: Republican
Term: January 20, 1981–January 20, 1989
President: Ronald Reagan

(See full biography, p. 132.)

During the 1980 primary season, George Bush frequently attacked Republican rival Ronald Reagan as an ultraconservative and called his fiscal program "voodoo economics." Bush was Reagan's second choice (behind Gerald Ford) to be his vice-presidential nominee but accepted when the post was offered and went on to become a Reagan loyalist, undertaking many official missions overseas for the aging president. Late in Reagan's second term, Bush began his own run for his party's nomination and

went on to win the presidency in 1988. He thus became the first sitting vice president elected to the presidency since Martin Van Buren in 1836. His stewardship in the 1991 Persian Gulf War earned high approval ratings, but a turndown in the economy led to a losing reelection bid against Democrat Bill Clinton in 1992.

Dan Quayle

Born: February 4, 1947; Indianapolis
Party: Republican
Term: January 20, 1989–January 20, 1993
President: George Bush

James Danforth Quayle III was the eldest of the four children of James and Corinne Quayle. Since childhood, James was called "Dan." His maternal grandfather, Eugene C. Pulliam, was a conservative Indiana newspaper publisher who amassed a fortune close to a billion dollars. In 1955 his family moved from Indiana to Phoenix, Arizona, where his father helped manage the family's newspaper interests in that state. When Dan was in high school, the Quayles moved back to Indiana, where his father took over as publisher of the *Huntington Herald-Press,* one of the family newspapers.

In 1965 Quayle enrolled in DePauw University, a small liberal arts college in Greencastle, Indiana, which was heavily endowed by his family. Quayle played on the golf team and compiled a mediocre academic record. Upon graduation in 1969 Quayle lost his student deferment and became eligible for the military draft. With the help of family friends, however, Quayle secured a place in the Indiana National Guard, an action that made military service in Vietnam unlikely.

While serving in the National Guard one weekend a month, Quayle held a series of jobs in Indiana state government and attended Indiana University

Dan Quayle

Law School at night. With the help of his family he was hired as a clerk in the attorney general's office and later as an assistant to Indiana governor Edgar Whitcomb. After graduating from law school in 1974, Quayle opened a law practice in Huntington and worked as associate publisher of the *Huntington Herald-Press.*

In 1976 local Republican leaders asked Quayle to run for Congress against eight-term incumbent Democrat Edward Roush. Quayle waged an energetic campaign and won despite his inexperience. He served two terms in the House before challenging Democrat Birch Bayh for his Senate seat in 1980. With the help of conservative groups, Quayle unseated Bayh after a tough campaign.

Quayle showed greater diligence in the Senate than he had in the House. As a member of the Armed Services Committee he supported most defense spending programs, including President Ronald Reagan's Strategic Defense Initiative missile defense system, but he also advocated reforms in the Pentagon's procurement process. Although Quayle

sided with Senate conservatives on most issues, he occasionally demonstrated independence. In 1982 he worked with liberal senator Edward M. Kennedy on a consensus job training bill that was enacted into law despite the initial opposition of the administration. In 1986 the Democrats were unable to attract a prominent challenger, and Quayle was reelected to his seat.

In August 1988 Republican presidential nominee George Bush surprised the nation by naming the forty-one-year-old Quayle to be his running mate. Quayle had been considered a long shot behind several better-known Republicans. Within hours of the announcement, Quayle became the subject of controversy. Commentators focused on Quayle's use of family connections to enter the National Guard. Negative reports also pointed to his unimpressive academic record and his apparent use of family influence to gain admittance to law school. The portrait of a wealthy underachiever who exploited his family's connections threatened to damage Bush's election chances. Some Republicans advised Bush to withdraw Quayle's nomination, but Bush stuck by his choice.

Bush campaign strategists sought to limit Quayle's visibility by seldom having him appear with Bush and assigning him to campaign in smaller cities. Most observers believed that Democratic vice-presidential nominee Lloyd Bentsen easily defeated Quayle in their one televised debate. Nevertheless, Bush and Quayle defeated Massachusetts governor Michael S. Dukakis and Bentsen 426–112 in the electoral college.

As vice president, Quayle was prone to verbal gaffes that perpetuated perceptions of him as inexperienced, inept, and prone to laughable malapropisms. Quayle sought to overcome these perceptions by taking on several high-profile assignments. He headed the Council on Competitiveness, a Bush administration working group charged with identifying and eliminating unnecessary or counterproductive regulations. Quayle also headed the president's National Space Council and provided advice to Bush on congressional matters. But like most vice presidents, Quayle spent much of his time on ceremonial and political duties and was not among the president's foremost advisers.

Before the 1992 election, many Republicans urged Bush to choose another vice-presidential running mate, but the president expressed his confidence in Quayle. During the campaign Quayle gained favor with many party conservatives by frequently promoting personal responsibility, the maintenance of two-parent families, the disciplined upbringing of children, and the preservation of religion in society. Quayle's activities may have helped to increase the ticket's popularity with conservatives, but support for Bush and Quayle among independents and moderates eroded. They were defeated by Democrats Bill Clinton and Al Gore.

Upon leaving office, Quayle returned with his family to Indiana. He wrote a regular newspaper column and a book about his vice-presidential experience. His performance during the 1992 campaign had made him a favorite with conservative Republicans, and he frequently appeared at party events. After considering a presidential run in 1996, Quayle announced in February 1995 that he did not want to leave his family to campaign. Most observers believed that he had made a strategic decision not to enter the crowded Republican field. After having moved his family to Arizona, Quayle announced in 1998 his candidacy for the Republican presidential nomination in 2000. He garnered little support from party loyalists and pulled out of the race in 1999 before any primaries. In 2004 Quayle was working at an investment firm in Phoenix.

Quayle married Marilyn Tucker on November 18, 1972. The couple met in law school and practiced law together briefly before Quayle entered politics. Marilyn Quayle functioned as a close political adviser to her husband and also was mentioned as a possible candidate for governor of Indiana. They have two sons and a daughter.

Al Gore

Born: March 31, 1948; Washington, D.C.
Party: Democratic
Term: January 20, 1993–January 20, 2001
President: Bill Clinton

Albert Arnold Gore Jr. was the son of Albert Gore Sr. and Pauline LaFon Gore. His father was a U.S. senator from Tennessee who served from 1953 to 1971. Before being elected to the Senate, Al Gore Sr., a New Deal populist, served seven terms in the House of Representatives. Pauline Gore was one of the first women to earn a law degree from Vanderbilt University.

Gore grew up in Washington, D.C., where his family lived in a hotel owned by a relative. He attended the elite St. Alban's, a Washington prep school, but dressed in a cousin's hand-me-down clothing, an indicator of his parents' frugality. He spent summers and vacations working on the family farm near Carthage, Tennessee.

In 1969 Gore graduated from Harvard University with a degree in government. Like his senator father, the younger Gore opposed the Vietnam War, but he enlisted in the army and served for six months as a military journalist in Vietnam without seeing combat. Gore's decision to enter the military rather than seek a graduate school deferment was influenced by his concern that his father's reelection chances could be harmed if he avoided service. Despite Gore's action, his father was defeated for reelection in 1970 largely because of his outspoken opposition to the war.

From 1971 to 1976 Gore worked as a reporter for the *Tennessean,* a Nashville newspaper, writing investigative pieces and covering local politics. In 1976 at

Al Gore

the age of twenty-eight Gore won his father's former seat in the House of Representatives and was easily reelected to the heavily Democratic district in 1978, 1980, and 1982. In the House Gore led the campaign for televising its floor proceedings. When that campaign succeeded, he delivered the chamber's first televised speech on C-Span in March 1979.

Gore successfully jumped to the Senate in 1984, winning with 61 percent of the vote despite Ronald Reagan's national landslide and carrying every county in the state. During his years in Congress, Gore gained a reputation as a moderately liberal, detail-oriented lawmaker. He became an expert on the environment, high technology, and many defense issues, most notably arms control. He displayed a firm grasp of ecological issues in his 1992 book, *Earth in the Balance: Ecology and the Human Spirit,* which reached the *New York Times* best-seller list.

At age thirty-nine Gore entered the race for the 1988 Democratic presidential nomination. He won five southern primaries but was unable to win a major primary in the North. Nevertheless, his third

place showing behind Jesse Jackson and the eventual nominee, Michael Dukakis, established him as one of the top southern Democratic politicians.

Reelected to his Senate seat in 1990, Gore was one of only ten Democrats in the Senate to vote for the authorization of the use of military force against Iraq in January 1991. Gore's vote upset some Democratic Party loyalists, but he repaired the damage by vigorously defending Democrats who had voted against the measure from charges that they were unpatriotic.

In 1992 Governor Bill Clinton of Arkansas surprised many commentators by picking Gore as his vice-presidential running mate. Presidential candidates usually try to balance the ticket with a running mate who is from another region and who has a somewhat different political ideology. In contrast to this norm, Gore shared Clinton's moderate southern Democrat outlook and was from a state that borders Arkansas. Moreover, they were only a year and a half apart in age. But Clinton and Gore used this close identification to project an image of unity and youthful energy. Gore's service in Vietnam also aided Clinton, who had been accused of avoiding military service. Clinton and Gore defeated incumbents George Bush and Dan Quayle by an electoral vote of 370–168.

Gore, with his extensive experience in Washington, became one of President Clinton's closest advisers. Gore took on many critical assignments, serving as the head of the president's effort to "reinvent government," a long-term project to reduce the size of and reengineer the federal government to achieve efficiency and cost savings. Gore also functioned as the administration's point man on congressional relations, environmental protection, defense, and high technology.

During the summer of 1993, after much partisan debate in Congress over Clinton's budget plan, Vice President Gore, presiding over the Senate, cast the deciding vote for the plan. Another celebrated moment for Gore came on November 9, 1993, when he debated the merits of the North American Free Trade Agreement (NAFTA) with billionaire H. Ross Perot on the "Larry King Live" talk show. Polls showed after the debate that Gore and the pro-NAFTA position had won decisively, giving proponents a big psychological boost. The outcome induced many wavering members of Congress to support the president and the agreement, which passed both houses.

In 1996 Gore and President Clinton faced Republicans Bob Dole and Jack Kemp in the general election. Gore again proved to be an effective defender of Clinton administration positions during the vice-presidential debate with Kemp, handily winning it, according to most political observers. The Clinton-Gore ticket defeated Dole and Kemp by an electoral vote margin of 379 to 159.

The second Clinton administration presented a number of problems for Gore, most pertaining to questions of his campaign activities for the 1996 race. He was accused of violating federal law by making phone solicitations from his Washington office and by attending a fund-raiser at a Buddhist temple in Los Angeles. But after a lengthy investigation by the Justice Department, Attorney General Janet Reno found no evidence of wrongdoing by the vice president.

During President Clinton's sex scandal of 1998 and his impeachment in 1999, Gore publicly supported the president, although Gore made it clear he disapproved of the president's behavior—placing some distance between himself and Clinton to demonstrate his own style of leadership.

Gore dominated the 2000 Democratic primaries, despite increasingly pointed charges by his opponent, former senator Bill Bradley of New Jersey, about Gore's truthfulness and changes of position on gun control and abortion. Gore's choice of Joseph Lieberman, a respected senator from Connecticut, as his running mate appeared predicated on Lieber-

man's role as the first Democratic senator to publicly criticize Clinton's behavior.

In one of the closest presidential races in history, with the election results from Florida hotly disputed, Gore lost his White House bid to George W. Bush of Texas. The outcome of the contest was not known until five weeks after the election. Although Gore won several states by razor-thin margins, he needed Florida's twenty-five electoral votes for victory. Both campaigns raised numerous legal challenges in state and federal court on the legitimacy of the state's final tally. Stepping in to end the dispute, the Supreme Court ruled in favor of Bush in a close 5–4 decision. Although Gore lost the electoral vote 266 to 271, he won the national popular vote by half a million, marking the third time in U.S. history that the winner of the popular vote did not advance to the presidency.

After the election Gore took a teaching position at Columbia University's Graduate School of Journalism. He and his wife, Tipper, published two books in 2002 on the subject of families, titled *Joined at the Heart* and *The Spirit of Family*. As the next presidential race drew closer, many expected Gore to run again. Although he would have been the automatic frontrunner, the former vice president announced in December 2002 that he would not seek his party's 2004 nomination. A year later, in December 2003, Gore endorsed former Vermont governor Howard Dean, passing over Lieberman, who also was running for president; both men eventually lost the nomination to Sen. John Kerry of Massachusetts. Gore, who had moved back to Tennessee after the 2000 election, spoke at the 2004 Democratic National Convention in Boston but generally kept a low political profile.

Gore married Mary Elizabeth "Tipper" Aitcheson in 1970. They had three girls and one boy. Tipper Gore gained national attention in the mid-1980s when she waged a campaign to put warning labels on record albums to alert parents about lyrics that glorified violence and casual sex. In 1987 she published a book, *Raising PG Kids in an X-Rated Society.* A former photographer on the *Tennessean,* she published a collection of her photographs, *Picture This: A Visual Diary,* in 1996.

Richard Cheney

Born: January 30, 1941; Lincoln, Nebraska
Party: Republican
Term: January 20, 2001–
President: George W. Bush

Richard Cheney

Richard Bruce Cheney was born in Lincoln, Nebraska, in 1941. His father, a soil-conservation agent for the federal government, moved the family to Casper, Wyoming, when Richard was thirteen. At Natrona County High School, he was cocaptain of the football team and president of the senior class. He also met his future wife, Lynne, there. Cheney won admission to Yale University on a scholarship but flunked out as a sophomore, he said, because he "goofed off." Returning home, he worked for a time for an electric utility stringing power lines, then returned to college, earning a bachelor's and master's degrees in political science at the University of Wyoming.

Cheney then entered a doctoral program in political science at the University of Wisconsin at Madison. While in school, Cheney got four student deferments from military service in Vietnam. In 1966 he married Lynne and won another military deferment.

In 1968 Cheney left Wisconsin without completing his doctoral dissertation to become a congressional fellow in the office of a Wisconsin Republican, William Steiger. Cheney's ideas about reorganizing the Office of Economic Opportunity (OEO) attracted the attention of another Republican representative, Donald Rumsfeld, who was helping reorganize the OEO for the administration of Richard

Nixon. When Nixon resigned the presidency in 1974, Rumsfeld became President Ford's chief of staff, and he brought Cheney to the White House as his deputy. When Rumsfeld became Ford's defense secretary, Cheney, at age thirty-four, became Ford's chief of staff.

Called a "boy wonder" by veteran Washington observers, Cheney was a low-key but effective aide to the new president, making sure the executive office ran smoothly. Cheney eschewed the trappings of power that came with his new post, turning down the limousine that came with the office and continuing to drive his ten-year-old Volkswagen to work at the White House.

When Ford lost reelection in 1976, Cheney returned home to Wyoming and won its one at-large congressional seat in 1978. Shortly after he began the race, Cheney suffered a mild heart attack and was unable to campaign actively. His wife Lynne took over for the last six weeks of the race, which Cheney won with 59 percent of the vote. He would go on to serve five terms, despite suffering two more heart attacks (he would later have a quadruple bypass).

While in Congress, Cheney amassed a highly conservative voting record. For example, he opposed the 1987 reauthorization of the Clean Water Act, the Endangered Species Act, funding for Head Start, and all gun control legislation. But despite his conservatism, Cheney made friends among his Democratic colleagues, who respected him as a scrupulous and ethical adversary with whom they could work. "The real secret to his success," The *New York Times* said, "may be an ability to wrap a staunchly conservative ideology in a mantle of moderation and civility to get people to trust him."

In 1983 Cheney and his wife coauthored a book, *Kings of the Hill,* which analyzed how House Speakers rose to power. One of the book's conclusions was that these leaders took an obscure, unwanted post and made it essential to the party leadership. Cheney followed this course, taking over the House Republican Policy Committee, which under him would become a launching pad for the new generation of Republican leaders, such as Newt Gingrich who would become Speaker in 1995.

In 1988 Cheney was tapped by President George Bush to become defense secretary. Cheney had little experience with defense issues, beyond being an ardent supporter of Ronald Reagan's military buildup and "Star Wars" proposal, but he studied military matters diligently and ably managed the huge department during the U.S. invasion of Panama in 1989. Later, working with Secretary of State James Baker and Gen. Colin Powell, chairman of the Joint Chiefs of Staff, Cheney was instrumental in ensuring American military success in the 1991 Persian Gulf War.

With the end to the cold war, Cheney also orchestrated a stringent cut in the military budget. He frequently clashed with entrenched congressional and military interests on such issues as base closings and weapons systems. Cheney was against let-

ting gays serve in the military, but when it was revealed that one of his chief aides was gay, he defended him, saying as long as the aide did his job well, his private life was his own business. During the 2000 campaign, it became known that the younger of Cheney's two daughters, Mary, was gay and an activist for gay causes.

Cheney briefly flirted with the idea of making his own presidential run in 1996 but decided against entering a race where domestic policies, and not security matters, were the primary issues. Instead, he joined the Halliburton Company, a Texas-based international oil services and construction company, as chairman and chief executive. His contacts proved valuable to the company, which experienced a doubling of its revenues during his tenure. Critics, however, argued that the company also had undertaken several unprofitable enterprises during Cheney's watch.

When he resigned in 2000 to be on the ticket with Gov. George W. Bush of Texas, the $20 million or more in stock options that Halliburton granted him raised ethical questions about whether Cheney, if elected, could distance himself from the oil business—a perception that also dogged Bush, who had strong ties to the industry. Then in 2002, amid a wave of corporate accounting scandals, the Securities and Exchange Commission (SEC) investigated accounting practices at Halliburton while Cheney was chief executive officer. In August 2004 Halliburton agreed to pay a $7.5 million penalty in a settlement with the SEC. Halliburton also won a no-bid multibillion-dollar government contract for work in Iraq, which led to questions from Democrats.

The vice-presidential slot was seen by many political observers as lending weight to the candidacy of the two-term governor who had never served in national office and lacked experience in foreign affairs. Laconic and unexciting as a speaker, Cheney was a well-seasoned Washington veteran whose long and varied experience in two branches of government was an invaluable asset to the ticket.

As vice president, Cheney had to answer many questions about his health, and in June 2001 he had a pacemaker inserted after tests showed an occasional irregular heartbeat. In August 2002 Cheney declared himself fit for a second term if invited by President Bush—which he was.

Cheney was a powerful figure in the Bush administration, serving as a trusted adviser, chairing an energy task force, and traveling on important missions abroad. In the wake of the September 11, 2001, terrorist attacks against the United States, Cheney often spent time in an "undisclosed location" as a security measure. Cheney's energy task force sparked a legal battle after congressional investigators asked for records from task force meetings and the administration declined to provide them. The case made its way to the Supreme Court, which in June 2004 sent the case back to a lower court.

Cheney was a forceful advocate for the Bush administration's decision to invade Iraq, and remained a vocal defender of the Iraq policy during the 2004 presidential campaign. While Cheney had kept himself out of the spotlight in the years following the September 11 attacks, he reemerged in 2004 as a combative member of the Bush reelection team. His debate with his Democratic counterpart, Senator John Edwards of North Carolina, held on October 5 in Cleveland, was hard-fought. The two nominees clashed on the administration's Iraq policy, on the economy and on the candidates' respective records. Cheney accused Edwards of being an undistinguished senator, while Edwards highlighted Cheney's past ties to Halliburton. After the debate, which was viewed overall as a draw, Cheney spent the remaining weeks campaigning hard around the country for the Republican ticket.

Cheney married Lynne Ann Vincent in 1964. They have two daughters, Mary and Elizabeth. Lynne was the controversial head of the National Endowment for the Humanities (NEH) under Presidents Reagan and George Bush. After leaving NEH, she was for a time the conservative cohost of Cable News Network's "Crossfire" program. She also was a senior fellow at the American Enterprise Institute. She is the author of several books.

Illustration Credits and Acknowledgments

Index